Redemptoristine Nuns
Mother of Perpetual Help Monastery
Esopus, New York 12429

A New Charter for Monasticism

A New Charter
For Monasticism

Proceedings of the Meeting of the
Monastic Superiors in the Far East

Bangkok, December 9 to 15, 1968

Edited and with an Introduction by

JOHN MOFFITT

Foreword by George N. Shuster

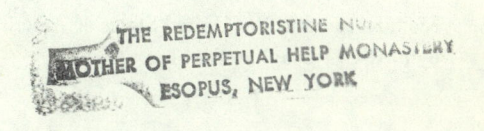

UNIVERSITY OF NOTRE DAME PRESS
Notre Dame   1970   London

Published under the Auspices of the
Institute for Advanced Religious Studies

Copyright 1970 by
University of Notre Dame Press
Notre Dame, Indiana 46556

"Marxism and Monastic Perspectives," by
Father Louis, O.C.S.O., copyright 1970 by
the Trustees of the Merton Legacy Trust,
% New Directions Publishing Corporation,
333 Sixth Avenue, New York, N.Y. All
rights reserved. This text may not be
published without permission from the Trustees.

Library of Congress Catalog Card Number: 70-122049
Manufactured in the United States of America
by NAPCO Graphic Arts, Inc.

CONTENTS

FOREWORD	ix
PREFACE	xiii
NARRATIVE INTRODUCTION	1

FIRST DAY (MONDAY, DECEMBER 9, 1968)

Speech of Welcome by Dom Rembert Weakland, Abbot Primate of the Benedictine Order	15
Reply by the Somdet Phra Ariawong Sankarat, Supreme Patriarch	15
Transplanting Ourselves or Just Finding Old Roots? Dom Rembert Weakland, O.S.B.	17
Present-Day Problems in Monasticism Dom Jean Leclercq, O.S.B.	23
Synthesis of Group Discussions: "Possibilities of an Asian Christian Monasticism"	44
Prayer and Readings at the Evening Office	48

SECOND DAY (TUESDAY, DECEMBER 10)

The Monastery in the Human and Social Context of the Theravada Buddhist Countries of Southeast Asia Father Jacques Amyot, S. J.	55
Marxism and Monastic Perspectives Father Louis, O.C.S.O. (Thomas Merton)	69
The Death of Father Louis	82
Prayer and Readings	85

THIRD DAY (WEDNESDAY, DECEMBER 11)

Western Observance and the Asian Mentality Dom Frans Hardjawijata, O.C.S.O.	91

Reorientation of Monastic Life in an Asian Context 109
 Dom Francis Acharya, O.C.S.O.

Synthesis of Group Discussions: "The Monastery in
 the Country" 124

Prayer and Readings 127

FOURTH DAY (THURSDAY, DECEMBER 12)

Varieties of Contemporary Hindu Monasticism 133
 John Moffitt

The Spirituality of Non-Christian Monasticism in Japan 161
 Father F. Enomiya-Lassalle, S.J.

Synthesis of Group Discussions: "The Missionary
 Aspect of Monasticism" (With an Intervention by
 Dom Rembert Weakland on Active and Contempla-
 tive Monasticism) 176

Prayer and Readings 181

FIFTH DAY (FRIDAY, DECEMBER 13)

Witnessing as a Catholic Sadhu 187
 Sadhu Ittyavirah

Toward a Vietnamese Monasticism 199
 Dom Marie-Joseph Ngoc-Hoang, O.S.B.

Synthesis of Group Discussions: "Problems of Recruitment" and "Problems of Formation" 211

Prayer and Readings 215

SIXTH DAY (SATURDAY, DECEMBER 14)

Brahma Vidya Mandir: Monastic Experiment 221
 Sister Shraddhananda Bahin

The Place of Monasticism in the Ecclesial Community 235
 D. S. Lourdusamy, Archbishop of Bangalore

Synthesis of Group Discussions: "Organizational Projects" 254

Prayer and Readings 257

CONTENTS

SEVENTH DAY (SUNDAY, DECEMBER 15)

    Conclusions of the Bangkok Conference   263

    Final Remarks by Dom Rembert Weakland, O.S.B.   267

APPENDIX A

    Telegram from Paul VI   273

    Letter from Cardinal Agagianian and Edward Pecorais, of the Sacred Congregation for the Propagation of the Faith   274

    Telegram from Dom Rembert Weakland to Paul VI   275

    Telegram from Dom Rembert Weakland to Cardinal Agagianian   275

    Scroll Presented to the Supreme Patriarch of Thai Buddhism   276

APPENDIX B

    Questionnaire (in Four Parts) Sent to Prospective Delegates   277

    Summary of Replies to Questionnaire   280

        Part I   282

        Part II   296

        Part III   301

        Part IV   315

APPENDIX C

    Excerpts From "Christianity Confronts Hinduism," A Background Paper Prepared for the Conference by John Moffitt   322

APPENDIX D

    List of Participants at the Bangkok Conference   332

Foreword

The day on which I read in *America* an article by John Moffitt about the Bangkok Conference was one bringing a special kind of surprise and good cheer. This conference had brought together, during the week beginning December 9, 1968, many Benedictines and kindred spirits to discuss the present and future of monasticism in the East. To be sure, the sudden, unexpected death there of Thomas Merton cast a shadow over the event even while focusing the attention of many throughout the world on a city known to most of them only as a tourist attraction. Good cheer? Yes, though gloomy facts galore dared everyone to ignore them.

Problems seemed beyond solution—Vietnam, the nuclear arms race, pollution, violence in the streets, the fanning of the embers of hatred in the Middle East. Yes, and there was spiritual disarray in and around the Church. Clerical and religious defection would seemingly never stop. Was it our collective destiny to be caught between the death of Thomism and the rise of the Pentecostals? Were we for or against the "death of God"?

But in Southeast Asia men were meeting for whom the monastic life appeared to be more important than everything else. Many in the United States were saying that this kind of living belonged once and for all in the history books. Yet some of us could not quite rid ourselves of the impact of evidence that the monastic witness is of the utmost importance if religious and spiritual values are to be preserved. Monasticism, the record insists, is "religious leadership." When this, which means seeing a worthwhile spiritual or ethical goal and striving to reach it, is thought of in purely individualistic terms it of course need not be denied either nobility or fruitful dedication. There have been, for instance, John Brown, whose body still keeps souls marching on, and St. Anthony of the Desert, whose ascetic achievements are well known even though he never wrote a line about them. Nevertheless, nearly all the majestic forward movements in religious history were led by groups. Jesus assembled a band of disciples. Augustine and Francis did the same. Newman had his confreres at Oxford and in the Oratory. What would Benedict have done without his brethren?

Granted such assumptions, what did the Bangkok Conference hope to achieve? It set out quietly to bring together the directors of Catholic monastic institutions in Asia and a number of men of wisdom and experience in the West to discuss what the goals of communal religious life are to be in the future. Were the men from the West to talk down to Eastern Catholic monks now aware as never before of the significance of Buddhist and Hindu monasticism? By no means. Rather it was almost the other way round. Christian was reaching out to non-Christian with respect and affection.

In a sense he was being driven. The impact of contemporary secularistic thought, in its American and Russian forms particularly, was being felt throughout the world. And the U. S. dollar, so often expended for great humanitarian as well as religious purposes, had been poured out during a series of wars and occupations to create such patterns of affluence, luxury and lust that whole cultures, including our own, had been infected with moral disease to which they had earlier been immune. Sexual indulgence, for example, had been paid for so cheaply, without the health risks that had once been unavoidable, that the appetites of millions had been whetted almost to the point of bestiality.

What in that kind of society would monasticism have to say to anybody? Moreover, the present discomfiture of the Roman Catholic Church, as well as of other religious communions in the West, is primarily due to the fact that many can no longer establish any kind of comradeship with authority. Why, it is asked, should those profess to lead whose right to do so is established only by the establishment? Putting such a question admittedly involves an assumption by the individual of rights whose righteousness is not apparent. How should the monastic community respond to such a query? So wide a gulf yawns between the permissive society and the monk, who elects to be governed by a rule whose objective is to create a climate in which the quest for holiness becomes natural and normal, that many wonder if that gulf can any longer be crossed.

That is the temper of our difficult time. That is why the conference and the papers written for it and now brought together in this book seem to me so vitally important. For here the response is made at the deepest level of the consciousness, where the person attains to selflessness and where prayer is the mode of speech. But that response is also life-giving in terms of the affection one man is to entertain for another. To be sure, the old rule needs to be redefined. It would be ridiculous to suppose that monastic farming in the United States could make any sort of contribution to the science and practice of agriculture, though it once did so in Europe during bygone days. But it doubtless could do so now, in an educational sense, in many parts of Asia, Africa, and Latin America. At the other end of the rule's gamut, the liturgy has today become "sacred dialogue"; and the fact that this concept has been primarily the creation of one branch of North European monasticism certainly indicates that the "houses of prayer" in our era will seek to renew and reinvigorate their practice of worship.

The conference went farther, however. It provided the first genuinely creative confrontation between Catholic and Oriental monasticism. This was an historic moment. The emphasis was on what Vatican II had glimpsed in a kind of vision—the moving of the Spirit over the waters, alighting where it thought best. In a common faith that this is the real meaning that lies at the heart of religious history, those who took part in the conference groped their way anew toward awareness of the ultimate essentials—the meaning of man's life spent in communion with God and accepting spiritual norms because only tyranny can impose others. Could we once again delight in the prayer that makes sacrifice meaningful? Indeed, could we pray together across barriers almost as old as the human race?

The men at Bangkok went still farther. It seems to me that they assented to what John Moffitt has said in one of his poems:

Faith[1]

Trouble no man's faith,
Faith is a precious thing;
It is the bird of life,
To drop it on the wing
Before its onwardness
Fulfills the arc of flight
Is to condemn a soul
To unredeemed defeat.

That its persuaded end
Belies the goal it sought
Need not disqualify
The zeal with which it thought
To overcome a world;

[1] Copyright, 1958, by John Moffitt. Reproduced by permission of Dodd, Mead & Company.

> For vision multiplies
> As the altitude's increase
> Reanimates the eyes,
> And fuller sense of space
> Cannot but countervail
> If only trust remains
> Some welcome waits the soul
> After its sojourn here
> Is perioded by death.
>
> Faith is a precious thing,
> Trouble no man's faith.

Let me add a word about this book.

John Moffitt, whose life includes years spent as a Hindu monk, conversion to Catholicism and brilliant work as a poet, agreed to prepare the volume. This has been truly a labor of love. It was no easy task to edit the translations from the French and the summaries of discussions, to make them both readable and accurate, and to interpret from within, as a participant, the significance of Bangkok. In addition, the Rockefeller Foundation generously gave the University of Notre Dame a grant that made possible publication of the volume through the University Press. This is being issued under the auspices of Notre Dame's Institute for Advanced Religious Studies, a recently established center of reflection and research. I remain deeply grateful to all who have helped to bring this book to the light of day.

GEORGE N. SHUSTER

Preface

This volume contains the complete proceedings of the Meeting of the Monastic Superiors in the Far East, held at Bangkok, Thailand, December 1968, under the auspices of the international Benedictine organization A.I.M. (Aide à l'Implantation Monastique).[1]

It was Dr. George N. Shuster, of the University of Notre Dame, who first conceived the project of publishing the proceedings of the Bangkok conference. After agreeing, at his request, to edit the volume, I began seeking some way to present these proceedings in a fitting manner—not as a dry-as-dust collection of lectures and discussions among delegates, but as a living witness to what those engaged in the missionary activities of the Catholic Church in the Far East are feeling and experiencing as they face the challenges of today's revolutionary world. As a result, I decided to arrange the materials in such a way that readers who were not present might get an inkling of the unforgettable atmosphere of the conference as the delegates experienced it.

The volume is divided into sections embodying, after a narrative introduction, the goings-on of each day. An appendix contains, besides certain important messages from Rome and other pertinent matters, valuable information received from prospective delegates in answer to a detailed questionnaire devised to obtain guidance for choosing topics for the planned daily discussion groups. I urge the reader, if he would experience

---

[1] The organization's program is an ambitious one. It convenes gatherings of superiors and representatives of monasteries by continents (as at Bouaké, Africa, in 1965 and at Rome in 1967) or by regions or parts of continents. It publishes a bulletin, sent gratis to all monastic communities in the Third World in order to keep them abreast with monastic developments elsewhere. It sends books and magazines for their libraries and medicines for their dispensaries. From time to time, it provides lecturers for these Third World communities. A.I.M.'s formation was first suggested in 1959 by Dom P. C. Tholens, abbot of the Benedictine monastery of Slangenburg, Holland, and the idea was approved by the Congress of Benedictine Abbots. At their congress in 1967, A.I.M. became one of the secretariats of the Benedictine Confederation. It collaborates with other Catholic monastic orders, such as the Cistercians and the Trappists, and all institutes concerned with the contemplative life that desire to collaborate. The headquarters is located in France, at 7, rue d'Issy, 92–Vanves, and is under the direction of Abbot Marie de Floris, founder of the monastery of Toumliline, Morocco.

the full impact of the conference, to read this volume from the foreword through the appendixes, without break.

We have felt justified in titling the volume *A New Charter for Monasticism* for a definite reason. It is not only in the Far East that Christian monasticism is in need of rethinking. Here in the West, curiously enough, the situation is not very different from that on the other side of the world. Just as in the Far East, here too, Christian monks and nuns are living in the midst of a society in some sense alien to them. In the East the difficulty arises from a lack of human contact with people—both monks and laymen—professing religions whose profundities our monks and nuns, even after centuries of devoted missionary activity, are scarcely aware of. In the West, on the other hand, believing Christians suffer from a woefully insufficient contact with growing numbers of people, nominally Christian for the most part, but drifting into agnosticism or atheism, whose values and aspirations and, indeed, positive virtues, our monks and nuns hardly understand. In my belief, what was learned at Bangkok can have a real meaning for monastic communities—and for Christians of all sorts—throughout the world. (Hence, too, the overriding importance for the West of the Secretariat for Non-Believers, with its remarkably open and truly catholic approach.)

My first debt of gratitude is, of course, to Dr. Shuster, not only for conceiving the project but also for asking me to edit the volume. I am equally indebted to Mrs. Otto Spaeth, of New York, and Swami Nikhilananda, of the Ramakrishna Order of India, for generously making possible my attendance at the conference as a participant. I am also much indebted for help and advice I have received from a number of other friends: Swami Kailashananda, of the Ramakrishna Order in Madras; Dom Jean Leclercq, O.S.B., Mother Pia Valeri and the staff of A.I.M.; Dom Bernardo Perez, O.S.B., and Dom Celestine Say, O.S.B., of San Beda College, Manila; Brother Patrick Hart, O.C.S.O., of the Abbey of Gethsemani, Kentucky, and Mr. John Howard Griffin, of Fort Worth, Texas; Mr. Joseph Campbell, of New York, and Mr. Joseph O'Connell, of St. Michael's College, Toronto, and others too many to name; and finally to Miss Carol Gaddis and Miss Rose Vaccaro, of New York, and Mrs. Patricia Mello, of Notre Dame, who typed and checked with me various parts of the manuscript.

The conference at Bangkok attracted worldwide attention not only because its members were welcomed to Thailand by the Supreme Patriarch of the Thai Buddhists, Somdet Phra Ariawong Sankarat, but also because one of the participants, Father Louis, O.C.S.O. (Thomas Merton), died there in the afternoon of the second day. Both these events, in their own way, signaled what were the main concerns of the conference: the understanding by monks and nuns of what they represent and what they are, and their wholehearted attempt to relate themselves, in no matter what part of the world they work, to the society within which they seek to bear witness to their Lord. A new approach is now required of them. In the words of the world-famous Trappist who at Bangkok gave his last message to the modern world: "What we are now asked to do is not so much to speak of Christ as to let him live within us, so that people may feel him by the way he is living in us."[2]

J. M.

[2] Reported by Dom François de Grunne, O.S.B., in a letter to the editor. These words were spoken, after Father Louis's lecture, in reply to a sister's query: "Why are we now asked not to speak any more of Christ to the people, when we have been sent to them precisely for that purpose?"

Narrative Introduction[1]

The Meeting of the Monastic Superiors in the Far East held in Bangkok under the auspices of the international Benedictine organization A.I.M. (Aide à l'Implantation Monastique) from December 9 to 15, achieved a true spiritual breakthrough. It brought together for the first time responsible representatives of all the monastic orders in the Far East under the Benedictine rule, for the purpose of hearing papers by experts on monasticism and discussing carefully chosen topics reflecting their common interests and problems as monks seeking to serve the peoples of Asia.

Again, through the inclusion of specialists on several of the non-Christian monasticism of the East, it represented a practical forward step in interreligious ecumenism. Perhaps even more significantly, daily contact was made with the monks of the nearby Buddhist monastery, Wat Asokaram. In no meeting of representatives of Christian denominations and non-Christian religions, to my knowledge, has there been such an opportunity for consideration, by those in authority, of the working of the Holy Spirit outside Christianity and of the possibilities of revitalization of the various great religions by each other.

The conference had been meticulously prepared for by the seemingly indefatigable Secretariat of A.I.M. Early in 1968 a questionnaire was sent to all the invited delegates and experts about all the important aspects of Christian monasticism in the Far East, and on the basis of the replies, summaries were prepared as guidelines for the group discussions to be held on each of the six working days.[2]

The delegates gathered on Sunday, December 8, at Samutprakarn, a suburb of Bangkok. The capital of Thailand is a very large modern city, teeming with activity and apparently far more advanced into the modern age than, say, the larger cities of India. In fact, many of the picturesque waterways along which much of the population still lives, and for which

---

[1] This account by the editor, adapted from an article published in the January 18, 1969 issue of *America*, pp. 60–64, is used here with the permission of *America*, the National Catholic Weekly, 106 W. 56th Street, New York, N.Y. 10019.

[2] For the original questionnaire and the replies from prospective delegates, see Appendix B.

Bangkok is famous, have now disappeared in the more central parts of the city. But the suburb of Samutprakarn is relatively peaceful, being situated perhaps twenty miles from the center of Bangkok and almost in the open countryside.

The conference site was the Sawang Kaniwat or Red Cross, a large compound with a small hotel and a number of cottages, a conference hall of very modern design, a large guest house called Happy Hall, three stories high and built around a vast roofed court, a long and narrow lake stretching between hotel and conference hall, a series of beautiful swimming pools, and an aquarium. Bright flowering plants and trees, including prolific red and purple bougainvilleas, orange flame-of-the-forest and many other less familiar varieties added a "typical" Oriental touch surprisingly lacking in many Eastern lands. A few languid and indifferent dogs strayed about the premises.

The participants in the conference, numbering between sixty-five and seventy, were drawn from almost all the countries of the Far East— India, Ceylon, Thailand, Cambodia, Indonesia, the Philippines, South Vietnam, Hong Kong, Taiwan, Japan, Australia and New Zealand—and from Belgium, France, Holland, Italy, Luxembourg and the United States as well. The majority were abbots, priors, prioresses, mother superiors and directors of novices—Benedictines, Cistercians, Trappists and members of related orders. The list of specialists included two Jesuits. Among the several auditors, in addition to a Dominican from Japan, were representatives of the European press and television. The meeting was under the presidency of Dom Rembert Weakland, Abbot Primate of the Benedictine Order.

Mass was concelebrated daily at noon by a principal celebrant and about thirty-five priest-monks (arranged in a semicircle); it was notable also for the inclusion of three Scripture readings. Each day a different priest offered the Eucharistic prayer. All present exchanged the "kiss of peace." At the evening Office the Lord's Prayer was sung each day by a different monk or sister in a different language: Chinese, Japanese, Korean, Vietnamese, Aramaic, Tagalog. Special prayers had been composed, and two readings from spiritual writings of East and West were included in either French or English.

The crowded schedule called for two lectures each morning, discussion groups in mid-afternoon and consideration of the findings of the group discussions in an after-supper meeting in the conference hall.

The most arresting feature of the opening session, at 9 A.M. on Monday, December 9, was the welcoming of the conference to Thailand by the Somdet Phra Ariawong Sankarat, the Supreme Patriarch of Thai Buddhism. It was the first official contact in a Buddhist country between Christian and non-Christian monasticism.

As the assembled monastic heads of all Christian Asia rose to their feet, the Sankarat entered and was received by Dom Rembert Weakland and Monsignor Jean Jadot, Apostolic Delegate for Thailand, Laos, Malaysia and Singapore. He was asked to sit on a small thronelike chair. The Abbot Primate now stood and, in the name of the conference, tendered a graciously worded greeting. Then, as is customary on such occasions in Thailand, two of the participants—an Australian prior and a prior from South Vietnam—offered the Patriarch a scroll with a message of greeting[3] and a few books as a token of esteem. In offering them, each bowed, then knelt, then again bowed as he withdrew.

The Patriarch next replied in Thai. "Generally, all religious believers are men of peace," he said. Welcoming the monks, he recalled the many good works of social service that Christians had done in Thailand. He expressed his desire that all believers should work for peace and justice, and his hope for the success of the conference. All again rose as he departed. (A half-dozen press photographers and television men recorded the ceremony of welcome, part of which was reproduced on the local TV in the evening.)

Dom Rembert, the thoughtful—and thought-provoking—Benedictine Primate, then spoke at some length. Western monks come now to Asia, he said, "not to 'civilize,' not to 'conquer,' not to 'convert,' but to live." And he continued: "We hope to find here, in a deeper way, what we are and to grow more deeply in our monasticism by our contacts here. But we do not come with empty hands."

The second lecture, at 10:45 A.M., was delivered by Dom Jean Leclercq, O.S.B., world authority on St. Bernard and on monasticism in general, and author of *The Love of Learning and The Desire for God*.[4] His prodigious experience in the field was evident in his paper, "Present-Day Problems in Monasticism." In it he stated: "The Christian monastic theory has always been a synthesis between permanent elements, primordial ones, those that come from the gospel and constant monastic tradition—and cultural elements, historical ones bound up with deter-

---

[3] See Appendix A.
[4] New York: Mentor Omega Books, 1962 (2nd ed.).

mined moments in evolution." He concluded by quoting the words of Dom François de Grunne, O.S.B.: "A religion flourishes with its monasticism, so much so that the decadence of the monasticism is not only the sign but also the cause of the decadence of the religion."[5] "Likewise," he added, "the vitality of a monasticism is the proof of the vitality of a religion."

The mid-afternoon group discussions on this first day were typical of all those held during the week. Exchange of ideas on the topic of "Possibilities of an Asian Christian Monasticism" was lively. It seemed the general consensus that the local institutions of the Eastern countries, especially the more deeply rooted ones, should be taken into account far more than in the past. What also emerged was the fact that in none of the Far Eastern countries, at present, is there a strong urge toward monasticism in the Christian communities.

Discussion topics on the days that followed were: "The Monastery in the Country," "The Missionary Aspect of Monasticism," "Problems of Recruitment," "Problems of Formation," and "Organizational Projects." The comparing of notes in the small afternoon seminars was most constructive. It contributed substantially to the conference's positive achievement. In the after-supper meetings, syntheses of the most important findings of the group discussions, prepared by the staff of A.I.M., were read. In this way all were able to share the thinking of the other groups. There was often spirited discussion at these evening gatherings.[6]

In addition to the group discussions, one of the most valuable aspects of the conference was the opportunity it afforded for informal conversations among delegates at meal time in the hotel building, or as they walked the long distances between their cottages and the conference hall. As far as I was concerned, such exchanges largely centered around the confrontation of Christianity and Hinduism.[7]

The second day of the conference, December 10, opened with an apostolic benediction and warm encouragement from Paul VI, delivered by the Papal Delegate to Thailand. A letter from Cardinal Agagianian, of the Sacred Congregation for the Propagation of the Faith, was also read.[8]

---

[5] *Rythmes du Monde*, 1967, p. 224.

[6] In the record of each day's activities, in this volume, the syntheses of the afternoon discussions are given immediately after the two lectures.

[7] Excerpts from a paper, "Christianity Confronts Hinduism," prepared by the editor in addition to his scheduled lecture as background material, are included in Appendix C.

[8] The telegram from Paul VI, conveying his blessing, and Cardinal Agagianian's letter are given in Appendix A.

There followed immediately an extremely informative and illuminating lecture on "The Monastery in the Human and Social Context of the Theravada Buddhist Countries of Southeast Asia," by Father Jacques Amyot, S.J., a Canadian-born professor at Chulalongkorn University, Bangkok. "They don't really need us," was the arresting lesson of Father Amyot's message.

He explained in lucid detail the popular Buddhism presently lived by the monks. Buddhist values, he pointed out, include mercy, compassion, respect for superiors; further, by doing goood deeds, one builds up merit, which will improve one's lot in the future life. He also explained the common people's animistic belief in spirits, and their worship and propitiation of them.

If there is to be a relevant Christian monasticism in Thailand or other Theravada Buddhist countries, said Father Amyot, it must satisfy a felt or latent need of the people and must be culturally intelligible to them. To this end, grass roots knowledge of popular Buddhism—not merely scholarly knowledge—is required. Even so, such an approach would merely make possible a Christian monastic presence in Thailand. The Church there is not felt to be needed: the people have no questions.

Father Amyot's talk provided an admirable model of the drastic rethinking of objectives that missionaries in the Far East will have to engage in if their work is to be meaningful outside the small Christian communities.

On this second day, at 7 A.M., one of the delegates visited Wat Asokaram, the large Buddhist monastery near the conference site, and became friendly with the abbot. As a result he attended the ordination of a young Buddhist monk. Each day thereafter, some of the delegates made the fifteen-minute walk to the very impressive compound, with its strikingly designed, dazzling white main building, whose central spire, tapering to a single point high above, was surrounded by a half-dozen lesser spires. At the base, within, sat a very Oriental-looking, large gilded Buddha. One could look down at him through a great opening in the concrete floor. Behind this building were several other shrines and the nuns' quarters.

All of us received a cordial welcome from the friendly, clean-shaven, orange-robed monks, who presented us with (and even tried to teach one of us) some of their prayers—printed, of course, in Thai.

Though no one realized it at the time, a talk suffused with special meaning for the conference was the one that followed, at 10:45 A.M., by Father Louis, O.C.S.O. (Thomas Merton). His subject was "Marxism and Monastic Perspectives."

Never having met "Father Merton" (as he was usually called), and never having read any of his writings before I returned to Christianity, I was gratified on arriving at the Sawang Kaniwat to find I was to be housed in the four-room cottage where he would be living. I met him on December 8, on returning from a morning of sight-seeing at the beautiful eighteenth-century monastic compounds in Bangkok, the Wat Po (Monastery of the Reclining Buddha) and the Wat Pra Keo (Monastery of the Emerald Buddha). I was interested to find he was well aware of the outstanding modern Indian saint, Ramakrishna (1836–1886), who had been such an influence in my life before I became a Catholic.

Of the non-Christian disciplines, it was Zen Buddhism that seemed to have captured Father Merton's imagination. At the evening meeting on the first day, December 9, we had heard and discussed the report of the various afternoon group discussions on the topic "Possibilities of an Asian Christian Monasticism." As he had done on several occasions during the day, when the regular interpreters were not available, he brilliantly translated into English the remarks of the moderator, the unfailingly genial Dom de Floris, O.S.B., of A.I.M. Subsequently he led the discussion. This for a time centered about the possibility—which appeared to interest several of the delegates considerably—of having married monks, as is the custom in certain forms of Buddhism.

After the meeting broke up, we were conversing about Hinduism and Zen, when Father Merton exclaimed with unfeigned enthusiasm: "Zen and Christianity are the future!"

In his talk, "Marxism and Monastic Perspectives," Thomas Merton spoke with earnestness, as if he very much wished to get something across to the delegates. Because of his fame, the TV men and photographers outdid themselves. All the time he was speaking, the TV cameras were whirring and the photographers wove in and out and around. They took pictures of him from every possible angle.

Father Merton pointed out that both Marxist thought and monastic thought have something in common: an attitude of criticism toward the established structures of society and personal life, and a movement toward change. But Marxist criticism of society, he reminded his hearers, is oriented toward its economic substructures, and it looks on the "superstructures" of religion, philosophy, and politics as attempts to justify an unjust situation. On the other hand, monastic thought is critical of any position that gives priority to the purely material over the spiritual. Both are, though from diametrically opposed directions, revolutionary. It was his opinion that the Marxist goal, "from each according to his capacity, to each according to his need," could not be achieved in society, but only in a monastic setting.

As a result of another sightseeing visit to Bangkok that afternoon, I was not present for the scheduled group discussion. But the discussion was never held. When we returned, about 5:30 P.M., we learned that Thomas Merton was dead. The first report, based on the diagnosis of the Thai physician from the Samutprakarn Hospital, who had been called, was that he had had a heart attack. But it soon appeared that the heart failure might have resulted from electrocution. What really caused Father Merton's death will probably never be known. As Dom Rembert Weakland said to me: "There is often something inexplicable about the death of great men. Perhaps we should just accept it as a spiritual mystery."[9]

Out of deference to the Thais' feeling, the other three of us housed in the cottage were asked to move. When I arrived at the cottage to remove my belonging from my room, Dom Rembert was seated outside, waiting for the police. They were slow in coming and arrived only about 6 P.M. As I passed the open door, I could see Father Merton's body lying where it had originally fallen, with a dark red burn down his right side. That night, by turns, monks kept vigil by his bed.

What we had been told by Father Amyot about the common man's belief in spirits now received striking confirmation. Almost immediately, everything was removed from Father Merton's room, the whole house was cleaned, the ceiling and partition of the room were removed, as well as the earth and plants from in front of the windows. Lights were kept burning for three nights.

The group discussion for Tuesday afternoon had, of course, been canceled. In place of the scheduled lectures the following morning, requiem Mass was said at 10 A.M. The three chief concelebrants were the Benedictine Primate, the Apostolic Delegate and a Trappist abbot from New Zealand. Thirty-five priest-monks assisted. Dom Rembert gave a moving tribute to this prophetlike monk and priest who, all his life long, "sometimes through strange and disconcerting ways," had searched for God and sought to show him to men."[10] The occasion was an affecting one, but not at all sad. All the delegates I talked with felt that this unexpected happening had given the conference far greater depth. It seemed

---

[9] For a brief account of the known facts about his death, see p. 82.
[10] See J. Leclercq, O.S.B., "Last Memories," *The A.I.M. Bulletin* 9, (1969), 17–21.

particularly fitting that Father Louis's final message had been one so pertinent to today's world.

From this time on, an even stronger sense of community began to manifest itself among the delegates. Shortly afterwards, I heard an abbot from South Korea propose to some of his brother monks that they should begin planning for a more modest regional conference on this same order, to be held yearly. The idea took definite form as a result of the final group discussions. The very real friendships one happened to strike up—with delegates from such places as India, the Philippines, South Vietnam, South Korea—seemed, as well, to take on added meaning.

During the following days of the conference, various other experts spoke, out of their own experience, about some of the problems and goals of Christian monasticism in the Far East. It became more and more clear that in Christian society in this part of the world, there was still very little real appreciation of the importance of monasticism to the Church. Whatever monasteries existed were largely the result of the efforts of Western Christians. Again, both in the talk by Dom Hardjawijata, of Indonesia, and during group discussions, the inadvisability of continuing to impose the strict Benedictine rule, with maximum frequency of community exercises, was stressed. It was also brought out that for many in the Christian communities, entrance into a monastery means a decided advance in economic security; the need for a life of greater poverty was therefore stressed.

Aside from the paper by Father Amyot, there were only two dealing strictly with non-Christian monasticism. On December 12, Father Enomiya-Lassalle, S.J., German-born professor from Sophia University, in Tokyo, a profound student of Zen and a naturalized citizen of Japan, spoke on "The Spirituality of Non-Christian Monasticism in Japan." He described the practices and aspirations of Zen Buddhists and stressed the fact that Christians, by using the Zen method of emptying the mind of all concepts, might substantially deepen their own meditation and prayer.

The other paper, entitled "Varieties of Contemporary Hindu Monasticism," had been delivered earlier that same morning by me. The reason why I, a layman, had been invited to deliver a paper on Hindu monasticism and to take part in the group discussions was my twenty-five years' experience as a monastic member of the Ramakrishna Order, the largest and one of the most important modern orders in India. In my paper I tried to give an account of the development and present state of Hindu monastic orders, concentrating on the activities and aims of the Ramakrishna Order, which I feel to be the most authoritative representative of modern Hinduism.

Two of the delegates from India, Dom Francis Acharya (born in Belgium and now a citizen of India), superior of Kurisumala Ashram in South India, and his colleague Dom Bede Griffiths, O.S.B., bore valuable witness not only to the profundity of the Indian mystical tradition but also to their own creative attempts to live Christianity in terms that Hindus would be able to appreciate. Dom Acharya's talk, "Reorientation of Monastic Life in an Asian Context," offered valuable insight into the relationship between Christian and Indian monasticism. (Though scheduled for Wednesday, where it is placed in this volume, it had to be postponed till later in the week.)

An especially appealing talk was that of the Christian monk, Sadhu Ittyavirah, delivered on Friday morning. A Jesuit scholastic, he had abandoned his studies to take up the life that Hindus most respected, that of a wandering monk with "no place to lay his head." His description of how he went about the villages teaching through simple parables won the admiration of the entire gathering. Immediately following his talk came a penetrating analysis by Dom Marie-Joseph Ngoc-Hoang, O.S.B., a superior from Hué, South Vietnam, whose monastery had been destroyed in the war. He spoke honestly of the problems of creating a valid Vietnamese Christian monasticism.

An absorbingly interesting—and indeed challenging—discourse by Sister Shraddhananda Bahin described the aims and ideals of Vinoba Bhave's ashram for Indian women, and her own experience of living in this Hindu retreat among believing Hindus. The sister had spent sixteen years in a convent in Germany, and only three years before had joined the ashram of the great Hindu leader (one of Gandhi's outstanding followers), living as the Indian women did but keeping her Christian faith. Her talk was given on Saturday.

A very carefully documented address, "The Place of Monasticism in the Ecclesial Community," by Archbishop D. S. Lourdusamy of Bangalore, was also delivered on Saturday. The archbishop held that before monasteries can become the centers of interreligious dialogue that they are destined to be, the Church in India will have to develop a greater appreciation of the contemplative life. Today is a critical period, he said, for the whole Church. It "can resolve itself . . . into a long era of contraction and dimunition of influence or into a new birth, a second spring of relevance and creativity."

Two days after Thomas Merton's death, four not very large crocodile-like creatures living in the lake came out onto the grass. There, in sight of several of the monks, including Dom Rembert, one of them seized and consumed a dog. (It seemed strange to me, in retrospect, to recall that in an Indian parable about the inevitability of death, the form taken by the god of death to complete his mission was that of a crocodile.) After hearing about the creature's attack, most of the delegates gave up their custom of walking to and from the conference hall along the water and chose a longer way.

As a result of complications having to do with Father Merton's death, Dom Rembert was forced to leave the conference a day earlier than planned. On the morning of Saturday, December 14, he bade the delegates farewell.[11]

In his opening address he had stated that one of the first purposes of a gathering like the Bangkok conference was to come to a "deeper awareness of what we are now." And he predicted that each area of the world would of necessity develop a different Christian monasticism. "Our monasticism should be pancultural," he said. Now, reviewing the achievements of the meeting, he seemed to feel that the delegates had moved measurably closer to the awareness of "what we are now" that he had hoped for.

Certainly it seemed clear to very many who attended the conference that Christian monasticism will have to be, indeed is already becoming, pancultural, and that, as Dom Rembert had also said in his earlier talk, the Church "must no longer remain the possession of Western culture." In his final remarks, the Benedictine Primate echoed the feelings of everyone when he said: "This has been a week to be experienced. It can hardly be described."

Sunday, December 15, was the last day of the conference. In the final meeting, Dom Marie de Floris, abbot of the Sainte Bathilde Priory, of Vanves, France, and director of A. I. M., read the "Conclusions of the Bangkok Conference," which were approved by the assembled delegates. Archbishop Lourdusamy gave the homily at Mass, immediately following the meeting, and the delegates returned to their various monasteries scattered throughout the East.

Two of the monastic participants, however, were able to implement the intention of the Bangkok Conference in an unexpected way. It was

---

[11] This talk has been placed at the end of the seventh day.

their privilege, for the twenty-four hours following the conference, to share the daily routine of the Wat Asokaram monastery.

There, beneath the snow-white pinnacles, in the presence of the serene gilded image of Buddha, the Compassionate, these children of Christ passed the night and the next day in the genial company of fellow pilgrims on the Way of Truth.

J. M.

FIRST DAY

Monday, December 9, 1968

One of the first purposes of a conference such as this should be a greater comprehension of what we are at this moment of our history as we come in touch with a new culture.

—Dom Rembert Weakland, O.S.B.

SPEECH OF WELCOME BY THE ABBOT PRIMATE OF THE ORDER OF ST. BENEDICT TO THE SUPREME PATRIARCH OF THAI BUDDHISM AND THE OTHER GUESTS AND DELEGATES

Your Holiness, Distinguished Guests and Fellow Participants:

We are indeed honored by your presence here this morning, Your Holiness. It is a sign to us of your personal esteem and kindness toward us. We monastic superiors wish to express publicly how deeply grateful we are to Thailand, your country, for the kind hospitality offered us. We express our gratitude to the officials of this country through you because of the great esteem with which you are held in our eyes and in theirs.

We chose to hold our meeting in Bangkok because we hoped to draw great profit from the ancient and rich traditions of spiritual life in this country, where Buddhist monks have been so numerous for so many centuries. We are honored that the Patriarch of the Buddhist monks has shown us his interest by his presence at our gathering.

We wish also to express our gratitude to the distinguished guests who have joined us on this occasion. To the Apostolic Delegate of the Holy See to Thailand, Monsignor Jean Jadot, and to the Director of Worship to the Minister of Education of Thailand—to all of you we express our gratitude.

As a remembrance of this occasion, we would like to present to Your Holiness a scroll commemorating the event, in which we again express our gratitude so that the event and our gratitude will here find a perpetual memorial.

We would also like to present to Your Holiness some small gift to be a symbol of the esteem of all our participants assembled here. We present these gifts in the hope and trust that every expectation of Your Holiness's heart may be always fulfilled.

REPLY OF THE SOMDET PHRA ARIAWONG SANKARAT, SUPREME PATRIARCH[1]

President and Directors of the Catholic Missions:

I am delighted to visit the seminar meeting of all Catholic missions in the Far East, here, at this time.

[1] The Supreme Patriarch's reply has been translated from the Thai language, in which he delivered it.

In Thailand, we know that our country has received Christians during many periods and epochs from approximately B.E. 2393 or A.D. 1851, in the reign of Ayudhia, up to the present. Many Christian institutions have come and brought much benefit to Thailand, such as in social welfare, education and medicine.

Among religious believers, each feels his own sympathies, preserving his own unity and maintaining his own general morality, which means righteousness in thought and perseverance in doing good. Generally, all religious believers are men of peace, showing their genuineness and friendly character to all fellow human beings and all religions. If, furthermore, the religious believers of all missions had concentrated their purposes on the means of peace, all together, our world would possess unity and justice in perpetual and permanent peace for all human beings.

I, in the name of the Thai monks, am therefore very glad to have this occasion to visit your seminar today, which can be recognized as a seminar of missions whose aim is peace. May the meeting of your seminar go on well and may it succeed in its purpose.

Transplanting Ourselves or Just Finding Old Roots?

REMBERT G. WEAKLAND, O.S.B.

Like most American boys, I grew up with a totally false notion of geography and a bad sense of direction. North and South were concepts that presented no confusion. I imagined that at these two ends of the earth, poles protruded, like those of a spinning top, and wherever you went on the globe you retained the same basic relationship to these poles. But East and West were confusing concepts. West meant principally California and everything on the other side of the Mississippi in a less rigid sense. East meant New York. I knew that if one went far enough west—beyond California—he would come, eventually, to Japan and China. If he went east far enough beyond New York, he would arrive in England or France, or Spain, or Italy. And then there was that area one could arrive at from either side, called India. My entire geography became confused, however, when I was told that by going west far enough I arrived at the Far East and that Europe, which lay to my east, was the heart of Western culture and civilization. After such confusion it did not matter to me when they told me that Jerusalem was in the Near East, since it was just as far away as the Far East, depending on which way one traveled and whether one started from California or New York.

No one ever told me—and I prided myself on having figured it out myself—that East and West are totally relative concepts from one point of view, namely, when applied to specific lands or regions, but very sure concepts for indicating direction from where one is standing. If the earth only revolved the other way, Commodore Perry could have put poles on East and West, and North and South would then have caused the confusion. Moreover, I became suspicious that when people talked of the Near and Far East and Western civilization, they had invented these terms for specific areas of the globe from a vantage point other than the United States of America and probably before Columbus sailed in the direction that the history books later called the West. I soon realized my European forefathers had brought these terms with them to America, and although they were no longer apt terms, these same forefathers were probably too busy fighting Indians to find time to change them.

It became even worse when I tried to speak a foreign tongue, because I knew that the sun rises in the East, but the East is really China, and the sun sets in the West, which is really Europe. Hence I must always remember that Oriental is Occidental and vice versa. From this I came to know, all too clearly, that I belonged to Western culture; that the pole I was looking for was far West—out in the Pacific Ocean; and that it was really a fence separating me from the East: that there were cultural ropes to my East that crossed the Atlantic Ocean and tied me to Western Europe—ropes I could not sever at will.

In many ways I was happy, however, about this confusion into which I was born. I was happy to think that my continent lay between East and West. My only regret was that China from the East had not discovered our Western shores at the same time Europe in the West discovered our Eastern shores. Perhaps some of the enormous cultural chasms we are trying to breach would already have been closed, and the relative concepts of East and West for designating areas of the world, and not purely relative directions from where one is standing, would have disappeared.

I have cited for a purpose the manner in which Western culture was brought to the United States of America without any change in geographic orientation. The manner in which the term "East" was applied not just to direction but to a territory came from the geographic concept of the world that Columbus set out to disprove. On a flat world East and West are more than directions. They are also lands. We must realize that Christianity took these concepts for granted and filled its liturgy with their symbolic meanings. The Magi came from the East—that land of untold wisdom and knowledge. The sun comes out of the East. It was here that paradise had been, and thus from the East must come the return of the second paradise. Turning toward the East for prayer, as Franz Dölger showed years ago in his masterly study *Sol Salutis*, was also a yearning for the return of the lost paradise. No wonder that the East had such a strong hold on early monasticism, with its eschatological yearnings. Need I point out the importance of this symbol for the liturgy of Lauds, especially the hymns, and for the whole

Transplanting Ourselves
Rembert Weakland, O.S.B.

liturgy of Advent and Christmas? Behind all these yearnings and symbols and false geography lay the basic truth of a relationship of Christianity to those lands that lay in the direction of the rising sun. A mystical yearning for its hidden wisdom filled men's minds.

Just as the terms East and West have been retained in Western culture even after the proof that the world is round, so Christianity has retained in its liturgy these allusions to the land that lay to the east of Europe as somehow an integral part of its eschatological yearnings. It would never have occurred to the first Christians who arrived on the shores of what is now the United States of America that these texts and allusions presented certain geographical problems. Although the rising sun in Pennsylvania still dispels the darkness, the East from which it comes has little relationship to the eschatological yearnings I mentioned. There is no longer, from the geographical location of someone standing in the United States of America, any relationship between the place from which the rising sun comes and the Far East. We stand, then, before a symbol that needs a readjusting in a new area of the globe. The rising sun can still be a symbol of Christ and the manner in which his light changes the darkness of history and of our lives; but it has no relationship to the whole body of Christian literature and symbolism that brought Christianity into an eschatological relationship to those countries we call the Far East. What is being alluded to is this: simple local transplantation of symbol and imagery, even within the same culture, can cause difficulties that can range from the ridiculous to the disastrous.

In this particular instance the Christological symbolism of the rising sun is still valid, although it has much less force than it did in the first four centuries of the Church's existence. It would be a significant loss, however, to forget the deep sense of relationship of origin that Christianity had to the East and that existed so strongly in the minds of the members of the early Church, simply because the symbol whereby it was expressed is no longer apt. It is of little import if paradise, in relationship to us, is in the East or in the West. This symbol, which was repeated so often among the Fathers, was founded on their reading of Genesis 2:8: "Then the Lord God planted a garden in Eden, to the east, and put there the man whom he had molded." This aspect of the symbol certainly can and must undergo a new analysis. What must remain, however, is that yearning for a close contact with the lands of the East, to which the early Christians felt instinctively they had an affinity of origin.

In purging the paradise concept of its false connotations, one is in reality helping the Church of today. It would be disastrous to perpetuate in our minds the notion that the Orient (I will now use the terms in their common territorial significance) is some mysterious unreal world—a world that should open up to us only at the end of time—and not a part of the real world in which we live. It would also be disastrous if it left a cleavage in our mind between two worlds that could never meet, or if it caused us to hesitate to search out that which we have in common.

From this rather lengthy example it should be clear that if such intricate difficulties arise from unthoughtful transplantations within the same culture, many more difficulties will arise if transplantations are attempted from culture to culture. The transplanted heart stands always in peril of being rejected by the new body.

In all of this, monasticism should play an important role. From a purely superficial survey it seems to be one link in Christianity to similar manifestations in the East. Historically the West develops its monasticism from the Near East. Historians of the last century thus took great pains to find the origins of Western monasticism in all kinds of Eastern cults and practices. Many of these claims of the rationalists of the last century were denied by Christians. Today we can take a less chauvinistic look at such relationships and rejoice in the affinities, even if evidence is not sufficient to support theories of origin. On the other hand, Western monasticism has developed greatly from its original Near East forms. It became an integral part of Western medieval culture and assumed forms that made any relationship to its primitive sources hardly discernible. Such transformations and reformations are a part of any living organism or ideal. It tended at times to be highly active in its missionary zeal; it tended to constant reforms to emphasize its basis in contemplative prayer; it emphasized at times its cenobitic possibility; at other times it tended again toward the hermitage. In general, however, it tended more in the West to emphasize its fraternal or communal aspect.

One thing, however, is certain: in the extensive missionary activities in the sixteenth century toward the Orient, Western monasticism played no part. It had lost its early medieval missionary thrust. Perhaps it was a blessing that our efforts at that time were not extensive. We might have attempted to come as conquering missionaries to perpetuate Western culture and symbols, and not as simple monks. I hope we can come now with a more open mind and heart. We come, not to "civilize," not to "conquer," not to "convert," but to live. We hope to find here, in a deeper way, what we are and to grow more deeply in our monasticism by our contacts here. But we do not come with empty hands. We

Transplanting Ourselves
Rembert Weakland, O.S.B.

carry a knapsack full of the history I have alluded to, a history full of its own values and worth, a history that has emphasized the horizontal community love, service and obedience, but that has not forgotten to make place for the hermitage. One of the first purposes of a conference such as this should be greater comprehension of what we are at this moment of our history as we come in touch with a new culture.

As I see it, then, one of the first purposes of such a conference as this should be a deeper awareness of what we are now. We have to examine—if only implicitly—the heart we are transplanting.

But perhaps the greater advantage of a meeting such as this should be the courage one receives to be truly himself as monk in the new culture in which he is sinking roots. This courage to rethink the symbolic and cultural expressions of Christ's message of salvation within a monastic context would be a missionary service to the Church today beyond any numerical statistics of baptisms. Perhaps one of the most important aspects of Vatican II—if not the most important aspect—when its history is written within a century or two from now, will be the first awareness in the Church that it must no longer be the exclusive property of Western civilization. Somehow it must no longer remain the possession of Western culture.

As the bishops would stream out of St. Peter's, one could see the breadth of the Church in a concrete form never expressed so clearly before. If today we are at a great turning point of Western culture itself because of the technological changes that have affected our thinking, we are also experiencing pancultural influences that are even more challenging. To meet this challenge the essence of the gospel message may at times have to be stripped of much of its historical and accidental accretions; at other times its prehistorical roots may have to be uncovered and fostered.

In every way, then, we are in an exciting era for Christianity and for monasticism in particular, especially here in the Orient. If, as I mentioned earlier, it may be an advantage that we were not a part of the great missionary movements to the East in the past, this means we may hope that today our monastic efforts will in some way be more thoroughly analyzed, studied and criticized. It presupposes our willingness and eargerness to bring to our efforts all the knowledge of history, of sociology, of psychology, together with a deepened theology and especially ecclesiology.

More than anything, however, it presupposes an openness that we may never have had before in monastic history. By this I mean that we should accept the beauty and riches of variety in the monastic witness that come from our *stabilitas loci*.[1] Each area of the globe, by reason of these local differences, will of necessity develop a different monasticism. The beauty of these divergent expressions is our wealth. We should no longer expect to transplant a tropical flower to Europe or vice versa. On the other hand, such a concept, which I feel sure is integral to the whole genius of monasticism, demands greater responsibility and awareness on the part of those engaged in the actual living. Our monasticism now must also, in its pluralism, seek to be pancultural.

In addition to helping us have the courage to be what we are, a meeting of this sort should be informative. Mutual exchange of insights is one of the necessities of our complicated age. From such exchanges we often see more clearly what we should be. We are forced to analyze ourselves and where we are going. This exchange, too, should not be just one of Christian ideals, but extend beyond to the Eastern manifestations of similar values and ideals. The field is vast and exciting.

My task, my role here, was simply to say a few opening words of encouragement. Just like you, I am here to learn. One thing I can promise you: I will try to learn from you what your aspirations and ideals are as you live here, and how you feel these must be expressed in your daily monastic living. And I will also try—insofar as my fallible comprehension permits—to protect your right to develop as you see fit. I will use whatever talents and influence I can bring to the situation to see that your monasticism here may flourish.

Lastly, I hope we all experience from this meeting a confirmation of our faith in the *Lux oriens ex alto*—in Christ himself—who, together with his Father and the Spirit he has sent, transcends time and place, culture and race. Our monasticism, as a way of expressing that Christian message, must share in its universality.

---

[1] That is, the promise to remain in one particular monastery.

Present-Day Problems in Monasticism[1]

JEAN LECLERCQ, O.S.B.

In contrast to the situation only a few years ago, the problems besetting monasticism today no longer have to do with observances.[2] The Council has ordered that these be subject to aggiornamento, and despite sporadic resistance its order is now being carried out. This resistance, we can confidently predict, will not last much longer. Life will have the upper hand over habit.

In particular, the forms of prayer are in full process of renewal. The use of the living language, which represented a minimum, a first condition, is henceforth within reach of all who wish it. The structure of the Divine Office is in course of transformation, and the experiments being carried out are already yielding good results. There will be no going back in this area. And much more than that, the conditions of all prayer in common—theological, philosophical, psychological, sociological and even economic—are being reconsidered in the light of recent acquisitions of Christology, ecclesiology and biblical and patristic studies, as well as of phenomenology and other schools of contemporary thought. We are still only at the beginning, but it is full of promise.

The possibilities of liturgical creation are being explicitly taken into account, and already we may draw hope from the valuable results pro-

---

[1] Reprinted, by permission, from *The Downside Review*, 87 (April 1969), 135.

[2] This was the case when a previous article of mine, entitled "Problèmes et Orientations du Monachisme," was written. It has been included in a volume containing several essays I wrote before and during the Council, *Chances de la Spiritualité Occidentale* (Paris: Cerf, 1967), pp. 7–66. A comparison between the problems then and now shows the progress that has been made.

duced so far.[3] In short, both the freedom that has been regained and the clear signs of an emerging culture at once traditional and contemporary allow us to look forward to the future with hope. Monasticism will find the forms and the observances it needs in the Church of today and tomorrow.

Institutional structures are also in the process of being transformed. In each institute, constitutions are being revised. The participation of representatives of a community in its own government (*regimen* is the word used in the Decree on the Appropriate Renewal of the Religious Life, n. 14) is little by little being introduced almost everywhere, in accordance with a demand of the Council. The length of the mandate of superiors is no longer what it used to be. Collaboration between the different orders is being intensified. Nuns are gradually coming to take their destiny into their own hands; the legislation concerning enclosure is being modified. The relations between motherhouses and their foundations of every kind are coming more and more to ensure that the latter may have the necessary help, but also autonomy. The "lay" brothers and sisters who came into being in the West during the Middle Ages are now a thing of the past. It is gradually being accepted on all levels—theological, psychological and even institutional—that the priesthood is not tied to the monastic state. In every way, structures are being renewed so as to return to tradition over and beyond recent historical forms.

This does not mean that there are no longer any problems: they are merely set at another level, a deeper one. They concern fundamental concepts. They are interconnected. In order to try to clarify matters, we may group them according to whether they concern the nature of monasticism, its designation, its relationship with its past in the West or finally its role.

THE IDENTITY CRISIS

During the Council, the Church as a whole asked itself: "What are you? What have you to say for yourself?" And it answered its own question. Today each of the organisms within the Church has to query its own identity. The great religious orders and groups of orders are querying their aim and their position within the Body of Christ; monasticism

[3] On these points consult *La Maison Dieu*, 95 (1968), where the proceedings of the congress of the Fraternity of Dominicans on liturgy and monasteries, held July 1–4 at Méry-sur-Oise, France, have been published.

cannot escape this challenge. Now, it happens that by reason of its very long past, of its greatly varying manifestations throughout history and in different parts of the world, it is not able to find a unanimous reply. To simplify things for clarity of exposition, and without taking sides, the major orientations may be reduced to two main ones. These will appear in connection with each of the aspects we shall review.

But first of all, does monasticism have to define itself, and can it do so? It has been objected, in the words of the Roman legal maxim: "Definitions are dangerous things." Doubtless that is so in the realm of law. It is not necessarily so in that of the specific aims of a spiritual group that must know exactly why it exists.

It is true that one of the inconveniences of a definition—the very word, according to its etymology, means a limitation—would be to exclude certain ways of living or forms of activity that are nevertheless in keeping with the Christian life. For this reason, some people are content with a deliberately vague and imprecise notion. It will be said, for example, that the monk is a "nonspecialized Christian," or that a monastery is a place where one lives "celibate life in common."

The monk is not even a religious, he is in no way specified, and thus he can do everything, and in fact in many places he does do everything, in the same way that others do it. Neither are his activities specific nor is the style of life they determine. This fact has recently been very clearly observed in the United States. According to Father Justin M. Ryska, O.S.M.: "For many years communities representing the five classical categories of religious life—monastic, canonical, mendicant, clerk regular, and congregation—(even though each professes a distinct style of community life) have engaged in identical apostolates. Thus Benedictines, Norbertines, Franciscans, Jesuits and Oblates, because of identical apostolates, have all modified their community life."[4]

Other people, more demanding, tend to think that a certain separation from the world, a major part of the day given over to prayer, a stricter asceticism, and activities determined by these facts are characteristic of the monastic state and distinguish it from other forms of life in the Church.

The two positions may be symbolized by two types of documents to which they refer or in whose words they express themselves. Those who hold with the first position invoke—readily, and exclusively—section 9 of

---

[4] "The Male Religious Community in Experiment for Major Authenticity," a paper given at the national convention of the Canon Law Society of America, Boston (September 2–12, 1968), p. 4.

the Decree on the Renewal of the Religious Life, which speaks of the "monastic order." Those who represent the second position quote in addition, and even with preference, section 7 of the same document, where it is a question of institutes totally dedicated to the contemplative life.

The former may find support in the "Propositions on the Benedictine Life," approved by the Congress of Abbots of the Benedictine Confederation in 1967. This text offers a sort of average doctrine on which men of very varied kinds of life can come to agreement.[5] The second group recognizes itself in the project of the "New Chart of Charity" of the Trappists,[6] or in the "Message of the Contemplative Monks to the Synod of Bishops,"[7] or again in the "Declaration of the Cistercian Abbesses," made in 1968 on their type of life.

This last document, which is little known and is valid for certain monks as much as for certain nuns, deserves quotation here as a witness to the tendency we are considering:

> [It is] a life . . . based on the sense of the transcendence of God which animates the entire Rule, and the central place that St. Benedict gives to Christ. The reply of one who is called to this life is the search for God and his will, in imitation of Christ, in obedience. When his heart has been purified by humility, he becomes ready for pure and continous prayer, and this penetrates his whole day, divided as it is between the *opus dei* and prayer, *lectio divina*—especially that of Holy Scripture—and manual work, in a style of life that is simple, poor and penitent, in a climate of silence and of that separation from the world which is necessary for attending to the things of God alone (cf. Decree on the Renewal of the Religious Life, n. 7) in contemplation. He pursues this search for God in the monastery where he has made a promise of stability in order to live in common with his brothers in the cloister in the charity of Christ, under a rule and an abbot. It is this same charity that urges him to practice Benedictine hospitality. Thus, throughout his life he wishes to respond to the mission that has been confided to him by the Church: to "bear splendid witness to the majesty and the love of God, as well as to man's

---

[5] The text has been published in French in the supplement to the *Lettre de Ligugé*, 128 (March-April 1968).

[6] Text prepared for the general chapter of 1968.

[7] In *Aspects du Monachisme* (Paris, 1968), chap. 1, I have presented and commented on this text.

brotherhood in Christ" (Decree on the Church's Missionary Activity, n. 40).[8]

This conception of the monastic life has been recently expounded, with many nuances, and clarified in the light of historical and doctrinal considerations. The most remarkable of such writings are those of Father Louis Cognet[9] and Father Ghislain Lafont.[10]

Without wishing to minimize the conflict between these two major tendencies in the heart of Western monasticism, we can say that a double problem underlies them, although it is rarely explicitly stated. Its two aspects are inseparable. The one has to do with vocabulary, the other with certain historical and philosophical facts.

QUESTIONS OF VOCABULARY

The mere fact that the word "monk" can designate men who lead entirely different kinds of life and give themselves to widely varied occupations shows that we are witnessing today a very real devaluation of monastic vocabulary. Thus a double question arises: Ought we to create new words? Or else, among the expressions inherited from tradition, may we select one that is still valid at least for one of the two tendencies evoked here?

We sometimes notice today that the vocabulary proper to Catholic Action is applied to those who wish to give themselves up solely to Catholic contemplation. Not long ago, the bishops of an entire apostolic region in France expressed their thought in the following terms:

> Those who live in the cloister pray, as did Jesus Christ, for the great intentions of the world. They listen in to the anguishes and the hopes of mankind. They are those who assure the permanence of prayer. . . . The life of these cloistered people is still largely unknown and misunderstood even among Christians. In this year of faith and in a spirit of fidelity to the directives of Paul VI, it is perhaps our

---

[8] The first draft of this text spoke of "monks," the second of "nuns." Here I have given it such a form as to be applicable to both.

[9] "Spiritualité Monastique et Laïcs d'Aujourd'hui," supplement to Écoute, 164 (May 15, 1968).

[10] "Réflexions sur la 'Vie Contemplative,'" in Lettre de Ligugé, 130 (July-August 1968), 5–27.

duty to find out in what way the cloistered life is a life in the heart of the world.[11]

Here the word "monk" was deliberately avoided. But "cloistered," that is to say "enclosed," will hardly be more welcome in a time when everyone is talking about "openness." Likewise, instead of "father" or "superior"—words to which one may attribute a Freudian tone, or a depreciatory shade of meaning veering toward authoritarianism—people readily speak, in certain circles, of the "animator" or of the one who "undertakes responsibility." Again, the oratory or chapel is called the "place of silence." For a long time certain orders have named their chiefs "ministers" or "guardians" in order to avoid the word "abbot," which from the idea of paternity had come to signify prelature. Now certain ones have come to adopt the expression "brother servant." That is what "minister" originally meant; but we all know what in our day a minister is.

Nowadays—and it is probably one of those manifestations of the acceleration of history—words wear out more quickly than before. It has been remarked how rapidly certain terms of recent ecclesiastical jargon have passed out of use, words like "apostolic," "missionary," "pastoral."[12] We could, of course, resort to neologisms. The French Academy, for example, recently admitted in one session the words "mazout," "commercialization," "bulldozer" and other imported terms.[13] But monasticism does not happen to have an Academy in every country.

Are we to remain attached to the vocabulary of a given period, for example, the period when the Rule of St. Benedict was written? Yet the patronage of this rule has now been claimed by many institutions that would have surprised its author. Not long ago, the creation of a "new kind of convent for married couples" was announced in the press. The couples, the account said, would live in small apartments, put their salaries in a common treasury, and in the matter of prayer follow the monastic Rule of St. Benedict and give themselves up to helping and educating children.[14] To want every word to be able to mean everything would be just as naive as to condemn words consecrated by tradi-

---

[11] "Collective Letter of the Bishops of the Apostolic Region Midi-Pyrénées," in *Documentation Catholique*, 55 (1968), 95*–96*.

[12] Cf. M. Bellet, *La Peur ou la Foi* (Paris, 1967), p. 91, n. 1; also H. Bourgeois and R. Schaller, *Nouveau Monde, Nouveaux Diacres* (Desclée de Brouwer, 1968), where it is noted how difficult it is today to define the words "minister," "missionary," "deacon," "diaconate."

[13] Account of this session in *Le Figaro* of April 21, 1967.

[14] Press report of November 13, 1967.

tion on the pretext that they were nonexistent at one period or another. Thus—and these examples are not pure invention—the argument has been brought forward that neither Abraham nor St. Martin called himself a contemplative.

This last word has been employed constantly, even if not by all representatives of monasticism without exception, from a time long before St. Benedict up to our own day. It is this word that was used in the "Message of the Contemplative Monks to the Synod of Bishops," which has already been mentioned. It is widely attested to by the contemporary magisterium,[15] and we know precisely what it means in the Decree on the Renewal of the Religious Life, section 7, as well as in other conciliar texts. Of course, it can still leave room for ambiguity.[16] But though rejected by certain monks, it is used by some scientists. "Scientific contemplation," writes Father R. Russo, S.J., "does not necessarily end in religious contemplation, but there exists between these two types of contemplation a certain affinity."[17]

All that is needed, perhaps, is that men concerned with spiritual matters should give a new lease on life to old words by charging them with a meaning that says something today. The following thoughts of Father Nicholas Lash are full of common sense:

> It was remarked that the received "language" of the "spiritual life" simply does not work for, communicate to, an increasing number of people. This does not mean that the problems this language has traditionally been concerned with are unimportant today; it means that, precisely by focusing on these problems from within our theological perspectives, we have to produce a viable language with which to discuss them. In the meantime, it remains true that the "old" language, which for so long had *droit de cité*, continues to affect many current theological debates (on the meaning and function of liturgical prayer, for example) more deeply than many of us might at first sight be inclined to admit. For this reason, the employment of the old

---

[15] Cf. my *Aspects de Monachisme*, chap. 4 (see note 7, supra).

[16] Cf. S. Walgrave, *Essai d'Auto-Critique d'un Ordre Religieux, les Dominicans en Fin du Concile* (Brussels, 1966), p. 127.

[17] R. Russo, S.J., "Expérience Scientifique et Ouverture à Dieu," in the supplement to *Bulletin du Cercle Saint-Jean-Baptiste* (January 1966); reproduced in the supplement of *Bulletin du Centre d'Étude des Conséquences Générales des Grandes Techniques Nouvelles*, 43 (September 1967), 8.

language by a man of Rahner's sanity and intellectual precision (I am thinking especially of the essays entitled "Reflections on the Problem of the Gradual Ascent to Christian Perfection" and "Some Thoughts on a Good Intention") could make a far more considerable contribution to the contemporary theological debate than the titles of these essays might suggest at first sight.[18]

Lastly, that new phenomenon which is the "encounter between religions" may have its contribution to make in once again giving value to the old vocabulary. It will be enough here to quote two witnesses. Dom Bede Griffiths, O. S. B., speaking of the relations between Christianity and Hinduism, wrote: "All Hindu teaching remains based, before all, on a profound mystical experience. And a dialogue in depth will never be realized except in the light of a real Christian mysticism or a true contemplation. . . . It is from such dialogue that we can hope for the development of a real contemplative theology."[19] And Professor M. O. Lacombe, of the Sorbonne, says in connection with the same problem:

> Christianity—at least in the Catholic Church—has always held mysticism in high esteem, and without confusing prophecy, prayer, mysticism, it has never wished to set up strict boundaries. It was to be the lot of the barbarity of our own times, dominated by *praxis*, to contest the rights of contemplation—under pretext that this word, or its Greek equivalent *theoria*, is not of Christian or Semitic origin. The mystic East will have none of this barbarity. Not that it is unaware of the problem of the relationship between spiritual experience and action, nor that it has refrained from finding varied solutions to it throughout the ages. The "Western Barbarians" will do well, then, to chasten their vocabulary if they wish to dialogue with the great mystical spiritualities of Asia.[20]

PROBLEMS OF DE-HELLENIZATION

Greek influence and Evangelical authenticity. In the last few years many voices have been raised against the influence that the thought of ancient Greece has had, and continues to have, on Western culture.

---

[18] *The Downside Review*, 86 (1968), 73.
[19] "Premiers Pas dans le Dialogue," in *Rythmes du Monde*, 41 (1967), 148.
[20] "Rencontre du Christianisme avec l'Hindouisme," *ibid.*, p. 141.

PRESENT-DAY PROBLEMS
Jean Leclercq, O.S.B.

31

The problem, which has now arrived at the level of theological vulgarization, and an almost outmoded one at that, is not new. Thirty years ago a Russian philosopher, Lev Shestov, in a remarkable and too little known work entitled *Athens and Jerusalem*,[21] brought up the subject of the connection between the Bible and Hellenism—especially in the chapter "Abraham and Socrates,"—and, as a consequence, the whole problem of medieval philosophy[22] and of religious philosophy in general. The theme has recently been taken up again. "Hyperplatonism" has been decried in connection with many areas.[23] In the Churches one talks about de-Hellenizing dogma,[24] and spirituality has not been left out of the debate,[25] nor monasticism either.

Ought we then to submit monasticism to the same procedure? And what will that lead us to? It cannot be merely a question of eliminating the Greek words. Modern language is full of them, and no one dreams of complaining about that. It is amusing to think that from the United States, via Austria, has arrived in France the adjective "metropolitan" applied not to a category of bishops or archbishops, but to an underground railway.[26] The Metropolitana of Rome is the most recent example of this proliferation that has taken place, and this time in the feminine. The Oxford Dictionary gives no less than ten derivatives in English of the Greek word *metropolis*,[27] and in the United States the adjective *metropolitan* is associated with other words of Greek origin: *museum, orchestra*. Let us not be ashamed of certain titles of nobility for our Western languages.

For us, however, the problem is much deeper. A recent essay by Father Markus Ohlislager has brilliantly set it forth.[28] If ancient spirituality in

---

[21] Paris, 1938; Athens, Ohio: Ohio University Press, 1966.
[22] *Ibid.*, pp. 366–380, in connection with E. Gilson, *L'Esprit de la Philosophie Médiévale* (Paris, 1944).
[23] This expression is in H. J. Barraud, *Science et Philosophie* (Louvain, 1968).
[24] J. F. Lonergan, "The De-Hellenization of Dogma," in *Theological Studies*, 28 (1967); P. McKewitt, "De-Hellenization of Dogma," in *Irish Ecclesiastical Record*, 109 (1968), 1–10.
[25] S. Walgrave, *op. cit.*, pp. 123–124; P. Duployé, *Les Origines du Centre de Pastorale Liturgique 1943–1948* (Paris, 1968), pp. 256–257, 267–268.
[26] J. Rey-Deboue, "Métropolitain et Métro," in *Cahiers de Lexicologie*, 5 (1964), 101–109.
[27] *Ibid.*, p. 106, n. 21.
[28] Cf. M. Ohlislager, O.S.B., "De-Hellenization of Monastic Life," in *American Benedictine Review*, 18 (1967), 517–530.

large part became monastic, it was because of the influence of Gnosticism, Stoicism, and Manicheism, but especially of Plato. The cultural setting that this determined led to a deviation of the meaning of Christianity. Adulterating the biblical fact, men went off into solitude in order to seek God apart from the world. In the same way, we can explain the vows, the conception of the abbot and his power, silence, asceticism, private prayer, the "so-called contemplative life, which seems to lack realism since it is cultivated by the spiritual element in man rather than by his whole person." [29]

This last phrase—taken out of its context, which is not wanting in certain nuances—is enough to show that there are in this presentation an extremely complex historical element and a great deal of simplification. The point was to prove that today we must give ourselves to "dialogue, communication and sharing of spiritual gifts."[30] The demonstration could well have been given with less party spirit, better information and more mature theological thought.[31]

History shows, indeed, that in the liturgy, for example, one has of set purpose "de-Semitized" in order to "Hellenize." And in many fields, even if unconsciously, the Hellenic Church thought after the manner of the Greeks because it was Greek, whereas the Judeo-Christian Church was gradually dying out. The Fathers Christianized Hellenism much more than they Hellenized Christianity.[32] It would be ungracious to reproach them with that in these present days, when we are so eager to rethink Christianity according to modern categories. Marx and Freud today play a role analogous to Plato's and Aristotle's roles in earlier times.

Moreover, Hellenization had already started in the time of the sapiential literature of the Old Testament and of the Septuagint. The vocabulary that these use is to be found again in the New Testament.

---

[29] *Ibid.*, p. 527.

[30] *Ibid.*, p. 529.

[31] For example, when one wonders in connection with one or another form of religious life, or its occupations, such as contemplative prayer, whether it is biblical or whether the Lord has counseled it (cf. *ibid.*, p. 521). Fr. J. Sudbrack has shown that a "biblical word-for-word criterion is naively antihistoric": "Das Neue Wagen und das Alte Gewinnen," in *Geist und Leben* 41 (1968), 179–181.

[32] G. Floyd, review of R. A. Norris, *God and World in Early Christian Theology*, in *The Downside Review*, 85 (July, 1967), 350–351.

PRESENT-DAY PROBLEMS   33
Jean Leclercq, O.S.B.

Must we de-Hellenize St. Paul, St. John, the whole of the New Testament, to make them Christian? Ought we not rather to stand in wonder at the fact that "the synthesis of Hellenism and Judaism preceded Christ,"[33] and in this sense paved the way for the diffusion of his message? It would seem that at Qumran, during nearly two hundred years of monastic life, the consciousness of sin and the need for grace was due not to Iranian dualism but to Messianic hope.[34]

If St. Paul is a Hellenist in certain points of his culture, he continues to have a Hebrew mentality. The Greek dualism of body and soul is absorbed, in him, in the contrast between sinful flesh and the glory of the spirit communicated by the Resurrection of Christ.[35] The concern to refer the gospel to a wider world than that of Hellenism appeared very early, and he independently echoed it. "It is in connection with the Christological hymn quoted in the Epistle to the Philippians," J. Murphy O'Connor has stated, "that it has been written: 'The Greco-Roman man is close to our contemporaries in many respects.' "[36]

Later on, Clement of Alexandria set about a "fully conscious and willed Hellenization of Christianity, and yet he is the most Christian of his contemporaries."[37] Tertullian objected: "What is there in common between Athens and Jerusalem?" Nevertheless, the evolution went on. St. Augustine played an important part, one that was decisive for the complete history of the West.[38] It is in connection with his conception of the monastic life that a study by Father Robert Javelet recalled and confirmed the results obtained by previous research: "On many points

---

[33] H. U. von Balthasar, La Foi du Christ (Paris, 1968), p. 172.

[34] This has been shown by Ringeren in The Faith of Qumran (Philadelphia, 1963).

[35] Cf. McLaslard, The Interpreter's Dictionary of the Bible (New York, 1962), art. "Man," vol. III, 235–252.

[36] In his review of P. Martin, Carmen Christi, Phil. ii, 5–11, in Recent Interpretation and in the Setting of Early Christian Worship (Cambridge, 1967), in Revue Biblique, 75 (1968), 115–116. An interesting link between the problems of the first Christian centuries and those of our times is likewise suggested by J. P. Audet, ibid., p. 149.

[37] T. Camelot, "Bulletin d'Histoire des Doctrines Anciennes," in Revue des Sciences, Philosophiques et Théologiques, 51 (1967), 685–686.

[38] A. Zumkeller, "Biblische und altchristliche Leitbilder des Klösterlichen Lebens in Schriften des heiligen Augustinus," in Augustiniana, 18 (1968), 17.

of doctrine, in spite of the well-known influence that Platonism had on him, he does not remain shut up within this philosophy; he lives in a theology born of Holy Scripture."[39]

One can observe signs of this integration of Greek thought with Christianity throughout antiquity and the Middle Ages. In the latter period we are struck by the coexistence of, on the one hand, a literature that gives expression to a certain contempt of worldly values and, on the other, a practical concern for beauty, hygiene, health, for artistic, literary and musical creativity, and for esthetics in all fields.[40] In every way we witness a continual deepening of certain values inherited from antiquity. A theme such as "to live with oneself," which was not very evocative with Epictetus or Persius, came to evoke more and more realities as it passed through the hands of Gregory the Great, St. Bruno, William of Saint-Theirry and St. Bernard, for whom the Christian contemplative "must know how to conciliate withdrawal into self with charity."[41] That, surely, is what may rightly be called a "transfigured Hellenism."[42]

Fashions pass rapidly, and after that of excessive de-Hellenization, today, on the basis of solid information instead of catchwords, there are some who are beginning to take sides with Platonism. This is not always done with impartiality. For instance, G. F. Pollard wrote recently: "What I ask to see is a return to the tradition of Christian Platonism, which continues to bear so much fruit in the Eastern Church, where the patristic Palamite doctrine has not been replaced by Thomist innovation."[43]

---

[39] The evolution is illustrated, in a chapter on Christian anthropology, in his *Image et Ressemblance au Douzième Siècle de S. Anselme à Alain de Lille* (Paris, 1957). He concludes that an optimistic conception (excessive, in his opinion) of man was held by the authors of the twelfth century. On his side, J. B. Russel, in *Dissent and Reform in the Early Middle Ages* (University of California Press, 1967), has shown that the elements of pessimism and dualism to be found in the Neoplatonic tradition were counterbalanced in orthodox Catholicism; the heretical teachings of Catharism upset the balance from about the middle of the twelfth century onward.

[40] This I have tried to show in connection with St. Bernard in *S. Bernard et l'Esprit Cistercien* (Paris, 1966) and in several articles on his esthetic, the first of which, "Essais sur l'Esthetique de S. Bernard," has appeared in the review *Studi Medievali*, 9 (1968), 688–728.

[41] The history of this theme has been set forth with immense erudition by P. Courcelle, in " 'Habitare secum' selon Perse et selon S. Grégoire le Grand," *Revue des Etudes Anciennes*, 69 (1967), 266–279.

[42] F. Guimet, in *Le Doute et la Foi* (Paris, 1968), p. 198.

[43] "Christian Mysticism," in *New Christian*, August 22, 1968, p. 15.

With greater balance, and no less energy, an English scholar, E. I. Watkins, has written:

> I strongly dissent from an unfavorable estimate of Neoplatonism as a distorting and baneful influence on Christian mysticism. Far from contaminating Christian mystical theology, Neoplatonism enabled it to achieve a precision and an understanding of itself otherwise unattainable. It was Neoplatonism—as derived on the one hand from Plotinus through Augustine, on the other from St. Gregory of Nyssa and Proclus through the pseudo-Dionysius—that taught definitively the "negative" way to God and experience of him, which is the center and substance of mysticism. For it cannot be said that the doctrine of adherence in blind faith to a Godhead beyond image or concept, such as is taught by the Catholic mystics and preeminently St. John of the Cross, is explicitly taught either in the New Testament or by primitive Christian writers unaffected directly or indirectly by Platonism. There is a fashionable but destructive tendency among contemporary Catholic thinkers to remove from the total Catholic religion its Hellenic constituent which, if successful, would deprive Catholicism of its claim to be genuinely Catholic.[44]

Is it necessary to add that this conception of mystical experience, inspired by Neoplatonism, is one of the points on which Christianity, perhaps more precisely in the tradition of Catholicism, comes nearer to the religions of the Far East? And again, is it necessary to remind ourselves that Plotinus, in his "passion" for Indian thought, had wanted to visit that country?[45]

Lastly, this principle of evolution has been set out by Karl Rahner. Everything in the Church that is "historical" as distinct from what is "revealed"—in other words, all that has arisen as a result of spatiotemporal influences—need not be eliminated from the Christian religion, which is eminently historical. In becoming man, God entered our history, and the Church shares in this.[46] The tendency of these last years toward a de-Hellenization bears witness to a generous "openness" in that it rejects certain elements that it had insisted upon too much during other periods. Nevertheless, another form of this same openness consists in respecting

[44] *The Downside Review*, 18 (1967), 342–343.
[45] Cf. H. de Lubac, *La Rencontre du Bouddhisme et de l'Occident*, (Paris, 1952), pp. 22–24.
[46] *Geist und Leben*, 18 (1967), 136.

values that for Christians have not only contributed toward civilization but also contributed within revelation itself to its historic development.

Concretely, the question for us is to know whether the Greek tradition helped our predecessors to grasp more exactly the sense of monasticism and of the contemplative life within the Church. We may say that the result has been positive. We may apply to its major concepts what has recently been written about the words they were expressed in, which "implied a cultural choice." Far from having a grievance against the early Christians for having gone out to meet their culture and having partly taken their words and mentality from it, we should, on the contrary, acknowledge that they only did what we wish to do today, and that on this particular point their effort contributes to the "recapitulation" in Christ of all the wealth of history or human thought.

The contribution of Greece and Rome is not a sign of decadence; it is, we grant, limited, directed, and we have perhaps dealt with it in a very "oriented" way, but the values to which it has in some measure given a basis have acquired standing in Christian thought. From this point of view, the monastic words of the Middle Ages challenge us today, just as they proclaim "essential truths about man's prayer."[47]

In short, the problem of the de-Hellenization of monasticism is a real problem, and not an imaginary one, and certain of the solutions that have been proposed will doubtless be found among those that the future will adopt. But the method does not have to be either radical or simplifying or impoverishing. We do not have to de-Hellenize on principle or to search for St. Benedict's fundamental idea under its cultural veils, which, anyway, it is impossible for us to do. As Father Ghislain Lafont has said:

> Our culture is made up of the intersection of Greco-Roman thought and the Hebrew religion, and it is not our business to deny either the one or other, or the fruits of their union. The correct and positive method is rather to pay attention to the real values that our times are discovering and to make place for them in *our living tradition.* Then certain elements of our life will fall away of themselves in order to leave room for others, but there will have been no rupture; we shall not have risked throwing the baby out with the bath water. The meaning of time, of "directed duration," of work, of the community as a meeting of persons and a place of exchange, will certainly

[47] G. Lafont, O.S.B., in *La Vie Spirituelle* (1968).

modify, in the monastic life, brotherly relations, the style of authority, the practice of silence, forms of economy.[48]

Will the changes be radical? Is the contemplative life—with what it has in the way of withdrawal from the world and search for union with God by a prayer as continuous as possible—destined to disappear? The future alone will tell: no one can decide about it in the name of any modern theory about monasticism. We may assume that within the Church there will always be forms of life inspired by the hidden life at Nazareth, by the withdrawal of Jesus into the desert and his nocturnal prayer. Let us avoid contesting, under pretext of de-Hellenizing, facts that are authentically evangelical.

Greek influence and universalism. There is another aspect of the process of de-Hellenization that is worth mentioning, according to the theory of its chief representative, the Canadian theologian Leslie Dewart.[49] In a broad sense, one we could admit, so long as we come to an agreement about the words used, this process consists, for faith and the Church today, in transcending the past—the whole past symbolized by a single one of the periods that have influenced Christian thought, that of Hellenism, which was first Platonic and then, during the Scholastic period, Aristotelian. From this point of view, de-Hellenization no longer signifies "de-Platonization," but, if one may say so, "de-Aristotleization." It designates the fact of consciously fashioning the historical cultural form that Christianity needs today in order to survive. In other words, in positive terms, we have to consciously create future belief.[50]

In the past, the fact that witnesses of Christian thought, from St. Paul to St. Augustine, adopted the cultural form of Hellenism allowed them to render the gospel message "catholic" by making it penetrate into the universe of their own times, which was entirely subject to Greek influence. If this process brought in its wake, as Adolf Harnack thinks, a substantial corruption of Christianity, we should have set about clearing away this influence, and the Church would not have waited until now to do so.[51] But Hellenization has not substituted a false Christianity for the

---

[48] Cf. the article of G. Lafont, referred to in note 10 above, pp. 14–21.

[49] *The Future of Belief: Theism in a World Come of Age* (New York: Herder and Herder, 1966). I shall present here only the general problem posed by this book which, moreover, claims to be nothing more than an essay. Several of the specific points it deals with, and the hypotheses put forward, have already been the object of remarks from several critics.

[50] *Ibid.*, pp. 49–50.

[51] *Ibid.*, pp. 112–13.

true one; it has enriched it and at the same time limited it. What we have to do, then, is merely to be discerning. We must maintain the riches and go beyond the limitation. We must set Christianity free from a particular cultural form in order to open it up to other forms—those of the scientific world (we can think here of Pierre Teilhard de Chardin), those of the Far East, those of Africa.

Hellenization was formerly a benefit: it made possible the universalization of Christianity. Thus what may perhaps no longer be excellent today was so during the first four centuries of the Church. But this alliance of Christianity to a culture, and to one alone, has in fact prevented Christianity from developing in other cultures and allying itself with them. Let us think, for example, of the quarrels over rites in India and China in the sixteenth and seventeenth centuries. From this point of view, de-Hellenization is perhaps essential for Indianization and Africanization. If we cease making Christianity dependent on one specific culture in its forms of thought, its expression, its conduct, we shall open it out to other cultures; we shall give it a chance to become richer, to assume new elements, to communicate itself, in Asia and elsewhere, to whole peoples entirely different from those who received Hellenized Christianity.

One of the intentions of the partisans of de-Hellenization is to liberate theology from a conception and a method that have been too speculative, in order to reintroduce an experimental dimension.[52] But this has never been wanting in monasticism, and it is even one of the elements that characterizes monastic theology. From this point of view, monasticism must be prepared to contribute to the integration of new cultures and new religious traditions in Christianity. It would at the same time favor the acceptance of Christianity by new peoples. It would be missionary in the way that is proper to it. It will doubtless share in what good there is in the de-Hellenization that has already started, but it must not cringe before it; it must look it in the face with optimism. Especially to the degree that monasticism is present among other cultures, particularly in Asia, it must see openness to these cultures as one of its functions.

It will also have to modify its structures and its conceptions if these prevent it from adopting what is good, valid for itself, in the monasticism of the countries where it happens to be. The witness of an Indian Cath-

---

[52] *Ibid.*, p. 174; R. Hinners, "Metaphysics and De-Hellenization," in *Continuum*, 5 (1968), 710–712.

olic, Sachit Dhar, will serve as a good illustration of this consideration. He wrote in 1965: "In our contacts with the West, we come up against men who have an arrogant belief in their own superiority, in their way of living, in their religious conception." After having remarked that already a minority of Asians "under the influence of Marx or of the dollar has lost its religion" and that this double materialism is a growing danger, he added: "A common resistance to this menace could come from the ashramic organization of Indian society. By Buddhism, the same idea has influenced the other Asiatic countries. It sees human life as constructed on four levels: that of the disciple of the holy tradition, that of father of a family, that of the solitary, that of the wandering monk."
And he continued:

> That does not mean that technical progress must be stopped or slowed down, any more in the Eastern world than in the West. No. But on all continents, religious men must unite their efforts so that technology remains within the limits of true necessity. Then the real values will have their place in the great synthesis, and it will lose its Promethean aspect.
>
> There are only little groups now keeping alive in Asia the sacred fire and preparing the future ashramic society. They are like those communities of monks who saved culture in the dark ages of history. Let this age of darkness over Asia come to an end, and let there be the dawning of a new age of spirituality; then these exceptions will multiply and become the reigning elite and will realize the dream of a truly evangelical and universal coexistence, of a brotherly society in Christ, who leads it to his Father.
>
> The darker the night, the more we should be grateful to those who are the outposts. Never has the service that religious render been more necessary than it is today. That is true for India and for the West, for priest monks and for lay monks, for those who remain inside their convents and for those who carry with them their invisible convent. Even the vocation of the solitary has rediscovered its meaning.[53]

The Christian monastic theory has always been a synthesis between permanent elements, primordial ones, those that come from the gospel and constant monastic tradition, and cultural elements, historical ones

---

[53] "L'Asie, la Chrétienté, l'Humanité," in *Rythmes du Monde*, 41 (1967), 158.

bound up with determined moments in evolution. The general conception of the world, of society and of the place that monasticism has within it has been modified more or less according to the times; it has known more or less lengthy periods of stability. It is now undergoing rapid and profound change. Monastic theory must, then, be constantly revised. We must avoid fixing it once and for all, but we must also avoid making it lose, in the course of its development, certain of its essential factors. And it is not easy to practice this discernment and this updating in a time when the knowledge we have of both the gospel and monastic history is undergoing change and, we may say, progressing.

One of the forms of monastic asceticism is that of accepting the fact that the theory of monasticism, the justification that monks have for their life, remains constantly insufficient, subject to revision and transformation. Let them never enjoy an absolute speculative security, but let them have confidence. The progress of their spirituality and of the forms of their existence entails a certain risk, which they must accept in the Holy Spirit. The charisma that was, and remains, at the origin of their life will allow them to continue to be within the Church, instruments in God's service and for the universal expansion of his work among men.

MONASTICISM IN A CHANGING SOCIETY

One of the aspects of the present-day crisis in monasteries is that certain monks within their ranks query their raison d'être in the name of contemporary anthropology and sociology and of theological considerations. Do contemplatives, then, all have to do something of immediate utility —and what? Will the solution come from "sociological experiments," kinds of "commandos," in which very small groups of religious will live without anything to distinguish their existence, prayer, activity, from those of other men? Will monks henceforth be obliged to find new raisons d'être solely in terms of a wider openness to the world?

One of the reasons advanced for a reduction of the number of monks in the priestly order and of the kinds of activities to which large numbers lead is that their continuance "would definitively impede a wide-openness of monasteries to lay Christians of those milieus toward which the Church today wishes to be particularly attentive,"[54] those that are less rich in the economic and cultural spheres. Must we find similar reasons for every aspect of monasticism?

[54] G. Lafont, O.S.B., "L'Appel des Moines au Sacerdoce," in *Supplément de la Vie Spirituelle*, 86 (September 1968), 443.

The problem is of a theological nature. Every state of life within the Church is only justified if it is a service, a "diaconate." But if all these services are services in and for the Church, they are diverse and, in fact, in the Church—just as in modern society, where professional competence is more and more the law—they are specialized. To quote Father Lafont once again: "Service can just as well consist in prayer carried out in withdrawal from the world as in a contribution to the technological and cultural betterment of the world."[55] It is also insisted upon more and more today that the relationship of man and God is lived in the relationships with other men.[56] One can only save oneself in helping to save them, in having had "experience of one's neighbor in love."[57]

We can guess at the meaning, as also the demands, that these considerations—the second, especially—introduce into every community life within the religious state. For it supposes that in the community there will be a real encounter between man and man, which in turn supposes that there are real men there, each with a real personality. Each shares in the other's life, and thus there is a mutual witnessing to faith—not in words, but by a life that is shared in all its aspects. There is exchange in charity, and this makes prayer and the other monastic activities bear fruit. The community as such must have a spiritual life, and not, or not only, each one of the individuals who make it up. The more personal each one is, that is to say, the more he differs from the others in his nature and grace, the more he will contribute to the wealth of the whole. He will stay himself and he will develop for God and the Church in the measure that he gives and receives.

Indeed, monasticism participates in the Church's mission of salvation with regard to the world. It must be open to it. There is, however, an illegitimate openness of monasticism to the world, and it must be warned against: the work done by monasticism in the pastoral, educational, social, and charitable fields has its limits. If it does not remain within these limits, it is unfaithful to its specific function, its special service in the Church for the world—to be a sign of eschatological hope.

But does that mean that the whole of the contemplative's life of prayer must become visible and perceptible? Does the fact of existing *for* others (*Da sein für andere*) necessarily imply "being *with*" (*Sein mit*)?

---

[55] Cf. J. Sudbrack, S. J., "Das Neue Wagen und das Alte Gewinnen," in *Geist und Leben*, 41 (1968), 184.
[56] *Ibid.*, p. 186.
[57] F. Wulff, S. J., "Der Auftrag des Mönchtums in der Modernen Welt," in *Liturgie und Mönchtum*, 43 (1968), 56.

There is room for a consented withdrawal, one that is a way of "being present to" and of "living for." In this sense there is a real relation of absence. If the Church is for the world, it is in order to announce the kingdom, and this is done according to the different charisms of men and communities. Is not one of the things the Church has to say to mankind that there should be men and communities that live withdrawn from the world? Is that not one part of its mission? Simply because the Church is sent to the world, we cannot conclude that all men and communities must live its mission out by directly participating in the world.

It is said that we must have an experience of our neighbor. But cannot this be realized in prayer, especially in a life where all prayer is guaranteed, upheld, stimulated, by an austerity that is a constant reminder of self-renunciation? For the experience of our neighbor takes place in faith, and the experience that can be had in a life consecrated to God may well consist in meeting this neighbor in the contemplative existence, or in those persons with whom one shares a common life, and beyond that, in all men in the name of whom, in union with whom, one prays and meets with God.

Can we draw any conclusions from all this? If we are attentive to the movement of the ongoing Church, one has the presentiment, contemplatives will have to have more and more contacts with the world, exercise more and more influence on it, without being less centered on prayer. It is our duty to foresee this evolution, to accept it graciously, as one of the signs of the times. We shall have to help monasticism find within the Christian social order the place that is to be its own from now on. The problem no longer concerns merely contemplatives themselves, but also the heads of the Church, the clergy, the religious of the apostolic life and all the faithful. Occupations must be found for them that will not only allow them to earn their bread but also contribute to the Church's efforts in the apostolic and cultural fields.

For contemplatives themselves, the first form of presence to the world will consist in an attention to the world: both to the cosmos and to all humanity—to the actions and the constructions, to the becoming and the progress, to the problems and dangers of men. Their first duty will be to be informed about the great problems of the times and of the renewal in theology.

But considerations of this sort lead us to a practical problem. Is this separation-communion best realized at a distance from the world, far from it, or close to it, within it? More and more, monks and nuns who are not yet in urban areas are being faced with the problem of an "urban monasticism." Must they move toward the cities, and in that case how will they organize their existence?[58]

Here again the search for an answer must bear on two points: the location and the type of community. One cannot just transplant into town a type of life thought out in terms of living conditions in the country or according to the forms, psychological or other, of rural life. Location in a city will determine the habitat, time schedule observances, occupations; more and more these will have to take into consideration the site and milieu. All this will raise problems, and the solutions will call for imagination. To mention only one aspect of the life of a monastery, the welcome and hospitality extended to visitors may be thought out along two different lines: either as a simple openness of the monastic family to anyone who may wish to take a serious part in its life; or else along the lines of a more marked apostolate after the manner of a retreat house or a residence for spiritual directors. And in addition to imagination in the practical sphere, it will be necessary to have some in that of theory. It will be necessary to elaborate what the title of a recent book calls a "town theology."[59]

Connected with the problem of location is that of the type of community. A good many signs seem to show that on the whole, and for a number of reasons, communities will be much smaller, more restricted than in the past. Not that the larger communities will cease to have a reason to exist. On the contrary, they will possibly find a new one—to serve as a support for the smaller communities. These will need to be part of a well-organized whole, in which links will be assured both between themselves and with larger monasteries. In each, charity will be lived on the level of human relations of a more personal kind, and for that reason it will be all the more demanding. Certain less organized forms of welcome, of a spontaneous nature, may also be encouraged.

We can readily acknowledge that under certain political or social conditions the practice of one particular monastery in Brazil is perhaps the only possibility. From the point of view of economy and employment, however, not everyone need imitate it. Quite near the Abbey of St. Benedict at Olinda, near Recife, is the little ecumenical foundation of

[58] The problem of the substitution of an urban civilization for a rural civilization is not the same in the West as elsewhere, nor is it the same in Japan as in other Asian countries. But everywhere psychology is being influenced by growing urbanization, and monasticism must take the consequences of this fact into consideration.
[59] J. Comblin, *Théologie de la Ville* (Brussels, 1968).

the monks of Taizé. It is made up of four Protestant brothers and a few Catholic monks from Olinda. They live quite simply in a rented house, work in town as drivers, bank clerks and so forth. They pray together and offer the witness of brotherly charity by the common life they lead, and of hope in the Resurrection by consecrated chastity. Their presence is a living question, posed expecially to youth, and many come to find an answer in talking with the monks.

"A religion flourishes with its monasticism," says Dom François de Grunne, "so much so that the decadence of the monasticism is not only the sign but also the cause of the decadence of the religion."[60] Likewise, the vitality of a monasticism will be the proof of the vitality of the religion.

SYNTHESIS OF GROUP DISCUSSIONS
December 9, 1968

POSSIBILITIES OF AN ASIAN CHRISTIAN MONASTICISM

Questions for discussion:[1]

1. *What, in general, are the local customs and institutions you feel should be integrated into community life?*
2. *Ought we to consider the possibility of eremitical life for members of the community, and if so, under what form?*
3. *Does it seem desirable to set up small monastic groups that would be supported by a community of the traditional type?*
4. *Does it seem opportune to establish a certain liaison between the different monasteries, and if so, under what form?*

1. *Customs and institutions to be integrated into the monastic life.* The discussion began with the pointing out of certain dangers inherent in this sort of integration: first, the danger of purely exterior and superficial imitation; second, the danger of going backward, whether to an inferior level of civilization or to the customs of another age that are destined to disappear; or finally, to practices contrary to the monastic or the Christian spirit.

To avoid these dangers, it seemed helpful to recognize three levels of customs. The most superficial of the levels is concerned with details of

[60] Review of K. Klostermaier, *Hinduismus*, in *Rythmes du Monde* (1967), p. 224.

[1] The questions are based on the questionnaire, Part I. A and Part IV (Appendix B, pp. 277 and 279). See also the summary of replies to Part I. A (pp. 282–286) and Part IV (pp. 315–321).

nourishment, clothing, manner of greeting, etc. These seem to be able to evolve easily enough.

Other customs more directly express a mentality proper to the country—for example, the way of expressing respect, obedience or filial devotion. Certain members of the groups pointed out that too many Europeans in a community make the development of an authentically local way of expressing itself difficult.

Finally, and more profundly, there are religious customs that are still more difficult to understand and whose study requires the help of specialists.

Among all these customs, it was felt, those ought to be chosen that faithfully interpret, according to the manner of the country, the authentic principles of the Benedictine life. Those European customs that are in contradiction to legitimate local usage ought accordingly to be dropped.

One of the obstacles to such adaptation is the difficulty certain Christians and certain monks have in understanding the need for these changes. It seemed prudent to adopt, if possible, only those usages that do not provoke division but, on the contrary, favor unity.

To stimulate this movement, a renewal of the traditions, the culture and the national religion that can be presently verified would certainly be profitable in all the countries of Asia.

Another problem that attracted attention was that of the impact of the modern world on traditional customs, which tend to disappear. One of the roles of the Church in a country should be to discover what is good in these traditions, both to preserve it and to help express it in a more modern way.

Once more it was insisted that specialists or institutes were needed to guide any attempts to study these questions.

2. *The eremitical life*. The non-Christian context of the eremitical life in the different countries of Asia is extremely varied.

The life of the hermit seems unknown in Vietnam. In Ceylon and in Korea, hermits dependent on cenobitic communities are well respected, but wandering solitaries are scorned. On the contrary, in India and in Cambodia the hermits or solitaries in the forest represent the state of mysticism and of the most exalted sanctity. In Cambodia, fervent monks are able to spend some weeks or some months in solitary hermitages.

In Christian monasticism there is much less variety. The eremitical life already exists, in fact, in India, and in Japan and Indonesia. In some other countries one can scarcely see how it can exist. But elsewhere some communities consider the idea of an eremitical life very favorably, be it permanent or temporary. It seems, indeed, that in countries where a non-Christian, serious and respected eremitical life exists, Christian hermits may be necessary to the Church in order to demonstrate that mystical prayer exists also among Christians.

For a practical realization of Christian eremitical life several solutions were envisaged: the hermitage could perhaps be an isolated place on the monastery property, if it is large enough, or even in a room in a solitary corner of a large house; on the contrary, it could be in a place far from the monastery but dependent on it. But whatever might be decided about the placement of the hermitage, an eremitical life, whether strictly enclosed or more or less open to contacts with people from outside, should be considered.

The form of hermitage chosen must be carefully studied—with the help of monks who show a real vocation for this state—in regard to the community, to the persons in question and to exterior circumstances.

3. *Small monastic groups.* It must be noted, first of all, that most of the groups did not have time to discuss the last two questions suitably. Only a few ideas were exchanged, and they will demand further study.

First, two types of "small groups" were envisaged: a group restricted to a few people in agreement, "commandos of experimentation"; secondly, communities of restricted size, not to go beyond thirty.

As for the small groups, it seemed, as a result of various sorts of experiences, that there must be at least five or six persons in the group. These groups have the advantage of greater adaptability to the country. Neither large buildings nor great amounts of capital are needed; there is also a possibility of the monks and nuns working like the people around them and living like them. Young people from the country would be able to enter, as a matter of course, into this kind of monastic life without feeling estranged from their normal surroundings. These small groups would depend on a more important central monastery, where the house of formation would be.

For those leading a more active life, the advantages are that such groups permit the deepening of the spiritual life in a simple community life, by avoiding being completely absorbed in activity, and create spiritual centers in the region for priests, religious and the faithful. This form of life has been asked for in Korea by many native bishops.

It was remarked, also, that if the communities are to be viable, their particular purpose must be clearly defined.

For want of time, there was hardly any allusion to the difficulties of realizing these projects. Certain delegates insisted only that these houses should be able to support themselves financially.

As for monasteries of restricted size, many recommended these in preference to the great monasteries, because they make possible a more simple and hence more human life, and because they allow the formation of the young in the sort of milieu where they will live, which is not the case with the smaller groups.

4. *Bonds between the monasteries.* The value was stressed of having more meetings like the present one, or meetings on a regional scale, so that

religious might get to know each other and help each other in reflecting on common problems. Besides, it seemed that an organization flexibly grouping the Asian monasteries in a kind of conference would give weight to the demands of monasteries presented to the civil authorities, to the hierarchy and to the authorities in Rome. It could also be used to organize mutual aid, such as loan of professors, and circulating of lectures, or to provide retreats and other common services.

PRAYER
(In English)

Wisdom of the Father, when thy earliest prophets were reminding Israel of the greatness and of the true nature of Yahweh, thy Father, and composing the inspired accounts of creation, the *rishis*[1] of our land were striving for the knowledge of the true Atman, who is the ultimate cause of the universe. That intense longing to know thee has been kept alive by thy Spirit in the hearts of many of our countrymen even today. Fulfill that desire and reveal thyself to our brothers so that they may come to know thee as Lord and thy Father who in his love sent thee into this world. Amen.

FIRST READING
(In English)

What is the description of the man who has a firmly founded wisdom, whose being is steadfast in spirit?

The blessed Lord said:

When a man puts away all desires of his mind, and when his spirit is content in itself, then he is called stable in intelligence.

He whose mind is untroubled in the midst of sorrows and is free from eager desire amid pleasures, he from whom passion, fear and rage have passed away: he is called a sage of settled intelligence.

He who is without attachment on any side, who does not rejoice or loathe as he obtains good or evil: his intelligence is firmly set in wisdom.

He who draws away his senses from the objects of sense on every side, as a tortoise draws his legs into his shell: his intelligence is firmly set in wisdom.

---

[1] Ancient Indian seers.

Even though a man may ever strive for perfection and be most discerning, his impetuous senses will carry off his mind by force.

When a man dwells in his mind on the objects of sense, attachment to them is produced. From attachment springs desire, and from desire comes anger. From anger arises bewilderment, from bewilderments loss of memory, and from loss of memory the destruction of intelligence; from destruction of intelligence he perishes.

But a man of disciplined mind, who moves among the objects of sense with his senses under control and free from attachment and aversion: he attains purity of spirit.

And in that purity of spirit is produced for him an end of all sorrow; the intelligence of such a man of pure spirit is soon established in the peace of the Self.

For the uncontrolled, there is no intelligence; nor for the uncontrolled is there power of concentration; for him without concentration, there is no peace; and for the unpeaceful, how can there be happiness?

When the mind runs after the roving senses, it carries away the understanding, even as a wind carries away a ship on the waters.

He, therefore, whose senses are all withdrawn from their objects: his intelligence is firmly set.

What is night for all beings is the time of waking for the disciplined soul; and what is the time of waking for all beings is night for the sage who sees. He into whom all desires enter as waters into the sea, which, though being ever filled is ever motionless, attains to peace, and not he who clings to his desires. He who abandons all desires and acts free from longing, without any sense of mineness or egotism: he attains to peace.

This is the divine state; having attained thereto, one is not again bewildered; fixed in that state at the end, at the hour of death, one can attain to the bliss of God.

—Bhagavad-Gita ("The Characteristics of the Perfect Sage")

SECOND READING
(*In French*)

In all things man must take hold of God and accustom his mind to having God constantly present in his deepest depths, both in his intentions and in his love. Mark well in what manner you should yearn after your God. The dispositions that are yours in church or in your cell, those same ones you must keep and carry with you in the heart of the crowd, amid the agitation and hostility of the world.

And when we speak of sameness, we do not mean that the same value must be given to every work alike, to every place or to every man. That would be a great mistake: it is more meritorious, indeed, to pray than to spin, and the church is nobler than the street. But in all your works you must be of the same mind and the same trust, and maintain the same gravity with regard to your God. Indeed, were you to persevere in such sameness, no one would hinder you from enjoying the presence of your God. Whereas to him who does not really possess God in this way in his deepest depths, it easily happens that he meets with some obstacle, for he does not possess God, and it is not God alone whom he seeks, whom he loves and whom he sets before himself. Thus he is hindered not only by bad company, not only by evil words and evil deeds, but even by good works, for the obstacle lies within himself: God has not come to be his all. If God were all for him, he would be at ease everywhere and with everyone, for he would possess God and none would be able to snatch him away, nor turn such a one from his work.

In what, then, does this true possession of God consist in such wise that he is truly ours?

This true possession of God has its source within the soul who, with fervent vigilance, turns to God and yearns for him. It is not a question of thinking constantly of him at all times; that would be impossible or most difficult for our nature, and it would not even be the best solution. Man must not content himself with a God who is a mere figment of his thought: when the thought shall have passed away, God too shall go. Far better, what we must possess is

God in substance, he who is beyond the thought of man and of every other creature. That God never leaves us—unless a man voluntarily turns from him.

He who thus possesses God substantially takes hold of him by the divine part of his own nature, and God enlightens him in all things. For such a man, everything savors of God; for him, God is reflected in all things and God shows himself to him at all times. Such a one, in his deepest depths, has withdrawn himself, has turned aside from all, and his God, whom he loves and who is present, takes form there. The same occurs when one is greatly parched and very thirsty: one may do all else but drink, and think of everything else but that; but whatever one does or wherever one may be, whatever may be one's plans, or thoughts or businesses, as long as the thirst persists one is obsessed with the thought of a drink, and the greater the thirst, the more vivid the thought of drink, the more deep, actual and constant.

Such a man is all the more pleasing to God in that he takes all things in their godly aspect and estimates them at greater value than they are worth in themselves. Of course, for this one needs zeal and love, attentive watchfulness over the human conscience, a vigilant, true and effective intelligence that directs the whole spiritual attitude with regard to things and men. Man cannot acquire this intelligence by an attitude of evasion, by running away from things in order to take refuge in solitude, far from the outer world. On the contrary, he must learn an inner solitude wherever he may be, in whatever company he may find himself.

He must learn to penetrate the depths of things, to take hold of his God there and be able, by a vigorous effort of his conscience, to give him form substantially.

It is thus that a man must be soaked with the presence of God, refashioned according to the form of his God of love, being one with him so that the presence of God may illumine him without the slightest effort, in such a way that he may grasp the eternal modes of all things and remain perfectly disentangled. Just like a schoolboy who learns his lesson, he must start by thinking about it and carefully assimilating it.

—Meister Eckhart (*Spiritual Talks*)

SECOND DAY

Tuesday, December 10

If you forget everything else that has been said, I would suggest that you remember this for the future: "From now on, everybody stands on his own feet."

—Father Louis

The Monastery in the Human and Social Context of the Theravada Buddhist Countries of Southeast Asia

JACQUES AMYOT, S.J.

I come to you this morning not as a theologian, not as a philosopher, not as an expert in Oriental religions, but as a working anthropologist who has spent several years in the Orient and, in particular, several years in this country of Thailand.

The original task assigned me was to give some idea of the human and social context of the monastery in Asia in general. I have concluded, however, that it would not be very meaningful to try to do such a thing for all of Asia. The subject would be much too general and also not very useful. Hence I have decided to limit the field of my description to Southeast Asia, and within Southeast Asia, to those countries belonging to the sphere of the Theravada Buddhism.

I fully realize that many points will be lacking if you want an understanding of all of Asia, but I see by the list of the talks to be given that you will hear about Japan, Vietnam and India. The Philippines, of course, are a very special case; the Muslim countries, too, are important. But they are so different from the field I intend to cover that it will not be practical for me to discuss either of these areas. So I will be talking primarily of Thailand, and through Thailand we will have a good idea of the other Theravada Buddhist countries, namely, Laos, Cambodia, Burma. I should also include Ceylon, though I am not certain it belongs to Southeast Asia. Nevertheless, the problem there resembles very closely what we will find in Thailand itself.

The problem I want to direct my attention to is this: to what extent can a Christian monastery be relevant and meaningful but also represent a value in this particular social context? I offer here a number of working hypotheses derived mainly from anthropological considerations.

Under what conditions can a Christian monastery be relevant and meaningful in this kind of context? I say that it must first of all satisfy a need, a need either felt or latent, a need of the population. In other words, the monastery, in what it stands for, in the doctrine it propounds and the services it gives, must try to make the world intelligible. It must contribute something to the understanding of the problem of suffering and of evil, to help toward self-identity, to help establish oneself in time and place. These are the kinds of problems that religions and religious institutions are called upon to fulfill.

Secondly, the role of the monastery must be understood by the people, and by that I mean that it must be intelligible in terms of cultural points of reference. If it speaks a language that is not understood by the people, its role will not be understood. If it employs symbols or behavior completely foreign to the population in which it finds itself, it will not be understood. For example, to attempt to shake the hand of someone who is not at all familiar with the meaning of such a thing might seem a hostile gesture. Likewise, if we present religion and religious institutions using symbols that are completely unfamiliar to the population in which it is found, those institutions will not be understood.

Third, it must be compatible with the way of life and values of the host population. For example, here in Thailand, in the self-view of the Thai, to be a Thai means to be a Buddhist. So for a Thai to become a Christian, to a certain extent means in practice that he must stop being a Thai. I ask a Thai: "Are you a Christian?" He will answer: "No, I am a Thai." If I speak to a Christian Thai, he will refer to the Buddhists as the Thais, and so on. These are the kinds of problems that confront us.

Now, before we can decide whether or in which form monasticism can take root in a given context, we have to know something about this context. I am going to try to give you some idea of this human and social context. Then I am going to speak at considerable length about popular Buddhism, and here you must always understand that my point of reference is not scriptural Buddhism, not textual Buddhism, but the religion of the people as it exists now, as it is understood by these people. You might call it contextual Buddhism. Then I shall also speak of Buddhist monasticism at considerable length. My reason for doing so is that Buddhist monasticism is highly successful as a monastic institution. If we are thinking of founding Christian monasticism in this part of the world, it is difficult to conceive that it can be introduced in the specific form in which it exists in the Western world. There will have to be some adaptation. Several models are conceivable, models of adaptation for this monasticism, but we have here one very successful model. So it will be at least very unwise not to take it into consideration. What I shall now attempt is to give some idea of the Thai, and through the Thai of the Southeast Asian, human and social context.

The Thai style of life, speaking generally, has its generalized Southeast Asian cultural substratum, namely, subsistence patterns based on wet rice cultivation and on undifferentiated kinship systems, weakly developed authority structures, and a mystical belief in spirits. These features have been retained in varying degrees from the distant past, but several very important factors have brought about changes in this basic Southeast Asian pattern—contacts with the civilizations of China and India. The influence of the first is rather diffused and difficult to determine. The influence of India is much more precise and was effected mainly through Cambodia in the formative years of the Thai nation. More recent influences that have contributed to the transformation of the Thai fabric of culture have come from Western nations—Great Britain, France, Germany, Holland, Portugal, and the United States in particular.

So if one could speak of the basic pattern of Thai culture in the modern era, it would be characterized by the following features: first of all, subsistence patterns based on the cultivation of wet rice, on a generally favorable position from the point of view of the fertility of the land and the pressure of the population. But these are rice-growing populations, peasants predominantly. In Thailand, over 90 percent of the population is peasant.

The second feature is a social organization recognizing social inequalities but lacking rigidity in political and religious structures. The social structure plan has been described as the loosely structured social system. Anthropologists are generally unhappy with this characterization, but it actually gives a general idea of what it is like. It is very different from a Chinese type of society, for example, where you have very rigid lineage and family organization and very definitely ascribed roles, with very little room for mobility within these ascribed roles. This is not the case in Southeast Asia, and even less so in Thailand itself.

The third feature of this culture is a political organization centered upon a king, who is conceived as the father of the people, invested with a magico-religious preeminence, and upon a nobility with analogous attributes derived from its closeness to the king. The king is an extremely important part of Thai society and culture—important not only in political terms, in social terms, but even in religious terms. The Thai monarch is the father of the people, but also, according to the old Indian concept, a divine king, one who embodies some kind of a magical preeminence. Because he is king, it implies that his *karmic* condition is very high, and this fact gives him this magical preeminence.

A fourth feature is Buddhism conceived as an essential element of the Thai way of life, a major source of influence. On it depend the sense of the sacred, of morality; it determines men's attitude toward the good life and toward human endeavor. In its institutional form, it is one of the most important focuses of social interaction. I shall come back to this point.

The last feature is animism, a Brahmanism-derived spirit worship and one of the main ingredients of the Thai view of the universe. It provides explanations for the phenomena of nature as affecting humans and is the object of magical manipulation for the pursuit of human aims. So the Thai, the Southeast Asian (and I feel this is true even of such countries as the Philippines and certainly of Indonesia) lives in a supernatural world, in a world of spirits, a world that is alive with spirits.

The several features I have just mentioned would need to be qualified and completed if they are to be applied to contemporary Thai culture as it has been affected by contact with the outside world during the past century and by modernization. One can point, for example, to the birth of nationalism, which in Thailand is more assimilative than aggressive. The changes in political organization and corresponding changes in attitudes toward royalty and political allegiance are problems that have to be solved. The changes of attitude toward the subsistence activity and rice culture, stemming from the growth of a cash economy, are still poorly determined, poorly defined, even in urban centers, where many of the traditional rural-based values have been either slighted or lost.

These, then, are the broad general features of Thai society and culture. From here onward I shall be talking mainly of rural Thai society and culture.

There is a great deal in common between Thai rural villages. The main concern, as I said, is wet rice cultivation. The communities range from 300 to 3,000 individuals, and they represent more than 90 percent of the population. In the center of each village is the *wat*, the monastery, and around it are the houses of the peasants raised on piles, the various granaries and so on. There is a great deal of intimacy between the people in these villages. Everybody knows everybody else.

The main unit of social interaction is the elementary family, but beyond that there are groups of people who cooperate more closely than with others, groups of people who help one another in agricultural pursuits, who attend one another's weddings, one another's housewarming ceremonies, one another's cremation ceremonies and the like. This is the group that can be called upon; this is the group of close people. Now, because the whole kinship system is so loosely defined, in this sort of group you will find many people who are not, strictly speaking, kinsmen. They are friends, they are neighbors, people who more or less grew up together and came to be closely associated.

The pattern of leadership is determined by many things. The leader of a large family group, for example, is considered important. Also considered a leader is a man who is richer than others, a man who is more generous, a man who has been a monk in a monastery for at least one Buddhist Lenten season of three months (if he has been there for a longer period, he obviously enjoys more authority), a man who has more learning than others. A man who is a good man is a leader. All this corresponds very closely to the value system of the Thai population.

Let me now address myself directly to the position of Buddhism in these countries. I shall be speaking of Thailand in particular, but we can be certain that the same proportions would apply in other countries.

To get an idea of the statistical importance of Buddhism, it will help to know that in 1966, for example, there were 24,105 Thai Buddhist monasteries; in 1962, as many as 238,570 Buddhist priests and novices, a population larger than the Christian population of Thailand. Out of these 238,570, roughly 155,000 would be priests as opposed to novices. In 1964, 73 percent of the schools of Thailand were located in the monasteries, in *wat* compounds in close proximity with the monks. Over the years, this role of the monk with respect to education in Thailand has been altered considerably. In the past, the monks were almost the only teachers in the land. For example, in 1908, there were 30,000 monks in over 12,000 monasteries teaching 200,000 pupils. At that time, there were only 471 lay teachers in the whole nation. In 1917 there were 146,734 pupils in state-operated schools, whereas, in monastery schools, there were 21,053. Today, all schools, or virtually all schools, are state-operated schools, depending upon the Ministry of Education; that is, the teachers are laymen. But as I mentioned, many of these schools, at least 73 percent of them, are in monastery compounds and use one of the monastery buildings. This will help one understand how extremely important an element and a force Buddhism is in the culture of Thailand.

Buddhism, as conceived and interpreted and lived in a rural environment, is a pervasive force in Thai culture. The *wat* and compound are certainly the focal point of the village. Religious, social and artistic events take place in the monastery rather than anywhere else. We have seen, also, that it is an educational center. When the need arises, it can also become a political center. But in Thailand the political role of the Buddhist clergy is discouraged by law and by custom. What I mean to say is that it becomes a political center in the sense that the *wat* is the natural meeting place in the village. Whenever a meeting of any importance is called, it takes place in the monastery, and obviously the monks are in a position to exercise influence.

It is the center of village life. Feasts of various kinds and funerals take place there. It is the center in sickness and distress and in joyful family events. The *wat*, the monastery, is the principal institution of the village. Its support is considered a very important responsibility of the town, and this by the villagers themselves. The abbot of the village monastery is often a community leader whose influence is directed toward peace and harmony.

Buddhism has acted as a symbol of cultural conservatism and serenity that binds together all the strata of Thai society in what is seen as a just and natural scale of status and rights. All this is based upon the understanding that these people have of the influence of *karma* and the extent to which one's fate can be determined by one's *karmic* condition, so to speak. So there is no need for envy or jealousy. What good things one has are the result of one's action, either in this life or in preceding ones. Buddhism reinforces the social virtues of mercy, compassion, confidence and respect for one's brothers, upon which the society rests. It encourages a certain amount of enjoyment, coolness in the face of trouble and indifference to disappointment—something that makes life easier and suffering bearable. And these different kinds of virtues, of course, are very important to assure cohesion in isolated and tight communities from which it is very difficult to escape.

When we speak of the influence of Buddhism on Thai society and culture, we must not imagine it is something unchanging. There is change taking place in the position of Buddhism within itself. In its traditional form, Buddhism is most completely adapted to the life of the wet rice cultivator. But now changes are taking place, such things as the influence of industrialization and modernization are coming to bear on traditional Thai ways of life, and so occupations change. New occupations are arising that no longer have a religious sanction. Wet rice cultivation is completely religion-sanctioned. For example, there are all kinds of ceremonies that relate to the cultivation of rice. But there is nothing equivalent to these ceremonies connected with industrial activities.

Another factor of change comes from changes in the pattern of education. In former times all education was given by the monks. In modern times all education is given by laymen in state institutions. As a result, we find that the monks are much less in contact with the people than they used to be. Here I am speaking of those villages rather close to larger urban centers, such as Bangkok. In more remote areas there is practically no change. People who live in the urban environment are usually very busy people. When I ask my Buddhist abbot friends, "What is the result of all this activity?" they tell me, "Well, these people simply do not have time to come to the monastery any more." It may not necessarily be that they are bad Buddhists, but they just do not have time. In earlier days, there were many periods of leisure in the year, but there was no other place to go except the *wat*, to meet with other friends and relatives, to chat and so on. As a result, the influence of the monasteries and of Buddhism in particular was felt much more strongly than it is at present. And so, inevitably, among these communities a certain amount of secularism is beginning to set in.

I pass on now to a consideration of Buddhist monkhood as we find it in the village context of Thailand and in other Theravada Buddhist countries. We find that what is expected of the monk is highly elaborated and formalized in Thai culture. In other words, people know exactly what a monk—or monkhood—is and stands for, and what he or it is supposed to do. You have two specific orientations: the monastic orientation, where the ascetic aspects take the front, and the pastoral orientation for the laity. These two roles are inseparable.

We have two different kinds of monks: we have permanent monks, that is, those who join the monastery and stay there for life; and we have temporary monks, those who become monks for a short period. It might be just for a few days or a few weeks or at most a few years. All, more or less, will have the same basic kinds of motivation, but in the permanent monks you find something more intense: you have motivations that are more altruistic than those of the temporary monks. What are the reasons that induce Thai males to enter monkhood? (You will notice that I shall be speaking only of males. There is a sisterhood, of course, in the Buddhist setup, but it is completely secondary in this country and is extremely limited in comparison with the monks.)

A man becomes a monk for one or more of the following clearly defined reasons. A very few, those who are more educated, enter to find an end of craving and an immediate attainment of Nirvana. I said that few have this kind of motivation, because very few have any idea of what

Nirvana actually is. But they will be striving for it. More frequently, the motivations are those of filial piety. By this I mean that merit is accumulated by a monk and a good portion of this merit may be given to one's parents or another benefactor. One becomes a monk often in connection with death, to donate one's accumulated merit to the departing soul. An important motivation is that which makes becoming a monk the equivalent of a "rite of passage." One does not become really mature in this society before having spent some time in the monastery under the guidance of wise monks, who will give the minimum training necessary for male maturity. This experience is very important. Parents inquire into it when looking for a marriage partner for their daughters. They will not trust a young man who has not spent some time in a monastery. He is not yet considered to be mature.

Another motive is that of improving one's fate, when one has had a particularly bad streak of bad luck. One way of changing this is to enter a monastery. In this way one can calm one's mind, and the like. Very frequently this is also done in gratitude for good fortune. Again, to become a monk, to join a monastery, is one avenue to educational opportunities. In rural communities the monks are the most educated and the most skillful men. A certain amount of instruction is given in the monastery, and though the standard is not very high, it is higher than the level of educational attainment of most of the villagers.

A more interested motive is that of prestige. The Buddhist *sangha*, the Buddhist monastic community, enjoys very high prestige in Thai society. By becoming a member of this group, one's position increases tremendously. Another motive is that which I have called insurance for the future. It is the duty of a young man who wants to get married to become a monk, even apart from the other motive I mentioned—that of acquiring maturity. By becoming a monk, one is in a position to acquire a great deal of merit. By acquiring this merit, one improves, one overcomes the *karmic* influences of the past, and one can prepare a future of happiness for one's future family. By first becoming a monk, when one later has a family, many misfortunes in the course of one's married life will be avoided.

Now I come to the next point. What is the rural influence of popular Buddhism? One of the main influences is that which I have already mentioned: the fact that Buddhist beliefs and practices and Buddhist institutions make for social cohesion. They make for peace, for happiness in these very closely knit areas. The Buddhist emphasis on serenity and outward calmness in human relations, tolerance for another's opinions,

Theravada Buddhist Countries
Jacques Amyot, S.J.

avoidance of showing displeasure or hatred, allowing oneself to be wronged without resorting to violence—all these are sanctioned as acts of religious merit. One must do good in order to receive good. If one does evil, one receives evil.

One aspect of popular Buddhism that needs to be strongly emphasized is the fact that there is a coexistence and intermingling, without conflict, with animistic and Brahmanistic beliefs. The animistic world of spirits and magic is certainly very strong. Sometimes the monks themselves take part in, or at least are present at, supplications to a rain god or the earth spirit, for example, so that this particular aspect becomes very important.

In the minds of the people, however, there are no compartments. We cannot say they practice three religions. Not at all. They practice one religion, the characteristics of which are that it is influenced by Buddhism, by animism and by Brahmanism. These animistic practices are performed mainly with respect to the preoccupations of this world. The mystical practices relate more directly to the preoccupations of the next world. Yet in spite of the importance of animism and the rest, we must say that the Thai village social life largely follows the Buddhist cycle, with its ceremonies for acquiring merit and its festivals.

Let me say a word about what I may call here the economics of acquiring merit. One would think, for example, that the richer you are, the more you should contribute. The acquiring of merit has other ways.

A little bit farther on I will give you a kind of catalogue of the different kinds of meritorious acts and their various values. Wealth and good fortune are explained by accumulated merit. The fact that you are rich means, in the first place, that you have accumulated a great deal of merit. Your *karmic* quality is very good; so if you want to maintain this position, you don't have to work too hard; you more or less have it. If you are poor, it means that your *karmic* quality is very poor. It means that you must accumulate much merit to improve it; so the richer you are the less you have to acquire merit, and the poorer you are the more you have to acquire it. Merit is a kind of capital investment in psychic well-being, so to speak. So, as I have mentioned, the average villager knows very little about Nirvana, *dharma*, philosophical meditation and so on. His ideas about *karma*, or fate, or rebirth, or merit, or right conduct are understood and meaningful for daily life.

The villagers believe that the present state of existence is the result of accumulated *karmic* actions, good and evil, past and present. They can hope for a better future if their present actions are directed to making that future better. Their present actions are directed toward bettering merit in order to achieve a better life, present and future. The dreams of the high myth of the "better life" have little relevance to the Buddhist ideal of the extinction of cravings, desires and so on. Religious concepts have been translated into practical terms understood by all. So a better life comes to mean wealth, prestige, power, health, beauty, little physical labor, and the like, and acquiring merit is the means to attain these kinds of things. So merit making becomes something very important. Now we are under the impression that people are selfish in acting in this way, but the means to attain this better life are selfless acts of charity and community help.

In the Thai population there is a ranking of meritorious acts. There really is a means of comparing what ways are better than others. At the top of all comes the feeding, care and protection of monks and the building or repairing or beautifying of the monastery in general and of the *bot*, that is, the central chapel, in particular. That is the most meritorious act of all. After that comes working for the success of religious festivals and following the teachings of the Buddha in one's daily life.

Then come giving food, comfort, money to one's parents, elders, the poverty stricken, the blind or the orphaned. These also produce merit, but of a lower order. Finally we find various phases of community development, such as working on village wells, roads, bridges, irrigation trenches and the like.

From all this we can see what things are considered to be more meritorious and what things less meritorious. But whatever may be the case, mostly everything is viewed by the Buddhist peasant in terms of acquiring merit. So a wide variety of everyday actions are understood in terms of merit or demerit, which latter is sin. Acquiring merit is the focal point of religious thought. Antisocial behavior is not only improper but it also affects the status of one's merits.

The one essential point in acquiring merit is this: it is not the giving of money or food or other things that produces merit, but it is the fact that the gift is accepted. Hence the very great importance, the very important role, of the monks. The monks are the ones who accept the gifts to make it possible for the laity to acquire merit. This brings me now to discuss the role of Buddhist monks as seen by the villagers.

By way of introduction, let me say that there are binding ties between the monks and the laity. This is a very important aspect of the situation. The monks and the laity in the village are the same type of people. They have the same culture, very often they are related by blood, they have

THERAVADA BUDDHIST COUNTRIES
Jacques Amyot, S.J.

been known to one another ever since childhood. The villagers are in contact with the monks every day. The monks are invited to meetings and asked for counsel in secular problems. There is a great correspondence between the affluence of the *wat* and the affluence of the villages, because the monastery belongs to the village; it is something the village takes pride in. If there is anything wrong with the villager, he can go to the *wat*.

The monks have several functions, of course. One of these has great importance; this is the social function. It has a welfare function. The monks make up for any lack of government services. If no schools or medical facilities or social welfare or other community services are available, the monks will step in and do whatever they can. They are called upon to settle disputes within their communities, to care for the orphans, to bring their influence to bear on difficult children. Very often, if parents cannot handle a difficult child, they send him to the monastery and let the monks try to straighten him out.

But no matter how important these kinds of functions may be, in the psychology of the population the function most proper to monks is a religious function. In other words, the villagers feel a desperate need for the monks in the realm of religion. The monks stand as a model of ideal religious behavior; they perform the necessary religious ceremonies; they receive the offerings and care of the laity. If there were no monks, Buddhism would become meaningless to its lay adherents. They have an indispensable function in the cycle of family life. Now this function is not what you will find to any great extent in textual Buddhism, but in fact this is the way things go on in the Buddhist environment. For example, monks are connected with marriage ceremonies, with housewarming ceremonies, with sickness, with death and with protection against all evil omens.

For example, for a wedding ceremony, although this ceremony is not, of itself, a Buddhist ceremony, you will always find that before the ceremony takes place, there is a ceremony for acquiring merit directed to the monks. The monks are invited to the home; they are fed. They have charge of sprinkling with lustral water and reciting verses from the *Tripitaka*, the Scriptures. They have the major role in the planning, preparation and execution of village festivals, since the *wat* is the center of these.

The visible presence of the *sangha*, the monastic community, is desired and needed so that more merit can be gained. They are present in village festivals and family ceremonies. They are present at the opening of a new road, a new dam, an irrigation tank, a school. They are present at the opening of a new business.

The Buddhist monkhood is seen by the villagers as a world apart, with its own standards of conduct. Monks cannot mix intimately with the lay population—not, certainly, on the same terms. But on the other hand, their presence is essential for the peace of mind and the tranquility of society.

The monastic aspect of monkhood is certainly primary in establishing the monk's identity. It is the ability of the monk to serve as a vehicle for merit by his own personal holiness, if you wish, that makes him really useful to the village population, and this monastic aspect of monkhood serves as the ultimate cultural reason for the monks' existence. They cultivate merit so that they also may improve their lives with merit.

Now what is the monkhood's involvement in the community cult? The monks in rural areas, especially the more remote areas, are very intimately connected with many secular activities dealing with community development, social welfare and so on. To many villagers, they represent a real source of authority, and they are the natural leaders. Endorsement by the monks of government projects is necessary for their success. If the abbot of the monks does not approve of a certain community development project, be it promoted by the government itself, that project will not be a success. If he does not approve, it will be impossible to recruit people from the village to work on this project. The monks often assist in the planning and directing of the projects. They lend a hand and they encourage the task to a meritorious conclusion. It is always the same aspect that keeps coming in all the time. If the monks are connected with this, then it is a potential source of merit. It receives a religious sanction.

Often the monks provide technical advice, which makes the performance of the project possible. They have certain skills and training—in architecture, for example, or in carpentry, in tile and brick making, in cement work and other skills. They have learned this either on the job, working with other monks, or after being trained by other monks to do the same kind of thing, or in vocational schools. The monastery provides acceptable channels of modernization to many villagers who might otherwise be slow in accepting any new ideas. Monks often collect funds for various cooperative community projects; they can do so more efficiently than laymen because they provide the donor with special kinds of merit.

Theravada Buddhist Countries
Jacques Amyot, S.J.

Many of the monks, especially in more remote areas, not only act as foremen in community projects but engage in active manual labor, pouring cement and so on. They act as part of the village community to enhance its community spirit. (Rural monks are more involved in this way than city monks.) The villagers think of the monks as having specialized kinds of knowledge and free time. It is natural to think, therefore, that this special knowledge and free time should be devoted to the welfare of the community, because this opportunity came from the village in the first place. Any way you look at it, you can see that the words and ways of the monks are so woven into the village pattern of life that the monks exert a profound influence, regardless of their own personal desires, by the simple fact that they are part of an institution that exercises profound influence.

I will conclude with a few reflections on the establishment of Christian monasticism in this area. To me they are highly unsatisfactory, and I must apologize for this. Whenever I start thinking on this subject I always find myself discovering new areas of problems, finding that the problem is much more complicated and complex than I had first imagined. I am more convinced than ever that to arrive at satisfactory decisions on this subject we need to study the problem very intimately. We need far more data than we have now; we need much more cooperation than what we have now between theologians and social scientists and people from the monastic orders themselves. So what I would say here is certainly not a complete statement of what I think can or should be done. It is just something to give direction, let us say, to our thinking.

We consider that Western monasticism could be imported unmodified into this part of the world and that it would have a certain impact, possibly a stronger impact than Catholic parishes as we find them at present. Inevitably, however, they would basically have the same problem as the Church in Thailand today. The Church in Thailand and in many other Theravada Buddhist countries is not felt to be needed by the Buddhist population. True Buddhism offers a total and satisfactory answer to their religious needs. Buddhists have no doubts; they do not feel they have any reason to doubt. We might not agree with the answers, but they have answers for everything that falls within the province of religion.

So the Church and the Western monastery is not felt to be needed. You will not find any Buddhist community in Thailand that will make a special call to a Western monastic organization to found a Christian monastery in Thailand. Secondly, a Western type of monasticism would not be understood—in the same way that the Church in its Western guise is not understood—precisely because it is a foreign thing, because it deals in symbols that are not sufficiently intelligible or meaningful. There is nothing, or very little, in the Thai social and cultural background that is applicable to what is presented, and this is partly because, as I have said before, Western monasticism would seem incompatible with the Thai way of life.

A Thai is a Buddhist. That is the way Thais look at it. And so monasticism needs to be reinterpreted to fit into the local context. As I said, several models are conceivable. The Buddhist rule is formal; it is a highly successful and very much respected one, as opposed to the kind of Buddhism that Matteo Ricci encountered in China. His first approach in China was to take on the guise of a Buddhist monk. He did this until he discovered that Buddhist monks were despised and even stoned, which is certainly not the case in this country.

So monasticism as it needs to be evolved, to really fit into the context of this kind of country, needs to be born again in and from the local context. One must build upon it and reinterpret it in Christian terms rather than destroy it. But theologians have learned to look for the action of the Holy Spirit. Everything is not bad; very much is excellent. The Buddhist ethic is excellent; so we don't need to destroy that. True, Buddhism can lead to agnosticism; but in this particular combination, as it exists here, you will find the population living in a world of the supernatural. The belief in God, it is my guess, will come not through Buddhism but through animism or spirit worship. These sorts of things are things we need to think about. So we must try to reinterpret local institutions, Christianize them from within, not destroy anything unless we are thoroughly convinced that it cannot be reconciled with our faith.

Finally, as I mentioned before, there is great need to form a new synthesis to be created through the joint effort of theologians, historians, specialists in textual Buddhism, if you will. Most important, all this needs to be kept very close to the grass roots of this kind of situation, and this is where the social scientist, which is my training, is best able to do something.

Marxism and Monastic Perspectives

FATHER LOUIS, O.C.S.O. (THOMAS MERTON)

After the very complete and authoritative lecture by Father Amyot, which you have just heard, I must apologize for giving you what will inevitably be a rather impressionistic treatment of something I do not know very much about, because I cannot possibly pretend to be an authority on Marxism. My purpose is perhaps to share with you the kind of thing a monk goes through in his, shall we say, identity crisis. (The term was used by Dom Leclercq yesterday and has been widely used in certain circles, anyway.) The monk, I mean, who questions himself in the presence of the Marxist—who has certain answers and certain views of the world that are not necessarily quite those of the monk—trying to find where he stands, what his position is, how he identifies himself in a world of revolution. And in speaking of this, I hope I will be able to give you at least a minimum of information about the kind of thought we stand up against, and against the light of which we try to identify ourselves.

This lecture might have been entitled "Marxist Theory and Monastic Theoria," because I am concerned much more with the thought, and indeed with a kind of mystique, of Marxism than with orthodox Marxist thinking and, still less, actual Marxist political techniques and tactics. I would say, too, that what I am going to be talking about will be much more Western than Asian. I am not talking about Asian Marxist thought because I do not know much about it. The Western Marxist thought against whose background I shall be speaking is Neo-Marxist and strictly Western; it is the kind of thought that underlies the riots and rebellions in the universities of the West. Specifically, my background is the work of Herbert Marcuse, who is a very influential thinker in Neo-Marxist student circles. And I would add, quite bluntly and brutally, that I regard him as a kind of monastic thinker. So if you wanted to be completely irresponsible, you could say this is a lecture on the monastic implications of Marcuse at the present moment.

This is *not* a talk addressed to the needs of those brethren here present who have been in a totally different and much more existential contact with Marxism, namely, those who have had to flee for their lives from Communist countries. This is not the problem I am talking about, the problem of life and death, when for bare survival one simply has to get away from an enemy who seeks to destroy or completely convert one. I don't see that there is much that can be said about this, except indirectly. You save your life by saving your life; you do what you can. Perhaps something I say may have an implication for the possibility of survival in a completely totalized society of the future, something that might very well take place. But, as I said, I am thinking much more in terms of the kind of Marxist thought that influences the youth of the West and will possibly influence some of the youth of Asia—and that will, I think, be influential with the kind of people we could really be in vital contact with in the East, that is to say, the intellectuals.

So I am addressing myself to the monk who is potentially open to contact with the intellectual, the university student, the university professor, the people who are thinking along lines that are going to change both Western and Eastern society and create the world of the future, in which inevitably we are going to have to make our adaptation.

An alternative to a strictly anti-Communist and negative attitude toward Marxism is, of course, the attitude of dialogue. I will not speak at great length about Western dialogue between Catholics and Marxists except to say that it exists. I shall breathe with respect the name of Roger Garaudy, the French Marxist who is notably in contact with Catholic thinkers. I would just make one remark about Garaudy and his attitude toward monasticism. The significant fact is that one of the points Garaudy sees to be interesting in Christianity, something that really strikes him as important, is the existence of somebody like St. Teresa of Avila.

Now, I think this is something we ought to keep in mind. This is something that concerns us deeply as people for whom the contemplative life is so important that we have dedicated ourselves to it completely and definitively. We will be relevant in the world of Marxism in proportion not as we are pseudo-Marxists or semi-Marxist monks, or something like that, but in proportion as we are simply monks—simply what we are. I think that that takes care of the point of relevance for the moment. I shall return to it afterwards.

Marxism and Monastic Perspectives
Father Louis, O.C.S.O.

At the head of my notes, which I am not necessarily following, there is an allusion to a remark that I heard in California before coming to Asia. I was at a meeting to which many revolutionary university leaders from France, Italy, Germany, the Low Countries had been invited. This meeting took place in Santa Barbara, California, at the Center for the Study of Democratic Institutions, and the purpose of it was to give these young people a forum in which to express their views and to state what they were trying to do. In a lull between lectures I was speaking informally with some of these students, and I introduced myself as a monk. One of the French revolutionary student leaders immediately said: "We are monks also."

This seemed to me to be a very interesting and important statement, and it had all kinds of interesting implications. One of the implications, for me, was a sort of undertone of suggestion that perhaps he was saying: "We are the true monks. You are not the true monks; we are the true monks." I am willing to accept that kind of challenge from people who are dedicated in this particular way.

What does such a statement, such a suggestion, mean? What was he alluding to when he said that the revolutionary student is the "true monk," and the monk in his monastery is not a true monk? I think it gets around to one of the things that is most essential to the monastic vocation, which we have to some extent neglected.

The monk is essentially someone who takes up a critical attitude toward the world and its structures, just as these students identify themselves essentially as people who have taken up a critical attitude toward the contemporary world and its structures. But the criticism is undoubtedly quite different. However, the student seemed to be alluding to the fact that if one is to call himself in some way or other a monk, he must have in some way or other reached some kind of critical conclusion about the validity of certain claims made by secular society and its structures with regard to the end of man's existence. In other words, the monk is somebody who says, in one way or another, that the claims of the world are fraudulent.

Now this, of course, is a dreadful thing to say—and especially now that it is being said on TV! But nevertheless there is something essentially valid in this kind of claim.

I think we should say that there has to be a dialectic between world refusal and world acceptance. The world refusal of the monk is something that also looks toward an acceptance of a world that is open to change. In other words, the world refusal of the monk is in view of his desire for change. This puts the monk on the same plane with the Marxist, because the Marxist directs a dialectical critique of social structures toward the end of revolutionary change. The difference between the monk and the Marxist is fundamental insofar as the Marxist view of change is oriented to the change of substructures, economic substructures, and the monk is seeking to change man's consciousness. Permit me, then, to spell this out a little for the information of those who have not been meditating on Marxism recently, and who have not really done much homework on Marxism, which I think would be important for monks.

Remember that in Marxist thought you have the priority of matter. Marxist materialism is a doctrine that insists that everything is grounded in matter, and that the explanation and the understanding of things amount to an understanding of processes that take their origin in matter and in material elements, so to speak. I could quote to you the famous statement of Feuerbach: *Mann ist was er isst*, which means "Man is what he eats."

In other words, the basic approach to reality that the Marxist takes is that if you want to understand man's predicament in the world, you have to understand the economic processes by which he makes his living. And if you fail to understand these processes, no matter how good your explanations and answers may be, they are wide of the mark. Because, ignoring this basic economic subculture, they build something that has no validity, on a different approach, which ignores this economic starting point and becomes what they call a mystification. In these terms, therefore, for Marxism, you have three great sorts of mystification: religion, philosophy and politics. Religion, philosophy and politics ignore the economic basis of man's being, and so forth, and therefore they are wide of the mark.

Now, I was speaking to a Marxist professor about this thesis the other day in Singapore, and I asked him what he thought about it. He said: "Well, you must be careful to note that Marxist thought is not essentially and militantly antireligious—that is to say, in Marx himself. Marx simply discarded religion as an honest and sincere attempt to answer certain fundamental questions, which had been attempted in the past but had not fully answered the question. It had been a good attempt but was now no longer valid." So the Marxist view of religion, according to this man, was not really that it was something to be militantly put down, but that it was something that would disappear by itself as soon

Marxism and Monastic Perspectives
Father Louis, O.C.S.O.

as man began to mature. This, of course, is tied in with the familiar cliché we hear these days about the maturity of man.

Teilhard de Chardin steps into the picture at this particular point and meets Marxism halfway by his scientific approach to man, and he is very well accepted by Marxist thought. Teilhard is the one Christian thinker today who is widely read in Marxist countries, and precisely because he moves in the direction of an interpretation that takes matter into account as basic. All right, I don't want to go any farther on that. This is just enough to give you some idea of what Marxism says; and of course it is very insufficient.

Traditional monasticism faces the same problem of man and his happiness, what his life is for—and approaches it from a different angle. When I say "traditional monasticism," I mean Buddhist monasticism as well as Christian. Buddhist and Christian monasticism start from the problem inside man himself. Instead of dealing with the external structures of society, they start with man's own consciousness. Both Christianity and Buddhism agree that the root of man's problems is that his consciousness is all fouled up and he does not apprehend reality as it fully and really is; that the moment he looks at something, he begins to interpret it in ways that are prejudiced and predetermined to fit a certain wrong picture of the world, in which he exists as an individual ego in the center of things. This is called by Buddhism *avidya*, or ignorance. From this basic ignorance, which is our experience of ourselves as absolutely autonomous individual egos—from this basic wrong experience of ourselves comes all the rest. This is the source of all our problems.

Christianity says almost exactly the same things in terms of the myth of original sin. I say "myth of original sin," not trying to discredit the idea of original sin, but using "myth" with all the force of the word that has been given to it by scholars like Jung, and people of the Jungian school, and those psychologists and patristic scholars who meet, for example, at the Erano meetings annually in Switzerland, where they understand the vital importance and dynamism of myth as a psychological factor in man's adaptation to reality. So our myth of original sin, as explained for example by St. Bernard, comes very close indeed to the Buddhist concept of *avidya*, of this fundamental ignorance. Consequently, Christianity and Buddhism look primarily to a transformation of man's consciousness—a transformation, and a liberation of the truth imprisoned in man by ignorance and error.

Christianity and Buddhism alike, then, seek to bring about a transformation of man's consciousness. And instead of starting with matter itself and then moving up to a new structure, in which man will automatically develop a new consciousness, the traditional religions begin with the consciousness of the individual, seek to transform and liberate the truth in each person, with the idea that it will then communciate itself to others. Of course, the man par excellence to whom this task is deputed is the monk. And the Christian monk and the Buddhist monk —in their sort of ideal setting and the ideal way of looking at them— fulfill this role in society.

The monk is a man who has attained, or is about to attain, or seeks to attain, full realization. He dwells in the center of society as one who has attained realization—he knows the score. Not that he has acquired unusual or esoteric information, but he has come to experience the ground of his own being in such a way that he knows the secret of liberation and can somehow or other communicate this to others.

Now, in patristic doctrine and in the teaching of the monastic fathers, you find this very strongly stressed. You find, for example, the Cistercians of the twelfth century speaking of a kind of monastic therapy. Adam of Perseigne has the idea that you come to the monastery, first, to be cured. The period of monastic formation is a period of cure, of convalescence. When one makes one's profession, one has passed through convalescence and is ready to begin to be educated in a new way—the education of the "new man." The whole purpose of the monastic life is to teach men to live by love. The simple formula, which was so popular in the West, was the Augustinian formula of the translation of *cupiditas* into *caritas*, of self-centered love into an outgoing, other-centered love. In the process of this change the individual ego was seen to be illusory and dissolved itself, and in place of this self-centered ego came the Christian person, who was no longer just the individual but was Christ dwelling in each one. So in each one of us the Christian person is that which is fully open to all other persons, because ultimately all other persons are Christ.

Now, I don't want to get into this deeply mysterious and mystical doctrine here. I have to keep on the subject of Marxism. But I would just point out that in Marx himself you can see something of this same desire to evolve from *cupiditas* to *caritas*, when you see the idea of Communism—which is a progress from capitalist greed (in their terms) to Communist dedication, according to Marxist formula in which Communism consists in a society where each gives according to his capacity and each receives according to his needs. Now, if you will reflect for two seconds on that definition, you will find that it is the definition of a monastic community. That is precisely what monastic community life has always attempted to realize, and it is my personal opinion that monastic community life is really the only place in which this can be realized. It cannot be done in Communism. It *can* be done in a monastery. (I am subject to correction on this particular point. This is just a personal idiosynscrasy of mine, perhaps, but that is what I believe.)

We come now to the ideas of Marcuse. I am not going to develop him at great length. I would simply recommend quite strongly that you make yourselves acquainted, in one way or other, with Marcuse's very important book, *One Dimensional Man*. This book is much more important for the West than it is for the East, but I still think it has considerable importance even in the East, because Marcuse's theory is that all highly organized technological societies, as we have them now, all so-called managerial societies, as found both in the United States and in the Soviet Union, end up by being equally totalitarian in one way or another.

Marcuse's thesis is that the society of the United States of America is just as totalitarian as the society of Russia, the only difference being that the totalitarianism in the United States is benign and benevolent and smooth and sweet, whereas that in Russia is a little bit tougher. (I am not preaching this; I am just giving you the stuff. This is what the man says, although I must admit that I agree with it to some extent.) Marcuse and the students who are revolting in the universities contend that, in fact, significant choices can no longer be made in the kind of organized society you have either under capitalism or under Soviet Socialism. The choices that are really important have all been made before you get around to trying it yourself. The choices that are left to us are insignificant choices, like the choice between which toothpaste I will use, which airline I will take, or what time I will go from Bangkok to Hong Kong, or what time I will go from Bangkok to San Francisco—whether I will go Tuesday or Wednesday, or whether I'll go this week or next week. But these, as far as Marcuse is concerned, are not significant choices.

I will not elaborate on this, but there is something to be said for Marcuse's statement. It has also been made, incidentally, by Erich Fromm, whom you ought to know, in works like *Escape From Freedom*, *The Sane Society* and the like, which are now quite dated but nevertheless still have validity.

Erich Fromm is an American psychoanalyst living in Mexico who has gone deeply into the idea of alienation in modern society. The idea of alienation is basically Marxist, and what it means is that man living under certain economic conditions is no longer in possession of the fruits of his life. His life is not his. It is lived according to conditions determined by somebody else. I would say that on this particular point, which is very important indeed in the early Marx, you have a basically Christian idea. Christianity is against alienation. Christianity revolts against an alienated life. The whole New Testament is, in fact—and can be read by a Marxist-oriented mind as—a protest against religious alienation. St. Paul is without doubt one of the greatest attackers of religious alienation. Alienation is the theme of the Epistle to the Romans and the Epistle to the Galatians, and it is something worth knowing about.

In the monastic life, it is extremely important that we take account of this concept because, in fact, we have to face with sorrow the bitter truth that the life of many monks and many dedicated women, and many other dedicated people, is a life of total alienation in the sense that it is a legal surrender of things that perhaps they should not have surrendered, and a failure to fulfill potentialities that the monastery should allow them to fulfill. Now, this is an enormous problem, but on this point we have to come together with the Marxists and admit there is something to be done about it.

I will pass on now to something that might be more interesting to you—some conversations I had with Tibetan monks who had gone through the experience of being thrown out of their country, driven out of their country, by Communism. First of all, I spoke of this to the Dalai Lama, and I asked his ideas on this whole question of Marxism and monasticism. I suppose there are few people in the world more intimately involved in this question than the Dalai Lama, who is the religious head of an essentially monastic society. The Dalai Lama is very objective and open about this kind of thing. He is in no way whatever a fanatical anti-Communist. He is an open-minded, reasonable man, thinking in terms of a religious tradition. He obviously recognized the problem of a ruthless Communist takeover, a power move that had to get rid of monks, that had to drive monks out of Tibet. The Dalai Lama himself made every effort to coexist with Communism, and he failed. He said frankly that he did not see how one could coexist, in the situation in which he had been, with Communism—on an institutional level, anyway. He then went on to admit the blindness of the abbots and communities of the great, rich Tibetan monasteries, who had failed to see the signs of the times and had absolutely failed to do anything valid to meet the challenge of Communism. They refused to do anything, for example, about giving land to people who needed it. They simply could not see the necessity of taking certain steps, and this, he said, precipitated the disaster, and it had to happen.

Marxism and Monastic Perspectives
Father Louis, O.C.S.O.

I would like to add now, while speaking of the Dalai Lama, that he had some very interesting questions to ask about Western monasticism. He was extremely interested in it. He had seen a film of the Trappist monks of Sept-Fons, and he was very much interested in everything they did in this film and wanted to know all about Trappist silence. Incidentally, the question of a married clergy amused him highly. He thought that the idea of priests of the West getting married was very funny. He knew he had some married monks in his outfit, but he was not exactly wild about married monks either.

But the questions he asked about Western monasticism were quite interesting. He started asking about the vows, and I did not quite know what he was getting at. Then he said: "Well, to be precise, what do your vows oblige you to do? Do they simply constitute an agreement to stick around for life in the monastery? Or do they imply a commitment to a life of progress up certain mystical stages?" I sort of hemmed and hawed a bit, and said: "Well, no, that's not quite what the vows are all about." But it was interesting to see that this is what he thought the vows *should* be about. When you stop and think a little bit about St. Benedict's concept of *conversio morum*, that most mysterious of our vows, which is actually the most essential, I believe, it can be interpreted as a commitment to total inner transformation of one sort or another—a commitment to become a completely new man. It seems to me that that could be regarded as the end of the monastic life, and that no matter where one attempts to do this, that remains the essential thing.

To get back to the lamas. I spoke to another Tibetan lama, a young one whom I consider a good friend of mine—a very interesting person indeed. Chogyam Trungpa Rinpoche is now about thirty-one or thirty-two years old—a Tibetan lama, a Rinpoche, that is to say, a reincarnation, who got the complete reincarnation treatment: a thorough formation in Tibetan science, monasticism and everything.[1] He had to escape from Tibet to save his life, like most other abbots.

---

[1] The term "Rinpoche" (literally, "precious one") is used here to indicate the reincarnation of a saintly personage who has returned to earth not as a result of his actions in the previous life (his past *karma*,) but by his own free will. The title, besides being given to such "incarnate lamas," was given to senior abbots and occasionally to kings. It should be noted that Thomas Merton, in telling Chogyam Trungpa's story, is relying on his memory, and hence certain of the details are not quite correct. For Chogyam Trungpa's life, see *Born in Tibet* (Harcourt, 1968), especially pp. 115–116 and p. 192.

When he was faced with the decision of leaving his country, he did not quite know what to do. He was absent from his monastery on a visitation to some other monastery, and he was caught out in the mountains somewhere and was living in a peasant's house, wondering what to do next. He sent a message to a nearby abbot friend of his, saying: "What do we do?" The abbot sent back a strange message, which I think is very significant: "From now on, Brother, everybody stands on his own feet."

To my mind, that is an extremely important monastic statement. If you forget everything else that has been said, I would suggest you remember this for the future: "From now on, everybody stands on his own feet."

This, I think, is what Buddhism is about, what Christianity is about, what monasticism is about—if you understand it in terms of grace. It is not a Pelagian statement, by any means, but a statement to the effect that we can no longer rely on being supported by structures that may be destroyed at any moment by a political power or a political force. You cannot rely on structures. The time for relying on structures has disappeared. They are good and they should help us, and we should do the best we can with them. But they may be taken away, and if everything is taken away, what do you do next?

The Zen people have a saying that has nothing directly to do with this, but is analogous in a certain sense: "Where do you go from the top of a thirty-foot pole?" You see? Well, in a certain way the answer has something in common. Where do you go from the top of a thirty-foot pole—which is where we all now sit? I think it is useful in this conference to take account of the fact that that is where we are.

Trungpa Rinpoche, then, on this advice to stand on his own feet, said: "O.K. I'm going to India." He had with him his cellarer (and this will be amusing to anybody who has lived in terms of abbots and cellarers). His cellarer had a whole train of about twenty-five yaks loaded with all kinds of provisions, and the abbot said to his cellarer: "Listen, Father, we aren't going to be able to take all those yaks. We're going to have to ford rivers and swim rivers, and we're going to have to travel light." The cellarer said: "Listen, we've got to take these yaks, we've got to eat." So they started off on their journey. The first thing that happened was that the Chinese Communists saw this train of yaks going down the road and got them. But the abbot didn't happen to be right there; he had gone on ahead, and was swimming a river somewhere, and he escaped.

Marxism and Monastic Perspectives
Father Louis, O.C.S.O.

I think there is a lesson in there somewhere, too. We can ask ourselves if we are planning for the next twenty years to be traveling with a train of yaks. It probably is not going to work. The ultimate end of Trungpa Rinpoche's story—which is, of course, still being lived out in full force—is that he got a degree from Oxford, speaks excellent English, has a thorough knowledge of both Western and Eastern civilization and is now running a Tibetan monastery in Scotland, which is quite a good place. It is incidentally a place where you can temporarily be a monk. It is a place where you can make a three-year Buddhist retreat in total silence, and so forth. I hope to visit him there.

Coming now toward a sort of conclusion, it is obvious that we have to plan the future. Let us look forward to the worst. Supposing that we are totally destroyed as an institution. Can we continue? It is the same question: Where do we go from the top of that thirty-foot pole?

What is essential in the monastic life is not embedded in buildings, is not embedded in clothing, is not necessarily embedded even in a rule. It is somewhere along the line of something deeper than a rule. It is concerned with this business of total inner transformation. All other things serve that end. I am just saying, in other words, what Cassian said in the first lecture on *puritas cordis*, purity of heart, that every monastic observance tends toward that.

Incidentally, I would say that the question of Asian monasticism for Christians should not be interpreted in terms of just playing an Asian part or an Asian role. It is not that we want to look like Asians; it is not sufficient simply to present an Asian image. Too often it seems to resolve itself into that. I think we have to go much deeper than this. For a Christian—as also, I believe, for a Buddhist—there is an essential orientation that goes beyond this or that society, this or that culture, or even this or that religion. When I said that St. Paul was attacking religious alienation, I meant that really he meant very seriously what he said about "There is no longer Jew or Greek, there is no longer Jew or Gentile." There is no longer Asian or European for the Christian. So while being open to Asian cultural things of value and using them, I think we also have to keep in mind the fact that Christianity and Buddhism, too, in their original purity point beyond all divisions between this and that.

So you respect the plurality of these things, but you do not make them ends in themselves. We respect these things and go beyond them dialectically. The kind of thing I am saying is that in Christianity you have a dialectical approach to this, and in Buddhism you have an essential dialectic called the *Madhyamika*, which is the basis of Zen, and so on. All these dialectical approaches (Marxism, of course, is also dialectical) go beyond the thesis and the antithesis, this and that, black and white, East and West. We accept the division, we work with the division and we go beyond the division.

I will close with a remark on Buddhist iconography, on one of those traditional representations of the Buddha in which with one hand he is pointing to the earth (he is seated in the lotus posture) and in the other hand he holds a begging bowl. This is quite relevant for monasticism. It is a kind of summary of Buddhism, too. The Buddha's gesture of pointing to the earth is made in response to an accusation on the part of the devil, Mara. Mara is not quite the devil, but the tempter, the one who represents all illusion, and so forth. Mara came to Buddha where he was sitting when he had obtained enlightenment, and said: "You have no business sitting on that little square of earth where you're sitting, because it belongs to me." And the Buddha pointed to the earth and called it to witness that it did not belong to Mara, because he had just obtained enlightenment on it.

This is a very excellent statement, I think, about the relation of the monk to the world. The monk belongs to the world, but the world belongs to him insofar as he has dedicated himself totally to liberation from it in order to liberate it. You can't just immerse yourself in the world and get carried away with it. That is no salvation. If you want to pull a drowning man out of the water, you have to have some support yourself. Supposing somebody is drowning and you are standing on a rock, you can do it; or supposing you can support yourself by swimming, you can do it. There is nothing to be gained by simply jumping in the water and drowning with him.

The begging bowl of the Buddha represents what Father Amyot was talking about this morning. It represents the ultimate theological root of the belief not just in a right to beg, but in openness to the gifts of all beings as an expression of the interdependence of all beings. This is the most central concept in Buddhism—or at least in Mahayana Buddhism.

The whole idea of compassion, which is central to Mahayana Buddhism, is based on a keen awareness of the interdependence of all these living beings, which are all part of one another and all involved in one another. Thus when the monk begs from the layman and receives a gift from the layman, it is not as a selfish person getting something from somebody else. He is simply opening himself in this interdependence, this mutual interdependence, in which they all recognize that they all are immersed in illusion together, but that the illusion is also an empir-

Marxism and Monastic Perspectives
Father Louis, O.C.S.O.

ical reality that has to be fully accepted, and that in this illusion, which is nevertheless empirically real, Nirvana is present and it is all there, if you but see it.

I think, by way of closing, that this kind of view of reality is essentially very close to the Christian monastic view of reality. It is the view that if you once penetrate by detachment and purity of heart to the inner secret of the ground of your ordinary experience, you attain to a liberty that nobody can touch, that nobody can affect, that no political change of circumstances can do anything to. I admit this is a bit idealistic. I have not attempted to see how this works in a concentration camp, and I hope I will not have the opportunity. But I am just saying that somewhere behind our monasticism, and behind Buddhist monasticism, is the belief that this kind of freedom and transcendance is somehow attainable.

The essential thing for this, in the Buddhist tradition, is the formation of spiritual masters who can bring it out in the hearts of people who are as yet unformed. Wherever you have somebody capable of giving some kind of direction and instruction to a small group attempting to do this thing, attempting to love and serve God and reach union with him, you are bound to have some kind of monasticism. This kind of monasticism cannot be extinguished. It is imperishable. It represents an instinct of the human heart, and it represents a charism given by God to man. It cannot be rooted out, because it does not depend on man. It does not depend on cultural factors, and it does not depend on sociological or psychological factors. It is something much deeper.

I, as a monk—and, I think, you as monks—can agree that we believe this to be the deepest and most essential thing in our lives, and because we believe this, we have given ourselves to the kind of life we have adopted. I believe that our renewal consists precisely in deepening this understanding and this grasp of that which is most real. And I believe that by openness to Buddhism, to Hinduism, and to these great Asian traditions, we stand a wonderful chance of learning more about the potentiality of our own traditions, because they have gone, from the natural point of view, so much deeper into this than we have. The combination of the natural techniques and the graces and the other things that have been manifested in Asia, and the Christian liberty of the gospel should bring us all at last to that full and transcendent liberty which is beyond mere cultural differences and mere externals—and mere this or that.

I will conclude on that note. I believe the plan is to have all the questions for this morning's lectures this evening at the panel. So I will disappear.

The Death of Father Louis

"There is no integral text of what is going to be given," said Thomas Merton in his informal remarks immediately preceding his lecture at the Bangkok conference, "because God alone knows what is really going to be given here, except for the general idea that this is a talk on Marxism and monasticism—and we will see how it turns out." The words with which he concluded were equally informal: "I believe the plan is to have all the questions for this morning's lectures this evening at the panel. So I will disappear." They stated by coincidence just what was to happen about two hours later. The following account, drawn mainly from the words of four of the first witnesses of the accident—and employing as little as possible even of what they said the others had said or done—attempts to give all that can be certainly known about the father's unexpected death.

On Tuesday, December 10, Dom Celestine Say, O.S.B., the Benedictine prior from the Philippines, whose room was on the ground floor opposite Father Louis's, sat across from him at lunch in the main building of the Sawang Kaniwat. After finishing the meal, Father Louis asked the prior for the key to the cottage, saying he wanted to take a nap since he had missed it the day before. He left in the company of Dom François de Grunne, O.S.B., the French monk who lived on the floor above, directly over the Philippine prior's room. The time was probably 1:40 P.M. Between five and ten minutes later, the prior followed. Since it took about ten minutes to walk from the main building to the cottage, he must have reached the cottage about 2 P.M. On entering, he went directly to his room, casually noting that Father Louis was not moving about in his quarters.

After entering the bathroom at the rear of the wide entrance hall between the two rooms on the ground floor, the prior began to brush his teeth. Perhaps just a few minutes before this time, the French monk had heard a sound, something like a cry and the fall of a heavy object. But since there was a good deal of noise coming from outside, he momentarily thought nothing of it. Shortly, however, he changed his mind and descended the stairs. Hearing sounds in the bathroom, he knocked on the door. To his surprise, it was the Philippine prior who opened the door. "I thought you were Father Merton," he said. "Did you hear any shout?" On the prior's answering in the negative, the monk returned upstairs.

Leaving the bathroom, the prior noticed that Father Louis's bed was empty. He did not, however, look into the room. The inside wall of the room was made of perhaps four feet of rather flimsy wood paneling, topped by screening that reached to the ceiling. Inside, just above the paneling, was a width of some sort of curtain material, which, if drawn, made it impossible to see into the room. The door was in the center of the partition and could be locked by a bolt from within. Since the prior could see the bed, which was located on the right side of the room as one faced it, the curtain on the right half of the screening must have been partly drawn back.

After unsuccessfully trying to sleep for more than an hour, the prior got up, took a shower, and returned to his room. Shortly thereafter, probably five or ten minutes before 4 P.M., the French monk, wanting to get the key to the cottage from Father Louis, descended and knocked on his door. When he received no reply, he peered into the room. The father was lying on his back in the far left corner. At once the monk called out to the prior that something was wrong with Father Louis, and the prior rushed out into the hall. They vainly tried to open the door.

Father Louis was plainly visible inside. He was wearing only a pair of shorts. On top of him lay one of the tall standing fans—with broad, circular base—used for ventilation in each of the rooms. The shaft was across Father Louis's legs and the fan itself rested to the right of his head. The monk said he would go to get help and left the Philippine prior alone.

As the prior stood there, looking in, he became aware of a strange odor of burning. At the same time, he saw sparks shooting from the large switch box of the fan. The sparks were making a crackling sound, and he now recalled that earlier, during the time he was trying to go to sleep, he had heard the same sound and smelled some sort of odor. All this was the matter of only a moment. Thinking Father Louis had merely knocked himself out in falling backward, the prior called to him. At that moment two abbots, Dom Odo Haas, O.S.B., from South Korea, and Archabbot Egbert Donovan, O.S.B., from the United States, burst in.

They had been alerted by the French monk, who then proceeded to the main building to tell the others.

The abbot from South Korea, who was the younger of the two, pushed hard on the upper panel of the door, which gave way. When the panel opened, the younger abbot climbed through and unbolted the door. A smell of burning flesh pervaded the room. Seeing that the fan was still turned on, the abbot tried to lift it from Father Louis's body. In doing so, he received a strong shock and his hands became paralyzed by the current. As quickly as he could, the Philippine prior unplugged the fan from the wall. At the point where the switch box touched Father Louis's body, just above the shorts, he saw a large and deep burn. A streak of red extended up toward the right armpit. The face was bluish, and the hands, too, had spots of discoloration. Both abbots gave Father Louis general absolution.

Immediately the young abbot from South Korea went to inform the Abbot Primate. But he must have been alerted already, for he reached the scene a few minutes later. With him was a sister from South Korea, who was a doctor, and she verified the death as being caused by electrocution or heart failure. The Abbot Primate administered extreme unction at 4:10 P.M. Later a Thai physician stated, in his report, that the death had been the result of acute cardiac failure and electric shock.

Perhaps the most balanced comment has been offered by Sister Pia Valeri, the secretary of A.I.M., in a letter written to the editor:

> I believe that no one can say with certainty what caused Father Merton's death. . . . One cannot say his death was caused by electrocution, as many newspapers have said; and one cannot say, either, that it was the result of a heart attack. Probably—but only probably —a heart attack began it and electrocution completed it. In fainting, the father may have dragged with him the large fan, which in falling was damaged and caused a short circuit. That is as far as we can go with our deductions. That would explain why Father Merton's hands were not burned and not glued to the fan. . . . I believe that no one can say more about this mysterious death, by which God wished to mark one of his elect. "This is my servant in whom I am well pleased."

> J. M.

PRAYER

(In French)

God of unspeakable and unseen mysteries, in whom are hidden all the treasures of wisdom and knowledge; thou who hast revealed to us the service of this liturgy and who, by reason of thy great love for mankind, hast established us to offer thee the sacrifice of our prayer for our offences and for the unwittingness of the people; thou, the invisible King, who makest great and inaccessible things, glorious and without number—cast thy eyes upon us, we who stand before thee as before thy throne of the Cherubim. Thou hast set us free from all impurity; do thou sanctify, by an indelible blessing, the souls and bodies of us all, so that, vivified by thy grace, we may unite ourselves to Christ himself, the true God who lives and reigns with thee, Holy Father, in the unity of the Holy Spirit for ever and ever. Amen.

FIRST READING

(In French)

Contemplating that peace of supreme silence
which takes hold of those who know,
those who possess high, perfect and solid knowledge
because they no longer are drawn to
the pursuit of worldly things;
contemplating this divine slumber that shuts nothing out,
  where all begins,
eternal, tranquil happiness,
calm freshness of true being;
contemplating again and again the eternal, perfect Being,
who from all witness and every beginning
leads to the supreme purity of wisdom

those who are beyond the three states
and neither wake, nor sleep, nor dream;
contemplating thee, stainless flame
of that light
which disperses ignorant multiple vision,
sea of happiness beyond the reach of
the six beliefs;
and thee, O Peace,
contemplating thee, vast ocean of joy,
reservoir of all life, delightful nectar,
brilliant gold, jewel, first essence of nonduality,
which dwells in me,
sovereignly infinite radiance enfolding all about,
infinity lighted up with glory,
joy—oh, joy!

—Ramana Maharshi ("Silence")

SECOND READING

(In English)

How well I know that fountain's rushing flow,
   Although it is night.

Its deathless spring is hidden, yet even so,
Fully I sense from whence its sources flow,
   Although it is night.

Its birth (since none it has) no one surmises,
But from it every origin arises,
   Although it is night.

I know there is no other thing so fair,
And earth and heaven drink refreshment there,
   Although it is night.

Well do I know its depth no man can sound,
And that no crossing of it may be found,
   Although it is night.

Its clarity unclouded still shall be:
Out of it comes the light by which we see,
   Although it is night.

Flush with its banks that stream impetuous swells;
I know it waters nations, heavens and hells,
   Although it is night.

The current that is nourished by this source
I know to be omnipotent in force,
   Although it is night.

From source and current a new torrent swells
That neither of the other two excels,
   Although it is night.

The eternal source hides in the Living Bread
That we with life unending may be fed,
   Although it is night.

Now to all creatures it is crying: Hark!
Come then and drink your fill, here in the dark,
   Although it is night.

This living source, which is so dear to me,
Within the Bread of Life I clearly see,
   Although it is night.

—St. John of the Cross ("Song of the Soul That Rejoices to Know God by Faith")

THIRD DAY

Wednesday, December 11

The Alpha and Omega is at the beginning and at the end of all religion, of whatever truth is found in the world.

—Dom Francis Acharya, O.S.B.

Western Observance and the Asian Mentality

FRANS HARDJAWIJATA, O.C.S.O.

I was really embarrassed when last October I received a letter from the secretariat of Aide à l'Implantation Monastique asking whether I would like to give a talk on "Western Observance and Asian Mentality" during the meeting of Superiors of Asian monasteries at Bangkok in December 1968. Even though for many years I have been a monk of a monastery keeping a Western observance, I had never explicitly reflected upon it. My embarrassment, however, was caused more on account of the words "Asian mentality," of which I had never made any study. Born of Asian parents on an island considered as part of Asia, I was educated in a rather Western way.

Nevertheless I accepted the offer. I accepted it not only because the letter from A.I.M. explained that all I had to do was state my personal opinion on the Western observance, but also because I thought the situation of most Asian Catholic monks was the same as mine. Like me, most of them never have had the occasion to study or make any research on the Asian mentality, and most of them have been educated in the Western way.

I do not know much about the Asian mentality. But—and this is my only consolation—being an Asian, I possibly have received a Western education in an Asian manner, at least as far as we can believe the well-known scholastic principle *Quidquid recipitur ad modum recipentis recipitur*, "Whatever is received is received according to the receiver's way."

When I began preparing this paper, I wanted to read something to get some inspiration. But in our monastery no books or articles were available of immediate use for this purpose. The only thing I could do was reflect on the matter. So the thoughts presented here are in no way results of serious study; they are no more than personal reflections. Perhaps it would have been exact to change the title of this paper to: "Personal Reflections of an Asian Monk on Western Observance." Nevertheless, the original title remains unchanged, because, reflecting upon the Asian mentality, I have met some problematics worthy of our attention.

The first part of this paper will deal with the problematic of the Asian mentality, and will be followed by a short survey of the problematic of the Indonesian mentality. This part may be considered as introductory. After that follows the main part, presenting my personal opinion about Western observance. In this part I shall give a description of the meaning of Western observance, the main elements of which will be subjected to critical examination. At the end I shall offer a concise conclusion.

As a matter of fact, when preparing this paper I already had at my disposal the summary of the answers given in response to the questionnaire of the A.I.M. in preparation for this Bangkok meeting. But of set purpose I did not make use of it, in order to avoid its eventual influence upon my reflection. Later on, when comparing my reflections with the summary, I found several parallel thoughts in both.

Here I have to say frankly that I have not been thinking for a long time about these subjects. Some of the thoughts here presented are, in fact, not yet matured. Hence the opinions I put forward in this paper are rather to be considered as a starting point for further consideration and as subject matter for exchange of thoughts. In this way, I hope the truth in them will be discerned from their errors, and their inexactitudes will be corrected.

PROBLEMATIC OF THE ASIAN MENTALITY

When we hear the term "Asian mentality," we spontaneously ask ourselves what it means and whether there is such a thing. Asia is a very large continent consisting of many nations, each having its own history and culture. Mutual relations between them are too limited to serve as a basis for a unity. Probably instead of speaking of Asian mentality we had better use the term "mentalities of Asian peoples."

This lack of contact between the Asian nations is the result of Western colonialism in the past, owing to which the Asian nations have had closer relations with their respective Western colonializing countries than with their Asian neighbors. Even nowadays independent Asian nations maintain special relations with their former Western colonial countries.

Western Observance and Asian Mentality
Frans Hardjawijata, O.C.S.O.

This is especially true of the Catholics, who are still under Western missionaries from the respective Western countries.

In fact, as members of Asian monasteries, we do not need to know the Asian mentality in order to continue to carry out our task of implanting monastic life in Asia, because we have either no connection or very little connection with one another. In my opinion more attention has to be focused on the local mentality. For us in Indonesia, for instance, it is more important to know the Indonesian mentality and to see what its attitude is toward Western observance.

When each monastery has explored the attitude of the mentality of its respective nation toward Western observance, comparative studies can be made that will bring to light whether there are common elements or not. Eventually whatever common elements there are should be compared with non-Asian mentalities so as to decide whether they are specifically Asian or rather simply human. Not until then can we know more exactly about the attitude of the Asian mentality—if there is one— toward Western observance.

So far as I know, at present no study has been made on the level of national mentalities, consequently no comparative research can yet be begun. So what is now necessary is to make research on Western observance and a given national mentality. This research is necessary to intensify the effort for the adaptation of monastic life to the nations concerned. More attention must therefore be paid to local mentalities on the national level rather than on an inter-Asian level.

As a matter of course the question occurs to us whether there is any need for the superiors of Asian monasteries to meet together as we are doing here and now. Of course there is, because our monasteries are usually very much isolated—without contact with other Asian ones and with no possibility of carrying on a dialogue with brethren of the same vocation. In our own countries each of us surely has contact with other religious institutes; but most if not all of them are not monastic ones. Consequently their experiences cannot always be applied to us without distinction. Moreover, although there is much difference in our mentalities and cultures, it may nevertheless be of great use to exchange experiences and become well informed about the process of adaptation occurring in other countries. Everybody can see and judge whether there are elements applicable for himself. Knowledge of the problematics of monasteries abroad makes us more sensitive to the problematics of our own countries.

PROBLEM OF THE INDONESIAN MENTALITY

Now that I have shown the impossibility of explaining at this moment the attitude of the Asian mentality toward Western observance, I intend to open the way for further exchange of thoughts by confining my attention to one of the Asian mentalities. Since I come from Indonesia, it is obvious that my further attention will be directed to the Indonesian mentality and to its attitude toward Western observance. In this connection, too, I must confess that actually I have no competence to speak about this subject because I have never made a study of Indonesian society and its mentality. My knowledge in this matter is rather that of the common man.

The question to be treated is this: How is Western observance considered by the Indonesian mentality? But here, too, we encounter problems. Allow me to explain briefly.

We want to know the Indonesian mentality in order to be able to implant the monastic life more deeply into the Indonesian soil and to promote its adaptation more intensively. In this context our attention must first be directed to the Indonesian mentality of the present time insofar as it can determine or at least influence the Indonesian mentality in the future. In other words, we have to focus our attention on the present and the future rather than on the past, because the Indonesian nation is experiencing a phase of development in which it is shaping its identity and building its future.

It is true that since the present situation is influenced by the past, the past, too, has to be considered. But research on the earlier mentality and on the treasures of a past culture should not be overestimated, because as a united country Indonesia is a newborn child. In this period of self-shaping, regional cultures of the past surely have a contribution to make to the present-day mentality, but we must not forget that the influence of the West is not less important. Both regional cultures and the culture of the West are influencing the present-day and so the future mentality. Nowadays it is very difficult to determine which influence will be the stronger.

Throughout history, the Indonesian islands, situated as they are in the midst of an international traffic, have shown themselves open to influences from abroad. Thus many kinds of religions and trends can be found there—for instance, Hinduism, Islam, Christianity, and Communism. Of course, these influences are received by the Indonesians in their own way, but the fact remains that they exist and have a real importance.

Western Observance and Asian Mentality
Frans Hardjawijata, O.C.S.O.

Lately there has been an explicit desire among the Indonesian people to find their "Indonesian personality." But side by side with this desire there is also a very strong tendency toward internationalization in several spheres, such as thought, social and economic life, social etiquette, political activity, fashions, and comfort.

Thus, the Indonesian mentality, being in a stage of development, is seeking after its own identity. In this process, as I have said, the influence of the regional cultures of the past is competing with the influence of the West. This statement applies also to Indonesian Catholics, who are actively taking part in promoting the development of the nation.

So far as the Catholic Indonesian mentality is concerned, certain comments have to be made. In this context we can pose the question: Do Indonesian Catholics Indonesianize their Catholic mentality?

Mission work among the Indonesian people did not begin until a hundred years ago. Up to the year 1945, the year of the proclamation of the Republic of Indonesia, Catholic Indonesians were passing through a state of receptivity in the sphere of Catholic life. Since 1945, an attempt has been made to assimilate Catholicism in the political sphere, where Indonesian Catholics have been active in fighting for and defending liberty. In this endeavor they have been exerting themselves to the utmost in order to obtain a place, a living space, among the other groups of people. Thus they have been forced to express their Catholicism in the forum of the national political life, and so they have Indonesianized their religion in the domain of politics.

But in the field of ecclesiastical life they are still in a state of receptivity. Many missionaries are still coming from abroad, and the native clerics receive a Western education in their philosophical and theological studies. At present the Indonesian Catholics' main preoccupation is still to fight for a living space; they have no occasion to think more deeply. Moreover they have no competent theologians able to take initiatives to promote the adaptation of theology to the Indonesian background. The books and periodicals in this field read by the Indonesian clerics are mostly Western ones, or at least translations of them. In the domain of liturgy there are some attempts at creativity, but they are still in the beginning stage. Thus in their way of thinking as well as in their mentality, Indonesian Catholics are undergoing Western influence more than their non-Catholic fellow citizens.

From this Indonesian Catholic society come our monks, members of our community at Rawaseneng. They too are much influenced by the situation of development in their nation and their Church. In the monastic domain, the monks of Rawaseneng are still in the receptive stage, for most of them are still in their formative years. They consider the Western observance followed in the monastery as something to be fulfilled in order to follow their vocation. They feel themselves obliged to adapt themselves to it.

Even though this is the case, there are signs indicating that they are beginning to look at the Western observance critically. This critical mentality is in part explicit, but it is a great question whether it is based upon the Indonesian mentality or upon the influence of Western books. The most trustworthy mentality is the implicit one, which is to be found in the way they live the Western observance. Some observances are understood and lived rather broadly and loosely.

As an example I may mention the case of silence. There are breaches of continuous silence. Sometimes these breaches are not felt as a transgression. The monks, especially the younger ones, feel a need to speak more normally and to have personal human contacts. But there are monks who feel this transgression of the rule of silence as a real transgression to be corrected. It is therefore very difficult to decide whether this loose practice of silence is the result of the Indonesian mentality or is due to the fact that the monks are not mature enough for continuous silence.

This need of contact is also found in their relation toward the people outside. It is still a question to me whether this phenomenon is specifically Indonesian or not because as far as I know it appears in other countries as well.

From what I have expressed in this introductory part, we may conclude that it is very difficult to decide what is the meaning of the Asian mentality. In my endeavor to decide about the mentality of even one nation, Indonesia, I experience difficulty—no less than in the endeavor to explore the mentality of a still smaller group, such as Indonesian Catholics or even Indonesian monks. What I can do is simply present their problematics.

Consequently, I do not dare explain the attitude of the Asian or the Indonesian mentality toward Western observance. All I can do is to present my personal opinion about this observance.

PERSONAL REFLECTIONS ON THE WESTERN OBSERVANCE

It is not merely by chance this part is entitled "Personal Reflections," because here I am speaking personally, not as the representative of a certain community or nation. It is not impossible that my thoughts are

Western Observance and Asian Mentality
Frans Hardjawijata, O.C.S.O.

not representative and that they are not agreed upon by my confreres. Although born and brought up in Indonesia, I received a Western education, and even a part of that—that is, from my entrance into the novitiate up to the end of my theological studies—took place in the West. Even now my reading materials are almost entirely Western. So I do not dare to say my views are Eastern.

I shall try to reflect on Western observance in the context of Eastern society, or to state it more precisely, of Indonesian society. I shall direct my attention to that part of Indonesian society in which our monastery is situated.

First I shall explain what I mean by "Western observance." Then I shall present personal notes on the observance. Here I shall do my best to express my views as sincerely as possible. All these will be brought to the fore merely as thoughts submitted for further consideration and, if need be, for correction. It is not my intention to propose changes based upon my views or opinions.

Before presenting my opinion about Western observance, I must explain what I mean by the term. In fact I am acquainted with only one of the Western observances, namely, the one followed by our order. Hence when I speak about the Western observance in this talk, I am dealing with the observance based upon the Rule of St. Benedict insofar as it is commented on and practiced by Trappist communities. The Western observance in this restricted sense can be defined as an observance consisting of many obligatory community exercises.

These exercises cover both spiritual and physical activities. Practically the whole day is filled by them, and they are binding even though there is a certain degree of gradation in them. Some are strongly obligatory, such as community prayer, meditation, conventual Mass, meals and rest. Others admit of variation, such as manual labor and spiritual reading. All of this is practiced in an atmosphere of silence and recollection in a community that has more members than normal families and that is characterized by enclosure. That is to say, everything, including searching for a livelihood, must be done within the monastery itself, which is usually set up at a place far away from ordinary society.

The life of the monks who follow this observance is continually bound by community exercises and rules and regulations, as many as possible, so that their whole life, at least as it is seen externally, is likewise tied up. The monasteries where this observance is followed belong to an international order, and a considerable part of the rules is put forward by the leadership of the order, that is, the general chapter.

Western observance as I have described it here is at present undergoing revisions and changes, because in the monasteries of the West, too, there are monks who think that their observance is no longer suited to the aspirations of today. I shall now give my personal reflections on the observance.

Large community. Western observance supposes a rather large community. Certainly no specific number is demanded, but if the whole community consists of less than twenty members, including old monks and those who are still receiving formation, it is difficult to keep the observance completely as it should be, especially if we pay attention to the requirements of formation as at present and to the custom of hospitality, which should be kept up.

Essentially, a community must be self-supporting financially, and its relations with the external world should be reduced to the minimum. To cover the expenses needed for a great community that has members whose work is not productive enough, a large amount of capital is required. Even though the monks have to work hard so that the capital may yield properly, still capital is required first. In this way monasteries have a position among those who have capital and are economically strong.

On the contrary, the people around the monastery—even the whole district—are mostly economically weak and do not have a large capital. Thus from the economic point of view the monastery is very different from the society around it. The financial position of the monastery is nearer to that of the rich than to that of ordinary people.

Entering the monastery, we leave everything—which is usually very little—to become members of a body having insured capital, while the family members left behind are struggling to maintain their daily life. The financial security of the monks is far above the financial position of the common people, except when they come from very rich families (and this seldom happens). The vocation to become a monk is usually accompanied by a certain promotion in financial affairs. It is a pity if, later on, a monk does not have the real vocation and has to leave the monastery and go back to the world, because then he has to come down to the low financial situation he had in the beginning. In a monastery the monks can experience how they are rewarded a hundredfold even in this world.

I wonder whether this is according to the original inspiration of monastic life. I do not dare give an affirmative answer. Can the counsel of Christ to leave everything and follow him be commented on in this way: that we leave everything only to be accepted by an institute that makes our life secure, so that, as seen from the economic point of view, we are better insured? If it is so, can we consider this "leaving everything" as something real? It is for me a paradox that we need a large amount of capital to give an occasion for monks to leave everything.

Closed community: withdrawal from the world. According to the rule of St. Benedict, the monastery should be arranged in such a way that the needs of the monks can be satisfied without their going outside, because it is not good for their souls. This regulation is often connected with withdrawal from the world, which is considered an essential element of monastic life. In other words, the necessities for living should be produced as much as possible within the monastery itself; the monastery should be a source of production for its inmates. This requires a large capital—with all the difficulties already mentioned.

But there is still another difficulty. At present it is impossible for a monastery to produce everything to satisfy the needs of life. Only a part of its needs can be produced in the monastery, and only a part of the particular produce is needed for the community. Hence we cannot prevent our having contact with the world outside, because the produce of the monastery must be sold outside and the articles needed must be bought outside. Thus in financial affairs the monastery cannot separate itself absolutely from the external world.

This fact is usually accepted, and the relation with the external world in this field is taken to be something normal. This relation is reciprocal. There are people from outside who come to the monastery for business reasons, and there are monks who have to go out for the same reason. For many people the monastery is thus more an industry than a place of recollection.

To keep the spirit of withdrawal from the world, contacts with the external world for other reasons are very greatly limited, so that sometimes monks go out only for business reasons. Traveling monks often act more as businessmen rather than as religious. And in economic transactions monks often act like other businessmen, as if there were no withdrawal from the world at all.

In Western observance this withdrawal from the world is often considered too materially and locally. As a consequence, when a certain monk has to go outside he feels that there is no withdrawal any more, because materially and locally the monk concerned is no more in the monastery and is no more separated from the external world. Thus there is a kind of dispensation, or more clearly, there is a kind of "suspension."

Nowadays, since it is impossible to live in a community that is completely separated from the world materially, absolute material separation from the world cannot be practiced. Relations with society cannot be avoided. This being the situation, might it not be better to consider separation from the world in a more spiritual sense? If it is, the reason for contact with the world must be reconsidered. If a monk has to leave his solitude at times, is it not more correct that he should go out as a messenger of God's kingdom rather than as an industrialist? This reflection invites us to review the activities of monks.

Earning a living. Monks follow the counsels of Christ, selling all their possessions and leaving everything to follow him. But as long as they live in this world they need the necessities of life. They cannot live on air alone. In some way the necessities of life must be satisfied. Monks have to earn their living or others have to do it for them. According to Western observance, the traditional way of seeking a livelihood is to work within the monastery itself in order to produce something based upon the capital—whether in the form of fields or cattle or industry or something else. This traditional way of earning a living presupposes a large capital. Are there no other possibilities? Can we not find another way of earning a living, one that does not require a large capital?

In our society people who are not very rich earn their living by contributing their energy. Their capital has the form not of riches but of competence and energy. They work as laborers, not in their own homes but in productive organizations belonging to others. For thus exerting their energy they receive a salary with which they can buy things needed for their life and that of their families.

Is this system not a possibility for monks too? Can monks not be like common people in the way they earn their living?

This possibility has some difficulties: for instance, material withdrawal from the world cannot be maintained. Moreover, since in Indonesia at present the economic situation is very unfavorable, when monks earn their living with only competence and energy as capital, they can earn only very little, not enough to live properly. Hence to cover the expenses needed for living properly they will have to look for some sort of business on the side, and as a result very much time will have to be spent on work alone. They will thus surely experience many financial difficulties, and the peacefulness of their life will certainly be troubled. And what to do if they are ill or getting old? There are indeed serious inconveniences.

Yet I wonder whether living with such difficulties is not closer to evangelical poverty than living securely in the monastery. Is this struggle for life not useful to make the spirit of confidence in the divine providence more authentic? Putting trust in divine providence in the midst of financial security is an illusion.

If monks earn their living by working as laborers, the structure of the monastery will be completely changed, and observances will have to be radically revised.

Contact with society. According to the Western observance, contact with the external world—thus with society as well—must be limited to the minimum. It can even be said that such contact is only tolerated. Minimal contact is considered as ideal—as a situation most closely resembling the spirit of the desert.

Monks from the West sent out to the mission to found a monastery, usually, on their arrival in the mission, go straight to their new monastery. The new monastery should be prepared in such a way that regular life can be started as soon as possible. Having entered the new monastery, the monks do not go outside unless it is absolutely necessary. There is practically no occasion for direct contact with society. Certainly there is some contact, because society visits the monastery in the persons of guests and meets the monks. But ordinarily only the monks appointed to receive guests or having something to do with the guests are allowed to have contact with them. In this contact with guests there is very little occasion for them to become acquainted with society, because usually it is the guests who desire to know something about monastic life. So the monks concerned speak, while the guests listen.

Native monks, too, are completely separated from society after entering a monastery. They live in the monastery as if on an isolated island, whereas at present society is undergoing a very quick development. Hence, if monks are separated from society for too long a time, they do not know the real society any more and they are strangers to it.

In such a situation, how can they adapt their monastic life to the mentality of society? And who has to arrange this adaptation? How can monks find out the riches hidden in society that can be taken over to enrich their monastic life? Is the recommendation to know society laid down by the Decree on the Appropriate Renewal of the Religious Life as one of the principles for renewing religious life not applicable to monks, too?

Without denying the importance of withdrawal from the world, I am of the opinion that direct contact with society is necessary. Even as monks we must try to know society. Contact with society should not be held as an unavoidable evil to be tolerated; it must rather be promoted consciously and systematically. Only in this way can our endeavor to adapt monastic life to the local mentality be properly realized.

In promoting direct contact with society, we must continue to maintain our monastic life with its withdrawal from the world. This should be shown in our mental attitude and in our outer way of life.

If this view is accepted and practiced, our observance has to undergo rather great changes.

International institute. As a Trappist monastery, ours is part of an international order together with all other Trappist houses throughout the world (though, in fact, direct contact with members of other houses of the order is very limited). This international organization has surely its advantages, but there are disadvantages, too. The general chapter is an intrinsic part of the order. Every two or three years superiors of our monasteries have to attend the general chapter. This is necessary for maintaining real contacts within the order. But from the financial point of view it is a very heavy burden, at least for monasteries in the Far East.

Though this burden can be easily alleviated thanks to the help of the order or of other houses, nevertheless the difficulty remains real. The fact that every two or three years a large amount is needed to pay for the travel to the general chapter is a fact worth considering. Ordinary people from our society are not able to pay for such expensive travel abroad. Here again we meet the problem of the need for a large capital. This financial difficulty is not the only one.

I wonder whether the Trappist monasteries throughout the world need to form such a strong juridical unity. Would it not be better if such an isolated monastery as ours at Rawaseneng were to be put under the protection and the supervision of the local bishop? It is a fact that liturgical matters in the vernacular are regulated and controlled by the liturgical commission of the order, of which not one of its members knows our language. This is also the case with problems concerning readings, formation, architecture, food, clothes and the like. I am completely aware that the possibility proposed involves also inconveniences and dangers, such as the danger of deviating from the pure tradition.

In this connection I must admit that our order has, indeed, flexible views in the matter and that we actually have so much liberty that the tie with the order does not cause many disadvantages in these matters.

Western Observance and Asian Mentality
Frans Hardjawijata, O.C.S.O.

Contacts with monasteries abroad, I agree, are necessary. Nevertheless I wonder whether these contacts must be of such a sort that all monasteries form an institutionally binding unit. Is there no possibility of looser and more flexible arrangements?

Frequency of community exercises. Inseparable from the questions already discussed, such as large community, closed community, the way of earning a living and contact with society, is the question of community exercises. Changes in these matters will surely cause changes in the community exercises, too.

In the observance presently in force there are very many community exercises. Though Prime has been abrogated, we must still come together seven times a day for the Divine Office. Moreover there are still daily conventual Mass, meditation twice a day, common meal, rest at a determined time, chapter and conferences. From rising to bedtime we are bound by bells and clocks. It can be said that in our observance the number of community exercises reaches its maximum. This situation differs considerably from the normal rhythm of life in society. In convents of active religious there is not so great a proportion of exercises.

These are my questions: What is the purpose of this maximal frequency of community exercises? Is it the promoting of the spirit of prayer? The living and deepening of the community life? Mortification? Creating the atmosphere of prayer and recollection? Or is it rather adapting to the rhythm of life of the time when the rule was composed?

I leave this last possibility to be investigated by historians. As for the other possibilities, my opinions are these.

Maximal frequency of community exercises presupposes that a great part of the members of the community have duties that can be easily interrupted. As a matter of fact, those duties must be performed within the monastery itself and form a way of earning a living based upon a large capital.

I am rather skeptical of whether maximal frequency of community prayer offers a good occasion for deepening the life of prayer. The danger of routine is very great, especially because the text of the prayers has been fixed beforehand. Moreover, there are certainly some members of the community whose work, at times, cannot be easily interrupted, so that they are not able to follow all the community exercises. Their absence, especially if it becomes a custom, can have an influence upon the community that is not good. On the other hand, if they try to be present at all community prayers, they are continuously in an atmosphere of unrest, as if tyrannized by time and always haunted by it. This causes an atmosphere of oppressive tension in the monastery. Everyone knows that such an atmosphere is not helpful for the development of the life of prayer.

I am of the opinion that in these matters quality should be preferred to quantity. It is better to reduce the frequency of community prayer and to make it more living, for instance, by introducing certain variations in its form and by leaving room for improvisation, so that the community prayer can be adapted to the aspirations of today. Thus, to deepen the life of prayer we do not need to have maximal frequency of community prayer.

Nor is such frequency needed for promoting community life. In the traditional community exercises there is no occasion for personal contacts among the members of the community. Their being together is of a nature more material than personal. More than community exercises, personal contacts are useful for deepening community life. It seems to me better, therefore, to reduce the frequency of community exercises in order to leave more time for personal contacts.

If maximal frequency of community exercises is meant as mortification, it may be said that this goal is attained. But it is still a great question to what extent such a form of mortification remains significant. All the disadvantages being considered, is it not possible to look for other more significant forms of mortification?

I dare not say that frequent obligatory community exercises are apt to create an atmosphere of recollection and prayer in the monastery, because the atmosphere of tension and hurry already mentioned highly disturbs peace and quietness. And, of course, if the way of earning a living is changed—for instance by the monks' working as laborers—the frequency of community exercises will be automatically reduced.

These reflections persuade me that the frequency of community exercises must be reduced so that more time may be set aside for the monks to use more freely and personally.

Obligatory community exercises. In Western observance, community exercises are obligatory, and in the case of community prayer the obligatory character is such that monks who do not attend one of the exercises have the obligation to pray it privately outside the office. I think that it is better to have more flexible regulations in this matter. For example, if a monk cannot be present at a community prayer because of some urgent work that cannot be postponed, it seems to me that this urgent work may be considered as a substitute for the community prayer he misses, on the understanding that for the rest he does his best to maintain and intensify his life of prayer.

It is quite another thing if the monk in question regularly cannot attend a part of the community prayers because every day he has to be elsewhere at the time of some of them. In that case he has to look for another time to do his prayer—though in my opinion it would be better if private prayers meant as substitute for common prayer were not bound by given text or structure. Let him be free to choose the way of praying that suits him best. In that way obligatory prayer may be understood in a more personal than material or formalistic manner.

It is with hesitation I bring up the following questions: Would it not be better if this obligatory character were slackened? Would it not suffice if, instead of monks' being obliged to follow all the community exercises, it was recommended to them? In that way, attending community exercises would be left to each monk's responsibility.

Of course, monks must be educated in such a way that they will love the community exercises and be convinced of their importance, and that they will want to be present at them not on account of obligation, but because of personal conviction. The community exercises, in their turn, have to be carried out in such a way that they can be lived as significant exercises. Possibly by making the obligatory character more relative, the danger of routine can be more easily overcome.

Personal relations among monks and the rule of silence. In Western observance as interpreted by the Trappist order, there is very little occasion for personal contacts among monks. Monks are permitted to have contact with one another only when it is necessary. Contacts are seen as exceptions. There must be valid reasons if they are to be authorized. Abstaining from contacts and keeping silence are regarded as the normal situation. Contacts with brethren must be reduced to the minimum in order to promote, as far as possible, contact with God. Of course, in this matter the practice is far more "human" than the rules.

It must be clearly affirmed that contacts with one's fellow men must by no means be regarded as in any way rivaling one's contact with God. By lessening one's contacts with one's fellow men, however, one does not automatically develop contact with God. Furthermore, the rigid rule of silence cannot be indiscriminately applied to all members of the community. Here development is needed. Development in spiritual life and the life of prayer is allied to an increasing need of silence. This development, however, is not the same in all monks. A forced silence is more harmful than profitable.

If occasion for personal contacts is restricted only to the most necessary occasions or work, the conversations of monks can be confined simply to material matters. Spiritual matters are spoken about only on official occasions, during community exercises or during conversation with the spiritual father. As a consequence the conversations of monks are usually superficial. Can it be supposed that their conversations with God are deeper?

If the life of prayer is an expression of a life of love of God, and if on the other hand man cannot love God unless he loves his fellow men as himself, must we not conclude that authentic love of one's neighbor is an absolute condition for the love of God and the life of prayer? How can we love our brethren without having normal and human contacts with them? Personal contacts among monks are as necessary as silence. Silence, of course, remains necessary, but it should not take away the possibility of personal relationships.

In any case, silence will be significant only if it is filled up with a content. To fill up silence, personal contact with God is needed. But this personal contact with God cannot be properly developed without personal contact with one's fellow men. Personal contact with one's fellow men can therefore be of great use in improving and filling up silence.

The quantity of rules and regulations. Western observance includes many rules and regulations that are explained even in minute detail. It seems there is a tendency to multiply rules to the maximum. Even the monks in the West feel them to be in excess. I am inclined to think that the rules and regulations should be reduced to the minimum. Things known to common sense need not be expressed in the form of a rule. In that way occasions of transgression of the rules are reduced, as well, and the monks' attention is not interrupted by rules of little importance.

It is especially important that matters intimately connected with the local situation not be decided from abroad. It is desirable that a community, led by its superior, should be given liberty to arrange matters like food, clothing, lodging, beverages and the daily schedule. Rules should be limited to general principles. The monks may then have opportunities to use their own common sense and act as adults.

If there are too many rules and regulations, too much attention may be given to them, especially by new members of the community, so that the rules will cloud the main inspiration of their monastic life. A monk can then become narrow-minded and his spiritual life will inevitably suffer.

WESTERN OBSERVANCE AND ASIAN MENTALITY
Frans Hardjawijata, O.C.S.O.

CONCLUSION

This is my personal view on Western observance as understood and practiced by the Trappist order. When I look back on what I have said, I am completely aware that my view has been mostly critical and negative. Nevertheless my criticism embodies structural elements that are fundamental. Once more I stress the point that what I have brought forward are only thoughts and reflections. I do not expect all my thoughts to be accepted and put into practice immediately. All I want is that they be received as material for further thought, revision, examination and correction of shortcomings. Only after mature consideration can they gradually be put into practice when the time is ripe.

In the first stage, a traditional monastery belonging to an international institution should be founded, maintained and developed. A traditional structure is necessary during the first stage, which will still be a stage of "tradition," that is to say, a stage of "channeling" the monastic life in its existing form.

As seen by the native monks, this first stage will be a receptive stage, a stage of receiving and living the traditional monastic life purely and authentically. Certainly this traditional monastic life should be adapted to the local conditions and culture, but without radical structural changes. In Indonesia we are still in this first stage.

The second stage can be begun only when the traditional monastic life has strong roots. Besides the traditional monastic life, experiments can be made in living a monastic life with a different structure in small communities that are open and that approach the condition of the common man in the way they earn a living and in external life. The monks who carry out this experiment should have lived the traditional monastic life long enough to have known the essence of monastic life by experience. Such experiments should have the support of a traditional monastery, and they can only be begun even then if the Holy Spirit inspires those who plan to make the experiments.

These experiments will not replace traditional monastic life. The traditional monastery will continue to exist, and it should remain. But besides it other experiments can be made when the time comes.

The stage following this one cannot be determined beforehand. It will depend upon the experiments already mentioned. It is possible that both forms will continue side by side; or one may flourish and the other fail. Pessimists may think that both will die out. But it is not for us to decide. Our task is simply to do everything in our power to live the monastic life sincerely and authentically and, following the rhythm of the Holy Spirit, adapt our monastic life to the local mentality. Thus gradually it will assume a form that the people around us can recognize as being suited to their own mentality.

Reorientation of Monastic Life in an Asian Context

M. F. ACHARYA, O.C.S.O.

> From the unreal lead me to the real,
> From darkness lead me to light,
> From death lead me to immortality.
>
> —Brihadaranyaka Upanishad, I, iii, 28

This Vedic mantra, a prayer to be initiated into the mystery of the Absolute, to be shown the path of Brahmahood—summing up the monastic aspirations of the Upanishadic sages—is still relevant today. It was Jawaharlal Nehru who, addressing the World Congress of Orientalists in New Delhi a few months before his death, stated that ancient civilizations had a remarkable depth. "The ancient way of thinking," he said, "concentrated itself on knowing oneself interiorly, from within." And he added: "It is still desirable to learn something of ourselves apart from the outside world, because it helps to keep one's balance in the tremendous technological changes of the modern world. But it is difficult to see how this depth of the past can be saved to remedy the superficiality and outwardness of the modern world."

The depth of the Indian culture is to a great extent the fruit of the monastic experience of India's *rishis*, or Vedic seers. It would seem, therefore, that the monastic life might help in correcting the spiritual imbalance of the world today, a monastic life however that does not close itself to the challenge of modern man. Many of the changes modern life is bringing about in the appreciation of human values can make a positive contribution to the progress of mankind.

First among these contributions is modern man's positive approach to earthly realities and a corresponding respect for all that pertains to the body. Next comes, with a greater understanding for the rights of each individual, an increasing consideration for universal human brotherhood. Similarly, the challenge of modern life, with the dynamism of urban and industrialized society diversified according to a great variety of functions, can be beneficial for the ancient, self-contained monastic establishments of the Middle Ages. Finally, with the increasing contacts of Christianity with the great religions of the world—in a spirit of mutual respect urged by the increasing place given to dialogue—a new challenge comes to Christian monasticism from its Asian counterparts in Hinduism and Buddhism. It is in the light of this last development, the encounter of Christianity with Hinduism, and also of the postconciliar renewal of the religious life, that I propose to examine here the new orientations that should be given to Christian monasticism in Asia.

CARDINAL FEATURES OF THE MONASTIC IDEA ACCORDING TO VATICAN II

It is quite true that the Vatican Council, as a whole, has confirmed the traditional teaching of the Church on the monastic life. Yet when we ponder more deeply the Pentecostal renewal initiated by the Council and presently prompting the Church and the whole of Christianity to a reappraisal of its life, we cannot fail to acknowledge that the traditional teaching is given new perspectives. And these throw a new light on the place of the monastic life in the Church and its meaning for the world at large.

Two trends of the conciliar renewal must claim our attention in this respect. The first is often lost sight of and is sometimes even completely ignored. It may be called the contemplative dimension of the life of the Christian. The second is more prominent in people's minds but remains open to much questioning. It may be referred to as the incarnational character of the economy of salvation.

The contemplative dimension of Christian life. While the Church is a community of men on earth, a society with a visible structure and its own proper laws, that which creates the communion among its members is their divine sonship, their sharing in God's own life. The Church is the place where the divinization of mankind is effected by sharing in the very being of God. Even when the Council addresses the whole of mankind and deals with basically human problems, such as the dignity of all human beings, man's activities and the development of his culture, it takes a sapiential view. This view of the fathers of Vatican II marks a return to a more biblical anthropology. In spite of the current trend of human history, leading mankind by its own discoveries and power to conquest of the universe, the Council champions the contemplative purpose of human life, "proclaiming the highest destiny of man and the godlike seed that has been sown in him" (Constitution on the Church in the Modern World, n. 3). Thus it takes its stand in the wake of the fathers of Christian monasticism (generally also of Christian mysticism), Origen and Gregory of Nyssa, Isaac the Syrian and Bernard of Clairvaux, by whom man is described not as *animal rationale* but as *capax Dei*, i.e., as having a divine dimension, a purpose, a destiny that can be fulfilled only by divine communion, by sharing in God's life.

In the Constitution on the Church in the Modern World, the Church reasserts its faith in the new earth and the new heaven when the creation "will be unchained from the bondage of vanity." It also declares solemnly that this new kingdom, the kingdom of Christ, is "already present in mystery," waiting to be brought into full flower when the Lord returns (n. 39). In spite of the contradictions begotten by the great changes taking place today, in spite of the imbalance arising from an ever increasing concern for practicality and efficiency, the Council expects man to achieve a more vivid sense of God. "When a man applies himself to the various disciplines of philosophy, of history and of mathematical and natural science, and when he cultivates the arts, he can do very much to elevate the human family. . . . Thus mankind can be more clearly enlightened by that marvelous wisdom which is with God from all eternity. . . . In this way the human spirit grows increasingly free of its bondage to creatures and can be more easily drawn to the worship and contemplation of the Creator" (n. 57).

Freedom from bondage and contemplation of the Creator are unmistakable monastic motivations. Even the philosopher and the scientist are expected to grow increasingly free from bondage. They seek and attain reality, and thus "steeped in wisdom pass through invisible realities to those who are unseen." The Council confirms the views of Jawaharlal Nehru, asserting very strongly that the modern world needs such wisdom more than bygone ages if its technical and scientific achievements are to find their true meaning.

In the light of the Church's concern to see every man, even when dedicated to the great tasks of the world, "grow in the ability to wonder and contemplate, and free himself from his bondage to creatures," it is difficult to see how monks could be content with less. Can they even be satisfied with being labeled as members of the contemplative state of life? Certainly the gifts of the Spirit are diverse even within the monastic family, and it is of the nature of the pilgrim Church to experience a tension between the earthly and the heavenly, between the human and the divine. Yet some of its sons, the monks, are definitely called "to give clear witness to the new heaven and the new earth and to keep this desire green among the human family." Such is the monastic charism within the body of Christ.

And this, precisely, has been the constant function of monasticism in Asia for three thousand years. There is little use in pointing to the deviations from the monastic ideal and the compromises entered upon by a number of its representatives. Religious institutions throughout the world and all along the course of human history have passed through similar crises. The wandering lawless monks censured by the Rule of St. Benedict have much in common with a certain type of *sadhus*, or holy men. We have indulged too long in this condemnation of our brothers. A more subtle temptation nowadays is to quote our non-Christian friends, Buddhist or Hindu, when they have disparaging remarks for their own monks. Could they also not make a good harvest of such criticisms in Western literature of the late Middle Ages and of the Reformation?

The contemplative dimension of man's life comes closer to us when we reflect on the incarnational principle of the Church's mission.

The incarnational economy. Man's achievements in the twentieth century are not seen by the Council as a tower of Babel, rising in challenge to the divine power. They are looked upon from a deeper level, as a flowering of God's mysterious design. They contribute to the realization in history of the divine plan. And this applies particularly to the human culture by which man refines his spiritual and bodily activities. Culture is like an incarnation of man's spiritual experiences and aspirations.

God revealing himself to his people has spoken according to the culture proper to different ages. "In virtue of his incarnation, Christ bound himself to the definite social and cultural conditions of the human beings among whom he dwelt" (Decree on the Church's Missionary Activity, n. 10). The first encounter of the Church was with the Mediterranean world. It was so deep that it has resulted in substituting Greek philosophy and theology, Roman law and institutions, to its original biblical world thought to such an extent that since then it has never succeeded in expressing the Christian mystery in any other great world culture.

Reorientation of Monastic Life
Francis Acharya, O.C.S.O.

In this respect, however, Vatican II has achieved a breakthrough to the point of creating a crisis in the missions. Drawing on the teachings of some of the early fathers and ecclesiastical writers—Justin, an Asiatic, and Tertullian, an African—the Council has rediscovered the hidden presence of God in the non-Christian cultures and the validity of religious experience outside the Church.

For the first time in history the Church has officially adopted a positive attitude toward other religions. It has recognized them as entities with whom it wishes to enter into dialogue and has created for this purpose a new Roman Dicasterium, with consultors throughout the world. Yet for many of us who are in the mission fields this is a fearsome confrontation, and it is painful to adjust ourselves to the new situation, though it seems to be based on fairly solid theology.

Three to four thousand years ago the Word of God came to Abraham, Moses and the Prophets. In the last days God has spoken to us through his Son. But seeds of the Word have been sown by him in the ancient religions and cultures of Asia prior to the preaching of the gospel. These seeds make up the cosmic covenant. The fourth Eucharistic prayer recently sanctioned by Rome praises the Father for the repeated covenants he made with man. These are seeds of the Word that have never ceased to sprout and bear fruit. And these again have continued to mature under the rays of light of the Word of God, who enlightens every man. The quest of the rishis for ultimate Reality, the attainment of enlightenment by the Lord Buddha, the transcendent wisdom and the infinite compassion of the Mahayanists, and the fervor of the many *bhakti* or devotional movements, insofar as they carry grace and truth with them, are so many gifts of God to the nations, for "whatever truth and grace are to be found among them" are a secret working of God.

Not that the Council fathers forget the unicity of the biblical revelation or close their eyes to the impurities that the ore carries with these bright particles; but the work of the missionary is to go in search of the kingdom, likened by our Lord to a treasure buried in a field, and to lay bare these precious pearls with the joy and reverence that fill the hearts of those who come in the presence of the Divine. Missionary activity must purify these treasures and ennoble them by restoring them to Christ, for they are part of his inheritance, of his kingdom. This is often very hard to realize, yet it is the unquestionable teaching of the Council.

Just as the Jewish Church moved outward and broke down its barriers when Peter, at Caesarea, was astonished that the gift of the Holy Spirit had been poured out even on the Gentiles, the fathers of Vatican II could not help being seized with wonder at this secret but unquestionably authentic presence of God. Hence they wish us "to learn by sincere and patient dialogue what treasures a bountiful God has distributed among the nations." They marvel at the "spiritual adornments and gifts of the various races and peoples." They look at the non-Christian cultures as to the "good ground watered by divine dew" and causing the seed which is the Word of God to sprout, while drawing "nourishing elements which it transforms and assimilates into itself to bear much fruit" (Missionary Activity, n. 22).

When they come to an official declaration of the Catholic Church on non-Christian religions, they remain below the expectations of those among us who have had a living experience of the presence of the Spirit in the hearts of those seekers of God and who are acquainted with their deep commitment to the unseen realities. Yet they nevertheless give us a positive exhortation that "prudently and lovingly, through dialogue and collaboration with the followers of other religions and in witness of the Christian faith and life [we] acknowledge, preserve and promote the spiritual and moral goods found among these men, as well as the values in their society and culture" (Declaration on the Non-Christian Religions, n. 2). This is a clear call to set out on a prudent but loving quest into the heart of Hinduism, Buddhism, Islam, in search of seeds of the Word as ways of meditation, practice of the divine presence, prayer of the name, ascetic ways, modes of worship and the like.

The integration of the Church with the thought world of the Greco-Roman empire was the work of a pleiad of monastic fathers who emerged very early from the monastic movement—the first generation of monks that followed Anthony and Pachomios, Basil and the two Gregories, Ephrem and Chrysostom, Jerome and Augustine, with Justin, Clement and Origen as their forerunners. Could it not be that the Holy Spirit has a similar purpose in bringing Christian monasticism to Asia at this eleventh hour of the Lord's day? If this is the case, there is a really gigantic task ahead of us: the integration of the Church with the religious forces still shaping the Asiatic continent; the formulation of the Christian mystery in the light of the experience of its sages and *rishis*, its *bhaktas* or devotees and all other seekers of God. There can be no doubt that these expectations were kindled at the Vatican Council. "In imitation of the plan of the Incarnation, the young Churches . . . take to themselves in a wonderful exchange all the riches of the nations which were given to Christ as an inheritance" (Missionary Activity, n. 22).

"Wonderful exchange," *admirabile commercium*, is the contemplative

REORIENTATION OF MONASTIC LIFE
Francis Acharya, O.C.S.O.

utterance of the Church in the celebration of the mystery of the Incarnation at Christmas. As matter for such sacred trading between the young churches and the nations the fathers enumerate the "customs and traditions of their people," their "wisdom and learning," their "rites," their "ascetic and contemplative traditions" (*ibid.* nn. 18, 22; also Constitution on the Sacred Liturgy, nn. 65, 77). The Decree on Missionary Activity mentions explicitly the whole life of faith, the teaching of the Church's doctrine, the liturgy and even the formerly untouchable canon law. We read that the faith "must be taught by an adequate catechesis celebrated in a liturgy which harmonizes with the genius of the people, and introduced into upright institutions and local customs by appropriate canonical legislation." Further it adds: "Theological investigation must necessarily be stirred up in each major socio-cultural area. . . . Thus it will be more clearly seen in what ways faith can seek for understanding in the philosophy and wisdom of these peoples" (*ibid.*, nn. 19, 22). There is not one facet of the life of the Church—its institutions, its teachings, its spirituality, its worship—that cannot be enriched by these wonderful exchanges between the nations and the Bride of Christ.

Organic relation between Christian and non-Christian monasticism. Vatican II has not only opened the way and shown the fields in which the seeds of the Word lie hidden and call for our searching. It has also provided the theological principle prompting the new approach. This pertains to the very nature of the Church, to its catholicity understood not as a prerogative excluding other men or non-Catholic Christians, as in the preconciliar usage of the word, but as a dynamic quality, a universal expansiveness, which must be attributed ultimately to the presence in it of Christ and of his Spirit. "This characteristic of universality which adorns the People of God is a gift from the Lord himself. By reason of it the Catholic Church strives energetically and constantly to bring all humanity with all its riches back to Christ, its head, in the unity of his Spirit" (Constitution on the Church, n. 13). The riches of the nations cannot be rejected by the Church, not even neglected as irrelevant or of little importance. Being part of Christ's inheritance they must by all means be brought in as a harvest to enrich the life of the Church and thus enhance its catholicity.

The doctrines of "man naturally Christian" and of the *spermatikos Logos*, the germinal or seedlike Word, imply that the Church is in continuity with the non-Christian religions. Augustine would even not agree with this qualification insofar as it conveys a negation of any relation to

Christ. For the Alpha and Omega is at the beginning and at the end of all religion, of whatever truth and goodness is found in the world. Did he not write that the Christian religion was in existence long before Jesus Christ gave it a name and form? And Newman added in greater detail:

> A great proportion of what is generally received as Christian truth is, in its rudiments or in its separate parts, to be found in non-Christian philosophies and religions.... The Moral Governor of the world has scattered the seeds of truth far and wide over its extent. These have variously taken root and grown up as in the wilderness, wild plants indeed but living.[1]

In this sense not only is the Church in continuity with non-Christian religions, but Christian monasticism is related to Asian monasticism. The fathers of the Vatican Council have acknowledged as genuine the strivings of the world religions to answer the restless searching of the human heart by proposing ways of conduct and of life, rules and teachings. They have praised the great Eastern religions in particular for their deep sense of God as well as for their monastic motivations: the Buddhist's experience of the radical insufficiency of this shifting world and his search for supreme enlightenment, the ascetical practices, the paths of meditation and devotion so representative of Hinduism.

NECESSITY OF DIALOGUE AT THREE LEVELS

It is therefore very urgent that we acquire a direct knowledge of indigenous monasticism and that we become acquainted with representatives of such monasticism. Long ago we should have shunned our ignorance and our complacency while pondering over the words of St. Paul to the Athenians, worshipers of the unknown God: "God created man that all nations might seek him and by feeling their way toward him, succeed in finding him. For he is not far from any of us, since it is in him that we live, and move and exist, as one of your own writers have said: 'We are all his children'" (Acts 17:27–28). Our monastic life should therefore grow under the enriching presence of our non-Christian brethren, and this mainly at three levels: study, friendly relations and dialogue, and ultimately an actual sharing in the experience of the monastic life as it is lived by our people.

[1] "Milman's View of Christianity," *Essays Critical and Historical*, Vol. 2 (New York: Longmans, 1887), 231.

REORIENTATION OF MONASTIC LIFE
Francis Acharya, O.C.S.O.

The study of their Sacred Scriptures. By this phrase I mean the study of their sacred texts, their Scriptures, to the extent that it could compare with the study of the Bible in the first three centuries of the Church, when the father sets to establish the Christological meaning of the Old Testament. Indeed, in the light of the gospel, for many generations the Old Testament remained a rather questionable document of divine revelation. We all know the letter addressed by Athanasius of Alexandria to a nun of his diocese who found great difficulties in using the Psalms to formulate her prayer in the light of the Sermon on the Mount and the parables of the kingdom.

Such a study of the Scriptures of the Gentiles as illustrated abundantly by Vatican II is warranted by the Bible itself, both the Old and the New Testaments. "The nations have to bring to Sion all their riches . . . to beautify the place of God's sanctuary" (Is. 60:13), while Israel (the Church) will suck the milk of the Gentiles, the breast of kings. "The nations walk by the light of God and the Lamb and bring into the heavenly city all their splendor" (Rev. 21:24–26; Is. 19:24). Similarly, there are passages (Wis. 7:22–8:1; Ezek. 14:10–20) where the best intercessors for the chosen people are Daniel and Job, two pagans, not to mention Melchizedek, the pagan priest of El-Elyon (Gen. 14; Ps. 109; Heb. 7:1–10) but also a prophetic prefiguring of Christ the eternal Priest, and therefore commemorated at the Anamnesis of the Roman Canon. In the New Testament there is a harvest of texts revealing the central place of Christ in history and in the cosmos (Col. 1:16–20, 29; Eph. 1:10; Rom. 8:19; Jn. 1:3, 9; Rev. 1:18) and pointing in the same direction.

The study of these texts will help us to realize that the spirit of God has been working in and among the Gentiles all down the ages, drawing them toward Christ and the fullness of his manifestation. And if this is true, then even today God is speaking to us through the Scriptures of the Gentiles, their religious traditions, their spiritual attainment. Through them he challenges us and calls us to draw nearer to him, as he does also through the calamities and trials that are never far from us as well as through the great conquests of science and technology.

Thus when we study the non-Christian Scriptures, we have to read them in the way our Lord read the Old Testament about himself in the providential circumstances of his Incarnation in Palestine. This Christian reading, or rather rereading of the non-Christian Scriptures, in the way the Hebrew Scriptures were constantly reread by prophets and scribes, and, later, for their integration in the New Testament and in the Christian liturgies, will be an unveiling in the spirit of their eschatological and real meaning. In the same way as the New Testament writers and the authors of the Church's liturgies detected in the Old Testament the presence of Christ and of the Holy Spirit, we are asked by the Church to go in search of the seeds of the Word and discover what the non-Christian Scriptures say of Christ. Our aim is not to confront the Hindu Scriptures with the biblical revelations, but rather to hear what the Hindu Scriptures say of the Word whose seeds have been scattered by God in them even prior to the gospel and have continued to sprout and bear fruit up to this day.

In India there is a quasi-canonical trilogy of texts constituting a Summa of *Brahmavidya*, or knowledge of supreme Reality: the Upanishads, the Bhagavad Gita and the *Brahma Sutras*. These three outstanding monuments of Hinduism are considered to embody the three constitutive elements of all religions: experience, discipline and knowledge. They do not form a religion, but they are "religion itself in its most universal and deepest significance." A long established tradition demands that everyone who reaches the status of *Acharya* (understood as teacher of salvation) should write a commentary on each of these texts. But the other lesser scriptures—the epics, the six great *darshanas* or systems of philosophy, the *Puranas* or mythological histories and the *bhakti* or devotional literature provide many other fields of research for the monastic quest.

Friendly relations. Academic studies of sacred texts will not suffice. The great faiths of the world carry their own Scriptures with them in a living tradition. Hence the need of friendly and protracted dialogue at the level of personal friendship with people who truly live for God, who live close to him. It is from them that we have to learn the language they use, the ways they express their knowledge of God and their quest of him, their approach to the great problems of man's relation to God and to the universe, their understanding of the human being: body and soul, with their respective parts in the spiritual quest, and so on. While doing all this, we have to perceive the presence and action of God in their lives.

Sharing of religious experience. The study of non-Christian Scriptures and the dialogue at the level of personal friendship will have true meaning only if they lead to an actual experience of the religious life of our non-Christian brothers. For this we have to share in their prayer and then also, by ourselves, to use their best prayers in our worship and devotional life. In India we have to join in their devotional singing (*kirtan* and

Reorientation of Monastic Life
Francis Acharya, O.C.S.O.

bhajan), not, however with the inhibitions or suspicions of an inquisitor, or with the interest of the scholar of art or religion, but with true devotion. We have to share in rituals like the *arati*, or waving of lights before the image, or *diksha*, initiation. We may have to seek spiritual guidance under some modern, open-minded teacher, or *guru*. We must draw closer, again with loyalty and with discernment, to the mystery of God's grace as present in our non-Christian brothers. Only on such a broad and deep basis can Christian monasticism discover its profound affinities with its Asian counterparts and come to share with them the light of the gospel and be in a way regrafted on its stock.

It is at this level only that a real encounter of Christianity with Hinduism may ultimately take place. Its outcome should be nothing less than the integration of the spiritual heritage of India into a new expression of the Christian mystery. This is a task for which hardly any foundation has been laid. There has been a good deal of study of texts and doctrines; yet too often it has been made with a view to contrasting them with our own theological categories. We remain unacquainted with, and uncertain about, the religious experience that Hinduism has been nurturing from the time of the Upanishads to the contemporary renascence.

SOME CHARACTERISTIC FEATURES OF ASIAN MONASTICISM

Canonically structured yet always charismatic. From its origins and all along the course of its history, Asian monasticism has preserved certain remarkable features. It can surely claim a very ancient juridical structure, as exemplified in the *Code of Manu*, for the life of the *vanaprastha* (recluse) and the *sannyasi* (monk), or in the Rules of the Sangha (*Pratimoksha*) and of various Buddhist schools such as the Mahayana, Zen, Lamaism, and so on—a juridical structure that has often resulted in amazing forms of legalistic observances persisting as such to this day. Yet at the same time it has never been subdued by legalism. It has always remained open to and positively oriented toward a charismatic life.

A particular example of this view can be found in the life of prayer. In contrast with Western monasticism, its ways of prayer, worship or meditation, its paths to spiritual attainment, have never been enforced under mortal or venial sin; they have remained a matter of response to the promptings of the Spirit. A more general illustration of this charismatic understanding of the monastic life may be given here by a *sannyasi*, revealing in his own words—a living testimony—his own ideal:

Sannyasa is not just an extension of the first three ashramas (stages of life): brahmacharya, garhastha, vanaprastha. It indicates a total break with the past, with a conditioned way of life perpetuating the illusions and bondages in ever changing forms, in a sort of modified continuity. If *sannyasa* is not a liberation from the conditioned way of thinking, feeling and acting, it can hardly by called by that name, despite the ocher robe, the staff, the vows of poverty and the rest. *Sannyasa* is an inner revolution exploding in a total liberation from the past. A new mind and a new man totally liberated from the past and daring to live from moment to moment in a state of intense inquiry into his real being is the crying need of humanity, precariously perched on the verge of catastrophe. Truth does not influence, impose or convert. It only liberates and spontaneously places man in a state of timeless compassion and love that holds the whole mystery of life within its womb—a kind of void, nothingness, or a creative emptiness.

Beyond the conflict affecting Western monasticism. Asian monasticism in its various forms—especially in the ashram life—has not suffered from the same tensions as Western monasticism almost all along its history, such as the tension between active and contemplative. Although the ashrams remain open to the world, virtually ignoring—with only a few exceptions—the law of enclosure, yet they often remain conspicuously unworldly.

Similarly, the awareness of the *sadhu* of belonging to a universal order of beings, not simply to a particular congregation or monastic family, is much deeper than in our Western monastic orders. An ancient *mantra* from the Rig Veda (9:13.2, slokas 1–2) recited at the opening of the *diksha* (initiation) ceremony reads:

> God enjoins this upon a man about to take *sannyasa:* As the sun sucks juice out of the earth, similarly a *sannyasi* should live on the juice of fruits and develop his spirituality so as to become as kind to human beings in general as the moon, and to give true advice to all people.

Never overshadowed by the priesthood. The vitality of Asian monasticism asserts itself again in the question of its relationship to the priesthood. Although some *sadhus* or *bhikshus* may seek an outlet for their lack of realization by acting as *pujaris* (priests), yet the status of the *sannyasi* always emerges as the real thing, unlike the status of the non-priest monk in the Church. In India, for instance (and this reflects the prevailing notion in the Western Church until very recently), the Chris-

Reorientation of Monastic Life
Francis Acharya, O.C.S.O.

tian nonpriest monk is commonly taken for a third-rate religious. He has no proper identity even in the official census of Church statistics, where only two kinds of religious are listed: priests and brothers.

Although the *sannyasa diksha* (initiation into monkhood), as one of the great sacraments of Hindu life, is an elaborate piece of ritual, yet the *sannyasi* who emerges from the ritual is expected to be above all a catholic being, a man free from all bonds, reborn to become a member of the universe. His vows bind him to a triple renunciation: renunciation of progeny for the love of all beings, renunciation of money, renunciation of fame. They bind him also to three fundamental dispositions of all seekers of truth: perseverance or forbearance, patience and fearlessness, the very same that St. Paul calls fruits of the Spirit.

There are colorful rituals in the *sannyasa diksha*. The whole ceremonial is conducted around the *havan*, sacrificial fire, on which *ghee* (clarified butter) is poured repeatedly and generously all through the service. There is the shaving of the head, leaving only a tuft of five hairs later to be plucked and to serve as food for the sacred fire. The sacred thread, which had dubbed the boy a student and made him "twice born," now also is removed and consumed in the fire. Before that there were one hundred and eight washings of the shaven head, and later the bath in a sacred river, consisting of ceremonial dippings and a protracted standing navel deep in the water to wash away the sins and extinguish the passions before donning the ocher robe. Yet with all this, no trace of illuminism.

The teacher's *upadesha* (instruction) during the initiation rite impresses upon the mind of the candidate the fundamental values of moral life: never to deceive anybody, always to adhere to the truth, to serve others to the best of one's ability without expecting anything in return (there is even a vow of not accepting any gifts). There is stress on control of the senses, unshakable belief in God, worship of truth and a commitment to give always true *upadesha*, i.e., to teach the true doctrine, and to devote at least two hours daily to meditation. To these are added a number of precepts reflecting much of the Sermon on the Mount but already found in the *Code of Manu*: to welcome those by whom we are belittled, to keep no grudge, no ill will, to see all beings as oneself, not to look for rewards but to sit in meditation listening to God and practicing *yama* (abstentions) and *niyama* (observances). The former are abstinence from injury, from falsehood, from incontinence, from appropriation, from acceptance of gifts; and the latter are purity, contentment, austerity of life, study of the Scriptures and surrender to the Lord.

REORIENTATION OF THE MONASTIC TRAINING

At this initial stage of dialogue, this first attempt at trying "to recognize, preserve and promote the good things spiritual and moral," the *monastica*, found in Hinduism, it is too early to give definite directions for the reorientation of our monastic training in an Asian context. We can, however, give some guidelines in conclusion.

Reevaluation of the monastic vocation in itself. If Christian monasticism is to spread in Asia, it will not be without a deep reevaluation of the monastic vocation in itself, independent of the ministerial priesthood. This reevaluation will have also to be made in the light of modern life. When monasteries come in contact with an increasingly secularized, industrialized and urbanized world, the monastic life will have to show great flexibility. In this respect large communities on the pattern of the Cistercian or Benedictine monasteries of the West may reveal themselves to be unwieldy. In order to bear witness more profoundly to the life according to the gospel, a priority may be given to smaller groupings of fifteen to twenty, or even less—four to six monks, provided they are sufficiently mature.

Emphasis on the charismatic dimension. This reevaluation will work in favor of the charismatic dimension of the monastic life, with a consequent loosening of the present juridical setup. For this it may prove necessary to remove the rigid class system of our novitiates and study houses—leading after one to two years to the first vows and, after another three years to the final vows—in favor of a personal growth toward monastic maturity. This would require doing away with any fixed limit of years, or at least adopting great flexibility in this respect. It might also lead eventually to a man's remaining permanently in the path of the *sadhaka* (novice) or of *brahmachari* (simple profession).

For this to happen, it will be necessary to focus obedience on spiritual growth and spiritual attainment. And such a development demands an insistence on the experience of spiritual conversion or *metanoia*—in India, *sannyasa*, the great renunciation—as the very core of the monastic life. And that, not only initially, at the first call, but also throughout the life of the monk. From this should follow the possibility of entering, at a later stage, more deeply into solitude or of taking up a more exclusively spiritual path.

Training through sharing the life of a community and by the guidance of a monastic theology. The training would consist mainly in sharing the life of a community, or even of a particular *guru*, with, however, a program of monastic theology extending over some ten years. This program would consist of a triple course: Bible, liturgy, monastic tradition. This last course would deal extensively with the seeds of the Word as already described with respect to the Summa of *Brahmavidya*. That this is not simply the province of experts and scholars of comparative religion is witnessed to by the Decree on the Church's Missionary Activity. Here the religious communities as a whole are told to strive to give expression to "the treasures of mysticism adorning the Church's religious tradition" and to hand them on "in a manner harmonious with the nature and the genius of each nation." They are asked also to "reflect attentively on how Christian religious life may be able to assimilate the ascetic and contemplative traditions whose seeds were sometimes already planted by God in ancient cultures prior to the preaching of the gospel" (Missionary Activity, n. 18).

It is difficult to see how the contemplative communities more especially dedicated to the Church's liturgy, in which is reached the highest contemplation of the divine mysteries, could assume this task and bring it to fulfillment without evolving a liturgy that "harmonizes with the genius of the people and [is] introduced into upright institutions and local customs by appropriate canonical legislation" (*ibid.*, n. 19). In this light should the Rule of St. Benedict and even Eastern monastic customs not give way whenever desirable to Indian or Asian monastic legislation?

The renewal of the religious life in the Church according to Vatican II, as it has commonly been observed, should be undertaken in the light of two principles. First is the following of Christ as set down in the luminous pages of the Gospels. Second, the concern to reflect more faithfully the spirit of the founders. The evangelical life and a return to the spirit of the early monastic fathers have been the springs of all monastic renewals in the West.

But in India and Asia, Christian monks have to read the gospel even in its preparations—the seeds of the Word sown by God in their ancient religions. For this purpose they have to detect the rays of light of him who enlightens every man and reverently and with joy bring to the full light the seeds of truth that lie hidden in the religions of their people, who yet belong to Christ's heritage. Doing this they will also be returning to their own resources. For the origins and the first flowering of monasticism are India's great contribution to world religion.

We can promise a plentiful harvest in the field of monasticism, both in the documents of the past and of the present, in India and all over

Asia. But we cannot forget our Upanishadic *mantra*, and we must allow ourselves to be led from the unreality of our narrow views to the reality of the divine workings in the world, from the darkness of ignorance of God's ways with the nations to the knowledge of his self-revelation to them and his repeated covenants with them, from the death of our sinful self-sufficiency to immortality, which is a sharing of all mankind in his own eternal life.

SYNTHESIS OF GROUP DISCUSSIONS

December 11, 1968

THE MONASTERY IN THE COUNTRY

Questions for discussion:[1]

1. How can monks take part in the true development of the human environment they are situated in?
2. Do you notice a need among young people, even in the monastery, to contribute to the development of their country?
3. How can the monk's work fit in with the general economy of the country where he lives?
4. How can the monastic community advance progress and peace in the country where it is established?

1. *Role of the monastery in a developing country.* Two aspects of the monastery's role were constantly stressed:

The monastery, as a spiritual center, should bear witness to the ideological orientation of the Church, directing all its activity toward God. The specific contribution of monasticism to development is prayer, which gives its spiritual weight to the work of our contemporaries.

The monastery, being an integral part of a human context, must also express the charity of Christ toward it. Charity is not only vertical but also horizontal, and it seems that men in our times wish also to nourish their contemplation itself through the search for Christ in men.

These two aspects—that of the original reaching out toward God and that of social charity—create a tension and lead to different solutions according to the different locations and traditions of the monasteries. Some insist on

---

[1] The questions are based on the questionnaire, Part III. A and C (Appendix B, p. 278). See also the summary of replies to Part III. A and C (Appendix B, pp. 301–304 and 308–313).

the principle that monasticism has no "secondary end"; others on the duty Christian charity common to all men and to all institutions.

2. *The attitude of monks, old and young, regarding this double duty.* A conservative attitude is often found among older monks; such monks wish to avoid change and content themselves with giving alms and doing their work in the monastery well, leaving others to their own problems. On the other hand, the ardent desire of most of the young monks is to work for the country's development. According to the circumstances, they would like either to participate directly in social work undertaken by the management of youth or to pursue their studies to the maximum, with the best professors, to become competent and useful to their country as informed monks.

In those cases where the work of development is already assured, one often finds a desire for "retreat and sublimation," leading to a life that is more detached and more prayerful.

3. *Social work undertaken by the different monasteries.* This work takes two forms:

Help is extended in individual cases. For instance, young people are sought out who can become leaders in their own neighborhood, and help is provided for their formation. Again, there is cooperation in local ventures that will help the neighborhood profit from the resources of the monastery in both men and material, from its skills and from its connections.

Such institutions as cooperatives and credit societies are created, and contacts are established between local needs and organizations or administrations that can fulfill them. There is also more general work, such as translation of books attractive to youth or to the intellectual elite of the country.

As for the monastery, it seemed more necessary than ever to listen to young people. It is they who bring to the monastery the mentality of the people of our times, permitting us to know it and to adapt to it here. It is sometimes useful, too, to inform the community of the social problems of those who surround them. It was also recommended that a monk in each community, prepared through special study, should follow these problems very closely so that through him the community might keep in contact with the country's evolution. And finally, when social work is undertaken, it is desirable that it be understood as a work of the monastery and not the particular affair of any one monk.

As for the social work itself, it was thought that to join ourselves with projects sponsored by the government or the region is better than to launch projects on our own initiative. At the same time, it is good that organizations founded by the monasteries should be open to people of all places and persuasions, not simply to Catholics.

It was thought desirable to free the monasteries, as soon as possible, from any regular assistance from foreigners or from purely capitalistic sources—

though this would not exclude temporary aid for a definite project.

To put it more generally, this work requires a certain suppleness in the organization and in the time schedule of the monastery, but not such as to turn it aside from its vocation and its proper work. On the individual level, it is the duty of superiors to discover and to respect the true spiritual aspirations of individual monks.

4. *The monk, a man of progress and peace.* In the words of an Indian nun: "To further progress, we must know the people and the country, study their culture and help elevate it to the fullness of Christ. There is the field for contemplatives. Our progress must be in Christ. Like Christ's, our mission is to provoke an interior change in men and to give progress a Christian motivation. After all, what has the West gained with all its material progress?"

The monk must also be a man of peace, having acquired that smiling serenity so typical of the old monks of other religions in the Orient. Again, the monastery, where men of different backgrounds often live together, must exhibit true charity among its members and toward its neighbors—a witness that will of itself command attention from each nation and from the world.

A practical means of observing this peace in relation to others is to avoid becoming involved in local political quarrels, while striving to promote social justice.

Certain members asked if the meeting could not make a declaration on active nonviolence.

PRAYER
(In English)

O merciful Lord, Lover of mankind, grant unto us that we may stand before thee in purity and holiness, with wisdom and reverence in the beauty of spiritual achievement, to serve thee as the Lord and Creator of all, to whom is due the obedience of every creature. At thy door, O Lord, we knock. From thy treasure, O Master, we beg for blessings. We have all turned aside and strayed from thy path. Aid us, O Lord, that we may be cleansed of our iniquity and live in the purity of thy holiness. Cleanse us, O Holy One, make us worthy to enter thy portals, and to stand in thy presence with joy in our hearts. Stir in us the promptings of thy love, that our hearts may cling to thee in loving adoration. Through Jesus Christ. Amen.

FIRST READING
(In English)

The One who, himself without color,
by the manifold application of his power
distributes many colors in his hidden purpose,
and into whom, its end and its beginning,
the whole world withdraws—he is God.
May he endow us with clear intellect!

Sacred poetry, the sacrifices, the ceremonies, the ordinances,
the past, the future and what the Vedas declare—
have been produced from the Imperishable.
This whole world the illusion maker projects out of this.
And in it by illusion the soul is confined.

Now, one should know that nature is illusion,
and that the Mighty Lord is the illusion maker.
This whole world is pervaded
with beings that are parts of him.

Not above, not across, nor in the middle
has anyone grasped him.
There is no likeness of him
Whose name is Great Glory.

His form is not to be beheld;
No one soever sees him with the eye.
They who thus know him with heart and mind
as abiding in the heart become immortal.

He who is without beginning and without end,
in the midst of confusion,
the Creator of all, of manifold form,
the One embracer of the universe—
by knowing him one is released from all fetters.

Some sages discourse of inherent nature;
others, likewise, of time. Deluded men!
It is the greatness of God in the world
by which the Brahma-wheel is caused to revolve.

He by whom this whole world is constantly enveloped
is intelligent, the Author of Time,
he is sinless, omniscient.
Ruled over by him, his work revolves—
this that is regarded as earth, water, fire, air and space.

Of him there is no ruler in the world,
nor Lord; nor is there any sign of him.

—*Svetasvatara Upanishad*, IV:1, 9–10, 19–20; V:13; VI:1–2, 9
("The One God of the Manifold World")

SECOND READING
(In French)

In order that a man may possess the sublime
gift of wisdom in all its perfection,
he must be inwardly pierced
with boundless love
and wholly bathed in divine sweetness;
amongst the other works that take their origin
in simplicity's abyss,
he must have unclouded meditation.

Whence is born admiration
of the many gifts
and of the unfathomable richness.

Admiration leads one to sigh after
and to cling by yearning
to high happiness.

Thus man must fix his gaze,
to slake his yearning,
above all activity.

Boundless Love
flames up in every being
in the furnace of oneness.

Whence comes liquefaction
and deep plunging
in the delights of happiness.

This man entirely penetrates,
and is swallowed up in,
the essence without change
as in a desert of darkness.
There, no more receiving nor giving,
nor exercising of love;
just pure and absolute simplicity.

But you must also be instructed
in what wrongs and hinders
sweet wisdom.

To contemplate, heedless of the works
that should flow therefrom—
that hinders the divine savor.

Those who are wanting in admiration
have less of that yearning
which springs from loving impatience.

And boundless love
burns them so much the less
in the deepest depths of the soul's realm.

To strain one's gaze toward the simple
without feeling love's burnings,
that prevents high purity.

I would now make known to you
the cause of ruin
and the loss of blessedness.

There are the ignorant and the blind,
who wander around and about
seeking alien satisfactions.

They cast their eyes upon and consider
wretched and miserable advantages,
and they take their rest in what is vile.

It is a perverse love,
which maddens their unhappy senses
and blinds their human reason.

Following an alien savor,
they can in no wise reach that place
where flow the delights of eternity.

Thus, it is a great hindrance
to receiving eternal brightness
not to live in purity.

—Ruysbroeck, the Admirable (*The Book of the Realm of God's Lovers*)

FOURTH DAY

Thursday, December 12

We can give much more of what we have to give if we adapt our ways as much as possible to the mentality of the people.

—Fr. F. Enomiya Lassalle, S. J.

Varieties of Contemporary Hindu Monasticism[1]

JOHN MOFFITT

For the first fifteen hundred years of its history, which began roughly with the second millennium before Christ, Hinduism so far as we know had no organized orders of monks. Ancient Hindu society, as reflected in the epics *Ramayana* and *Mahabharata*, was itself in a sense monastically oriented. The total life span of its individual members was divided into four progressive stages: celibate studenthood, or *brahmacharaya*; householder life, or *garhasthya*; life of a recluse, or *vanaprastha*, and monkhood, or *sannyasa*. The aim of this social organization, with its four levels of caste—the intellectual and spiritual, the political and military, the agricultural and economic, and the level of the manual laborer—was to prepare the individual member of society for his ultimate encounter with God. And this social setup may explain why no need was felt for monastic communities to bear witness to the reality of the Spirit.

Monks there were, of course, some of whom had even entered the fourth stage of life without passing through all the others. The *Brihadaranyaka Upanishad*, one of the earliest of the more mystical Hindu Scriptures, mentions (4.4.22) those who had renounced the world for a higher goal in terms that show that monkhood was already well known in India somewhere between 1000 and 600 B.C. The reference here is not so much to those individual hermits and forest recluses dedicated to a life of contemplation in an ashrama, or retreat, as to wandering *sannyasis*, members of the fourth stage of life, who in exchange for alms shared the spiritual insights gained through their life of medita-

[1] Reprinted, by permission, from *Vedanta Kesari* (June and July 1970), Madras, India.

tion and renunciation. But Scripture makes no mention of a communal life among these wandering monks.

By the time of the early Upanishads, it appears, the original healthy spirit of Vedic Hinduism had begun to decline. The Upanishads themselves, expressing as they do a highly refined mystical philosophy, constitute to a great extent a protest against the religion of the brahmin priests, which centered around ritual. Something of this same sort of protest may be seen in the surprisingly rapid spread of Buddhism in the several centuries directly following the early Upanishadic period, from 450 B.C. onward.

Gautama Buddha, the first great spiritual luminary in the post-legendary period of Indian history, must have been keenly aware of the religious decline. He was born the son of a petty prince in North India about the middle of the first millennium before Christ. Despite the luxury that surrounded him, he saw enough of the sufferings of life to make him question the values of the society he lived in. Brought up a Hindu, Gautama began his spiritual search in traditional fashion, but disillusioned by the sterile asceticism of the monks of his day—as well as, we may imagine, the dogmatism of many of the priests—he finally struck out in a novel direction. After a heroic quest, through meditation, for the truth behind the appearances of the world, he achieved, through his own efforts, as he insisted, a state of mind he called Nirvana, the blowing out of desire. But so ineffable was his experience that all his life he refused to define it or even to say anything about the soul or God.

After his illumination, out of compassion for men he renounced the bliss of Nirvana and began to preach his "eightfold path," a way of spirituality based on moral discipline and meditation. He steadfastly refused to consider the many philosophical and theological questions his followers and others put to him; these, as he told one and all, did not "tend to edify" a spiritual seeker. During the eighty years of his life, this religious reformer wandered the length and breadth of India, preaching his message of the existence of pain and the way to release from pain. A great following gathered around him and his teaching.

So far as we know, it was Buddhism that developed the first organized collective life of monks for the purpose of spiritual culture.[2]

---

[2] For some of the information in this and the two following paragraphs, I am indebted to "Monasticism in India," by Sukumar Dutta, in the *Cultural Heritage of India* (Calcutta: Ramakrishna Mission Institute of Culture, Vol. 3.)

Contemporary Hindu Monasticism
John Moffitt

The Hindu monks of the Vedic tradition and the Jaina monks looked upon the several months of the rainy season as a period of special sanctity. Like them, Gautama and his wandering monks also spent this time in company, celebrating it ceremonially and meditating together in a shelter provided by devout householders. But as early as the fourth century B.C., these Buddhist communities, unlike the others, became permanent. The wandering life for the most part ceased. Each community developed certain requirements for admission, and each had its own monastic rule.

In the Buddhist monasteries, significantly, all member were equal. The traditional Hindu institution of a spiritual master, or *guru*, which had been accepted by the earlier sects of religious wanderers, was replaced by practice of reverence for elders and teachers, and politeness and consideration toward those of the same age or attainments. Though they never gave up the institution of the *guru*, the already existing sects in India almost certainly derived the idea of communal monastic life from these Buddhist monastic communities. Thus monasticism in India, which from all indications had until now been an individual affair, took a new turn. Incidentally, it is Buddhism, too, that gave India and the world, between the fourth and sixth centuries of our present era, their first great universities, such as far-famed Nalanda, to which scholars came from as far away as China.

About the ninth century, Buddhist monasticism, though it had spread widely in the East, fell into decline in India. This may have been due to the acceptance into monastic life of monks and nuns without true vocations. Nevertheless the example of Buddha left a permanent mark on Indian religious life. During the succeeding ten centuries, a succession of Hindu spiritual leaders have arisen, all of them monks. And the orders they established have had as profound an influence on India's culture as Buddhism had during the twelve hundred years of its ascendancy. It should be noted that, after Buddhism, very few women were accepted into the monastic life until the twentieth century.

The first of these Hindu spiritual leaders, the mystic and scholastic philosopher Shankaracharya, flourished in the early ninth century. In certain ways he resembles St. Thomas Aquinas, though he constructed his system upon canonical Scripture alone rather than upon the work of an alien philosopher. It is he who is credited with the reestablishment of the Nondualistic Vedanta as the leading religious philosophy of India. After strenuous effort, he succeeded in unifying many of the Hindu sects that had proliferated in the centuries before his time.

Legend has it that he established *maths*, or monasteries, at the four cardinal points of India—the Himalayas in the North, Mysore in the South, Orissa in the East and Gujarat in the West. Monasteries are in existence in these places today.

It was in Shankaracharya's time, perhaps even earlier, that a most significant institution, which continues to flourish even today, came into being. At an auspicious date monks gather by the tens of thousands, every three years, at four especially holy places: Allahabad, Hardwar, Ujjain and Nasik, in what is known as the Kumbhamela. No notice is sent, but unfailingly these men, together with many devoted laymen, congregate to enjoy the blessings of the holy place, share spiritual insights and benefit by association with other spiritual seekers.

After Shankaracharya came many other outstanding saints, among them two Vedantists of differing schools: Ramanujacharya in the eleventh century and Madhvacharya in the thirteenth. Both these men, like Shankaracharya, wrote elaborate commentaries on the Vedas and built systems of philosophy on them. And each made disciples, as Gautama Buddha had done, who became the nucleus of an order of monks. Another outstanding leader was Shri Chaitanya, who in the sixteenth century developed a highly sophisticated religious philosophy based on the love of the Lord Krishna. Among these spiritual figures who either founded or provided inspiration for the founding of monastic orders, the latest has been Ramakrishna Paramahamsa, who lived in Bengal in the nineteenth century. It was his foremost disciple, Swami Vivekananda, who founded—at Ramakrishna's urging—India's newest great monastic community, which is called the Ramakrishna Math and Mission.

So it is that today, in the twentieth century, there are innumerable monks in India, perhaps a million of them, attached to all the sects I have mentioned, and to others as well. Comparatively few of these monks are leading "enclosed" lives. We are told that one of Ramakrishna's several spiritual teachers was a monk from a monastery in the Punjab claiming 700 members. Numerous monasteries of the Vedantic sects and of the worshippers of Siva and Vishnu are to be found in South India, though for the most part they are small. And there are more modern sects in the North, including of course the Ramakrishna Order, where monks live in communities. But most of India's monks still wander, homeless beggars, as monks have wandered from time immemorial, bearing witness to the Spirit throughout the length and breadth of the land. Some of them live in caves in the Himalayas, or in isolated spots in the plains, either alone or surrounded by small bands

CONTEMPORARY HINDU MONASTICISM
John Moffitt

of disciples. Some even go without clothes, smearing their bodies with ashes and leading lives of great austerity.

Since it is impossible to describe the life of wandering monks, or *sadhus*, in precise detail, and since Christian monks in modern times chiefly share a spiritual life in common, I shall limit myself to a discussion of the monasticism of a few of the most important traditional denominations, and finally of the far more highly organized modern order with which I was associated for many years, the Ramakrishna Order.

LIFE IN HINDU MONASTIC COMMUNITIES

Before entering on these particular discussions, it will be useful to consider some of the general characteristics of communal monastic life in India. Though there are differences in the rules of various monastic orders, there are, too, in all communities a number of activities shared more or less universally and varying only as the beliefs of the sects vary. I think I should state at this point that though I have tried to be as accurate as I could, since India is a vast country it is entirely possible that a few of my assertions may not apply to monasticism in all parts of the country.

The daily schedule of monks in an orthodox monastery begins with brief ablutions, followed by a meditation, solitary or in company, either on a personal ideal of God—such as Krishna or the incarnation Rama, or the so-called mythological figures Shiva or Kali—or on the ineffable suprapersonal Brahman, the absolute Godhead. Thereafter they might attend the *puja*, or ritualistic worship of the Deity in the temple. Those who require it then have a very light breakfast; many have none at all. Certain of the monks perform allotted manual work for the upkeep of the monastery. Others pursue Scripture study or hold conversations with visiting lay devotees. Others have duties in the office, and so on.

If the community is an orthodox begging community, the monks then begin rounds of begging for vegetarian food. Before the noon meal, they bathe by pouring water over themselves or taking a dip in a river or pool. At this time there is another worship service in the temple. After the meal and the midday siesta, there may be study or discussion of Scripture; some of the monks may also instruct householders in spiritual discipline. At twilight there is again meditation, followed in many instances by the evening service called the *arati*, when ritualistic worship is performed and lights are waved before the image in the shrine. There may be an evening meal; afterwards there may be light conversation, or perhaps study of Scripture or spiritual conversation with older monks or visiting lay devotees. Finally there is another meditation, this time in the individual monk's room. Many holy days are observed in Hinduism, and on such occasions there are appropriate observances.

The most important spiritual practices pursued by monks are prayer and meditation. Though there are no orders that are wholly contemplative, individual monks may take a vow of silence for a period long or short; others may remain shut up in a cell without seeing anyone. But these are not the rule. Neither are extreme ascetical practices generally undertaken, despite the notoriety of certain individual *hathayogis* pictured lying on beds of nails or standing with one hand perpetually raised, or the like. The more advanced the aspirant, the longer the time spent in prayer and meditation. In the devotional sects, the most usual form of prayer consists in a natural outpouring of the heart to the personal ideal chosen by the individual monk. The Bengali Vaishnavas' chief disciplines are repetition of the Lord's name and the singing of devotional songs.

Followers of the path of love, which is known as *bhaktiyoga*, adopt one of five recognized attitudes toward the Deity: the peaceful approach, the approach of a servant, of a parent, of a friend or playmate, of a lover. There are three other paths that may be followed by monks: *jnanayoga*, or the path of intellect; *karmayoga*, or the path of motiveless work; and *rajayoga*, or the path of mental control. Usually a monk combines several of these, according to his temperament. Most of the various types of prayer described by Western mystics would perhaps be included in what the Hindus call "meditation" or "contemplation."

The techniques of meditation are included in *rajayoga*. According to the classical Yoga doctrine, after passing through moral disciplines, learning what posture makes it possible for one to forget the body, and training oneself to breathe correctly so as to calm and control the mind, the aspirant progressively learns how to (1) withdraw the senses from their objects; (2) return the mind again and again when distracted to the object of meditation (i.e., God); (3) fix the mind for a certain period on that object; and (4) meditate uninterruptedly on it. The last state is called *samadhi*; it has several stages. The final stage results in a complete transformation of character, making the one who has experienced it a saint. The disciplines of Yoga are used for meditation by many monks of all schools, including those who worship the Deity as one with their own inner self. In connection with the first stages of meditation, repetition of a sacred formula, or *mantra*, is often practiced, with or without the help of a rosary of 108 beads.

CONTEMPORARY HINDU MONASTICISM
John Moffitt

Nowhere is attendance at temple worship compulsory for monks, but seldom is it discouraged. The monasteries of the Shankaracharya school of Nondualistic Vedanta, which teaches that there is no difference between the reality behind the self and the reality behind the universe, place less emphasis on ritualistic worship than do those of other schools. But even the strictest of these Nondualists allow such worship as a concession to human limitations.

All monks in the orthodox sects must undergo ceremonies of initiation into the equivalent of holy orders. These ceremonies have come down from very ancient times. Since I was a member of the Ramakrishna Order, which traces its descent from the Puri division of Shankaracharya's order, I can describe its ceremonies of initiation from personal experience. The ceremonies I took part in occurred in 1949 and 1959.

The tradition governing initiation in *brahmacharya*, or the novitiate, and into *sannyasa*, or monkhood, goes back to Vedic times, when Agni, the god of fire, was looked upon as mediator between men and God. In those early days, many of the ceremonies of both monastic candidates and laymen were performed before a sacred fire. In the pre-dawn ceremonies of *brahmacharya* in the Ramakrishna Order, when postulants are initiated into the novitiate, the candidates, after a day-long fast, are given white clothes (a skirt-like *dhoti*, as it is called in Bengal, and a voluminous *chaddar*, or shawl). Seated around the sacred fire, they take temporary vows of poverty, chastity and reverence for elders, as they do so making oblations, into the fire, of leaves of the bel tree dipped in clarified butter.

At the time I was initiated as a novice, in 1949, the candidates lived together for the several days of the initiation period, sharing food cooked by themselves in brass pots, cleaning their utensils with grass roots according to ancient custom and not associating with other than candidates. The purpose of the whole proceeding was to remind the candidates of their spiritual origin. Those who had not already been formally initiated by a *guru*, or spiritual teacher, with a *mantra*, or sacred formula for repetition, could accept the venerable Abbot of the Belur Math, the head monastery of the order, as their *guru*. Each novice received a spiritual name. At the conclusion of the initiation period of three days, the new *brahmacharis* were given a talk by the abbot embodying basic spiritual instructions to guide them in their new life.

The same sort of observance of Vedic custom took place when I was initiated into full monkhood in 1959. On the first day, in a long and elaborate ceremony, the candidates, shielded from the eyes of all beholders, performed their own funeral rites and memorial rites for their ancestors. From this time on, they were considered dead men so far as the world was concerned. After a day's fast (slightly dispensed in cases of physical incapacity), the candidates appeared shortly before dawn, completely unclothed, before the abbot, in token of having renounced all ties with the world. They were then asked by a monk, peremptorily, if for any reason any one of them wished to change his mind about the serious step he was about to take. After a ceremonial bath in the sacred Ganges, on whose bank the monastery stood, the candidates received new monk's clothes—a pair of strips of cloth as loincloths, a *dhoti* and a *chaddar*—all dyed in the traditional *gerrua*, or ocher color, worn by most monks.

On this occasion, too, as the candidates took their final vows (including those of poverty, chastity and reverence), they sat about the sacred fire performing what is called the *Viraja Homa* sacrifice, making oblations into the fire while repeating a long series of sacred *mantras*. Prior to this ceremony all had received *dandas*, or staffs, tied with a small piece of *gerrua*-dyed cloth, signifying that they were now *dandis*, Nondualistic monks still bound by certain rules. Afterward they broke the staffs, signifying that they were now *paramahamsas*, monks of the highest order, who had gone beyond all rules. They then threw the broken pieces of the staff into the Ganges. In this way the new monks were reminded that though they had not personally reached such a stage, because they were the spiritual children of Ramakrishna Paramahamsa they were now members of his free order and shared a free spiritual state that very many Vedantic monks, those who wander from place to place with staff and water pot, never aspire to.

At the time I was initiated, each forenoon for three days there was barefoot begging for cooked food. This observance was in token of the fact that in earlier times most Vedantic monks threw themselves entirely upon the mercy of God. After all had brought their alms back to the monastery, the new monks partook of it together as sacramental food. For myself, a Westerner, the experience was one of a most moving sense of the protecting presence of God. At the conclusion of the initiation period, the abbot of the order gave the new monks a charge to lead the spiritual life as best they could "for realization of God and service of humanity."

It has often been claimed that many of India's wandering *sadhus*, or holy men, like vagabonds anywhere, have taken up this sort of life as an easy escape from worldly duties. Gullible laymen will always give something to a beggar, it is said, however unworthy he may be. What is not usually remarked is that communal living, too, can provide those lacking ambition with an opportunity to lead a life free of challenge. No doubt there are more than a few cases where a monk of either kind has fallen from his ideal but still keeps up the appearance of being religious. It is not likely, however, that many deliberately set out from the start to deceive people by masquerading as men of religion. As a Hindu monk said to me about this question: "After all, one must remember that these men at least began their lives with a generous act of renunciation."

There is a certain difficulty, of course, connected with life in a community. As the monk under whom I served, Swami Nikhilananda, pointed out to me before I joined the order: "Though an organization tends to raise spiritually all those below its level up to its own level, it also tends to pull down to its own level those few who are spiritually above its level." This is the price that must be paid so that the majority may be lifted up. It is perhaps a temptation for those whose understanding goes beyond the limits set by the community to rebel against some of its dictates.

Another source of difficulty found in modern Hindu monasticism, however, seems to be common to both East and West. As I learned from Swami Nikhilananda, himself a disciple of Ramakrishna's saintly wife, Sarada Devi, the monastic disciples of Ramakrishna were in the habit of scolding their disciples in public. There is no better way, certainly, to help an earnest aspirant overcome his ego. After the guru had observed one of his disciples transgressing the rule a few times without anyone's apparently having noticed, the young man would suddenly be taken to task when he committed some minor offense, and all his seemingly unremarked faults would then be brought to his attention. The favorite occasion chosen for such scoldings was at meal time, when the whole monastic community was gathered. I myself have received scoldings of this sort. Even in my time, however, I noticed that younger monks at the monastic headquarters near Calcutta expressed shock or even resentment when one of them was scolded in public. Perhaps, though, the love that superiors of the original generation of monks constantly showed their disciples has with the passage of time somewhat decreased, so that the original purpose of such discipline is no longer apparent.

Finally, in this brief consideration of common characteristics of contemporary Hindu monasticism, mention should be made of another development. Perhaps for the same reasons as in the West, namely, the existence of other channels through which idealistic young people could express their urge to serve society, the number of vocations noticeably fell off in recent years. In the Ramakrishna Order, however, after the early 1950's the number again began to grow.

THE TRADITIONAL ORDERS

The first great denomination whose monasticism I shall consider is one that is usually identified by modern Western writers as best representing "Hinduism." It is the denomination of the Nondualistic or Advaita Vedantists. Nondualistic Vedanta, as elaborated by Shankaracharya (A.D. 788–820) has indeed influenced many other schools of thought in India, and I myself now believe that, in a dialogue with Hinduism, Christianity will have to make its approach through this school. Though only about 12 percent of Hindus subscribe to its doctrines, it accepts all other schools as valid; and its interpretation not only does little violence to their beliefs but is in closer conformity with the central teachings of the Vedas, the revealed Scriptures of the Hindus, than other interpretations.

Nondualistic Vedanta affirms the existence of a "nondual" Reality that is the unchanging substrate of the sensible universe. Without that unconditioned first principle, known as the Nirguna Brahman, nothing could exist. This school of Vedanta also affirms the existence of a nondual Reality that is the unchanging substrate of the individual self of man. This unconditioned self, or Atman, is in actuality one with Brahman. The relative world of discrete objects appears to be independent of Brahman and absolutely real in itself, and the individual self of man appears to be independent of Atman and absolutely autonomous, said Shankaracharya, because of *maya*, a principle of veiling and projecting inherent, as it were, in the Godhead. This same *maya* makes the soul, at other times, think of itself as limited and full of desires. Through its power, too, the absolute Brahman appears both as the Creator of the universe, or personal God, and as the universe itself. There is a state, says Shankaracharya, in which both the Creator and the universe disappear, and Reality alone shines. It is given to man to attain such consciousness in his present life; at such a time, far from being merely "absorbed" in Brahman, he discovers at last his true identity, Atman, which is nondifferent from Brahman, ultimate Reality.

It is with regard to the individual soul, or *jiva*, under the sway of *maya*, that the doctrine of *karma* and rebirth is posited: the apparently limited soul, to satisfy its mistaken desire for completeness, performs various actions, which bear fruit in the present life or in future lives.

It is born in various bodies that will help it fulfill its desires left unfulfilled in its present life. Again, it is with regard to the universe under the sway of maya that the doctrine of the fourteen planes of existence, or *lokas*, and the recurring cosmic cycles, or *kalpas*, is posited. Even the heaven a man attains as the result of his good deeds, or the hell he reaches as the result of his wicked deeds, is part of the relative universe. They are not eternal, but come to an end when the momentum of those deeds is exhausted. When the soul exhausts the fruit of its good or bad *karma*, it returns to earth, where alone it can take up the search for true satisfaction, which comes only from communion with God.

Shankaracharya, of whose philosophyical system I have given only the briefest hint, founded in his short lifetime of thirty-two years an order of monks (with ten subdivisions known as the *dashanami*) dedicated to the teaching of the truths he had discovered through personal experience and through reasoning based on study of Scripture. Vedantic monks of the Nondualist school are to be found in all parts of India today, either as traditional wandering monks or as solitaries (sometimes surrounded by a few disciples), or as members of small or large organized communities (either independent or affiliated with a larger group). Though perhaps the distinction is not as strictly observed as during the last century, these monks are divided into two broad groups: the *dandis*, who carry a staff (*danda*) and water pot, or *kamandalu*, made of a gourd, and are bound by certain restrictions as to food and the like; and the *paramahamsas*, who have no identifying insignia, have gone beyond all restrictions, and may be found living in any style of life.

Aside from the common characteristics of monastic life that I have already discussed, the Nondualist Vedantic monks manifest a few particular characteristics. These monks wear no distinguishing mark on the forehead such as is worn by members of several other sects. Their traditional garb, which, however, is shared by members of a few other orders, is what has been called the "ocher robe" of the *sannyasi*. It is the sign of renunciation, in contrast to the white clothes of laymen; the white garb is also used by Vedantic novices. The monk's clothes are dyed—by the monks themselves—with a kind of natural iron oxide. They consist of the skirtlike lower garment I have already referred to, and a long shawllike piece of cloth used as an upper garment. Modern monks often supplement these two with a shirt without a collar and with sleeves slightly open at the wrist, known in Bengal as a *panjabi*. Some orthodox Nondualist Vedantists wear no more than a brief loincloth, or *kaupina*, made of two strips of cloth. Old-style monks usually go barefoot, but more modern monks use simple sandals. A traditional monk, if he does not completely neglect his hair, shaves his head and face once a month. In most parts of India, a Nondualist Vedantic monk observes strict non-injury to animals and so abstains from eating meat or fish.

The generally accepted leader of the orthodox sects of Nondualistic Vedanta is the current *guru*, or Shankaracharya as he is called, of the Sarada Math at Sringeri, in Mysore, South India. The monastery at Sringeri is one of five monasteries said to have been established by Shankaracharya himself in the ninth century. A number of its abbots have been not only great scholars but highly advanced saints. The manner of choosing a successor to the abbot is interesting. If the *guru* finds any man whom he considers qualified, he gives him spiritual initiation and appoints him as his successor. In some instances the successor is chosen at an early age and kept in seclusion for a time during his period of training. At Sringeri, as at the other chief Shankaracharya monasteries, the community consists of the abbot and his several monastic disciples; only *brahmacharis*, that is to say, celibates, are accepted as monks. In addition to pursuing their own spiritual practice, they carry on the monastery's various activities and help their *guru* to spread the teachings of Nondualistic Vedanta to laymen throughout the surrounding country.

Shri Sachidananda Narasimha Bharati (A.D. 1879–1912), the thirty-third Shankaracharya of this *math*, or monastery, is a good example of a traditional leader.[3] In addition to administering the Sringeri Math, he founded a branch math at Bangalore and a school for philosophical study, and opened a number of other centers of learning. Under his encouragement a monastic disciple published a twenty-volume edition of the works of the original Shankaracharya, a scholarly achievement of high importance. He was also responsible for the founding of a number of temples, the reforming of rituals and the education of priests. The library of the Sringeri Math contains a collection of five hundred valuable palm-leaf manuscripts, some as yet unpublished. The present *guru* supports modern movements for the national welfare that do not, in his eyes, run counter to the country's spiritual ideals. Like other *gurus* in South India, he makes extensive propaganda tours to spread the faith.

Other Shankaracharya monasteries, such as the Sarada Pitha at Dvaraka,

---

[3] For much of the information about the Nondualist *(Advaita)*, Qualified Nondualist *(Visishtadvaita)* and Dualist *(Dvaita)* monasteries given in this and the following paragraphs, I am indebted to the *Bulletin of the Institute of Traditional Cultures* (Madras: University of Madras, 1957, 1958), and to Swami Kailashananda, abbot of the Sri Ramakrishna Math, Madras.

in Gujarat, and the Kanchi Kamakoti Pitham, in Tanjore, though interested chiefly in spiritual matters, are coming to be more concerned with social and educational matters as well. The Kanchi monastery, for instance, has undertaken prisoner reform by arranging weekly lectures for prison inmates. The chief monasteries of the order are seven in number; some of them have numerous branches within the parts of India over which they have jurisdiction.

There are, of course, individual monasteries founded in modern times that adhere to the basic teachings of Nondualistic Vedanta. In the year 1959, I visited one of these, outside Puri, in Orissa. Here a *sadhu*, or holy man, known as Langa Baba, lived with a number of disciples. The establishment consisted of three or four buildings. The *guru* remained completely naked, and his disciples, I was told, looked on him as the embodiment of God, conducting *puja*, or worship, before him at the stated hours as before an image. With several other monks of the Ramakrishna Order and several lay devotees, I visited his ashram, or retreat, one evening after dark. The Swami was sitting on a four-poster bed in a dimly lighted room. He was reputed to be very old; some said he was 135 years old, others 85. Though his body was well preserved, he gave an impression of great age, perhaps because his eyes, flushed with much meditation, seemed to be covered by an opaque film. A palpable joy emanated from his person as he gave his replies to the monks' questions. One of the monks asked: "Sir, are you praying for the welfare of India?" "Why India?" he asked spiritedly. "I pray for the whole world. All existence is one."

The second denomination whose monasticism I shall discuss represents probably the great bulk of orthodox Hindus. It includes the Qualified Nondualists and the Dualists, all of whom base their philosophy, like the Nondualists, on the revelation of the Hindu Scriptures. The monks of this persuasion worship what they call a personal God, or Saguna Brahman. The God they recognize is, in contradistinction to the Brahman of the Nondualists, endowed with qualities such as infinite power, majesty, fame, knowledge, beauty, renunciation—and, of course, compassion. They are followers of the great scholastic philosophers Ramanujacharya and Madhvacharya.

Ramanujacharya (A.D. 1017–1137) held that God, the universe and souls constitute one interrelated whole (hence the term "Qualified Nondualism" to designate his school). For him, Brahman, the Absolute of the Nondualistic Vedantists, means simply the luster of God's body; the term he used to designate the Lord is "Bhagavan." The physical world and souls are "modes" or "attributes" of God, even "parts" of God. God is, as it were, the cosmic soul, and the universe and individual souls constitute his body. Though matter and souls are thus intimately related to him, even in the final state of *moksha*, or liberation from ignorance, the distinction between God and the worshiper remains; there is no state of consciousness in which the distinction disappears. God, the universe and souls are ultimately real.

Like the philosopher Shankaracharya before him, Ramanujacharya accepted the doctrine of the cyclic evolution of the universe and the doctrine of *karma* and rebirth for the soul. In his interpretation, too, the creation is made by God, not "out of nothing," but rather out of the eternally existing subtle material, known as *akasha*, that forms the physical world. Matter is looked upon by him as the potency of God.

Madhvacharya (A.D. 1199–1276) likewise held that the distinction between God, the soul and the universe is eternally real. But in his view God alone exists, absolutely and independently; the physical universe and souls radically depend on him (hence the term "Dualism" to designate this school). From this point of view, Dom Bede Griffiths, who has made a study of these three Vedantic schools, declares that of the three, Madhvacharya's is closest to Christianity. None of the schools, however, conceives of creation in Christian terms.

The deity worshiped by followers of Ramanujacharya and Madhvacharya is Vishnu, the all-pervading Reality, known also as the Preserver of the universe. Salvation is attained through complete and loving *prapatti*, or self-surrender to him. The form in which Vishnu is usually worshiped is Krishna. From the point of view of Western scholars, Krishna is largely a mythological figure, friend and adviser of royal princes, who preached the message of selfless action and love embodied in the Bhagavad Gita. To worshipers of Vishnu, however, Krishna is Vishnu, or God himself, in his entirety. He is not an *avatara*, or "incarnation," in the same sense that Rama, the ideal king, and others are. (The ideas of the worshipers of Vishnu about Krishna and Rama are derived from secondary scriptures such as the epics *Mahabharata* and *Ramayana*, and the various mythological histories, or *Puranas*, all post-Vedic but based on early tradition).

The doctrine of the *avatara* is accepted by both Qualified Nondualists and Dualists. As enunciated in the Bhagavad Gita, it states that whenever virtue declines and vice flourishes, God comes to earth for the establishment of righteousness and the punishment of the wicked. Worshipers of Vishnu, whether Qualified Nondualists, Dualists or members of other

Contemporary Hindu Monasticism
John Moffitt

sects, are known as Vaishnavas. There were, of course, worshipers of Krishna and of Rama long before the Vedantic schools of Qualified Nondualism and Dualism came into existence in the eleventh and thirteenth centuries.

Vaishnava monks, like Nondualist monks, are found in all parts of India, whether they are wandering monks or live in a fixed place along or in community. Unlike those of Sankaracharya's school, monks of the schools of Ramanujacharya and Madhvacharya renounce the world after having married and fulfilled the duties of the householder stage of life. On their foreheads Vaishnava monks wear a mark made with white ash in the form of the letter V. Their garb is usually dyed with *gerrua*, though Vaishnavas of the school of Shri Chaitanya, who do not generally receive monastic initiation before renouncing the world, continue with the white garb of a householder. In all parts of India the Vaishnavas' diet is vegetarian. In most respects their life resembles that of other monks, whether solitary or living in community—aside, of course, from the content of their meditation and worship, which centers around their own chosen ideal of the personal God. Ritualistic worship naturally assumes great importance in their daily routine.

One of the oldest *maths*, or monasteries, of the sect of Ramanujacharya is the Ahobila Matha at Tiruvellore, in South India, which was founded in A.D. 1398. It has branch centers in important cities and towns in this section of the country. Most of the *math's* leaders have been scholars and outstanding religious teachers. Annually there is a Visishtadvaita (Qualified Nondualism) conference of scholars at the central *math*. The leader makes extended tours in South India and also in the North to bear witness to the truth of Qualified Nondualism. Another such *math*, the Vanamalai Matha in Tiruneveli District, was founded in A.D. 1400. Besides carrying on the regular activities of a *math*, it has established rest houses for pilgrims in many holy places and conducts a dispensary. There are at least ten such *maths* in South India with subsidiary branches.

The school of Madhvacharya also has a large number of monasteries in South India. The eight monks originally ordained in the thirteenth century by the great scholastic philosopher to carry on the worship of the Lord Krishna at the town of Udipi, in Kanada, all established monastic lines of their own. Eight monasteries are now in existence that are said to have been founded by these swamis. The monks of the *maths* hold office by turns as high priest of the Krishna Matha at Udipi for two years at a time. Those not in office tour the country on propaganda missions and help collect funds. Numerous schools and a Sanskrit college have been started in modern times by the Krishna Math, which interests itself not only in Dualist philosophy but in social work among the poor of the sect. It also publishes several journals and supports a hospital. In addition to the eight monasteries tracing their descent from Madhvacharya's disciples, there are several other important *maths* adhering to Dualist tenets, all with numerous branches. As in the Nondualist *maths*, the communities of the Qualified Nondualist and Dualist monasteries consist of a single leader and his several monastic disciples. All of them are supported by the service and donations of lay people; in the past certain of them were generously helped by maharajas.

The third denomination whose monasticism I shall discuss is that of the Shaivas, or worshipers of Shiva, the Dissolver of the universe, a so-called mythical deity who is the symbol of meditation and austerity, and of the Absolute as well (as opposed to the female divine creative power, or Shakti). Their philosophy attained its fullest development between the eleventh and fifteenth centuries and is known as the Shaiva Siddhanta, or "absolute intellectual finality." Worshipers of Shiva, of course, were in existence many centuries before the development of this philosophy; the Pasupatas, for instance, are said to have flourished in North India since the first century.[4]

Perhaps this is an appropriate place to note that when Hindus speak of a god as being "mythical," they do not mean that certain religious persons merely wrote myths about him and then others began worshiping this imaginary deity. On the contrary, the deity was first experienced by devotees in prayer or meditation, and gradually a number of stories and legends grew up about him, based on the witness of those who had experienced his presence. To a follower of such a god, whether Shiva or Vishnu or Mother Durga or Kali, the "myths" about them constitute spiritual history.

Like all the important schools of Hindu thought, the Shaiva Siddhanta allies itself with the other ways of belief yet claims to be itself the final goal of religious truth to which the others are perhaps necessary, but in any event preliminary, steps. According to this school, which is in many ways very close to Nondualistic Vedanta (with the addition

---

[4] Much of the information in this and the three following paragraphs is derived from the brochure *Mutt and Temples*, published by the Dharmapuram Adhinam, and from the *Bulletin of the Institute of Traditional Cultures* (Madras: University of Madras, 1957).

CONTEMPORARY HINDU MONASTICISM
John Moffitt

of a personal Godhead), there are three eternal truths: the Supreme Being, or Shiva, known as *Pati*; the individual soul, or *pasu*; and the ignorance, *pasa*, that hinders the soul from realizing the Supreme Being. The last term also stands for *karma*, the accumulation of merits and demerits through action (the cause of future birth, joy and sorrow), and for primordial matter, the basis of the phenomenal world, which forms both the human body and the plane of existence for the soul's purification. The nature of Shiva, the absolute Lord, is love, and through his grace the soul is released from its bondage to ignorance. Purified and enlightened, the soul enters into communion with him, sharing his nature and yet distinct from him.

Shaivite monks are found in all parts of India. On their foreheads they wear a sect mark of three horizontal lines of white ash, and they prominently display a rosary of large beads. Many of them, especially wandering monks of the ascetical Pasupata sect, carry a trident. In most other ways their daily life resembles that of the Nondualists, Qualified Nondualists and Dualists.

The earliest *math* of the Shaiva Siddhanta school, as legends suggest, was founded by Gurugnanambandha Swamigal between A.D. 1561 and 1566. It is known as the Dharmapuram Adhinam Mutt and is located in the town of Mayuram, in Tanjore, South India. With it are associated twenty-seven Shiva temples, many of them with the monumental *gopurams*, or entrance gates, prevalent in this part of India. During its long history, its *acharyas*, or teachers, have produced a number of great philosophical works. In recent times the Adhinam has founded several modest schools for the teaching of the hymns sung at worship and in festivals, and for instruction in the correct performance of temple ritual and correct interpretation of its meaning. Like the orthodox Vedantic *maths* of the three schools, the Adhinam has interested itself in educational and scholarly matters. In 1946, it founded an Oriental College affiliated with Madras University, for Tamil and Sanskrit studies, and it runs a high school and a higher elementary school with free education for about five hundred pupils. It publishes a monthly journal and many religious and philosophical works. After constructing a maternity and child welfare hospital, it turned the institution building over to the town of Mayuram. It runs an orphanage of its own and also supports many charities and temples. There are about eighteen such Shaiva *maths* with subsidiary branches. In addition to their other duties, the abbots of the *maths* arrange propaganda tours and convene frequent religious conferences.

After the development of the various monastic orders we have considered, perhaps the single most important spiritual phenomenon in India prior to the modern era was the appearance in the early sixteenth century of a new type of Vaishnavism in Bengal and Orissa. The St. Francis-like saint and philosopher Shri Krishna Chaitanya (A.D. 1486–1533), began his life as a typical scholar. Overcome with the love of the Lord Krishna, he spent his remaining years preaching total self-dedication to God, something to be attained by repeating his name and singing his glories. This new form of Vaishnavism, or worship of Vishnu, was carried on after his death by several of Shri Chaitanya's householder disciples. The *guru* and his followers developed a philosophy of love that has had a strong influence on devotional religion in India, and especially in Bengal, ever since their time.

Among Bengali Vaishnavas, the stationary community of celibate monks under one head appears to be the exception rather than the rule.[5] The aspirants' ideal has been to live alone or with one or a few disciple-attendants in a secluded spot near Vrindavana, which is located in the district where Krishna is supposed to have spent his childhood and youth. Normally in Bengal it seems not to have been customary for a Vaishnava aspirant to receive formal initiation into monkhood, or *sannyasa*. Ritualistic worship of the deity in the image, repetition of the Lord's name, singing of his praises and meditation on his activities occupy the individual's time. Passage from the role of householder to that of recluse is more a matter of gradual personal dedication than of formal change of state in life.

Nevertheless, in the nineteenth century, as the result of certain reformist trends in the Bengali Vaishnava community, communal monasticism began to manifest itself. One of the more significant of the modern Bengali monastic organizations is the Gaudiya Math in Shri Mayapur, north of Calcutta, which claims fifty subordinate houses in Bengal and Orissa, and one in Madras. Its membership includes between one and two dozen professed *sannyasis*, or monks, and between one and two hundred postulants and novices. This organization bases its teachings directly on those of Shri Chaitanya, whom his followers look upon as an incarnation of Krishna.

The Gaudiya Math is an offshoot of the Gaudiya Mission, the most

[5] For the information in this and the four following paragraphs, I am indebted to Mr. Joseph O'Connell, of the theology faculty of St. Michael's College, Toronto, Canada. Mr. O'Connell is submitting his doctoral thesis, *The Bengali Vaishnava Religion and its Social Implications*, at Harvard University. In preparation for writing it, he spent two years of study in India.

impressive of the attempts to give Bengali Vaishnavas an organized monkhood. The Mission itself was founded in the early twentieth century as the result of the efforts of a layman, Kedar Nath Datta (known in religion as Bhakti Vinode Thakur), who wrote prolifically on Vaishnava themes, and of his celibate son, Bhakti Siddhanta Sarasvati, who preached against alleged abuses that had grown up in modern Vaishnavism. A disciple of the latter, Bhakti Vilas Tirtha, now heads the organization known as the Gaudiya Math, which resulted from a factional split after the death of his teacher. The head of the *math* is alone empowered, as in most other modern monastic orders, to give spiritual initiation within his division of the denomination. He makes a yearly circuit of the major *maths* and temples of the order.

The daily routine of the monks at the Gaudiya Math is much like that of the individual Vaishnava recluse. The monks rise well before dawn and sing the praises of the deity, circumambulate the image in the temple and witness the early morning *puja*, or ritualistic worship, which includes the waving of light, incense, water, cloth and fan before the image in a graceful ceremony. (The same ceremony is repeated at midday and in the evening.) There is a modest breakfast. The monks then assemble for Scripture reading, instruction and (if it is required) reprimanding by the head swami. Thereafter monks and novices take up their allotted tasks: cleaning of the rooms, preparation of food for offering to the deity (after which it is eaten as *prasad*, or sacramental food, by the monks and novices), arranging of outside trips for the swami, and begging. This last duty is performed every morning by monks and novices individually or in small groups. Along with bequests, interest from endowments and receipts from publishing, it makes up the main source of the *math*'s income. The food eaten is vegetarian, and rather bland; any food thought to incite sensuality or to dull the consciousness is avoided. A smaller meal is eaten in the evening. On the eleventh day of each fortnight, known as the *ekadasi*, the diet is restricted to fruits and sweetmeats; rice and other staples are withheld.

At the main *math* various types of instruction are given daily. Novices are trained by means of various techniques, including lectures with colored slides. Fifty to one hundred lay persons join the monks and novices every evening to hear the head swami's spiritual instruction and attend worship. Special devotees spend some hours, even days, taking further instruction from the swami or those whom he had delegated to teach. During the frequent Vaishnava festivals, special services are held, sometimes with displays of manikins illustrating particular events of the Lord Krishna's or Shri Chaitanya's life on earth. Pilgrimages to holy places are occasionally organized for the monks and laity. Because of the great variety of pastoral activities required of them, Gaudiya Math monks do not spend as much time repeating the Lord's name or meditating on the incidents of his life as recluses do. They are also not much inclined to meditate on those aspects of the relationship of the Lord Krishna and his beloved Radha that are of a symbolically erotic nature. The somewhat Puritanical bias of the *math* disposes them to favor a more abstract religious philosophy.

The relationship of this math with the tradition of Madhvacharya appears to be ambiguous. Its philosophy is denominated by the not typically Dualist definition of the soul's relationship with God as an "incomprehensible difference and nondifference."

Probably no more than a few hundred persons ever assemble for a Gaudiya Math activity. But this is no indication of the number of monastic and lay disciples the head Swami has made. In fact, no strict census of followers is feasible; but it is safe to state that the original Gaudiya Mission, and to a lesser extent its daughter *maths* such as the Gaudiya Math, have gained the support of a considerable number of middle class disciples as well as a large following among the poor. The swami of the *math* does not see social service as a matter of direct religious concern. If men become truly religious, to his way of thinking, they will take care of their social obligations automatically, without being prompted. Politics and social reform seem to him to be laymen's duties.

About monastic groups other than those representing the orthodox traditions, it is difficult to obtain accurate information. Contemporary religious practice in India is not well documented; neither is it uniform throughout the country. In addition to the orders of Shankaracharya, Ramanujacharya and Madhvacharya, and the maths of the Shaiva Siddhanta school and of the Bengali Vaishnavas, there are in modern Hinduism at least ten other monastic sects or organizations of a certain degree of importance. Some of them were established in past centuries; others—such as the Divine Life Society of the late Swami Shivananda, a Vedantic organization—have been founded within the present century. Certain groups, such as those of the Hathayogis and the Tantriks, are notorious for seeming exhibitionism or for certain bizarre customs.

There are a few modern groups devoted to women. (Though one of Ramakrishna's important teachers, the Bhairavi Brahmani, was a woman Vaishnava adept, monasticism has been confined in India mostly to

Contemporary Hindu Monasticism
John Moffitt

men.) Prominent among these at present is the following of the woman teacher Ananda Mayee, and the women's *math* recently organized by, though independent of, the Ramakrishna Order.

Many individual monks, too, have founded independent organizations. The ashrams of the late Shri Ramana Maharshi and the late Shri Aurobino Ghosh, two outstanding spiritual personalities of this century, are not strictly monastic and so do not fall within the scope of our present discussion.

THE ORDER OF RAMAKRISHNA

In conclusion I shall consider the particular modern order that I believe represents the best modern trend in Hindu monasticism, the Ramakrishna Math and Mission. I myself belonged to this order for about twenty-five years as monastic novice and finally as monk. Founded at the turn of the century, it serves better than any other organization to point up the contrast between modern Hindu monasticism and the traditional monasticism represented by the orthodox *maths* of South India or by individual recluses and wandering monks. Indeed, the ideals for which it has stood have strongly influenced many of these organizations toward social service, just as its founder, Swami Vivekananda, may be said to have influenced Mahatma Gandhi toward organizing the masses of Indians.

Ramakrishna Paramahamsa (A.D. 1836–1886), whose life and teachings provided the inspiration for the founding of the order that bears his name, was born into an orthodox Vaishnava family of brahmins in a village in West Bengal. His father, a worshiper of Rama, was exceedingly strict in his orthodoxy; but because of poverty, the son accepted a position as priest in the temple of the Divine Mother Kali, near Calcutta. Seized with a hunger to know if God really existed, he was at last blessed with an almost continuous awareness of God's presence in the form of the Mother. He then set out, under the guidance of experts, to practice the disciplines of the recognized sects of India—all those we have discussed (except Nondualism), and several others as well. He read the Bible and the Koran with the help of devotees of Christianity and Islam, and to the best of his ability conformed to their customs. At the end of each course of discipline he attained communion with God. He thus came to the conclusion that all religions were valid as ways to experience transcendental Reality if they were practiced (as he practiced them) with utter fidelity. In a convocation of Bengali pandits and religious leaders, in the early 1860's, Ramakrishna answered questions about his experiences during his first period of discipline, when without the help of anything but untutored longing he had attained God-consciousness. At this time the scholars declared him to be an *avatara*, or incarnation of God.

Finally, in 1864, Ramakrishna received initiation into Nondualistic Vedanta and into *sannyasa* by a naked wandering monk, Totapuri. In this far more austere discipline, too, he achieved success, but this time with a difference; for now he experienced the *nirvikalpa samadhi*, complete union with suprapersonal Reality. In this state he remained for six months. After returning to the normal plane of consciousness, Ramakrishna's personality was completely transformed. Before, he had been simple and direct, like a saint, but now he remained always a child—completely an instrument of the Divine Mother. Almost everyone who met him felt irresistibly attracted.

During the period of his spiritual disciplines, Ramakrishna had come in contact with innumerable wandering monks and other devotees of all the sects he had been following. Many of them stopped at his temple on their way to visit the temple of Jagannath at Puri, an important place of pilgrimage. His firsthand experience of what their Scriptures taught helped them gain a deeper comprehension of their own faiths. He thus unknowingly left an indelible impress on all orthodox India.

Now, after completing his spiritual disciplines, Ramakrishna came in contact with modern India—first through the members of the nonmonastic Brahmo Samaj, a Unitarian-like movement of Bengal, and then through university students, who heard about him from the Samaj. From these he chose sixteen monastic disciples, who were later to form the nucleus of an order. He also had a following of gifted and intensely spiritual householder disciples. Chief among his disciples was Sarada Devi, to whom he had been married in youth but who remained always a nun. Ramakrishna began active teaching about 1879 and thereafter taught day and night till the end of his life. After a year of intense suffering from cancer of the throat, he died on August 15, 1886. Swami Vivekananda, his foremost monastic disciple, organized Ramakrishna's young disciples—according to his master's wish—into a monastic order.[6]

During the first difficult years of the order's history, most of these young men were seized with the desire to lead the life of a traditional

---

[6] The information in this and the following paragraphs is derived largely from the *General Report of the Ramakrishna Math and Mission* (Belur: 1966–1967).

wandering monk. But because of their great love for their master and for Vivekananda, they finally consented to live together. All this time, one of the disciples, Swami Ramakrishnananda, remained at the monastery and conducted the worship of his master as God. Between 1897 and 1899, the monastic disciples, together with the householders, brought into being the organization now known as the Ramakrishna Math and Mission. Its purposes were two: to create a band of monastic teachers of Nondualistic Vedanta and, in conjunction with lay members, to carry on missionary and philanthropic work, looking on all men as manifestations of God. The headquarters of the math was transferred in 1899 to Belur, a village near Calcutta, where on the bank of the Ganges an important monastic and educational center has grown up, including a residential college and a large temple of Ramakrishna.

Swami Vivekananda, during his travels in America and Europe from 1892 to 1897, and again in 1899 and 1900, was able to study and admire Western organizational methods. He clearly perceived the weaknesses of the West, however, and foresaw that great political and social convulsions lay ahead. The swami also studied the rules of several of the important Christian monastic orders and incorporated some of their features in his own rule. Nondualistic Vedanta as expounded by Shankaracharya, which teaches the absolute identity of the reality underlying the individual soul and the reality underlying the Creator God, is the order's philosophy. But according to Ramakrishna's own experience, allowance is made in the order for men's need to worship a personal God. Thus the insights of Ramanujacharya, pointing to the interrelatedness of God, soul and universe, and those of Madhvacharya, stressing their eternal separateness, are respected as valid degrees of spiritual evolution. The same is true of the systems developed by the worshipers of Shiva and of the Divine Mother, and of the teachings of Shri Chaitanya and other spiritual leaders.

Daily worship is performed in the great temple of Ramakrishna. The most impressive and moving service is that held at dusk, known as the *arati*, when the "Hymn to Ramakrishna" composed by Vivekananda is sung in chorus by the assembled devotees as the priest in the shrine concludes the worship with the waving of lights before Ramakrishna's image. Most important of the many religious festivals celebrated at the math—and these include Christian festivals—is the birthday of Ramakrishna. At this time vast numbers of persons come to the math grounds from Calcutta (in my own time it was said that hundreds of thousands came), until the whole extensive place is a sea of humanity.

The daily routine of the monks at the headquarters, and at the other monasteries of the order throughout India, is much like that of the orthodox monks already described. Individual monks, as time allows, practice various spiritual disciplines, depending on whether their tendencies are basically intellectual, devotional, active or mystical. No one set of dogmas is imposed on all. Poverty, chastity and reverence, of course, are enjoined upon every monastic member. The influence of the Ramakrishna Math and Mission is widespread, especially in Bengal and Madras. It has branches in almost every part of the country, and its following among the laity is probably the largest of any modern—perhaps even traditional—order. It numbers among its lay supporters and friends members of the government. In 1949, for instance, Prime Minister Jawaharlal Nehru addressed the gathering in New Delhi on Ramakrishna's birthday. At present the total number of monks, or *sannyasis*, is somewhere between 400 and 500. The total number of monks and novices is about 700.

Next to the extensive monastery grounds at Belur is a residential college, which was started in 1941 in partial fulfillment of Swami Vivekananda's desire to found a university that would one day have the importance that the Buddhist University at Nalanda once had. It teaches the arts and sciences to between 250 and 400 students. An industrial and technical institution offers courses in electrical, civil and mechanical engineering to well over 600. There are also a free junior technical school, a free trade school, a department of adult education, a social education organizers' training center and a residential teachers' training college with over a hundred students.

The Ramakrishna Math and Mission has in all about 120 branch centers inside and outside India. Of the latter, a few are in Pakistan, Burma and Ceylon, and about twenty-eight are in other countries, including ten in the United States. All the centers are well-established organizations with swamis permanently in residence; there are also thirty subcenters in India where monastic workers live more or less permanently. The affairs of the Ramakrishna Math and Mission are administered by a board of nineteen trustees, all swamis of the order. The president of the board, and thus of the Math and Mission, is the Abbot of the Belur Math. It is he who gives initiation to both monastic and lay disciples.

Most of the Ramakrishna monasteries in India minister as much to the physical as to the spiritual needs of the public. There are in operation ten hospitals, which accommodate almost 26,000 patients a year, and 65 dispensaries which treat about 3 million cases. The work done for women is especially noteworthy. The large maternity section of the Seva Pratisthan, a hospital that pioneered in this work among Hindus, has been in operation since 1932.

The order runs four general colleges, several of them much larger than the one at Belur Math, two teachers' training colleges and an art college. It has over 28 other specialized schools, including a school of agriculture, 90 students' homes or hostels, and 215 elementary and secondary schools. In all, according to the latest available figures, a total of 47,189 boys and young men, and 16,946 girls and young women are studying in its schools and colleges. Work is also done among aboriginal hill tribes, among former untouchables and among villagers.

Two of the order's largest publication centers are the Advaita Ashrama in Calcutta and the Shri Ramakrishna Math in Madras. In the United States are two other active publication centers: the Vedanta Society of Los Angeles and the Ramakrishna-Vivekananda Center of New York. It is the latter center that has published the English translation of the epoch-making *Gospel of Shri Ramakrishna*, embodying many of Ramakrishna's fascinating spiritual conversations with householders and a few monastic devotees. Of interest culturally is the impressive Ramakrishna Mission Institute of Culture in Calcutta, where Indian scholars offer courses in various fields and visiting scholars from abroad are invited to lecture.

In the period between 1900 and the achievement of Indian independence in 1947, the monks of the Ramakrishna Math took upon themselves extensive relief work in times of famine, flood, cyclone, drought and epidemic. The former British government of India, after a few years during World War I when it looked on the order with suspicion as a possible breeding ground or hiding place for revolutionaries, regularly turned over large sums of money for the Mission's use in such emergencies. After independence, the Indian government has itself taken over most of such activities. But in 1964, when thousands of refugees crossed over from East Pakistan into West Bengal, again the Mission opened temporary relief centers. In the year 1966–1967, the Mission spent Rupees 72,600 for flood relief and Rupees 314,750 for drought relief.

The evolution of the ideal of social service in India, as illustrated in the programs of the Ramakrishna Math and Mission, and to a lesser extent in those of the other organizations we have considered, it is one of the arresting phenomena of modern India. In traditional monasteries, and among all orthodox monks, it had been customary throughout Indian history for the spiritual seeker to devote himself completely to spiritual practice. It has been taught in India that the only true and lasting help one can render to others is that which one offers after having "realized" (i.e., experienced) God. This, I submit, and not simply a selfish preoccupation with personal salvation, has been the best reason behind the seeming lack of concern for underprivileged members of society on the part of monks—as witnessed by the fact that every great "realized" soul throughout India's history (such as the Buddha, Shri Chaitanya and many other saints) has devoted himself to the welfare of others. It has also been assumed that any truly religious-minded layman would, out of natural human sympathy, try to share what he could with those less fortunate than he.

Such an interpretation would perhaps shed the most charitable light upon the rather perplexing question of why, during the first decade of the present century, traditional monks usually looked down on the monks of the Ramakrishna Math for helping the poor and the sick, and those overtaken by natural calamities, as betraying the monastic ideal of bearing witness to the Spirit. Even in Vivekananda's time, of course, there were isolated Hindu groups that carried on social service.

Opposition did not discourage Swami Vivekananda's brother monks, however, and in time various forms of social service and educational work have become part of the daily routine of many monastic orders. Responsible for the change is the teaching of both Ramakrishna and his disciples that by sincerely trying to help others, by worshiping God through man, the individual can make spiritual progress and incidentally guard himself against the self-deception of thinking himself more evolved, spiritually, than he really is. A concept implicit in Hinduism was thus made explicit in modern times by these two religious leaders.

Given the Hindu persuasion that nothing is ultimately worthwhile unless it leads to God-consciousness, such teaching was needed to enable most Hindu monks to take up a duty that might otherwise have seemed to deflect them from their goal. Another factor that certainly contributed more than a little to the change was the extensive work done in India by native Christians and Christian missionaries to alleviate the suffering of neglected Hindus, especially untouchables. But it is curious that even today few Westerners are aware of how much the Hindus have been doing, in the twentieth century, to better their own social conditions.

There are at least two reasons why Vivekananda and his followers felt that the initiative toward social service should come, in India, from monks. Because of increasing poverty in India, in the end of the nineteenth century, a large percentage of middle-class families had had to

Contemporary Hindu Monasticism
John Moffitt

think first of themselves. Again, after a thousand years of foreign rule, the Hindu laity had become demoralized and lacked initiative. Swami Vivekananda saw it as the duty of all-renouncing monks to set an example for such householders, who otherwise could not be expected to recognize what was now required of them.

But thanks to Mahatma Gandhi, who was powerfully influenced by Vivekananda's ideas about nation building, India has gained independence. Indians are now responsible for their own fate, and there is no longer the same need for setting an example to lay people. The problem at present is how modern Hindu monks are to return to the original ideal of Indian monasticism: bearing witness to the reality of the Spirit. The Ramakrishna Math and Mission—like the Roman Catholic Church in the United States—must find a way to divest itself of its many worldly institutions and, of its own free will, turn over its facilities to the public. The action of the Burmese government in 1965 seems a portent of things to come. In that year the great Ramakrishna Mission Hospital, one of the most important non-Christian hospitals in the East, was nationalized by Burma in a move to lessen outside influence.

Even now, of course, there is ample scope for spiritual striving in the Ramakrishna Order. It is this fact that explains the constant attraction that the order's study classes and worship services, like those of all the more traditional monasteries, have for lay devotees. It is also important to note that both among those in authority and those who carry out the order's day-to-day activities, genuinely dedicated and even saintly souls continue to develop.

In an age that is increasingly influenced by materialism, the order that Swami Vivekananda founded has grown with surprising rapidity. It has covered India with a network of *maths*, large and small, and other organizations, just as Buddhism did at the beginning of the fourth century B.C., and as the Nondualistic Vedanta of Shankaracharya did at the beginning of the ninth century of our era. What we observe in the Ramakrishna Math and Mission is thus not something new, something wholly dependent for its inspiration on the West. True, Vivekananda was quick to recognize the value of Western organizational methods, as exemplified particularly by those of the United States. But his master, Ramakrishna, was a poor and unlettered orthodox brahmin. It was on his realization that *jiva*, the individual soul, is one with Shiva, the absolute Godhead, that Vivekananda built a fresh religious orientation for Indian monasticism.

Now that lay people, with the help of the government, are assuming their social responsibilities, the total monastic community of India will be grappling with the problem of how to serve, once again, as a purely spiritual reminder that God alone is the goal. It is here that the orthodox monastic orders, though they never really felt the need to awaken the laity by direct action, can contribute powerfully to an awakened laity. As Dom Jean Leclercq has reminded us, in his article "Monastic Life after the Second Vatican Council," in the *The Downside Review*, Vol. 86 (1968), the Church "teaches that the main purpose of the monastic life is not so much to do something as to be something: a sign, and an efficacious sign."

In the years to come, perhaps Westerners can learn much by observing how successfully Hindu monasticism meets this challenge.

The Spirituality of Non-Christian Monasticism in Japan

F. ENOMIYA-LASSALLE, S. J.

There can be no doubt that the implantation of Christian monasticism is a very important part of the introduction of Christian faith and spirituality into any non-Christian country. But this is particularly important in Asia, because there we find a tradition of several thousand years of monasticism in the great religions of this continent. Besides this, it is often easier to come to an understanding with other religions in regard to monasticism and—what is closely connected with monasticism— contemplative prayer than in regard to doctrine.

Everybody knows how important a part was played by the monastic orders in the conversion of the European countries to Christianity. Of course, times have changed and methods of evangelization, too, but from ancient times to the present day, wherever the Church has sent its apostles, it has sent also monastic and contemplative orders to take part in spreading the message of Christ.

So far, however, monastic life has been introduced into other countries almost or even completely unchanged in regard to rules, liturgy and way of living. In Europe and other areas that had almost no culture of their own, this was perhaps the obvious way, since the Church was simultaneously the vehicle for religion and civilization. But we must confess that it was a mistake in the case of countries and peoples that had their own culture, often one older than any culture in Europe. This method was followed, of course, not on account of any lack of good will, but simply because these cultures were not yet sufficiently known in the West. At present the situation is different.

Fortunately the mistakes made have been recognized as such by the Church, and we are now aware that we must change our methods. It is true, no doubt, that Christian monasticism has something to give to the East even in the form in which it has grown up in its homeland. For instance, a Benedictine monastery, established in Japan even without any change in language and liturgy, would be a great benefit for Christians and non-Christians. I wish to add that the Trappists, who came to Japan about a hundred years ago, have played an important role in the reentry of Christianity into Japan after centuries of seclusion and even persecution. It was only a few years ago that a very important Zen monk spoke to me of his great admiration for the Trappists in Hokkaido in the north of Japan. And he added that the Zen monks of our days would not be able to live as they do.

But it remains true that we can give much more of what we have to give if we adapt our ways as much as possible to the mentality of the people. In order to do that, we must know that mentality, and especially insofar as it concerns religious life, which means in our case the spirituality of non-Christian monasticism.

This is of course one very important task in our present meeting. I hesitated when I was asked to speak on this subject, because I thought it would be best to have somebody give this talk who had experience in monasticism. But there seemed to be nobody else available, and so I accepted. Since, however, my knowledge of monastic life is very limited, I should like to concentrate on one particular point that is very important for the spirituality of non-Christian monasticism in Japan, rather than speak about many things that I do not know much about. The special point is Zen meditation, or zazen—to use the Japanese expression already well-known in the West.

PRESENT SITUATION OF MONASTICISM IN JAPAN

Buddhist monasticism. In Japan we can speak about monasticism only in regard to Buddhism, because it does not exist in the original religion of Japan, which is Shintoism. That does not mean there is no such thing as mysticism in this religion; in fact there is. But it is very little known outside Japan. Moreover, in spite of the fact that there are eleven different Buddhist sects in Japan, counting only the old ones, there are only a few that have preserved any kind of monasticism. The most prominent are the two Zen sects, Soto and Rinzai.

Those sects that first came from China and introduced Buddhism into Japan had large monasteries. This was the case of the Tendai sect on Mt. Hie (Hiesan) and the Shingon sect on Mt. Koya (Koyasan). At times they even had troops of their own and took part in politics and war. But

Spirituality of Non-Christian Monasticism
F. Enomiya-Lassalle, S.J.

those sects that were founded in Japan in the twelfth and thirteenth centuries, the Jodo and Shinshu, concentrated on Amida pietism. They never had monasteries in the strict sense. Shinran, who represents the last step in the development of Amida pietism, abolished celibacy and ecclesiastical life. He himself was married.

In the course of time other sects followed their example—all except the Zen sects, which continued for many centuries to observe celibacy. But in the great changes during the Meiji period, which brought about a hostile attitude toward Buddhism in Japan, the Zen sects too dispensed their monks from celibacy.

Strange to say, they found a way to continue monasticism while being married. The families of these monks do not live in the monasteries. They have a smaller temple of their own, sometimes far away from the monastery, where their wife and children live. These temples are like parishes, and a certain number of families are attached to them. The services held there are partly performed by the wife of the monk; he himself lives most of the time at his monastery. At certain times when services for the deceased are very frequent, he comes home. This is regularly the case during the month during which memorials for the deceased are held. Many people then come to visit the cemeteries attached to the temple where their ancestors and relatives are buried and have services offered for the rest of their souls.

The Japanese in general are very faithful to their deceased parents and relatives. It is a kind of ancestor worship. These services to some extent provide a living for the monks. Up to now, the combination of monasticism and married life is unfamiliar to us. But that is how it works for Zen monks at present. Of course, there are also monks who, for religious motives, do not marry, but their number is small. Sometimes I have heard Zen monks say it was a mistake to abolish the vow of celibacy.

The recruitment of Zen monks is assured to a certain degree. The eldest son of a monk who is in charge of a temple has to get a certain amount of training before he can take charge of it. This training requires about two years. It consists first of all in the practice of Zen meditation. Besides that, the young monks have to study and to work inside and outside the monastery. They also have to go begging at certain times. This is done by visiting houses of lay people and asking them for rice and other eatables, or for money. Some also go away for several months of begging and practicing *zazen*, meditation, under the direction of a famous master. This is in fact a very old custom with Zen monks and has been kept up to the present day.

Of course, there are also those who do not enter a monastery in order to take over a temple, but for spiritual reasons only. They are the more serious ones, because they feel some vocation to this kind of life. Sometimes they are not satisfied with a life in the world and wish to faithfully follow the way of Buddha up to enlightenment. It may be that some deep disappointment has made them think about the meaning of human life. One young man I met in a Zen monastery told me that he had read St. Teresa and St. John of the Cross and had also studied the catechism and had thought of becoming a Catholic, but finally had entered this Zen monastery. I do not know if he has persevered. In fact there are not a few who do not persevere, though they had come with a firm resolution to stay.

As I have said, the most important part of a young monk's training is the practice of *zazen*. The monks have two meditations of forty minutes a day, one in the morning and one in the evening. But there are periods when they meditate much more. Those exercises are called *sesshin*, that is to say, "recollection of heart." They are held several times a year. Usually they take a whole week. During this time the monks rise at 3 o'clock in the morning and go to sleep at 9 in the evening. But there are also *sesshin* where they sleep only three hours, and that in the position of meditation. This means that they have to stay in the meditation hall in the place where they practice *zazen* during the day. One kind of *sesshin* is still more severe. There is no sleep at all during the whole week. During these exercises the monks stay almost the whole time in the hall and meditate. Even meals are taken in the meditation hall.

The *sesshin* is held six times during the year, but it varies according to custom of the monastery. The food is, as always in Zen monasteries, strictly vegetarian.

Even outside these periods of concentrated exercises the monks get up early in the morning, most of the time at 4 o'clock. They are kept busy during the whole day and have very little free time. Manual work is part of the training no matter whether it is cleaning the house or something else. It is meant to be a continuation of the meditation, but in another sense than we perhaps would expect. It is concentration on the work itself, just as one is supposed to concentrate on the meditation when he is sitting in the hall. This is something very particular to Zen and explains the fact that Zen monasteries, although often rather poor, are always very clean. They are cleaned every day by the monks.

What are the conditions for being received into a Zen monastery? The rules are not so strict as in Christian religious orders at present. For those who have no intention of doing any studies, a normal education is sufficient: six years of grammar school and three years of high school. But most of the young men enter after having finished a university course.

Now a word about how young people are first received at the monastery. According to an old tradition, when the candidate arrives he is refused entrance to the house. For one or more days, no matter how earnestly he may ask he is refused and has to stay all that time at the entrance unless he prefers to give up the idea of joining the Zen monks and goes home. It is a severe trial: he has to undergo it in order to show that he has firmly decided to persevere, no matter what is demanded from him. This is done because it is not easy to lead the life of a Zen monk. Of course, such practices are mitigated to some extent now, but there is still something left. After being received, too, he has to pass through many trials.

In regard to food we may add that the monks eat anything offered to them, when they are outside the monastery. This is reasonable under the present conditions in Japan, and to some extent necessary. The clothing is traditional, but many young monks at present often go in ordinary civilian clothes, though the head is shaven all the same. How long this will continue in Japan remains to be seen.

The rooms where the monks live are very simple: they correspond to the standard of middle class people in Japan, which is, however, far below that of Christian religious orders. The heating, if any, is by the old method, that is to say, by charcoal, which keeps the hands warm but nothing more. Central heating and the like have not yet found their way into the Zen monasteries.

What has been said so far concerns the monasteries for men. But there are also those for women, that is to say, Zen nuns. For them the requirements for admittance are different, and often also the motives for asking to be received. The first motive for men, as we have mentioned, is to take over the temple of the father; but this does not apply to the daughters. The motives are different according to the individuals, but in most cases they are religious. For instance, the woman may have had some material or spiritual misfortune and now wishes to find peace of mind. But sometimes non-Christians are also apostolic; for instance, they may wish to help other people along the spiritual way. Among them, however, entering a nunnery is often considered as a last refuge. (That is why parents who are not Christians are opposed if their Catholic daughter wishes to join a religious order. They consider such a step as a disgrace for the family, and it takes often a long time to make them understand that the situation is different with the Christian religious orders. They do not understand how a girl who has the best chance of making a good marriage and enjoying everything else that the world can offer can leave all that and join a religious order.)

The training in the Zen nunneries is very much the same as in the men's monasteries; sometimes it is even more severe, and this concerns also the practice of *zazen*. The nuns sit for hours and hours without interruption.

It would take too long to speak in detail about the different activities Zen monks or nuns are occupied in, or may be busy with, after their training is ended. They continue the daily meditation, of course, and have their Office to say at definite times together. This consists to great extent in reciting the *sutras*, a part of the Scriptures. They have a kind of matins and vespers every day if they are at home. Added to this there are frequent offices or services for the deceased. But that is not all. They also go out in order to give lectures, by preference on a famous *koan* (we shall see later what a *koan* is).

Zen masters also go to other places to give retreats for groups of lay people. Zen monks are therefore not contemplatives who do not go outside to work. The same holds good for the nuns. They have sometimes very efficient women Zen masters who themselves have obtained deep enlightenment. It sometimes happens that Catholics go for advice to Zen monks or nuns because they do not find understanding of their troubles among the priests.

Christian monasticism. About this point there is, of course, not so much to say as on Buddhist monasticism in Japan. Nevertheless Christian monasticism is present in Japan. We have already mentioned the Trappists. The monastery in Hokkaido has sixty-five monks, most of them brothers. It is the only Trappist monastery in Japan for men. There was a plan to found a second one in the South, because the climate in Hokkaido is too severe for some Japanese people. But it seems to have been given up for the time being. Besides vocations at present are few. This is better with the Trappistines, who have one monastery also in the North and three in other parts of Japan.

The Trappists, although strictly contemplative and without any direct apostolic work, have rendered very valuable service to the Church in Japan. They are very well known and have for some time been considered as the most genuine representatives of the Catholic Church. Japanese people in general have great admiration for the Trappists and have often compared them with the Zen monks, who are generally considered at present as the best of all Buddhist monks in Japan. They even believed that, just like the Trappists, all Catholics were not supposed to marry.

The Benedictines founded a monastery before the war, but unfortunately it had to be given up after a few years on account—as far as I know—of financial difficulties. Since then we have all been waiting for a new and lasting foundation, but so far nothing has been settled. If this meeting of ours could contribute to the realization of this project, it would be of great benefit for the Church in Japan.

There are Benedictine nuns. I regret I am not able to give any detailed information about them. There are other contemplatives, too, in Japan who have many vocations—Carmelites, Passionists and Clarisses. The women Carmelites have five convents. Among the men Carmelites there are both contemplative and active monks. The Passionists also have both, and the men are very active in giving retreats and popular missions. How far all these come under the heading of monasticism, I do not know, but they certainly belong to the contemplative life, which is important for Japan and may justify their being mentioned here. So, compared to the small number of Catholics in Japan (about 350,000), the contemplatives are very well represented. If we ask how far all these are adapted to non-Christian monasticism in Japan, we have not much to say. But it is encouraging to see that recently many of them have shown a great desire to know more about Zen and Zen meditation.

INTEGRATION OF BUDDHIST MEDITATION AND OTHER METHODS OF PRAYER INTO CATHOLIC SPIRITUALITY

Zen meditation. Let us first remember what Vatican II has said in regard to this point. The Decree on the Church's Missionary Activity (n. 18) says:

> Working to plant the Church and thoroughly enriched with the treasures of mysticism adorning the Church's religious tradition, religious communities should strive to give expression to these treasures and to hand them on in a manner harmonious with the nature and the genius of each nation. Let them reflect attentively on how Christian religious life may be able to assimilate the ascetic and contemplative traditions whose seeds were sometimes already planted by God in ancient cultures prior to the preaching of the Gospel.

In order to define Zen meditation (zazen) we have to consider three things: the position of the body, the breathing, and the mental attitude.

1. As for the position of the body, one sits on a cushion in such a way that the feet lie on the floor or on a blanket in front of it. Then one draws the left leg (or the right) toward the body, bending the knee in such a way that the outside of it touches the floor or the blanket, and the foot, as far as possible, is drawn toward the thigh of the other leg. Then one puts the foot on the other thigh, turning the sole of the foot upward. This however is not yet the perfect way to sit, called the "lotus posture." In this latter, one puts the right leg on the left thigh and the left leg on the right thigh. It may be added that using a cushion and blanket are meant to help in performing this rather difficult way of sitting. There is of course no objection to doing without such help if one prefers it.

The torso should be kept straight, but in such a way that the point of gravity lies in the abdomen, half an inch below the navel. The shoulders should not be pulled upward. The head is kept high, but the chin is drawn toward the "y" of the collar bone. Without strain the hands should be held in front of the abdomen. The traditional way of holding the hands is to place the left hand palm up in the right hand, and the thumbs should touch each other. The eyes are kept slightly open and one looks at a fixed point in front of one on the floor or, if one sits near a wall, on the wall.

2. The right way of breathing is very important, too, though it is not so much insisted on as in Yoga. Complex exercises in breathing are not demanded. One should breathe in and out deeply and quietly but without overdoing it. It should be done normally through the nose, not through the mouth. If possible one should breathe by way of the diaphragm, not as we usually do with the chest. This is very important for the efficiency of zazen.

Both the position of the body and the breathing have an influence on the circulation of the blood and on the nervous system, in the sense that the circulation of the blood works well throughout the whole body and the nerves are at rest. This position of the body is no doubt difficult and painful in the beginning, but once one gets used to it, he finds it most appropriate to its purpose, which is meditation.

3. The mental attitude is the most difficult part. One is supposed not to think about anything. Hence in this kind of meditation no object is used. And yet one should not drop into the state of daydreaming, which would mean that all spiritual activity is stopped. What should

Spirituality of Non-Christian Monasticism
F. Enomiya-Lassalle, S.J.

be obtained is a state of complete emptiness of mind. This state may also be called pure consciousness or a deeper consciousness. Some authors have called it "interior gaze [intuition] without pictures." The Japanese used to call it "munenmuso" (without ideas and without thoughts). It is very difficult, or rather impossible, to explain this state through words. Only by one's own experience can one know what it is.

Since it is very difficult to come to this deeper consciousness, several means are applied. There are three different ways to achieve it. The first is to concentrate on one's breathing. This may be done by counting the inhalations and exhalations in succession from one to ten, and again from the beginning, and so forth, during the whole time of meditation. Or one counts only the inhalations or only the exhalations. Again, another way is not to count the breathing, but to concentrate on the inhalations and exhalations without counting them. This first means is usually applied by beginners.

The second means is to use a *koan*. Literally, a *koan* means a public document or something the like. But with *zazen* it has a different meaning. It is a problem given by the master to the student to be solved. But the problem is of such nature that no solution is possible by logical thinking. Let us take an example: "If you clap both hands there is a sound. What is the sound of one hand clapping?" When you clap both hands there is a sound, no doubt. But with one hand only, how can there be a sound? Nevertheless the student must find a solution to present to the master. If he goes to him without one, he will be scolded. So he will try to find some sort of solution that seems to make sense. But however much he tries he will never find a solution that may satisfy the master, because there is none.

Since the student is urged again and again, he finally gives up searching for a logical solution. But the problem remains all the time on his mind, day and night. He falls asleep at night with the *koan*, and the first thought when he wakes up in the morning is the *koan*. If he continues like this for a long time, he will finally get the impression that he himself has become the *koan*. In the case mentioned he will feel as if he has become the one hand himself. But not long after this the *koan* will suddenly disappear from his mind. At this moment he has reached the state of complete emptiness of mind, because just previously there had been nothing else on his mind but the *koan*. Now he is very near to enlightenment and will obtain it if only he continues in *zazen* with the greatest possible effort and without any reflection.

The third means is just to sit and breathe, observing the prescriptions of *zazen* and not paying attention to anything that may happen inside or outside of oneself, and stopping at no thought that arises in the mind, no matter whether it is good or bad. One should strictly follow the advice of the famous Zen master Rinzai, who probably lived in the ninth century: "Put all hindrance out of the way.... If you meet the Buddha, kill him! If you meet your ancestors, kill them.... Only if you do that, you will obtain redemption. Escape the nets and become free."

Effects of Zen meditation. Three effects of *zazen* are named as the most typical and important: the so-called power of meditation (*joriki*), insight (*chi-e*) and enlightenment (*satori* or *kensho*). The first and second will be felt more and more if one continues the practice of *zazen*. Let us examine them a little more in detail.

"Power of meditation" means here power to stop the distractions of the mind and to establish spiritual equilibrium and peace of mind. This produces a greater ease in concentration and a greater spiritual freedom and self-possession. One is not so easily disturbed if things occur that are annoying, and if one loses his temper he easily regains the state of serenity. Yet this is not a kind of apathy or indifference that hinders activity. Zen is by no means quietism. Despite their peace of mind, these people have a strong will and great energy. Ease in concentration, again, helps one work with greater efficiency in any branch of work and profession. It is, of course, also helpful in the religious sphere. It is a help for recollection of mind, which is so important for any kind of prayer and the performance of liturgical functions.

"Insight" here means the intuitive side of the human intellect in opposition to the discursive one. The latter is always at hand and is mostly employed in daily human life. But it is different with the intuitive side, which normally is ready to be used only in regard to "first principles." Discursive thinking proceeds from one truth to another and has as its object first of all the differentiated world, while intuitive thinking is directed to the nondifferentiated and spiritual, particularly the absolute Spirit, God, and also to the Absolute if it is not conceived as a person, as in Buddhism. It goes without saying that this power is at work in other kinds of mental prayer, where intellect and will are working separately. With us in the Christian realm, one usually starts with this kind of meditation. But it is different in Zen, which starts from meditation by intuitive thinking, although in the beginning it has to overcome great difficulties.

"Enlightenment" itself is again very difficult to explain. A Zen master,

Spirituality of Non-Christian Monasticism
F. Enomiya-Lassalle, S.J.

if asked what it is, will not even try to explain. The most famous masters in the history of Zen have answered this question in such a way that an inexperienced person knows still less what it is than he did before. To give one example: when asked about it, the master answered: "Look at the oak tree in the garden." This answer has become a famous *koan*.

We may certainly say, however, that enlightenment is on the intuitive side and not on the discursive; that is to say, it is not the result of analytical or logical thinking. What then is the content of enlightenment? Properly speaking there can be no talk about content, because it would mean a limitation, and that does not fit this experience. It is an experience of complete unity and unique completeness. There is in it, therefore, nothing like opposition, and therefore no limitation. It may be said, however, to be the direct intuition of the Self, but in such a way that the Self is not the object of anything. With the Self thus recognized there is an intrinsic—an inherent or essential—connection with the Absolute. That is why Buddhists who obtain this experience recognize in it an all-oneness and an absence of any kind of individual self. A Christian or anybody who has faith in one God recognizes in the same experience of enlightenment his being united with God.

There are still many things to be said about the effects of Zen meditation, but let us now examine its relation to Christian practice.

Integration of zazen into Christian spirituality. In the case of Japan, the integration of *zazen* is not just one item of adaptation out of many others. It is so fundamental that, if applied properly, it will have an effect on the whole spiritual life. Surely if we go back to Christian spirituality as it existed in the Middle Ages, we can find methods of prayer and other matters that are strikingly similar to methods that we still find in East Asia. But sometimes, at least, our present spirituality appears so much in contradiction to those methods that it may at first seem impossible to integrate these Eastern ways into our Christian life. I should therefore like to consider some of these difficulties before trying to find how such integration might be carried out.

One objection, one that has often been made, is concerned with the origin of this method. It is said that the origin is Buddhist and so closely connected with Buddhism that it cannot be separated from Buddhism itself. It may therefore be very good for a Buddhist, but for a Christian there is a danger of being misled into monism or pantheism. Some go so far as to say that it is dangerous for the whole of Christian culture, because it is incompatible with everything that concerns the concept of personhood, whether it be in regard to the one personal God or to the human person. They are perhaps not against Zen as an exercise of concentration, but they would not allow it to penetrate any deeper into Christian spirituality.

Another objection is against any willingly attempted emptiness of the mind. Those who oppose it say that such an endeavor is contrary to the traditional teaching of Christian spiritual directors—in the first place, of St. Teresa of Avila, who points to the danger that the devil may take advantage of this emptiness and mislead the soul. Such emptiness should only be admitted, they say, if it comes to pass by the grace of God.

A third objection that is brought up is that a method like *zazen* would lead to quietism and a passivity that is not in accord with the genuine Christian spirit, which always includes action, particularly action of charity toward our fellow men. In regard to this objection, we have already given an answer in speaking about the effects of *zazen*.

In these objections and others that might be mentioned, there is still to some extent a theological question involved. But to meet these objections on the ground of theological arguments would take a long time for investigation and study. Besides, we are not sure of coming to a satisfactory conclusion, at least not as long as we work with the traditional theology. Already Meister Eckhart has tried to do it, and he was punished for it. Although I am far from underestimating the importance of the theological question, I prefer not to go into it now. Instead I should like to present a few facts and thoughts that are in favor of the integration of Zen meditation and similar Eastern methods into Christian spiritual practice.

First of all, there is the fact that again and again Christians who had lost their faith came back to God and to prayer by practicing this kind of meditation. No matter how unlikely this may seem to some people, it is a fact, and one that is not very difficult to explain. Many people at present are losing their faith through the overestimation of rationalistic thinking even in matters of faith. But modern man cannot bear this any more; he needs the experience of religion, of faith, of God. Now, in Zen meditation all rationalistic thinking is put aside, and with it all the difficulties with regard to faith. Thus a man comes to a deeper part of his mind and to his own surprise discovers that he has not lost his faith and can believe in God, and that it is only natural for him to do so. Or to express it in the words of a recent author, Hans Urs von Balthasar: "The entrance to the innermost Self is at the same time always the exit of the

Self to the all-highest God."[1] We may remember the words of St. Augustine: "God is nearer to us than we are to ourselves." Thus if a man comes to his real Self, he cannot but meet God. And it is just the real Self that the Zen meditation wants to lead to. The fact that the Buddhist does not find the personal God there does not disprove this. He too finds God, but without any label or concept attached.

It is not correct, either, to say that Zen meditation is a hindrance against charity. The facts stand against it, because Buddhists also have charity. Compassion for all suffering creatures has been known as a quality of Buddhism since the days of its founder. This is true also of the Zen Buddhists who practice zazen habitually. And this effect is not surprising, because zazen takes away all attachment, which is always the greatest hindrance for practicing charity.

Also the widely spread practice of zazen in Europe and America by Christians, whether they be fervent or not, seems to indicate that they have a profound desire for religious experience. This can be explained neither by saying it is a fashion nor by suspecting that they want to become Buddhists. Neither the one nor the other would be true. If one only sees how great a sacrifice these people make in order to learn this kind of meditation, one cannot but understand that here is a very serious desire at work. Unfortunately these people in most cases do not receive much understanding or even guidance from their pastors.

Perhaps the most convincing argument for the assimilation of Zen meditation and other Eastern methods is their striking similarity to the practices of our Christian mystics. Many sayings of our mystics could have been produced by one of the famous Zen masters, and the same holds good for the works of these Zen masters in regard to the Christian mystics. To mention only one, we may remember the *nada* of St. John of the Cross, which corresponds so well to the *mu* of the Zen. Both mean the same: "nothing." On this point books have been written and more could be written.

The extent to which Zen meditation should be integrated. There is, of course, no objection to using Zen meditation as psychological help, or merely the way of sitting and breathing used in that method. Practically speaking, if somebody is used to meditating every day, he may sit for a few minutes in the Zen fashion before he starts his meditation in order to get recollected. After that he can do his meditation as he is

[1] *Das betrachtende Gebet* (Einsiedeln, 1955), p. 18.

used to doing, taking, say, a text from one of the Gospels and meditating on it. But the question to be answered is rather: Can Zen meditation, just as it is performed by a Buddhist according to the respective prescriptions, take the place of Christian meditation if it is performed by a Christian? I believe it can, for the simple reason that there is no object. It is a way to go to the depth of the soul, and as such it is at the same time a way of purification. And it is, so to say, an existential purification. There is no Buddhism in this.

Remember: "If you meet the Buddha, kill the Buddha!" It is a Buddhist meditation only insofar as the one who performs it is a Buddhist. In the same way, it is a Christian meditation for the Christian, because he always has the Christian faith even when he does not think of it. His attitude toward God remains the same. In other words, for him Zen meditation becomes ipso facto a Christian meditation.

But there may be difficulties arising from the traditions of the religious orders, monastic and contemplative. They are supposed to preserve the spirit of their founders, as at present after the Council the Church also wants them to do. There may be methods of other religions that are good in themselves and worthy to be integrated, but in conflict with the tradition of one particular religious order. They may perhaps not fit into the structure of that order, or they may be incompatible with the way of instructing the young people who wish to join it. For it is not, I believe, just narrowness of mind to speak of the spirituality of St. Benedict or St. Francis or St. Ignatius. There is no doubt that this variety has its value and beauty. Changes may be necessary according to the time, but so far as we all think, these should be made in such a way that the original spirit is not lost.

To make things clear, let us take a practical case. For instance, you are used to introducing your novices to mental prayer by having them meditate on the life and passion of our Lord or on a text from the Gospels; but from now on you are asked, when the hour of meditation strikes, to have them sit on a cushion and think of nothing. Perhaps you will answer that this may be done after they have learned to meditate in the ordinary Christian way. But that is not the same as if you make them do it from the beginning, and only after having obtained enlightenment start to meditate on the Gospel text. It is just the opposite of our way.

As far as the Japanese are concerned, this difference of procedure applies also to the average man. With us, in the West, things start with the understanding and from there they go to the heart and to the "ground," but with the Japanese things start from below and finally come to the understanding. Now I ask you: Can we and should we force

SPIRITUALITY OF NON-CHRISTIAN MONASTICISM
F. Enomiya-Lassalle, S.J.

a Japanese to go our Western (I do not say Christian) way, starting from the head, and from there go down? Is that the way to get the best out of their qualification for religious life, as we certainly should do?

Now on this deadlock we are hitting a very important point of our discussions, it seems to me. The point has been mentioned in one of the answers to the questionnaire. It is the question: should we gradually introduce Oriental methods into our religious institutions, or should we —even must we—create something new? This new creation would start from the structure and ways of the non-Christian religions, and particularly of their monastic traditions, and try to introduce gradually what we have to give of Christian values from our side.

I do not intend to give an answer now to this difficult question. But it is no doubt a very important question, one that must be solved if we are to find the right way to implant of Christian monasticism. I am afraid that some or most of us, if we were told to start the instruction of the novices by having them sit and think of nothing, would feel like a man who is jumping from a plane without knowing whether the parachute will open or not.

Invocation of Amida and its integration. There is one other method of mental prayer very common among Buddhists in Japan. It is called *nembutsu*, and it consists in repeating an invocation to Amida with the conviction and confidence that one will be saved by his power. There is, however, a difference between those who are saved in this way and those who come to enlightenment by their own efforts. The difference is that the former will be reborn after death in the "Pure Land" and receive Buddhahood there, and the latter can receive Buddhahood already in this life, if they are qualified.

In Japan the practice of *nembutsu* is widespread. In fact, more than half the Buddhists in Japan belong to the sects that teach Amida pietism and with it *nembutsu*. It may be noted here that Amida is not a historical personality, but a name for the idealized Buddha. In other words, it is the Buddha who saves the people who recite this prayer. Now this *nembutsu* could be integrated into Christian spirituality by introducing the Jesus prayer. In fact, it seems that the Jesus prayer developed from an Oriental method, very likely from Indian Yoga. The work is done in this case; we need only make use of it. It would certainly appeal to the Japanese Christians, particularly to those who were formerly Buddhists and as such used to practice this prayer. It has no doubt two great advantages compared with *zazen*: it is easy enough to be practiced by anybody, and it is *prima facie* Christian.

WHAT HAS BEEN DONE SO FAR IN THE WAY OF ASSUMING THE ZEN MEDITATION AND OTHER METHODS?

This question may be quickly answered. With zazen for Christians we have just made a start. We had to overcome many difficulties, but about eight years ago we built a small Japanese house for this purpose twenty-five kilometers from Hiroshima. Since then there has been regular practice of Zen meditation. Most of the participants are Catholics, but non-Catholics are also invited and take part. We are now about to establish a bigger center for the same purpose near Tokyo. The first experiments have greatly appealed to Japanese Catholics and even to a number of Buddhists.

With the *nembutsu* we have not progressed as far. But the Jesus prayer is already known to Catholics. Once a former Buddhist who had become Christian was saying to a Catholic friend that he was afraid that the words of the *nembutsu* might come to his lips when he came to die. One of the others then told him about the Jesus prayer, and when he heard of this, he was very glad and said: "Now I am saved."

SYNTHESIS OF GROUP DISCUSSIONS

December 12, 1968

THE MISSIONARY ASPECT OF MONASTICISM

Questions for discussion[1]

1. In the specific sociological context of the country, how can the monastery convey a truly Christian witness of charity, prayer and poverty?
2. What should be the site of the monastery and its relations with the neighborhood?
3. What part can the monastery play in the evangelization of the aborigines?
4. How can Christian monasticism undertake and develop truly religious exchanges with representatives of non-Christian monasticism?

1. *Helping people understand the properly Christian witness of charity, prayer and poverty.* The Church being missionary, the monastery should also

---

[1] The questions are based on the questionnaire, Part III. A, B, D, E (Appendix B, pp. 278–279). See also the summary of answers to Part III. (Appendix B, pp. 301–314) and to Part II. (Appendix B, pp. 296–300).

be missionary in its own way. To clarify what the word "missionary" should connote for the monastic community, the following guidelines were proposed: that a community should demonstrate the gospel to non-Christians as well as Christians around it, while opening itself to the non-Christians' own proper values and contributing to their development. Seeking to interpret the meaning of charity, prayer and poverty, the group members came to the following conclusions: First of all, it should be noted that charity, prayer and poverty depend primarily on the authenticity and sincerity of one's search for God.

It is within the community that charity must begin. Its witness will then shine through to the outside and be spread by those who work with the community. Charity is involved also in the reception of guests. The whole monastery, and sometimes the whole Church, is often judged simply by the contacts visitors enjoy in the guest house. Special consideration is called for in receiving priests who came to refresh themselves spiritually and physically.

Outward charity implies, first of all, social justice toward employees of the monastery, a justice that often goes beyond strict legal requirements and implies an atmosphere of cordiality in the community's relations with them.

There are in addition, of course, the services that are rendered as good neighbors. But the help we can bring must look to the development of the people by themselves rather than what is to be accomplished through almsgiving. A Thai proverb was cited: "To teach someone to pick up rice is worth more than giving him a whole bag." But the bag must often be given, too, if the man has nothing to eat. Many examples of sharing of goods and of intelligent aid were cited: medical aid, distribution of seed and of young animals to be raised, and the like.

Second, like charity for men, the search for God will become authentic and profound only through prayer. One is always in danger of becoming superficial. It is important to develop a taste for contemplation; for it is from union with God that charity for men and evangelical poverty flow. Moreover, men are hungry not only for material goods but for spiritual values, and true conversion is not a response to some gift but a discovery of the supernatural.

On the practical level, the taste for contemplation can be developed by allowing time and freedom for the *lectio divina* and silent personal prayer. Contemplation can be encouraged in the monasteries if the superior takes the occasion of meals and community reunions to improvise simple prayers.

It is to be expected, besides, that a monastery will provide the example of a simple liturgy that can be understood by the people. It seems essential that it be in the language of the country, and it seems normal that the monks should try to complose suitable melodies.

Retreats will serve to develop a more personal prayer. It is desirable that retreatments should be able to participate in the prayer of the community and that on this occasion the prayer should take freer forms. Retreats seem to be especially fruitful for the clergy and religious, and for preparation of lay people for the sacraments, as well—marriage, communion and so on.

Third, in a country in the process of developing, poverty is an evil that must be combated. On the other hand, the concept of poverty is a relative one; it is to be understood in terms of the country's standard of living.

The monastic virtue of poverty, above all, consists in sincerity, detachment and sharing. It expresses itself differently according as the monastery is large or small; each expression has its advantages. The large monasteries find it difficult to bear witness to poverty, because they are necessarily cut off from their surroundings, but they can give more efficient aid.

A good example of detachment and of integration with the environment is provided by certain monasteries that have ceded their administration and a part of the ownership of their schools to the laity. The monks receive only their salary as professor or chaplain.

The small monasteries find it easier to adapt themselves to their surroundings, even though they must expect great difficulties when their standard of living is very low.

Certain small things aid, sometimes, in this adaptation: wearing the clothing of the country, the possibility of monks giving alms while traveling and so on. In general, experience proves that it is better to give a little money outright than to lend larger sums.

2. *The site of the monastery.* Everyone expressed the desire that monasteries be founded in a place at once sufficiently calm and solitary to safeguard monastic contemplation, and yet easy of access and near a great urban center that could be also an intellectual meeting place. Such a location would permit religious to enrich their own culture and to respond to the particular needs of those who frequent the center.

3. *Relationship to the aborigines.* A beautiful example of how to deal with these populations is the foundation of the Benedictines of Vanves on the high plateau of Vietnam. Ways must be sought to raise these people while safeguarding their own original approach to life. This sometimes presupposes, as has been discovered in Australia, obtaining information from specialists and collaborating with other organizations working with these people.

INTERVENTION OF THE ABBOT PRIMATE

I would like to say a word here about active and contemplative monasticism, because they are still causing a great deal of concern in the Benedictine family. And this is the only family I can speak for.

It seems that the Congregation of Religious has three slots or divisions: one is called contemplative, one is called mixed and one is called active. And they even divide their work according to the three different types of people who are in charge of these sections. I think we all realize that these categories are not so absolute, in reality, that there should never be a really totally active community that does not pray; and that the praying community, as it were, has to live. And so, in a way, we are all in the middle category in varying degrees.

At the Council, what happened was that the Decree on the Appropriate Renewal of the Religious Life, in its formation, involved a great argument. And so a new category was put in for the monks, so that the monks are not thrown into one of the three slots, but placed in a separate category. The difficulty is that the Congregation of Religious has never created a fourth slot to take care of us, and so there is a tendency always to throw all the monks together into slot number one, and this creates a great deal of difficulty for those who have taken on some sort of apostolate—as one of the sisters has said.

There has always been, and I suppose there always will be, in the Benedictine family I am speaking about, a kind of tension between these two poles: between a kind of total isolationism and a total activism. And perhaps this tension has been felt very much in the meetings this week. I can sense it tonight. I can sense it constantly when the Benedictine Congress of Abbots comes together. This tension and these poles are always present, and I think it would be a bad thing if they were not present. Perhaps they are present even in the Rule of St. Benedict, when he says that some monks have to be given work with the hands, and so on, and that those who are in the chapel should not be disturbed.

So it is that even within the same family there are those who are more prone to a certain contemplation; there are those gifted by grace toward greater interest in helping others. And the beauty of the Benedictine family —and I think the duty of Benedictine superiors—is to safeguard these different characteristics within the same family. As for me, it is the duty of the Abbot Primate to safeguard within the Benedictine Confederation the beauty of this variety. All attempts to split the Benedictine family into two categories (and this is a constant tendency)—into, as it were, the active and the contemplative—I have tried to avoid and will continue to try to avoid.

And so, Sisters, I do not know how you feel, but we consider you truly Benedictine.

I think the point was made by Father Merton in his paper. The real test is not to be so bound to your apostolate that your existence dies or develops with it (if you see what I am getting at). You need a certain detachment also from your apostolate, so that your institution as nuns is not really bound to doing whatever work you are doing now—so that tomorrow you could throw that work off and continue to exist where the need of your community or the Church would dictate.

I am trying somehow to get through to you that kind of detachment I think is necessary for your community to be truly Benedictine. Have I talked too much?

---

4. *Relations with non-Christian monasticism.* Monasticism is, in our areas, that institution of the Church which is nearest to non-Christian religions, and it is perhaps the best means of access to them. One of the objectives of the Christian monks of Asia is to establish contacts with the monks of other religions.

Superficial relations with them are easy. They are hospitable and often come to us willingly. But difficulties are not lacking. We do not know their religions well enough; they too are ignorant of ours. And often they are incapable of describing their own—not to mention the added difficulty of the technical language proper to Buddhist monks and of a religious vocabulary that differs between the two religions.

We ought, then, to try to deepen our contacts and to be tactful in welcoming non-Christian monks to the monastery. But above all it is imperative for us to encourage study of their religions. Such study should normally be part of the formation of young monks and should be encouraged in each community through lectures given by specialists. When it is possible, it is good to plan, also, for some of us to spend periods of time, more or less long, in non-Christian monasteries.

Finally, in several instances, the creation of small experimental groups to study how to achieve a more complete adaptation was asked for.

PRAYER
(In French)

O Lord, thou God eternal, unbeginning and unending Light, Master Craftsman of all creation, wellspring of compassion, ocean of kindness, fathomless abyss of love for men, let the light of thy countenance shine upon us. Shine forth in our hearts, O spiritual Sun of Justice, fill our souls with thy joy; teach us constant meditation, teach us to speak forth thy judgments and to praise thee unceasingly, thou our Master and our Benefactor. Bestow upon the works of thy hands an uprightness in keeping with thy will; lead us to the fulfillment of whatever shall please thee, of whatsoever thou dost love, so that, even by such unworthy ones as we, thy Holy Name may be glorified, Father, Son and Holy Spirit, sole Godhead and King, to whom is due all glory, honor and adoration for all ages. Amen.

FIRST READING
(In French)

What is Nirvana? The only reasonable reply that can be given is that it is impossible to reply completely and satisfactorily in words, because human language is too poor to be able to express the true nature of Absolute Truth, of the Ultimate Reality which is Nirvana. Language has been created and used by the mass of human beings in order to express things and ideas that their minds and sense feel. A superhuman experience like that of Absolute Truth does not belong to this category.

Words are symbols that represent things and ideas familiar to us; these symbols do not translate, do not have the faculty of expressing, the real nature of even the most usual things. We must understand that language is disappointing and deceiving when it is a question of grasping Truth. We cannot, however, do without language. But if Nirvana must be expressed and explained in positive terms, we at once risk holding to an idea that is associated with the terms used and that might be quite the opposite. That is why we generally use negative expressions, which is perhaps safer.

Let us take some definitions and descriptions of Nirvana: "It is the total cessation of longing; it is to abandon it, to give it up, to set oneself free from it." It is to calm all that is conditioned, to abandon all impurity; the extinction of longing, cessation. O Monk, what is the Absolute? It is, O Monk, the extinction of desire, the extinction of hate, the extinction of illusion. That, O Monk, is called the Absolute.

In Nirvana the four elements of solidity, fluidity, heat and movement have no part. The notions of length, breadth, fine and thick, of good and evil, name and form, are absolutely destroyed; neither this world nor the other, neither coming nor going, neither standing nor sitting, neither death nor birth, nor any objects of sense are to be found. Because Nirvana is expressed in this way, in negative terms, many people have the false idea that Nirvana is negative and expresses the destruction of the self. It is not its destruction at all, but the destruction of the illusion that gives a false idea of a self. Elsewhere Buddha uses, without ambiguity, the word "Truth" instead of the word "Nirvana": "I am going to teach you Truth and the path that leads to Truth."

Here, Truth certainly means Nirvana. Now, what is absolute Truth? According to Buddhism, the absolute Truth is that nothing is absolute in this world; that everything is relative, conditioned and meaningless, and that there is no absolute substance that does not change—that is eternal, like the Self—within us or without us. This is the absolute Truth.

Truth is never negative. To understand this Truth, that is, to see things as they are, without illusion or ignorance, is the extinction of desire, of longing and the cessation of suffering, which is Nirvana.

It would be wrong to think that Nirvana is the natural result of the extinction of desire.

Nirvana is not the result of anything at all. If it were a result, it would be the product of a cause. Nirvana is neither cause nor

It is not produced as a mystical, spiritual state of mind. is. Nirvana is. The only thing you can do is to see it, to stand it.

—Walpola Rahula (*The Teaching of the Buddha*)

SECOND READING

(*In English*)

While yet the state of faith endures and the substance of the clear light is not yet made manifest, the contemplation of pure truth can yet anticipate its action in us, at least in part. . . .

For when something from God has momentarily and, as it were, with the swiftness of a flash of light, shed its ray upon the mind in ecstacy of spirit, whether for the tempering of this too great radiance, or for the sake of imparting this to others, forthwith there present themselves, whence I know not, certain imaginary likenesses of lower things, suited to the meanings that have been infused from above, by means of which that most pure and brilliant ray of truth is in a manner shaded, and becomes both more bearable to the soul itself and more capable of being communicated to whomsoever the soul wishes. I think that these images are formed in us by the suggestions of the holy angels, as, on the contrary, evil images without any doubt are "innoculations" by bad angels. And very likely in this way is fabricated, as by the hands of angels, that mirror and enigma through which the apostle saw, out of such pure and beauteous imaginations, in such wise that we both feel the Being of God, which is conceived as pure and without any fantasy of corporeal images, and attribute to angelic administration whatever kind of elegant similitude wherewith it appeared worthily clothed withal.

—St. Bernard (Serm. in Cant. XLI: 3, 4)

Those angels may not make the light of grace in thy soul, for that falls to God himself only; for he, through his unseeable presence, makes might, light and love, and gives them to the soul. But angels, by their spiritual presence, shall help you and comfort your soul much when you are in this grace. For they drive out the press of unclean spirits.

They cleanse the soul from fantasies and vain imaginations, and they form firm likenesses in words and in reasons, and temper the light of grace sufferably in feeding of your soul. They urge your heart to the love of all goodness and, if you offend by frailty, readily they blame you; you shall bear it no further, for they will suffer no sin to rest on you. They comfort you in bodily disease and tell you of the joys of heaven, wondrous privily, that you should not think too heavy the prison of this life.

—Walter Hilton (*Qui Habitat*)

FIFTH DAY

Friday, December 13

Many Hindus are at heart Christians. They will tell you there is no need to be a Catholic in order to be a Christian, just as there is no need to be a Jesuit in order to be a Catholic.

—Sadhu Ittyavirah

Witnessing as a Catholic Sadhu

SADHU ITTYAVIRAH

Ten years ago, in May 1958, I started out from the Jesuit Theological College in Kurseong, West Bengal, as an itinerant witness to the love of God. Some of my companions said to me sorrowfully: "You are returning to your native Kerala, where the Communists are in power. Would to God we don't hear next about your death at the hands of the Communists." With copious tears they bade me farewell.

In fact, I had a mind to turn back, timorous and shy as I am by nature, to face the unknown. But the Lord helped me not to turn back; to take the leap into the dark, leaving the sunshine and the security of the Society of Jesus.

I was a Jesuit theologian, and in the normal course should have been ordained priest in March 1959. But since for about two years I had felt like making a sacrifice of my priestly vocation and beginning life as a Catholic *sadhu* (holy man) witnessing to the love of God in the weakness and helplessness of Christ crucified, I came away from the Society of Jesus after obtaining the necessary dispensation from the vows.

Some of my superiors and companions thought I was under an illusion, and that the illusion would blow up once I faced the hard realities of life as a homeless vagabond.

Ten years' experience as a Catholic *sadhu* has strengthened my faith in the loving providence of God. During these years, I have been to schools and colleges, hospitals and prisons, factories and farmhouses, railway stations and street corners, meeting all sections of the people with the message of God's love. It was given to me to witness unto the love of the Father before Hindus and Muslims, Catholics and Protestants, Communists and Congressmen, and it is with a heart filled with joy and thanksgiving I write about this. During these years I have given thousands of talks, written nearly two thousand articles for the Catholic newspapers and magazines in Kerala and published sixteen books, in English as well as Malayalam. My book *The Witness* has been published in America by the Franciscan Publishers, Pulaski, Wisconsin.

Communists in Kerala have not murdered me. I have seen the love of the children of God in them, too. They too have given me food and drink, and a place to stay overnight. I am convinced of the intrinsic goodness of man. His evil is only the *vikrithi*, the mischief, of his basic nature, which is goodness and love.

A CHANGE IN ATTITUDE

Ten years ago, in the preconciliar days, I had to face a lot of indifference, though not active hostility, on the part of orthodox Catholics. To them the idea of a Catholic layman going out to non-Catholics and non-Christians was tantamount to repudiation of the faith. In those days, at least in Kerala, only priests were supposed to have the commission to preach and to witness to the Word of God. As a lay preacher I was doing something out of the way—heretical in the eyes of many. *Quidquid novum hereticum.*

Today, after the Council, there is a complete change in this attitude. Nowadays I am invited to give talks in parishes, seminaries, religious communities.

In the beginning, I walked from place to place, eating what I got and sleeping where I happened to be at the end of the day. Now, since I am invited to give talks in many places, I also have to travel by bus and train.

In *sadhu* fashion I used at first to go to the heads of educational institutions and ask their permission to give a talk to their students about the love of God, the ethical and religious aspects of education, the unity of man, and so on. The great majority of the principals and headmasters of the schools and colleges have been very cooperative. On several occasions Hindu and Muslim headmasters of schools have canceled their English and mathematics classes to give me an opportunity to address their students.

TELLING PEOPLE ABOUT GOD

In Kerala, as is elsewhere in India, people on the whole want to hear about God. In our hardships, our people are glad to be reassured of the

Witnessing as a Catholic Sadhu
Sadhu Ittyavirah

love and goodness of God. They are happy to know about Christ even when they reject the claim that outside the Church there is no salvation. Many Hindus are at heart Christians. They will tell you that there is no need to be a Catholic in order to be a Christian, just as there is no need to be a Jesuit in order to be a Catholic.

In my life as a *sadhu* I have not been trying to make converts. My idea is to help my hearers to think of God our Father and to live as his loving children.

I speak with the help of analogies taken from nature. Ordinary men do not think syllogistically; they think analogically. For instance, when I tell them that just as they are more closely related to their mother than to the shirt they wear, they are more closely related to God whom they do not see than to their mother whom they see, they seem to understand my point easily. Or when I tell them that though the sun seems to rise and to set, yet the truth is that it is the earth that goes round the sun, and in a similar way, though God seems to be a nobody, he is in fact everywhere, they have no difficulty in getting what I mean. By means of similar analogies I tell people about God's fatherly love and goodness.

Persuaded that we are first sons and only then philosophers; that before we began to ask "why," we had learned to kiss our mothers; that love is anterior to reason, my approach has been filial and *kerygmatic* rather than philosophical and apologetical. My witness has been in the weakness and helplessness of Christ in the manger of Bethlehem and upon the cross of Calvary.

The realization that we have the truth should in no way make us proud. On the contrary, it must make us all the more humble. It is the tall coconut tree, and not the lowly grass, that is rent asunder by a stroke of lightning during a thunderstorm. God gives it to the lowly paddy and wheat, which belong to the grass family, and not the majestic oak and teak, to feed millions the world over. Rice, not teak, is the staple food of the people of Asia.

We are what we are by the grace of God, and we are what we are for the sake of others. I cannot see my face. In a mirror, I can see only the image of my face, and that, too, in reverse. As such, my face is to be seen directly by others and only indirectly by myself. I cannot sit upon my shoulders. It is others I can carry on my shoulders and lift up with my hands. So I am what I am for the sake of others. Naturally, I am not to glory in what I am and what I have.

The great sin of the Scribes and Pharisees at the time of Christ was their pride, their feeling of self-righteousness and their contempt of others. We have to guard ourselves against such Pharisaical pride.

In the Bhagavad Gita, one of the sacred books of Hinduism, it is as a *sarathi*, a chariot driver, that Krishna speaks to Arjuna about the intimate relations between the *jivatma*, the individual soul, and the *Paramatma*, God. At the Last Supper, it is only after washing the feet of his disciples that Christ speaks to them in most endearing terms about unity and love and gives them his commandment of fraternal love.

In Kerala, I have observed, every mother teaches her little son to make the sign of the cross and to pray after making him sit comfortably in her lap. The gospel must be proposed in a like spirit of humility and love.

We will not care to listen to a singer, however charming his songs may be, if he wants to sit on our back while he sings. If a priest wants to be lifted high on the shoulders of his parishioners for his sermons, they will show no interest in his sermons. If they try to run away from him, let him not say: "These devils have no mind to hear the word of God."

NEW APPROACH IN PREACHING THE GOSPEL

In the East, the gospel was often preached from the vantage point of power. For long it was associated with colonial powers and with power politics in the West. This has to a certain extent prejudiced the people of the East against the gospel, though at heart they long for it.

Water is good for plants. But if we pour it—be it even the living water come down from heaven—from a height of fifty feet, at the root of the plant, the plant is bound to be uprooted and destroyed. The gospel preached with the trappings of power and in the phraseology of *scientia subtilis* tends to produce similar results.

I am reminded of an incident in my life when I was a boy ten years old. One day I had gone to a neighbor who was a farmer. He was watering his tapioca plants by means of two pitchers. I offered to help him, and taking hold of one of the pitchers, I filled it with water from a pool. Then, without bending low, I poured the water on a plant. In doing so, I almost uprooted it. My neighbor saw this and came running to me saying, "Oh no. Not that way. You must pour like this, bending low." Stooping forward, he watered another plant and showed me the right way to water.

There is an object lesson for Christian witnessing in what that farmer taught me on that day. We have to bend low in order that the living waters may not become killing waters in our hands. In our thinking,

Witnessing as a Catholic Sadhu
Sadhu Ittyavirah

in our expressions, in our mode of life, we have to be prepared to bend low, for self-emptying, in order that our Christian witness may be life-giving and efficacious. Our concepts, our manner of life, our witnessing, must be adapted to the people.

We are not to be surprised if the sheep run away from the shepherd when he goes to them dressed like a wolf. Or take another example: Our body needs sodium and chlorine. But if they are given us separately, and not as common salt, we will get sick and may even die. The "salt of the earth" can also be killing if not administered properly.

We have to be careful about our mode of presenting the gospel. The scholastic method is distasteful to the people of the Orient. In religion, they expect the simplicity of the manger, the renunciation of Calvary, the forthrightness of the Sermon on the Mount. Our theological formulations, our circumlocutions, our hair-splitting distinctions, are distasteful to them.

It was with similes and in parables that Christ taught. He seldom spoke philosophically. He gave no philosophical arguments for the existence of God. His witness was filial. He spoke about the Father, not about the *Ens a se*. You cannot love the *Ens a se*. With the Infinite and Supreme Being the finite and contingent being cannot have any dialogue. Christ came to give us a lesson in dialogue with the Father, not to give a philosophical and theological exposition of God. There is no subtlety in his teaching.

Such has been the mode of teaching of the *rishis* and *bhaktas*, the sages and devout people of the Orient, too. They too have taught in analogies and parables. It is good to remember that ordinary people think analogically rather than philosophically.

METHODS OF TEACHING

In my peregrinations as a *sadhu*, I too have been talking to people with plenty of similes and parables.

To a group of villagers I may speak like this: "You have your head and hands. Seemingly, the head is an idler, it does no work. Yet really it is the head that does much more work, though the work of the hands is more easily seen. You can live without your hands. But you cannot live without your head. In the same way, God seems to be doing nothing for us. Yet it is he who helps us much more than anybody else. You see me. But you don't see your eyelids just in front of your eyes. Similarly we do not see God, who is always present with us.

"You have your clothes, and you must take good care of them. But for your parents you must have greater concern. You can buy clothes, but you can't buy parents. Your face will never be like the clothes you wear. It will always be similar to those of your parents. With your clothes, you have only *samipya*, extrinsic nearness, whereas with your parents you have *sarupya*, intrinsic nearness.[1] In the same way, though God remains unseen, we are more related to him than to our parents.

"If I ask you whether it is the earth or a bus that moves faster, you may feel like saying that it is the bus, as you can see the bus moving, while the earth appears to be still. Yet the earth in its apparent stillness is traveling faster than a jet plane. Similarly God appears to be unconcerned about us, though it is he who is most concerned about us. You cannot remember your birth, but you can remember your marriage. You can marry a second time after the death of your first wife, but you cannot have a second birth and a second mother. In the same way, we cannot remember our birth as children of God before our birth from our parents."

To a group of school children, I may speak in this way: "You are now *in* the school. But you are not *of* the school. It is from your home, which you cannot see now, that you come. In the evening you will return home. You cannot remain here in the school all the time. In the same way, though we are *in* the world, we are not *of* the world. One day we will have to go from this world, to a world we don't at present see. In school you have teachers who love you. You can see them here, and perhaps they call you 'my children.' But they are not your real parents. Your teachers don't love you as much as your parents love you, though in the school you cannot see and hear your parents as you can see and hear your teachers. You are first of all children of your parents, and then only students, even when you are in school. Similarly, we are first of all children of God, even though at present we cannot see him. Your parents loved you before your teachers began to love you. Just so, God our Father loved you before your parents could love you. You are first of all his children, even as you are your parents' children before being your teachers' children."

This is the way I have been telling people about our Father's love and goodness, and they have always listened to me with attention. On many occasions I give anywhere from five to eight lectures a day.

---

[1] In Hinduism, four kinds of nearness are mentioned: *salokya*, presence in one and the same place; *samipya*, contiguity; *sarupya*, resemblance; *sayujya*, living unity. The first two kinds are extrinsic; the other two are intrinsic.

Witnessing as a Catholic Sadhu
Sadhu Ittyavirah

I have no institutions. I do not remain permanently anywhere. In *sadhu* fashion I go from place to place, meeting people on the human level with the love of a brother.

My work is primarily a work of prayer, in the sense that I pray for all just as a mother prays for her children, even when they are far away from home. As Christ prayed from the cross, I pray for all. Now, for instance, I am praying for all those who may be hearing this paper. Again, mine is a work of presence. Where atheistic propaganda is trying to wedge its way in, I try to be present as a humble witness to the love of the Father.

Mine is a work not only of the spoken word, but also of the written word. I am persuaded that books, because they work like a chain reaction, can also do a lot of good. I have been writing books, both in English and Malayalam (the language of Kerala) and distributing them, sometimes freely, in the course of my peregrinations.[2] Besides, I have been writing regularly in eight magazines and newspapers in Kerala. So far I have published more than two thousand magazine and newspaper articles in Malayalam. Moreover, I write many letters in an attempt to console people in distress.

As a *sadhu*, I have had occasion to meet many people. I thank the Father for allowing me to share their bread and board, joys and sorrows, in a spirit of Christian involvement and love. I would like to share with you some of my observations and reflections, based on personal experience.

RELIGION IN THE EAST

Religion is very deep-rooted in the East. Religious values have greater significance than political and economic values. With people in the Orient, for all the propaganda atheistic materialism makes, *sannyasa*, the life of total surrender to God, is held in great esteem.

Vivekananda, a great modern Hindu thinker and *sannyasi*, has said:

> I have been in the countries of the West and have traveled through many lands of many races, and each race and each nation appears to have a particular ideal—a prominent ideal running through its whole

---

[2] Published works: *The Witness, Echoing the Father's Love, To the Father, 1 + 1 = 1, Solving the Food Problem, Redeeming Pain, We Are One*. In addition to these books in English, a number have also been published in Malayalam. All are available from St. Thomas Press, Palai, Kerala, India and from Deepika Book House, Kottayam 1, Kerala.

life; and this ideal is the backbone of the national life. Not politics, not military power, not commercial supremacy, not mechanical genius, furnishes India with that backbone, but religion, and religion is all that we have and mean to have.

I think these words are applicable not only to India but to the whole of the East.

In India, according to traditional Hinduism, sannyasa is the last of the four ashramas, the stages or periods in the life of man as a pilgrim here on earth. These are called brahmacharya, garhasthya, vanaprastha and sannyasa.[3] During sannyasa, a man takes to a wandering mode of life. He does not remain attached to any particular place, whereas during vanaprastha he lives a retired life, giving himself to the practise of sadhana, spiritual exercises. A sannyasi follows more or less the mode of life of Christ during his public ministry. He can say with Christ that he has no house of his own, though in a way all houses are his. Once I asked a sannyasi where his house was. He pointed to his body as his house. The sannyasi keeps moving from place to place as a witness to God's love. He tries to be meek and kind to all.

Many Hindus in India look upon our religious who live in monasteries and regular communities as living only in the vanaprastha stage. There are some who hold that our religious are stagnating, instead of making progress to sannyasa, as if the apostles had pitched their tents around the empty tomb of Easter Sunday and lived there for the rest of their lives singing the praises of Christ.

The sannyasi, with his life of simplicity and absolute trust in God, has a great appeal in India. True, there are false sannyasis who make sannyasa a career, a way of living. But even their presence has not undermined the faith of the people in sannyasis. This shows their profound respect for sannyasa. Often people from the West seem to identify sannyasa with the saffron dress, even as people in the East often identify the Catholic priest with his cassock. This is not correct. Sannyasa is much more than mode of dress or mendicancy. It is something dynamic, even as the power of Christ dying upon the cross. If a sannyasi keeps moving, it is not for a bowl of rice. His itinerancy is in fact an indication of his total involvement with the world.

[3] Brahmacharya refers to childhood and youth, when the young person is devoted to study of the Scriptures and the sciences and to the practice of virtue; garhasthya is married life; vanaprastha is the life of retirement; sannyasa is the life of renunciation and absolute trust in God.

Witnessing as a Catholic Sadhu
Sadhu Ittyavirah

THE EXAMPLE OF GANDHIJI

Gandhiji had such a great appeal in India because, besides being a politician, he was a true *sannyasi*, though he never wore saffron. He lived frugally. His was a life of prayer and renunciation. He considered his political activities as a *karmamarga*, a way of duty for God-realization. For him, his prayer meetings were more important than his political meetings. To quote his own words:

> I am a man of faith. My reliance is solely on God. But for my faith in God, I should have been a raving maniac. It is at God's behest I have become a servant of India and of humanity, and it is only at his behest that I can relinquish that charge. What I want to achieve, what I have been striving and pining to achieve these thirty years, is self-realization, to see God face to face, to attain *moksha*. I love and move and have my being in pursuit of this goal.

He was fully conscious of his involvement with the world, and he took upon himself the sufferings of his people. He worked hard to achieve the independence of India. He was not sorry because he did not have the military powers of a Napoleon or an Alexander. He found his novel method of *satyagraha*, nonviolent resistance, suited to the genius of the people of India, and he won independence for India. He taught us Indians that we do not have to feel inferior to anybody, that the dove is not to feel sorry because it cannot gallop like a horse, when God has given it wings to fly. He urged us to make use of our resources efficaciously and to live a happy life in gospel simplicity. A watch, a pair of sandals, a few books, a pair of spectacles and some other items of this type were all that he had in the way of personal belongings upon his death.

If we go to Gandhisamadhi, the place of Gandhi's cremation, at Rajghat, in New Delhi, we will find for his epitaph his last words, "Ram, Ram!"—"My God, my God!"—a symbol of the eternal longing of the East, and in fact of the whole creation, for God. There we do not find any mention of his great services to the nation.

Gandhiji was a typical *sannyasi*, in whom the traditions of the past and the aspirations of the present were happily blended. What people in the East, especially in India, look for in the lives of the religious is such a synthesis. In many *sannyasis* and *sadhus* this ideal is not realized. It is up to us Christians, and especially the religious, to show that in us such a synthesis and such a redemption are feasible through the power of the Father, even as it was in the life of Christ.

RELIGIOUS LIFE MUST BE REDEMPTIVE

In Christ is the bridge between spirit and flesh, grace and nature, heaven and earth, eternity and time. He was not a hermit who lived away from the world, unconcerned about its good and evil, absorbed in contemplation of the Absolute. Though he was from the Father, he knew that he was in the world. He knew the Father; he also knew the world. He loved the Father; he loved also the world—so much that he laid down his life for it.

In Gandhiji, religion and politics achieved a similar synthesis. It may be said that he gave politics its soul and that he redeemed it. We religious have likewise to be redeemers. Religious life has to be dynamic. It has to be a living force that can change people and redeem them from their slavery. It has to be redemptive. We are not to witness unto the *Verbum divinum*, but to the *Verbum caro factum*, to the *Deus homo factus*. As such, we must be concerned about the problems of man in this world and all forms of human activity. We have to be prepared to take upon ourselves the woes of our people. Their problems must become our problems.

In the East, especially in India, though we have political freedom, to a great extent we still have economic and scientific servitude. This lack of economic, social and scientific equilibrium is not conducive to world peace and order.

We religious, witnessing to the redemptive life of Christ, must work to help the people in the East to win scientific, economic and social independence, just as Gandhiji worked to win political independence for the people of India. People in the East must be helped to make their specific contributions in the realm of economics and science. They should be encouraged to know their own resources and make an efficacious use of them, and enabled to develop from receiving sons into bestowing fathers.

In the East we have great possibilities. It is a great pity our people in the East are never able to recognize and make use of them. Our religious must encourage our people to see the potentialities God has given them to solve their problems for themselves. In the Bhagavad Gita (2.3) Krishna exhorts Arjuna: "Arjuna, you are the terror of your enemies. Be manly. Don't be a coward. Get up and leave aside your faint-heartedness." Even so, we must help our people to rise to self-confidence and a feeling of human dignity as the children of God.

Witnessing as a Catholic Sadhu
Sadhu Ittyavirah

THE CENTRAL PROBLEM

The chief problem of Asian countries is the problem of food. The great majority of our people are underfed and live on subnormal rations. We should therefore do pioneer work in the line of food production, with the love of a mother for her starving little ones, as Christ in his pity for the multitude multiplied the loaves of bread, or as he prepared even after his Resurrection a nice repast for Peter and John on the shores of Gennesaret. We must not think we are incapable of doing something like this. Gregor Mendel did not have first-rate equipment for his program of study and research. He experimented with garden peas and formulated the laws of heredity that have won him world recognition.

Christ was born in a manger. Mary, our mother, did not require any elaborate labor room to give birth to her son. The manger and the swaddling clothes were quite enough for her. All great inventions and discoveries are made in circumstances analogous to the finding of Christ in the manger by the Magi. There is a measure of simplicity and poverty about them. Faraday needed only a cigarette tin, a bar magnet and a coil of wire to invent the dynamo and to usher in the era of electrical engineering. If we are prepared to do pioneer work, we religious can make like discoveries and inventions.

Present-day methods of extensive and intensive cultivation alone will not be able to solve the food problem. The dearth of books was met not be multiplying the number of copyists but by the invention of printing. In the same way, the food problem is to be solved by learning the food production techniques of nature and gearing them to our industrial methods of mass production, and by producing food artificially. All the constituent elements of our food—carbon, nitrogen, hydrogen, and so on—are found in nature in abundance. We have to learn how to synthesize these, and then we will have food in abundance.

I wish our religious would do pioneer work in this line, as the monks of old in Europe worked for the good of the people. For your information, I may tell you that for nearly a year I have been doing a series of experiments in this line and have published a book entitled *Solving the Food Problem*. I have only made a beginning. Maybe it is a long way from the goal. Nevertheless, I believe that the artificial production of food is possible, and God will give us the joy of finding it if we keep up the search.

TWO PHASES OF THE RELIGIOUS LIFE

Such a line of work is not to be considered as foreign to the mode of life we have embraced. For us religion is not a way of living, but a witness of love. As such, it should be capable of adaptation and ready for change. Religious life is not confined to one phase only. Just as a tree has to be heliotropic and geotropic, turned toward the sun and also toward the earth, so we have to be turned both toward the Father and toward the world. Such was the life of Christ. Such ought to be our life.

The higher the branches and leaves of a tree grow, the deeper its roots and rootlets have to strike into the dark recesses of the soil below. To ascend to the Father, the Son has to descend to the world. Religious poverty and renunciation are not a repudiation of the world but an indication of total involvement with the world, even as Christ's death was the prelude to his glorious Resurrection.

Besides being the beloved of her husband, a married woman is the mother of her children and the mistress of the house. Beside attending to her husband, she must attend to her children and to the house.

A son is not to remain forever in his mother's womb, where he began his life. He has to come out. His life is not to be centered in his mother forever. It has to be mother-centered, brother-centered and home-centered too. He must love his parents, his brothers and sisters, and the things in the house. Along with his sonship he has his membership in the family. It is by taking similar interest in the affairs of the world and in the problems of our brothers that we shall grow from being sons to being fathers.

CONCLUSION

If this talk of mine helps all of us to grow in this way, I shall be blessed. I wish it may do so. It has been my great joy to meet you all in the love of Christ. Thank you for your love and kindness to me. I am deeply grateful to Father Abbot Dom Marie de Floris for inviting me to take part in this meeting. In my peregrinations as a *sadhu*, I shall keep prayerful remembrance of you all. Let me, dear Fathers, have your blessings and prayers.

The peace and the joy of our Father in heaven be with us always.

Toward a Vietnamese Monasticism

MARIE-JOSEPH NGOC-HOANG, O.S.B.

This paper in no way pretends to be an exhaustive study about what could or should be a Vietnamese monasticism. That would require long research, calling for a great deal of competence. It would be more the business of the Institute of Monastic Studies that will one day, we may hope, be founded by the A.I.M. in Vietnam. My aim here is more modest. I merely wish to encourage reflection on a conscious and reasoned adaptation of Christian monasticism to the religious and cultural traditions of Vietnam. I wish also to bear sincere witness, in profound gratitude, toward all missionaries—and in particular the founders of monasteries—who have brought us the Christian religious life and who, conscious of the high mission that was theirs, have always done their best to hand on to us the ideal of the monastic life in all its purity.

That was their essential mission. They had no intention of incarnating monastic life in the flesh and blood and soul of the Vietnamese people. It is up to us monks of Vietnam to bring about, for the greater glory of God and the joy of our brothers, this final work of Christianizing both the Vietnamese culture and the Vietnamese soul. The Council has invited us to do so. It is now or never that Christian monasticism in Vietnam must become adult, take full consciousness of itself and show forth its specific originality.

Since what we are concerned with is the conscious and reasoned adaptation of Christian monasticism to the cultural and religious traditions of Vietnam, let us first see what the Church thinks about the matter. Then we shall take a look at the spiritual physiognomy of Vietnam today. And finally we shall consider what a Vietnamese monasticism could be under present-day conditions.

THE CHURCH'S THOUGHT CONCERNING ADAPTATION

Urged by the Holy Spirit, the Church has undertaken a general aggiornamento in all domains. It has invited all its sons to reflect, profoundly and serenely, on Christian living. But it has above all invited those sons and daughters whom it specially cherishes—that is to say, religious men and women, monks and nuns—to set about a serious revision, an appropriate renewal, of the religious and monastic life. In obedience to the voice of the Church, superiors of every religious and monastic institution have convoked provincial or general chapters in order to work out this appropriate renewal. The Magna Charta of this appropriate renewal of religious life is the Decree on the Appropriate Renewal of the Religious Life.

But for mission countries, we must also mention the Decree on the Church's Missionary Activity which opens up a really new era for the evangelization of the peoples and for the implantation of the monastic life. The words that occur most frequently in the conciliar documents are *adaptare, adaptatio, adaptus*. The synopsis of the conciliar texts prepared by J. Deretz and A. Nocent gives thirty-two cases of the use of these words by the fathers of the Council. (Many more could certainly be found, for it would seem that the synopsis has not drawn up an exhaustive list.)

Concerning the implantation of Christian monastic life in mission countries, the word *adaptatio* is a key word. It is my belief that it is of capital importance in the elaboration of the theology of monastic implantation, which forms part of missionary theology. Faithful to its millenary tradition, the Church of Vatican II desires that adaptations should be made everywhere and in all domains: religious life, liturgy, monastic implantation, relationships with the modern world. The Council has resolutely chosen the method of incarnation or of adaptation that was Christ's own and that the apostles continued, a method that the Church itself has frequently recalled throughout the centuries. Its basic theological principle is that grace does not destroy nature, but raises and transforms it: *gratia non tollit naturam sed perfecit eam*.

In order to save the human race, the Word of God became man. He was made in all things like to man, except for sin. Christ adapted himself to man. And in order to win all for God, St. Paul, as he says in 1 Cor. 9:19–23, made himself all things to all men.

The Church has always forbidden its missionaries to use the *tabula rasa* method. That is only wisdom. For every country existing in this

Vietnamese Monasticism
Marie-Joseph Ngoc-Hoang, O.S.B.

world necessarily has a land, men who live there, a language, a culture, traditions and a religious soul that the missionary must Christianize and offer to God. We should have infinite respect for local human and spiritual values when they are not contrary to faith and morals. It is this respect, this esteem, that touches the people and inspires trust.

St. Gregory the Great gave a very wise bit of advice to St. Augustine of Canterbury:

> There are some things, some institutions, that Holy Church graciously corrects; there are others that she gently tolerates; there are others that she seems to ignore, but it is just those things that she tolerates or pretends to ignore that she often manages to do away with, merely because she knows how to wait and close her eyes.

In view of its divine and human nature, the Church, sent to all peoples of all times and in all places, is not bound exclusively and indissolubly to any one race or nation, to any particular kind of life, to any ancient or modern custom, to any one culture. And that is precisely why it can enter into communion with every culture. The gospel has the marvelous power of adapting itself to all cultures, just as Christ has the power to take up into himself all men.

Nevertheless we must recognize that the gospel has penetrated deeply into the Greco-Roman culture, which is that of the West. And since the men who announced the good news to peoples of different cultures were themselves imbued with Greco-Roman culture, they were not always able to set themselves free from it, and especially during the colonial period.

But as it has been pointed out in *Rythmes du Monde*, from the year 1622 onward the Sacred Congregation for the Propagation of the Faith has done its best to set Catholic missions free from any undue influence of Western culture that impedes adaptations to local cultural conditions.

In 1659, Pope Alexander VII gave a series of directives to the first apostolic vicars destined for the East. And though these instructions seemed to show a new spirit, it was a spirit that had always been in the Church. One could almost say that it is connatural to the Church, for it is in its nature to be supra-cultural and supra-national. He wrote:

> Never seek, in any way whatsoever, to persuade the people you are evangelizing to change their customs, their habits and their way of living unless they be contrary to faith or morals. What is more

absurd, indeed, than to transplant France, Spain, Italy or any other country of Europe to China! Do not take our countries out there, but our faith, the faith that rejects neither rites nor customs of any people, so long as they are not detestable, but that, on the contrary, wishes to maintain and protect them. It is, so to speak, written in the nature of every man to esteem, love and extol above everything else in the world the traditions of his own country and the country itself.[1]

In 1951, in *Evangelii Praecones*, Pius XII reiterated:

From the beginnings up to our day, the Church has always followed the wise rule according to which the gospel neither destroys nor extinguishes, among the people who give themselves to it, whatsoever is good, honest and beautiful in their character and their genius. Indeed, when the Church calls to the peoples to raise themselves, under the guidance of the Christian religion, to a higher form of humanity, she does not act like someone who cuts down a luxuriant forest, respecting nothing, but destroying and ruining (the *tabula rasa* method) all that he comes across; she imitates more the gardener who grafts a pure strain onto wild stock in order that it may produce more savory and less bitter fruit.[2]

To crown this traditional teaching of the Church concerning adaptation to local cultural and religious traditions, some conciliar texts, selected from many others, may be quoted: "The Council . . . looks with great respect upon all the true, good and just elements found in the very wide variety of institutions that the human race has established for itself and constantly continues to establish" (Church in the Modern World, n. 42). Just as grace raises and transfigures nature, so the Church "takes nothing away from the temporal welfare of any people. . . . Rather does she foster and take to herself, insofar as they are good, the ability, resources and customs of each people. Taking them to herself she purifies, strengthens and ennobles them" (On the Church, n. 13). "The Catholic Church rejects nothing that is true and holy in these religions. She looks with sincere respect upon those ways of conduct and of life, those rules and teachings that, though differing in many particulars from what she holds and sets forth, nevertheless often reflect a ray of that truth which enlightens all men" (Relationship of the Church to Non-Christian Religions, n. 2).

[1] *Instructions XII*, quoted in Rythmes du Monde 10, No. 2 (1962), 2.
[2] *Ibid.*

Concerning liturgical adaptations, the Church is even more generous. Let me quote a few texts from the Constitution on the Sacred Liturgy: "She respects and fosters the spiritual adornments and gifts of the various races and peoples. . . . Sometimes in fact she admits such things into the liturgy itself, so long as they harmonize with its true and authentic spirit" (n. 37). "Provided that the substantial unity of the Roman rite is maintained, the revision of liturgical books should allow for legitimate variations and adaptations to different groups, regions and peoples, especially in mission lands" (n. 38). "In some places and circumstances, however, an even more radical adaptation of the liturgy is needed and entails greater difficulties—*profundior liturgiae adaptio* urgent. Therefore the competent territorial ecclesiastical authority . . . must, in this matter, carefully and prudently consider which elements from the traditions and genius of individual peoples might appropriately be admitted into divine worship" (n. 40). These elements are recalled in connection with music and musical instruments (nn. 119, 120), the Asian style (n. 123), sacred furnishings and vestments (n. 128), and, of course, the language of the country (n. 36).

About adaptations in keeping with local ascetic and contemplative traditions, we have the following texts:

> Working to plant the Church, and thoroughly enriched with the treasures of mysticism adorning the Church's religious tradition, religious communities should strive to give expression to these treasures and to hand them on in a manner harmonious with the nature and the genius of each nation. Let them reflect attentively on how Christian religious life may be able to assimilate the ascetic and contemplative traditions whose seeds were sometimes already planted by God in ancient cultures prior to the preaching of the gospel. . . . Worthy of special mention are the various projects aimed at helping the contemplative life take root. There are those who while retaining the essential elements of monastic life are bent on implanting the very rich traditions of their own order. Others are returning to simpler forms of ancient monasticism. But all are striving to work out a genuine adaptation to local conditions. For the contemplative life belongs to the fullness of the Church's presence, and should therefore be everywhere established (The Church's Missionary Activity, n. 18).

I have quoted these long texts from the Council in order to show you that the Church wishes to Christianize man in his depths, right to his very marrow, with his environment, his culture and every fiber of his heart, and that we have to imitate the Church in following this method of adaptation in matters of monastic implantation.

Moreover this was the method used with brilliant success by Matteo Ricci in China (A.D. 1583–1610), by Robert de Nobili in Madura (A.D. 1606–1645) and by Alexander de Rhodes in Vietnam (A.D. 1625–1645) as well as in our days, from the monastic point of view, by the late Father Monchanin and Father Le Saux in India. These great missionaries wanted to get at the roots of the souls they were evangelizing. And so they studied the language and culture of the countries to which they had come to announce the good news.

Since it is a matter of adapting ourselves to the cultural and religious traditions as they are now, I propose to say a few words about the physiognomy of Vietnam today. For it is to the Vietnamese of today that the message of the monastic life is being addressed.

PHYSIOGNOMY OF VIETNAM TODAY

A meeting point of peoples and civilizations, Vietnam today has a very painful physiognomy. In the first place, it is a country split in two and has known nothing but war—a real, atrocious and murderous war—since World War II. And it is just this cruel war that has imperiled the most precious thing that Vietnam has, that is to say, its soul, its long cultural past. The war has brought to Vietnam 500,000 Americans and 75,000 Allies.

This alien presence has profoundly modified the economic and social structures of the country. Contemporary Vietnamese society is modeled on that of the Western countries. A republic has replaced the monarchy. And it is especially among the youth of the country that we notice a frenzied enthusiasm for Western civilization. The universities and schools have programs almost identical with those of the European or American universities and schools. In town, the girls wear miniskirts and blue jeans, and they disdain the gracious traditional feminine dress so admired by foreigners. Happily, not all the girls act in this way. As to men's dress, no young man, even in the country, wears the traditional costume of trousers, a white coat and a black tunic. Only in the novitiates is it worn by the postulants. They do not dare to wear it in town because they would be laughed at for being old-fashioned.

There are some who have reacted against this rush for Westernization in all spheres. Associations now exist for the purpose of spreading the national traditional culture. But will they be able to hold out against the tide of general Westernization? The future will tell.

Vietnamese Monasticism
Marie-Joseph Ngoc-Hoang, O.S.B.

This phenomenon of Westernization astonishes me. It has spread even to the religious and monastic life. For what are our churches, our cathedrals, our monasteries, our prayers and our liturgical music? They are nothing else but churches, cathedrals, monasteries, prayers and liturgical music imported or transplanted from Europe.

I was talking to a European missionary about this, and he said: "You cannot do anything about it. The flow of history is irreversible. Vietnam will become more and more Westernized." I think he is right. And this must be taken into account when implanting or adapting monasticism, in order to avoid being anachronistic. It is a fact that all about us we see a frenzied life modeled after Western civilization. Radio, television, transistors—so many elements have penetrated even to the most secluded corners of the hamlets, which formerly knew nothing but a very tranquil life.

I also spoke about this matter to a specialist in Vietnamese cultural questions. This is how he expressed his opinion: "Do not worry. This Westernization is only skin deep. Once peace has come again, we shall get back to our own rhythm of traditional life." Personally, I think that Vietnam is in full evolution. Even when the war comes to an end, Vietnam will certainly have a quite different physiognomy. But I, too, think that the Vietnamese soul is not to be found in this superficial Westernization. In order to discover it, we must examine its fundamental religious beliefs and the philosophical and religious systems imported from China at the beginning of the Christian era.

There are at present in Vietnam about two and a half million Catholics, strongly organized, five million Buddhists, and Protestants, Hoa Hao and Caodaists, out of a total population of thirty-eight million inhabitants (of whom seventeen and a half million are in the South, and twenty and a half in the North). Thus about a third of the population adheres to one or other well-defined religion. The rest, although not connected with a definite religion, nevertheless have a religious background.

Vietnam is a very religious country. The most general and the most fundamental belief is the belief in spirits. It seems to have existed since earliest times among the people of Vietnam, as is witnessed by numerous legends. The spirits are either the souls of the ancestors venerated by each family, or else the souls of the more or less legendary heroes of antiquity. Another belief, just as general, is the belief in "heaven." By some profound instinct, the Vietnamese knows, more or less confusedly, that heaven is the supreme principle upon which all nature, and especially man, depends. Among the people, one often hears them have recourse to heaven in their difficulties.

This heaven is not the material heaven, but heaven conceived of as a personal Being, both Creator and Providence: one speaks of "Mister Heaven" as the one who causes the floods, destroys the harvest, causes rain and drought. Heaven intervenes in human life: "Heaven engenders; heaven nurtures." Life and death are in the hands of heaven: "Happiness and misery are in heaven's power." Heaven is thought of as a supreme and universal Being who examines all hearts and penetrates all man's thoughts, of which he is the most enlightened judge. In short, we may say that the Vietnamese have a very pure notion of God, one that is close to that of the Bible, and one that missionaries were quick to baptize.

Thus we see that the Vietnamese have a very rich religious sentiment, fed by two basic beliefs deeply rooted in their soul.

Among the cults, the one that dominates the spiritual horizon of the Vietnamese people is the cult rendered to ancestors. And this is even more true since the Holy See, on October 20, 1964, authorized this cult for Vietnamese converts to Christianity. This step taken by the Holy See will do much to help toward the conversion of the people, because all, without exception, are attached to this cult.

But apart from the belief in spirits and in heaven, and the cult of ancestors, the Vietnamese soul is dominated by a synthesis of three systems: Confucianism, Buddhism and Taoism.

Vietnamese culture is fundamentally Confucian, especially among the higher and the intellectual class. Only thirty years ago, our men of letters were so deeply concerned with it that they saw nothing else, with the result that nowadays no one studies Confucianism as in the past, that is, as being all that could signify intellectual formation. Confucius is studied now in the same way as one studies any modern philosopher, that is, without the veneration that men of letters felt for him.

Buddhism seeped into North Vietnam via China, though fairly transformed by the Chinese genius, in the form of the Great Vehicle (Mahayana Buddhism), and into South Vietnam via Cambodia, in the form of the Little Vehicle (Hinayana Buddhism). In the course of centuries it has acquired a number of adepts. The reason for this probably lies in the fact that the Vietnamese, being profoundly religious, find in Buddhism a method of recollection, of spiritual concentration, that allows them to experience the spirit that is their own soul; and since this spirit is open to the universal, there is a means of entering into communion with all. On the other hand, many among the Vietnamese take to Buddhism on account of its ethics, entailing

Marie-Joseph Ngoc-Hoang, O.S.B.

asceticism, purity, renunciation, gentleness and universal brotherhood with all beings.

In Taoism a twofold distinction must be made: there is the philosophical part, accessible to only a small elite; and a second part which consists in magical practices rather similar to witchcraft. Often uneducated people bound up by a certain secret initiation with dark forces offer a cult to a whole pantheon of immaterial beings.

All these religions and sects must be known, and from them we have to select and assume those elements which are compatible with Christian monasticism.

WHAT A VIETNAMESE MONASTICISM COULD BE TODAY

After all that we have considered, what, we may ask, could monasticism be in Vietnam today? Before answering this question, it should be stated that we must at all costs maintain the absolutely transcendent nature of Christian monasticism in order to avoid ending up with a distasteful syncretism under pretext of adaptation and acculturation. What is Christian monasticism if not perfect Christian living? And Christian living is essentially the life of grace, participation in the life of the Divine Trinity itself. *Ad Patrem—per Filium—in Spiritu Sancto*, here below in faith, and above in the vision face to face. The Christian monk wants to live fully his baptismal grace, his grace of adoption as God's son, and that within the appropriate setting, which is normally a monastery, under a rule and an abbot. That is what is specifically Christian. And this Christian base cannot be changed. That means that all the adaptations now about to be suggested are only means; they are not the end.

In Vietnam there is an authentic Buddhist monasticism lived by the *bonzes* and *bonzesses* in the pagodas. This monasticism, well integrated into the Vietnamese mentality and culture, is made up of a mass of observances very similar to those of Christian monasticism. Some of them must be intelligently adapted, while others may simply be adopted as they are, taking care, nevertheless not merely to copy them.

The *bonzes* and *bonzesses* live in pagodas built in local style, of medium proportions, that is, in keeping with middle class standards. They live in poverty and celibacy. Their habit is very simple: grey or chestnut color. Wandering monks wear the yellow robe of Hindu monks. They do little manual work and devote many hours to prayer, meditation and spiritual concentration. They have a keen sense of renunciation, of fasting and abstinence. Their food is strictly vegetarian.

It must be acknowledged that this monasticism has a very real value. In matters of prayer—techniques of meditation and spiritual concentration—as well as in those of poverty, we have much to learn from the bonzes.

Confronted with this deeply rooted monasticism in Vietnam, Christian monasticism—and every other form of Christian religious life—seems to be only an imported product. What can we do about it? What sort of Christian monasticism must we decide on?

1. Considering the rush for Westernization now taking place in Vietnam, the monasteries already established there can only intensify their adaptation to present conditions—intensifying their effort for effective *poverty*, both individual and collective; for *spiritual radiation* (by living an authentic contemplative life, a life of intense prayer; by becoming really spiritual men, real contemplatives); for *cultural radiation* (by uniting all their intellectual energies for the purpose of translating the Bible and books of spirituality, theology and philosophy).

It is not a very pleasant thing to have to say, but after more than three centuries of evangelization, Vietnam has not yet a complete and exact translation of the Bible. One day a German doctor asked one of our monks for a complete Bible in Vietnamese, and he was obliged to admit: "I am sorry, but we haven't yet got a complete Vietnamese Bible." What is also especially needed is a translation of the Divine Office and the liturgical texts into our language. It is by reciting the Divine Office in his mother tongue that the monk, offering to God every fiber of his heart and soul, helps the life-giving sap of monasticism to penetrate into the substance of his flesh and blood, and into his soul.

2. There is no one of our Vietnamese Benedictine or Cistercian monasteries that offers higher studies. Faced with modern Catholic youth athirst for knowledge and learning, the type of monastery that runs a college or a university would be welcome.

3. As to the new foundations, they will have to set their minds resolutely on an Oriental and Vietnamese monasticism in what concerns habit, architecture of both monastery and church, and vegetarian diet. It has been pointed out that the medieval type of monastery, with its show of power, fits in badly with our natural and psychological scenery: it risks betraying our witness of poverty. It is high time that the monastic rule be lived *in a Vietnamese manner*. But this must come about by organic growth and not by arbitrary decisions.

St. Benedict thought the monastery out along family lines. The example of the small monastery, like the one he built at Subiaco, fits in well with the idea of a middle-sized family in Vietnam. Certain pagodas have quickly taken root thanks to this sort of monastery. Within the framework of the limited dimensions it offers, it is easier to practice poverty and evangelical simplicity.

The big monasteries that actually exist in Vietnam will meet with difficulties everywhere: they require monks to leave the monastery for business matters, and one has to ask a great deal of help on all sides in order to obtain public assistance (from the Army, for example). Christian monks in Vietnam have acquired the bad reputation of being businessmen and not monks at all. The small monastery, in which it is possible to live a very simple and poor life, would do much to help monks set themselves free from the complications bound up with big monasteries of, say, two hundred monks.

But another monk pointed out to me that in our days people like to see efficacy in our life. So we must show it to them. In a little monastery of about a dozen monks, he says, not much could be done in the way of monastic formation. We need a decent staff of professors; and this is also necessary for the cultural radiation I have already spoken of—for the translation of books, for example. Furthermore, one cannot give what he does not possess. A small monastery, where a poor and simple life is led, necessarily has very few financial resources. Generally, in the neighborhood of a monastery one finds very poor people who need material assistance. Sometimes whole villages ask the monks for help. Thus he suggests a type of monastery that would be a motherhouse in Vietnamese style: no imposing buildings, yet large enough to house suitably one hundred to one hundred and fifty monks together with the novitiate. This would be the center of a large number of little monasteries like the one at Subiaco.

Yet another monk writes excellently on this subject:

> In Vietnam, several-storied buildings stuffed with little closed-in rooms are not the ideal thing: those who arrive there feel often lost and shut in. On the other hand, a little community is wanting in spiritual warmth and future prospects; it does not inspire confidence.

If we expect Vietnamese monks to personalize and deepen their monastic life, we must not go beyond a medium-sized community, harmoniously set on a piece of land that favors recollection. Whatever the case, the failings of a large building can be to a large extent corrected by a setting that creates a climate of open intimacy and reasonable freedom (varying, for example, from the setting out of a large solitary park to the discreet decoration of the corridors on each story).

4. Another project of monastic life is that which Paul VI is trying out. He aims at founding a supernatural community of persons based on the ideal of the community of the three Divine Persons. Vietnam, like many another country where Chinese culture is found, has been influenced by Confucian formalism for nearly two thousand years, and by Roman juridicism from the time of the evangelization of our country. Thus it happens that in the monasteries much attention is sometimes given to exterior observance of the rule, without equal attention to the deep inner life of the monk. One is sometimes tempted to designate as a "good monk" someone who observes the letter of the rule. But the inner meaning of monastic life is to unite the monk intimately with God. That is why Paul VI aims at living, in Vietnamese style, the community of the three Divine Persons. In such a community every human person will be harmoniously developed according to the divine measure, that is to say, will become totally "sons in the Son"—*filii in Filio*.

Paul VI envisages a return to the sources: a return to effective poverty, to the simplicity of the gospel—a return to the poverty and simplicity of Asia, of Vietnam; to the poverty and simplicity of primitive monasticism (that of Egypt and of Subiaco, where there were twelve monasteries each containing twelve monks).

In this perspective, the young monks would be sent to study in a seminary, the community would go to Mass in the parish church, and so on. As to cultural adaptation, there would be some attempt at making a synthesis of all that is beautiful and good in the spiritual traditions of Vietnam, in the three great religious systems: Taoism, Buddhism, Confucianism and in Hinduism. All these good elements would have to be integrated, insofar as possible, in order to give rise to a truly Vietnamese monasticism.

For the moment Paul VI is alone. But he has decided to attempt this form of life. His project is certainly worthy of attention. It replies to a desire coming from the Holy Spirit, one that is springing up everywhere in the world—in Europe and America as well as in Asia. He should be helped to realize his project for the greater glory of God.

To conclude these few short notes, only too brief and sketchy, I would like to ask you to pray for all the monks in Vietnam. May they be real monks, simply and purely monks, that is to say, men "all for God," men for whom God is all—the God who is to be found wholly in Christ, for in Christ there is neither Jew nor Greek, neither Westerner nor Oriental, but only brothers, sons of the same Father, who is God. Christ alone is all in all, the center of creation, of all human history.

SYNTHESIS OF GROUP DISCUSSIONS

December 13, 1968

PROBLEMS OF RECRUITMENT

Questions for discussion[1]

1. What means are used to find out something about the postulant before his entry?
2. What natural tendencies do you expect to find in a subject seeking admission to the postulancy?
3. What are the obstacles to recruitment originating in the environment: social, familial, political, religious?
4. What tendencies should be considered as favoring recruitment?

1. *Inquiry before admission.* The process begins in general with the submission of "testimonials" from the pastor of the candidate's parish or from other priests who know him. Then follows a search for information on the family background; it is often difficult, however, to rely on such information. A medical certificate is demanded, and sometimes, also, a psychological test, the results of which are compared with information from persons who know the postulant well.

2. *Tendencies required of postulants.* These group themselves around four themes, developed rather lengthily in the discussions: simplicity and sincerity; sociability and good character; good judgment and a sense of humor; strong will and balanced feelings helpful in adherence to chastity. In brief, mental and physical equilibrium, as found in the type of youth who likes sports.

Attention must be paid, however, to the fact that the monastery is made for the monks and not the reverse. This implies serious obligations for the monastery so as to assure proper adaptation and formation.

It must also be recognized that the particular tendencies of certain people make it difficult in many countries for men of different races to live together.

[1] The questions are based on the questionnaire, Part I. (Appendix B, pp. 277–278). See also the summary of replies to Part I. (Appendix B, pp. 282–296).

But being Christians we ought to be able to surmount these difficulties.

3. *Obstacles from the social background.* The first of these is a misunderstanding of monastic life still often found among the laity, and among the clergy as well, which sees no immediate efficacy in this kind of life. The materialistic and worldly spirit of modern civilization, capitalist or Marxist, leads young people to desire more attractive and lucrative professions.

On the part of families, opposition is sometimes encountered because of a lack of religious spirit. Above all, however, there is opposition for economic reasons when the postulant is able to procure material advantages for the family, or promises to be able to in the future. Such advantages are often considered in Asia as of prime importance. But in other circumstances, the same reasons could persuade a family to make sure—by exerting tremendous pressure—that certain of its members choose to enter religion or remain there, even if they have no vocation.

Converts sometimes come up against opposition from their former coreligionists. New Christians converted from certain sects rarely have those human qualities required by the monastic life. As for others, it is customary to ask them, first of all, to lead a good Christian life in the world for some years in order to take root in Christianity.

4. *Conditions favoring recruitment.* First of all, there must be no propaganda; we must be what we are, in a realistic and human manner. We should provide simple information about our environment for the young and should not be afraid to use modern means of diffusion. For this purpose, it would be good if monasteries cooperated with each other in producing the necessary documentation.

Young people are habitually attracted by retreats at the monastery, by preaching, by vocation days or by contacts with young monks returning to spend some days in their family surroundings. The monastery should also remain in close touch with priests who appreciate the monastic life and are habitually in touch with youth.

But the community itself must constantly make an effort to renew itself and adapt itself to the mentality of the young, at the same time practicing a faithful observance; for this alone attracts true vocations. The "grilles" of nuns, for example, seem archaic. Finally, the quality of the hospitality received in a monastery is very important.

A special question poses itself in certain regions where neither Latin nor a language of general culture is taught in the schools any longer. It would be necessary to establish there a kind of "seminary for late vocations" to teach Latin, together with a language of general culture and an advanced course in religion. If such institutes are founded and if they have an open spirit, there would seem to be no objection to sending postulants there.

PROBLEMS OF FORMATION

Questions for discussion[2]

1. How does the community understand the monk's vocation?
2. How long is the postulancy, and after how long is the candidate allowed to undertake a definite engagement?
3. How do you work out a synthesis of obedience and responsibility?
4. What specific aspects of fraternal relations would you like to see more evidence of?
5. How does your community put into practice its withdrawal from the world?
6. What do you think of the suggestion about a center for monastic studies?

1. *How the vocation of the monk is understood in the community.* Each monastery has its distinctive nature. Some tend to be more contemplative, others less, following their own traditions and the needs of the local Church. But this diversity is also a common trait of the Order. It has its source in the Rule itself, which allows the option of a longer silent prayer or of replacing the reading by work, according to need. In the discussion, the general desire, which affirmed itself very quickly, was to insist less on these differences than on the common characteristics of the communities, centered about the primacy of the search for God.

2. *Steps in the monastic life.* The duration of the postulancy varies. The very young sometimes need many years to achieve intellectual formation; the time is shorter for adults. Serious difficulties also arise from the fact that the conditions of the postulancy in a closed milieu scarcely permit one to know what a candidate's reactions will be when he is not under constraints.

The novitiate itself is often a life too much "enclosed in an ivory tower," something far removed from the real life led by professed religious. The situation is all the more inconvenient in that Orientals possess, in general, a great aptitude for adapting outwardly but a real difficulty in coming to a definitive commitment.

Also, in order that decisions may be taken with eyes open, it seemed necessary that there should be a very great flexibility, even a lack of precise determination of the length of different steps of the monastic life—if they are to be adapted to individual needs.

On the other hand, some of the delegates questioned the necessity of simple vows. The aspect of legal formality in them shocks certain young

---

[2] The questions are based on the questionnaire, Part I. B (Appendix B, pp. 277–278). See also the summary of replies to Part I. B (Appendix B, pp. 286–296).

people. Others remarked that they give to the professed a feeling of security that renders them freer and more natural in their monastic life. If they were to be suppressed, it would be necessary to find something else to express the acceptance of the novice by the community.

Finally, the recommended flexibility would permit the Order to envisage a "temporary monasticism," which seems to be the general rule of non-Christian monasticism in Asia and is perhaps at present the form best adapted to certain countries. It must be remarked about this proposal that there exists in the Buddhist monastic ritual a provision that has no counterpart in Christian monasticism, namely, the ceremony of blessing a monk who is returning to the world. His secular clothing is given back to him, and he asks that they pray for him in his life as a lay person.

Because of a lack of time the problems of formation were scarcely touched upon. Questions 1 and 2 received attention in some of the groups, but questions 3 to 6 had to be passed over.

PRAYER
(In English)

O thou Lord of the nations, thou who givest breath, from whom comes strength, whose command all the sons of God wait upon—thee we worship with the oblations of our minds and hearts. O thou King of the world, Lord of the two-footed and the four-footed, to whom belong the snowy mountains, the wide oceans and the mighty rivers, Lord of the whole earth—thee we worship and thee we adore. O thou who hast fixed the heavens and the earth in their paths, who hast established the sun in the firmament and filled the middle sky with air, God of the two realms, Lord of the Universe, thou art the Lord of Lords. We invoke thy blessed Name. Bless us, O Lord, through Jesus Christ thy son, who lives and reigns with you for ever. Amen.

FIRST READING
(In English)

The best man is like water.
Water is good; it benefits all things
  and does not compete with them.
It dwells in lonely places that all disdain.
This is why it is so near to Tao.
The best man in his dwelling loves earth.
In his heart, he loves what is profound.
In his associations, he loves humanity.
In his words, he loves faithfulness.
In government, he loves order.
In handling affairs, he loves competence.
In his activities, he loves timeliness.
It is because he does not compete that he
  is without reproach.

To yield is to be preserved whole.
To be bent is to become straight.
To be empty is to be full.
To be worn out is to be renewed.
To have little is to possess.
To have plenty is to be perplexed.
Therefore the sage embraces the One
    and becomes the model of the world.
He does not show himself; therefore he
    is luminous.
He does not justify himself; therefore he
    becomes prominent.
He does not boast of himself; therefore he is
    given credit.
He does not brag; therefore he can
    endure for long.
It is precisely because he does not compete
    that the world cannot compete with him.
Is the ancient saying "To yield is to be
    preserved whole" empty words?
Truly he will be preserved and will
    come to Him.

He who stands on tiptoe is not steady.
He who strides forward does not go.
He who shows himself is not luminous.
He who justifies himself is not prominent.
He who boasts of himself is not given credit.
He who brags does not endure for long.
From the point of view of Tao, these are like
    remnants of food, which all creatures
    detest.
Those therefore who possess Tao turn away
    from them.

He who knows others is wise; he who knows
    himself is enlightened.
He who conquers others has physical strength.
He who is contented is rich.

He who acts with vigor has will.
He who does not lose his place with Tao
    will endure.
He who dies but does not really perish
    enjoys long life.

—Lao-tse (*The National Way of Lao-tse*, 8, 22, 24, 33.)

SECOND READING
(In French)

God of magnificence, when my reason, which you created, did not yet know you, when my will had not yet set out on the road toward you, when I did not yet know that all things that exist in the universe strain silently toward the highest goal of existence, the feeling of the absurdity of myself weighed me down and I very much wanted to give myself up to the unconsciousness of the world of nature.

Really, I loved life and wanted to live. That was why I tried painfully to know what purpose my existence would fulfill—mine, that of the things around me, and all that is in the visible world; this desire oppressed me exceedingly. And even though this awareness of living caused me to suffer, I wanted, seeing all things in the world of nature silently obey a law that was beyond me—I wanted to return to the world of unconsciousness.

If I have begun to appreciate, in keeping with its nature, as an inalienable gift from you, this alienated faculty of my conscience, it was because I met you, a personal God, and that changed everything for me. After I had met you on the narrow path that leads to the inner depths, my reason was sufficiently filled with the knowledge of you and my will by the desire for you. Already my consciousness is going toward the springing light of your glory. And your creature has spoken almost familiarly with you, O personal God.

—Japanese student witness

SIXTH DAY

Saturday, December 14

There is evidently no single solution valid for every place and all times. The diversity of mentalities, milieus and values, in the context of an evolving society, imposes on the Church a corresponding diversity of missionary approach and Christian presence.

—Archbishop D. S. Lourdusamy

Brahma Vidya Mandir: Monastic Experiment

SISTER SHRADDHANANDA BAHIN

It was nine years ago, on March 25, 1959, when Sri Vinoba Bhave, one of the most outstanding personalities in India today, saw his long cherished plan fulfilled: to establish a place for spiritual life for women in India.

Vinoba himself, like St. Benedict, had in his youth left home and study for the sake of *Brahma Vidya*. *Brahma Vidya* means *cognitio Dei per experimentum*. When he gave to his foundation the name Brahma Vidya Mandir, "House of the Knowledge of God," he expressed thereby his own high aspiration and the purpose of the ashram, as well.

The foundation group was formed by twelve young Indian women who were working with Vinoba in his country-wide Bhoodan movement (land reform on a voluntary basis, and uplift of the village community). These women had already left behind careers and important jobs in order to serve the poor and oppressed people in their country. Now they were inspired by Vinoba to devote their lives to the search for God.

MONASTIC EXPERIMENT

With the foundation of the Brahma Vidya Mandir, Vinoba went ahead of the traditional forms of monastic life in Hinduism and other religions. He made his ashram, or monastery, a place of existential experiment, where a serious attempt would be made. This experiment is still going on, and the community insists that the ideal is not yet fulfilled. But it is a thrilling experience to see how, step by step, the community is approaching the goal.

Because of my completely different background in monastic formation, it was not very easy for me, in the beginning, to understand the value of this experiment. Nearly everything we consider essential in monastic life I missed in the Brahma Vidya Mandir. But in the course of the years I have realized that actually only the exterior, the accidental form, of monastic life was different in this ashram. The center of our monastic vocation is preserved: total engagement in the search for God, the ultimate Reality.

Constitution of the community. One might have expected that Vinoba would go with the foundation group in order to initiate the young and inexperienced community into the path of monastic life. But this was not the case. He remained in far away Bihar, guiding the community only by correspondence. Two years ago he ceased even to write letters to us, when he decided to take up *sukhshma karmayoga,* "work on the level of the spirit."

One might think that he would have sent at least an experienced and mature personality with the foundation group to guarantee the continuance of his work. But it is one of the most significant symptoms of his experiment that the Brahma Vidya Mandir does not have a superior or spiritual master. It was Vinoba's intention that the community should not rely on individuals, but on the ideology.

Perhaps there has never been a founder of a religious order or congregation who did not give his followers a rule or at least a constitution. But nothing of this kind was provided for the Brahma Vidya Mandir, not even certain regulations and disciplines. Vinoba left it to the community to build up the plan of life in the ashram. He regards imposing discipline on others as an indication of weakness. Every member is expected to keep self-discipline and to act with responsibility according to her conscience, in a spirit of freedom.

One may ask what monastic life in the Brahma Vidya Mandir is like, when two of the seemingly essential elements of community life, authority and rule, are absent. Especially for any of us of St. Benedict's school, where such importance is given to the authority of abbot and rule, it is difficult to imagine that monastic life can stand without these two pillars.

In the Brahma Vidya Mandir the authority is with the community, and all the members of our ashram have expressed their readiness to surrender to the decisions taken by the community. This is our form of obedience, and we consider it a direct means to attain self-realization, perfect union with God. For the individual it may not make much dif-

Brahma Vidya Mandir
Sister Shraddhananda Bahin

ference whether he renders his obedience to a superior or to the community, but the community gains much spiritual strength when each member obeys it. It is the combined effort of all to come to a decision, to find out a solution in every situation, that strengthens the community. Obedience in this form, according to my experience, is a very constructive element in community life and a strong means of union between the members. Decisions are taken only when unanimity is achieved. In this way we are forced to be one heart and one soul; otherwise our community life is impossible. And this was exactly Vinoba's intention when he started the ashram on an experimental basis: the community must be one mind, one spirit. The main force to achieve this oneness is the power of love.

It may come as a surprise that Vinoba, who himself is a Hindu, has chosen the words of Christ to mark the goal for a community of Hindu *sannyasinis*: "Love one another as I have loved you." And indeed the spirit of love is most significant for the community in the Brahma Vidya Mandir. It is a genuine, human love for each other, accompanied by a deep respect for the freedom of conscience of every individual. Love and freedom are creating in our ashram a unique atmosphere, which inspires everyone who comes in close contact with the community.

Management and administration are distributed among the members of the community according to their capacity and inclination. At the present time there are twenty-two sisters and three brothers at the Brahma Vidya Mandir.

Principles of life. Although the founder of the Brahma Vidya Mandir did not feel the need to give a rule to the community, he nevertheless gave certain principles on which the life in the ashram should be based. These principles are called the "eleven vows." They had originally been Gandhi's "ashram observances" at Sevagram. Not the objects of a solemn promise, they are rather considered to be guidelines for our life and a uniting element for our community. For those who are not acquainted with Gandhi's ideology, I shall briefly explain these principles here. In many aspects they remind us of the fourth chapter in the Rule of St. Benedict.

1. *Ahimsa*, nonviolence. The positive meaning is love and regard for every creature of God. To use any violent means in order to achieve a certain result is against love. The principle of nonviolence does not allow us to kill animals in order to maintain our life.

2. *Satya*, truth, truthfulness, honesty, sincerity, loyalty. Gandhi con-

sidered *satya* to be the sovereign principle; it includes numerous other principles. The literal meaning of *satya* is "existence" and refers to God. God is existing in us and guiding us from within. Faithfulness to our conscience is therefore included in *satya* as well.

3. *Asteya*, not stealing. Gandhi considered it already as theft if we take things with the permission of the owner that we do not really need. We should not receive a single thing we do not need. It is against the principle of *asteya* to increase our wants.

4. *Brahmacharya*, a life devoted to the service of God. It is the first of the four stages of life in the Hindu tradition. Generally the word is translated as "celibacy." *Brahmacharya* is a condition for membership in our ashram.

5. *Asangraha*, not collecting things. It is the vow of poverty in a very concrete form, and it implies not keeping superfluous things, whether as an individual or as a community. This principle has a deep impact on our life in the Brahma Vidya Mandir.

6. *Sharir Shrama*, manual labor. This principle has its special significance in India, where manual labor is still considered to be inferior. It was Gandhi's conviction that everybody should produce what he is consuming.

7. *Asvada*, not eating for enjoyment's sake. Control of the palate is very important and not quite easy, even for spiritual people. *Asvada* is observed in our ashram very strictly; even fasting has its due place in the ashram life.

8. *Sarvatra Bhaya Varjana*, fearlessness. Conquest of fear comes through faith in God: "He who takes refuge in the Lord has no fear." Such a man can resist threats and violence even unto death.

9. *Sarvadharma Samanatva*, the equality of religions. This principle emphasizes that all religions have their origin in God, and we should not consider any other religion as inferior to our own, but we should have regard for other religions and try to see them with the eyes of their followers.

10. *Swadeshi*, solidarity with the country, especially our neighbors. As a consequence we should be content with things easily available in our own neighborhood.

11. *Sparsha Bhavana*, the removal of untouchability. This is to be striven for because we are all children of God.

Apart from the eleven vows, there are two other important principles that shape the life in the Brahma Vidya Mandir. These are *karmayoga* and *samuhik sadhana*.

Brahma Vidya Mandir
Sister Shraddhananda Bahin

Karmayoga means every kind of work necessary to achieve purity of mind. After physical labor, it includes prayer, meditation, worship and study of spiritual books.

The daily routine in our ashram includes four hours of productive work by which we try to earn our livelihood. We are working for the publication of Vinoba's books, setting type and doing book binding. Some time every day is given to work in the vegetable garden. Every member has to do two hours of household work, by which we serve each other. The remaining time, apart from these six hours of work, is free. But we should not consider it to be our time; rather we should be always ready to help each other with our study or any other kind of service.

Three times a day there is community prayer in the temple for from twenty to thirty minutes. Whoever feels inspired to come will join the prayer. In the morning, at 4:30 o'clock we chant the *Ishavasya Upanishad* in Sanskrit. At noon we chant the *Vishnu Sahasra Nama*, the thousand names of God—a litany that is a theology in a nutshell. In the evening a part of the second chapter of the Bhagavad Gita is recited in Marathi, the regional language. These prayers are the same every day. Prayer, worship, meditation, are voluntary; but if anyone neglects this side of our daily routine, his experience will be incomplete, because man achieves a conception of the Infinite only when he is in a living contact with the spirit, the Atma, within himself.

There is no fixed time for meditation. Every sister has her meditation according to her convenience, and for as long as she wants. No methodical meditation is practiced in the Brahma Vidya Mandir; rather the members should do their entire work in an attitude of contemplation, i.e., complete absorption in the work of the moment, combined with internal and external purity, and they should make a special effort to reflect these attitudes in all their work. Once a week the community assembles for fifteen minutes common meditation. This custom was introduced two years ago in order to develop the community spirit.

For study, full freedom is given to everybody to choose her own subject. The members of the community are supposed to teach each other, but if by chance some scholar is coming to our ashram, we take advantage of his knowledge. From morning till evening, classes go on in the Upanishads, Bhagavad Gita, the *Ramayana*, the Bible, devotional music, languages, even Latin. Every sister can join the study group she is interested in. Six months a year Vinoba's brother lectures on the *Brahma Sutras* with Shankaracharya's commentary, the main source of Advaita philosophy.

Samuhik Sadhana is a word coined by Vinoba. It means "collective striving for Brahma Vidya," and according to the importance he has given it, the members of the Brahma Vidya Mandir regard *samuhik sadhana* as the center of their community life. We should go the way to perfection together. Nobody should be left behind, even if it takes a longer time to progress. Not the growth of *one* individual, not the growth of *one* mind, should be our concern, rather the growth of the community mind. We should grow into one mind, into one life. It is Vinoba's and our conviction that the explosive power of this collective mind can become the saving force for mankind.

Spiritual Life. Spiritual life in the Brahma Vidya Mandir is based on the *Advaita* philosophy. *Advaita* means "not two." There is only one principle of existence, the Supreme Being, from which creation has emerged. Shankaracharya is the main representative of the Advaita school, and his philosophy influences the spirituality in the Brahma Vidya Mandir to a very great extent.

Another source of spiritual life in our ashram is the Bhagavad Gita, which sometimes is called the Gospel of Hinduism. The sisters know it by heart, and often one can hear them reciting verse after verse while working or going through the ashram compound.

Spiritual life in the Brahma Vidya Mandir is simple and sincere. Most of the sisters are *bhaktas*, devotees of the personal God, whom they love with all the affection of their hearts. With an amazing simplicity they will pray and sing whenever the impulse from within urges them. *Bhakti* or devotion, however, is considered by the more intellectually oriented *jnanis*, followers of the way of knowledge, as a transitory stage in spiritual life, one that will vanish when full self-realization is obtained. Some of the sisters in our ashram may be of this *jnani* type, who search for final liberation through the way of knowledge. Their spiritual goal is not so much union with God through love as the realization that they are identical with God. Their experience is summed up in the classical formula: *Tat tvam asi*—"That thou art."

In all the forms of spirituality, scholarly differentiations have been made about these two concepts: union and identity. Among our Christian mystics we can find authentic witnesses for both forms of research. Indeed, the word "identity," as used with such a meaning, sounds always a little blasphemous in our ears. Yet St. Paul is not afraid to state: "I live, now not I, but Christ lives in me." He identified his own life, as it were, with the life of the Lord.

Brahma Vidya Mandir
Sister Shraddhananda Bahin

I am convinced that mystical experiences are really analogous in every religion; only their interpretation, their statement, is different, since it is impossible to express them adequately in human language.

Brahma Vidya. In the beginning we heard that Vinoba has started his ashram in the name of Brahma Vidya, knowledge of God. Brahma Vidya, or better, the striving for Brahma Vidya, is the center of the life in this ashram, and all our activities are directed to this center. We came in the name of Brahma Vidya, and in the name of Brahma Vidya we are living together. Brahma Vidya is the strongest impulse for our monastic life of prayer and work and perseverance.

Brahma Vidya is not intellectual, theoretical knowledge of God; it is the experience of the all-pervading Spirit, the experience of the existence of God. This experience cannot be communicated; it is the ever new finding of one's own Self after a long period of search. Shankaracharya has described the preparatory requirements to obtain Brahma Vidya in the first chapter of his commentary on the Brahma Sutras. According to him, an aspirant for Brahma Vidya must have:

1. Viveka, discrimination between real and unreal. This is the capacity to distinguish between God, the only eternal substance, and all other things, which are not eternal. Such a discrimination is not the result of theoretical knowledge. It is the innermost experience: *todo est nada—Dios solo basta*.

2. Vairagya, nonattachment to the objects of pleasure here and hereafter. This means complete detachment from any kind of self-relation in our actions and the forgoing of any desire for merit. Only then is God free to act in us and through us.

3. Shatsampatti, the six essential qualities or "treasures." These are sama, mental and spiritual equipoise; dama, control of the senses; uparati, detachment from the pleasures of the senses; titiksha, forbearance in every kind of difficulty and hardship; samadhana, meditation; shraddha, faith.

4. Mumukshutva, desire for final salvation. It is a program for a lifetime that Shankaracharya is giving us here. It is nothing else but total engagement in the search for God. And here it becomes apparent that the monastic vocation in Hinduism and Christianity are the same: the call to the Absolute.

SYMBOL OF HARMONY

Up to now this account of my experiences in Brahma Vidya Mandir has been concerned only with the monastic aspect. Before I come to the conclusions deriving from these experiences, we have to see the other, not less important aspect of this ashram, the ecumenical aspect. Since I came to Paunar three years ago, the ashram has developed a second dimension; it has become an interreligious meeting place, and as such a symbol of harmony between the religions.

For many Catholic Christians it is quite a surprise that a nun can live alone among Hindu *sannyasinis*, sharing their life in such an intimate way. The more this ecumenical experiment becomes known in our Church, the more its significance and providential character appears.

Encounter between religions. Sympathetic, peaceful encounter between the religions is of rather recent origin. Although valuable attempts of contact and dialogue have already been made, we are still in the beginning of this venture. It is my impression that a real encounter has not yet taken place, at least not on a large scale. The dialogue is carried out by a few experts on a scientific level; but not many have ventured to meet other religions on the level of their spiritual experience, where words are no longer of great importance. In Brahma Vidya Mandir the encounter between Hinduism and Christianity takes place on the existential level. We are actually living the dialogue between the religions. This is, according to my opinion, the best way to come to a genuine understanding of the substantial values in other religions and the only way to penetrate to their very depths.

When I came to India, I had no experience or even theoretical knowledge about dialogue with people of other religions, and it seemed a big risk to start my life in India right from the beginning in a Hindu ashram. But because of many circumstances there was no other choice for me, and to my great surprise I found myself ready for interreligious dialogue—not for scholarly discussions on controversial points, but for the encounter on the level of experience.

From the first moment we realized that we are one, and this experience of oneness has been the basis of our dialogue ever since. We are very much aware of the apparent differences in our religions, but the conviction of our oneness has never been shaken. We achieved in the beginning the experience that in the depth of our existence we are united in God, and this experience has stood every test. I believe this is the only starting place from which dialogue between religions can be carried out.

Another experience in this line may be of interest. It is the process of conversion of my own thinking and feeling regarding other religions.

Brahma Vidya Mandir
Sister Shraddhananda Bahin

Certainly, I was convinced even before coming to India that non-Christians can attain salvation through their own religion. But it was quite a new experience for me to realize how very near these young Indian *sannyasinis* have come to God and how the Spirit is guiding them. And the most unexpected experience: I found Christ in them. I was able to encounter him in their hearts—even more than in many of my Christian brothers and sisters. I believe that unless this experience has become common among us, we are not qualified for the dialogue with other religions. The consequence for the dialogue of the discovery of the divine life in these people is quite evident: we are partners on equal levels. Both Hindus and Christians have to give up their complex of superiority, regardless of their deep love and high appreciation of their own religion.

Dialogue is exchange of views and experiences, and it comes to an end when one party tries to impose his own opinion on the other or to try to convince him about the uniqueness of his own religion. Certainly, regard and understanding are not the last goal of interreligious dialogue; but I regard every attempt to shake or to destroy other people's belief as a crime.

Sometimes our dialogue came to a critical point when we discussed Christ and the *avataras* of Indian mythology. I tried to explain the uniqueness of Christ and his mission on earth; but love and regard for my partners did not allow me to insist upon a truth that only faith can reveal to us. I realized that in discussing philosophical or religious subjects with members of Brahma Vidya Mandir or Hindu friends, it is absolutely necessary to speak in their terms about our religion. Otherwise they are unable to understand. Knowledge of the holy books, the philosophical schools and the spiritual literature of other religions is indispensable for those of us living among non-Christians, since we want to make the Lord's message understandable to them.

Mutual enrichment. Not seldom we find among Christians the opinion that, in the encounter between religions, it is only we who are giving anything. But according to my experiences there is a mutual enrichment, provided both the parties are ready to accept the spiritual treasures of the other religion. I have to restrict myself to my personal experiences in this regard.

In fact, I have gained very much for my monastic and spiritual life while living with my Hindu brothers and sisters in Brahma Vidya Mandir. It is not an exaggeration to say that my monastic life has found its fulfillment here. It is here that I discovered the deepest meaning of a monastic community: making the pilgrimage to the Absolute together, serving each other as your real Self and growing together into one spirit. Such a community, I feel, has its meaning in itself, not in any other exterior reason. It is a community of life and not of purpose.

It is not possible to convey through words the atmosphere of love and affection that unites the community of this ashram. Next to the joyful and peaceful atmosphere, this has been the greatest experience and enrichment for me as well as for all my guests.

The spirit of freedom in our ashram has also contributed much to my spiritual development, because it became clear to me that only in complete freedom of conscience, in full responsibility for our actions and decisions, can we gain the capacity to encounter God.

Indian philosophy and spirituality have had a deep impact on my life. The first encounter with *Advaita* philosophy somewhat changed my relations to God. The evening after our first *Brahma Sutras* class, I spent in silent meditation over the discovery of the God immanent in creation, the central idea of *Advaita* philosophy. This aspect of the Supreme Being, I believe, is one of the great contributions of Eastern religions to Christian theology. Besides this, the living contact with spiritual people in our ashram and with other friends of mine is a constant source of enrichment for my own spiritual life.

Sometimes I scandalize our Catholic Christians when I speak to them of the spiritual treasures I have found in Hinduism. They say to me: "Don't we have all this as well, and even more than this? Isn't Christ sufficient for us?" But I think this is a wrong attitude, a ghetto attitude. And besides this, it is a fascinating experience to discover the face of God in another religion. This actually is the uniting element between us in Brahma Vidya Mandir—love of the same eternal God whose face we are searching for with ardent desire. We know that time has not yet come for humanity to be united in one religion, but we believe that it is always time to unite our hearts and minds in the love of God, the Father of all.

Fulfillment in Christ. What, in turn, can Christianity contribute to the mutual enrichment? Is there anything we have to offer the non-Christian religions, which are rich themselves in manifold gifts of the Spirit?

I am omitting all the secondary contributions, of a supplementary character, which generally non-Christians will accept with appreciation.

So far we are on the level of their own religious values. But our actual and substantial offer to the great ancient world religions is Christ himself (and not merely his teaching), in whom they will find their fulfillment. We can say this only with deep humility, because Christ is not in our hands and we are very incompetent and often even untrustworthy "mediators" of his message. Our contribution to the fulfillment of these religions has only a preparatory character, the more so as Christ is already present among them, hidden, unknown. Our humble service will be to hasten the time when God fully reveals him. Again I must limit the discussion to my personal experience in Brahma Vidya Mandir. In terms of this experience—face to face with my Hindu brothers and sisters, whom I sincerely love and to whom I have to be loyal—I see a threefold way to prepare the ultimate fulfillment of non-Christian religions in Christ.

1. First of all, we must have a strong and invincible faith in the presence of Christ in these religions. Through the power of this faith, we can believe that the light of Christ in them will grow and grow until it radiates in its full splendor. To be more concrete: it is up to us to live out the great religions of Asia Christically and to prepare their fulfillment by our own life in Christ. By this means, we may hope to be able to show that Christ is present there and that he is really their ultimate fulfillment.

One day, we ourselves will come to realize that Christ's teaching is the keystone, the acme, of all the sublime findings of Asia's ingenious philosophers; that the sacred books of Asia's religions achieve their full sense in the divine Logos, whom Hindu tradition considers "incarnated" (though in a special sense) in the Vedas. Then the day will come, perhaps it will even be after centuries, when India and Asia will realize it is actually Christ whom, unawares, they were searching for; that he is their long awaited Savior; that it is he whom they have already foreseen, more or less, in their *avataras*, and whom they have ever revered in their very hearts.

2. A second means, still stronger and more effective, is to love Christ with all our heart and strength and affection in the midst of non-Christians, so that this love may finally kindle the whole world by its irresistible power.

3. The last way open to us is, by the purity of our lives, to be his witnesses through our very presence. It was Gandhi who told the Christians: "Let your life speak to us." Once I realized the power of this testimony when somebody said to me: "I believe in Christ because

you believe. I see that he means everything to you and that you have dedicated your life totally to him."

In my opinion, only these means are lawful and effective to prepare the world for its fulfillment in Christ. We have to work from inside, on the spiritual level, for the fulfillment of all religions—including our own—in Christ.

CHALLENGE TO CHRISTIAN MONASTICISM

It remains to give account of the conclusions I have come to after three years of close contact with Indian spirituality and monastic life. My experiences are of course limited; three years are far too short a time to come to definite conclusions. But one thing I realized very early: Hinduism and Hindu monasticism are a challenge to the Church, and especially to Christian monks.

It is quite evident that a great deal of misunderstanding still burdens the relations between the Church and other religions. As Monsignor Capio, pro-nuncio to India, has said:

> It is perhaps one of the failings of the Church in this country that the full spectrum of Catholic religious life has not been presented before the eyes of the Hindus. Active orders and congregations predominate. The monastic institution that concentrates on prayer, silence, and toil is unfortunately all but unknown in this ancient land, and hence the image the Church projects is incomplete and therefore less attractive.

It is thus very difficult for non-Christians to get a true picture of the Church. A real encounter between the Church and India has not yet taken place. What would enable the Church to encounter Asia in its existential religious depth would be a bearing witness to the deep spirituality in the Church, the evident manifestation of its religious and mystical experience.

Life of inwardness. It is here that the great challenge lies for us to lead a life of inwardness that will finally lead us to the experience of the divine mysteries. In the course of these three years I frequently realized that non-Christians are interested not in what we *know* about God, but in what we have *experienced* of him. While studying the *Brahma Sutras*, I was often told by my teacher that India's sacred books and philosophical systems are based on experience and that we cannot understand them fully unless we have the same experience. Such deep spiritual experience is notable in the apostles and prophets and saints of the Church. "That which we have heard, which we have seen with our eyes, which we have looked upon and touched with our hands . . . we proclaim to you" (1 Jn.: 1,3).

What we need in today's Church—especially in India, in Asia—is men who speak about God from their own experience. This is the challenge of Asia to the Church, and it is the monastic institution, especially, that is called upon to take up this challenge. If we have monks and nuns who really have the *cognitio Dei per experimentum*, our monasteries will radiate the divine light and diffuse the divine Spirit without limit.

It was Vinoba's intention, when he started Brahma Vidya Mandir, to establish a spiritual power house that would cast the vibration of the Spirit throughout India and even the whole world. What a deep influence on the life of the Church, the fate of nations and of souls, our monasteries could exercise if they were such power houses. They really could renew the face of the earth.

Integration into culture and spirituality. The second conclusion I have drawn from my three years' experience in a Hindu ashram is that the Church in the Third World has to integrate itself with the culture and spirituality of Asia. Many discussions are going on about this vital point, and some experiments in this line have already been made. But I cannot overcome the feeling that they are imitations, more or less fortunate attempts to "adapt," while the spirit still remains Western. Such adaptations do not convince, because they are not the result of an inner *metanoia*.

Brahma Vidya Mandir can contribute a valid means of judging genuine integration. Many ecclesiastical leaders in India consider the form of life in our ashram an example for our Christian monasteries. It has become a touchstone for me, in judging whether a monastery or a convent is "Indian," to ask if our sisters would like to live there. But with very few exceptions they do not stand this test. We cannot even invite non-Christians to our table, because they cannot share the food with us.

We have to go farther in our attempts at integration. Exterior forms may be changing, but we should not make them anything absolute. Spiritual integration seems to me far more important. And here, so far as monastic life is concerned, we come to the most critical point. Our monastic spirituality is completely Western. The Rule of St. Benedict reflects a purely Roman spirit, something completely alien to Asia's mentality. By its very content it will always remain a foreign body. Whoever is acquainted with Asia's monastic spirituality will agree with this statement. If we want to implant Christian monastic life into the soil of Asia's countries, it has to undergo a deep change. Only then can it take root; this is my conviction. Otherwise our Christian monasteries will remain isolated from their non-Christian brothers.

I feel that for a real integration of Christian monasticism in India it is necessary for our monks and nuns to be trained according to Asia's ascetic norms, which are entirely different from ours. Indian Christian monks should practice their prayers in Indian style; they should meditate with the help of *mantras* (holy words) and *asanas* (meditation postures). A Christian monk should be initiated into *viveka* (the fundamental distinction between the real and the unreal), into the methods of realizing ultimate Reality, the attainment of *moksha* (final salvation) and especially into *Brahma vidya*. I strongly believe that Christian monks in Asia should choose the ascetic path of Asia's *sannyasis*.

My final conclusion, as the actual consequence of my experiences, is that monasticism in Asia cannot follow the traditional path, which, in many aspects, is being questioned even in Europe. A new way is to be searched for, one that is truly Christian and truly Asian. It cannot be less than a new creation in the spirit of the gospel and of the great heritage of Asia's countries. I am completely aware that this is a tremendous venture, but I believe that the time has come to set out toward new horizons.

The Place of Monasticism in the Ecclesial Community

ARCHBISHOP D. S. LOURDUSAMY

The scholars who have addressed this assembly before me have already read learned papers on the subject matter of our conference. As for me, without pretending to give in any way new insights or shed more ample light on it, let me just give my personal witness to the problem under consideration.

I shall consider the matter in three parts. First I shall show the relation between the Church and monasticism, or how monasteries are incorporated in the ecclesial community. Secondly, I shall make a few suggestions for the renewal of monasteries as a means of their better incorporation into the Church. Finally, I shall show how monasticism is providentially a steppingstone for encounter with the ancient religions of the East, especially in India.

HOW MONASTERIES ARE INCORPORATED IN THE ECCLESIAL COMMUNITY

Contemplation as the goal and essential element of the Church's life, and monasticism as its contemplative institution. The Church "is a kind of sacrament, or sign of intimate union with God, and of the unity of all mankind. She is also an instrument for the achievement of such union and unity"—so the Constitution on the Church (n. 1) sums up the Church's nature and mission. Man was made and the Church constituted for the union of men among themselves and for their union with God himself, namely, for a life of contemplation. This is the glory of God and the supreme bliss of man. To attain it, man made in the image and likeness of God must seek and discover him, respond to his call and realize union with him in knowledge and love, in adoration and praise, in dedication and service. This man must do not only as an individual, but as a member of the community of men. Now, the community essentially set up for this end is the Church. It is a community united with God in the risen Christ through the Spirit. And as such it is a sign and instrument of mankind's union with God, dedicated to the adoration of the triune God, standing as the witness to man's supreme goal and essential duty. The contemplative life of the Church is also an anticipation and foretaste of its eternal existence in the bosom of the Trinity.

Every man is made for contemplation of God; the call to contemplation is addressed to every Christian by virtue of his baptism, and the whole Church as a community is dedicated to this supreme task. Some members, however, receive a special grace to undertake it as their main apostolate to contemplate and adore God in the name of the Church and mankind. Thus monasteries are the contemplative institutions of the Church and stand as living signs of its contemplative goal and role. That is why Popes and Councils have not hesitated to emphasize the value and necessity of the contemplative life. In an allocution on October 20, 1960, Pope John said: "How precious is contemplative life in the eyes of God, how precious to the Church. . . . It constitutes one of the fundamental structures of the Holy Church." And Paul VI, in his discourse at Monte Cassino on October 24, 1964, said: "The monk has a very special place in the Mystical Body of Christ." The Decree on the Missionary Activity of the Church has a stronger expression: "Contemplative life belongs to the fullness of the Church's presence and should therefore be everywhere established" (n. 18). Here contemplative life and monastic life are equated and identified; and they are given a place within the mystery of the Church among the elements necessary for the fullness of its presence.[1]

Community nature of ecclesial life and the monastery as the privileged realization of it. The relationship between the Church and monasticism can also be illustrated by the fact that monasteries are evident signs of the authentic community life that characterizes the Church. The monks living together as a single family bound by fraternal charity and guided by the father abbot exemplify in themselves and radiate around them the essential reality of the Church. The Rule of St. Benedict (Chap. 72)

[1] Cf. J. Leclercq, "The Contemplative Life and Monasticism in the Light of Vatican II," in *Gregorianum* 47 (1966), or *Cistercian Studies* 2 (1967).

on the good spirit of the community is an echo of the gospel ideal of the community life:

> Let monks practice with fervent love the good zeal that separates from vices and leads to God and life everlasting: that is, let them in honor anticipate one another; let them bear most patiently one another's infirmities, whether of body or character; let them endeavor to surpass one another in the practice of mutual obedience; let no one seek what is useful for himself, but rather what is profitable to another; let them practice fraternal charity with a chaste love; let them fear God, let them love their abbot with sincere and humble affection; let them prefer nothing whatever to Christ; and may he bring us all alike to life everlasting. Amen.

That is why the Decree on the Appropriate Renewal of the Religious Life (n. 15) makes a comparison between the ideal Christian community life lived by the primitive Church and the fraternal life that religious and monks should strive to lead:

> The primitive Church provided an example of community life when the multitude of believers were one heart and one mind (cf. Acts 4:32), and found nourishment in the teaching of the gospel and in the sacred liturgy, especially the Eucharist. Let such a life continue in prayerfulness and a sharing of the same spirit (cf. Acts 2:42). As Christ's members living fraternally together, let them excel one another in showing respect (cf. Rom. 12:10), and let each carry the other's burdens (cf. Gal. 6:2). For thanks to God's love poured into hearts by the Holy Spirit (cf. Rom. 5:5) a religious community is a true family gathered together in the Lord's name and rejoicing in his presence (cf. Mt. 18:20). For love is the fulfillment of the law (cf. Rom. 13:10) and the bond of perfection (cf. Col. 3:14). . . . In fact, brotherly unity shows that Christ has come (cf. Jn. 13:35; 17:21); from it results great apostolic influence.

Evangelical counsels strengthen this relationship. Another means of incorporation into the Church is also open to monks by the profession of the evangelical counsels. The monks, as religious, are more intimately united with the Church under the new and special title of the evangelical counsels, and because of this intensified union they espouse the cause or mission of the Church more than anyone else. In the words of the Constitution on the Church (n. 44):

> By the charity to which they lead, the evangelical vows join their followers to the Church and her mystery in a special way. Since this is so, the spiritual life of these followers should be devoted to the welfare of the whole Church. Thence arises their duty of working to implant and strengthen the Kingdom of Christ in souls and to extend that Kingdom to every land.

The monasteries are to be not only missionary centers but "seedbeds of growth for the Christian people" (Decree on Religious Life, n. 9).

Contribution of monasteries to the life and growth of the Church. Their place in the ecclesial community can also be seen from the important contribution they make to the Church's life and the special functions they fulfill in its bosom. "The monks who assiduously fulfill the duty of prayer and penance," said Pius XI in his apostolic letter *Umbratilem* (1923), "contribute much more to the increase of the Church and the welfare of mankind than those who labor in tilling the Master's fields." This was echoed by John XXIII in a letter addressed to Cardinal Cento:

> Time and again we have spoken of the apostolic yield of contemplative life. . . . We now want to affirm that the Church, for all her being urged on the active apostolate so necessary in our day, still attaches a far greater importance to contemplation, particularly in our day when people insist so much on external activity. . . . Those who endeavor to live this hidden aspect of Christ's mission practice the apostolate in an eminent degree even though they do not devote themselves to any external work.

It is not out of place to repeat here the message of praise addressed to them by the Decree on the Religious Life (n. 7):

> Members of those communities that are totally dedicated to contemplation give themselves to God alone in solitude and silence through constant prayer and ready penance. No matter how urgent may be the needs of the active apostolate, such communities will always have a distinguished part to play in Christ's Mystical Body. . . . They offer God a choice sacrifice of praise. They brighten God's people with

the richest splendors of sanctity. By their apostolic fruitfulness they make this people grow. Thus they are the glory of the Church and an overflowing fountain of heavenly graces.

The Decree on the Missionary Activity of the Church pays high tribute to monks when it asserts: "Religious communities of the contemplative and active life have so far played, and still play, a very great role in the evangelization of the world. . . . By their prayers, works of penance and sufferings, contemplative communities have a very great importance in the conversion of souls." And the contribution of the Benedictine family was singled out by Paul VI, in his discourse of October 24, 1964, as "the faithful and zealous guardian of the treasures of Catholic tradition, a workshop for the most patient and vigorous ecclesiastical studies, a training ground for religious virtues and, above all, a school and a model for liturgical prayer."

The fate of the Church associated with and reflected in monasticism. The fate of the Church, its growth or decline, its states of fervor and tepidity, are all reflected as in a mirror in monasticism. Today, the Church has reached a crossroads; this is a watershed of its history as surely as was the eleventh century or the sixteenth. It is a critical period that can resolve itself for the Church into a long era of contraction and diminution of influence or into a new birth, a second spring of relevance and creativity. This chiaroscuro of hope and trepidation is projected in the history of monasticism since the war. In the West there was a great increase of vocations to monastic institutes, the Trappists being the main beneficiaries. Protestantism, traditionally so hostile to the monks, broke new ground with the foundation of the community of Taizé, which has since extended to the United States. At the same time, Mount Athos, a cradle of Eastern monasticism, is being depopulated with frightening rapidity.

Monks today are entitled therefore to a sober optimism; but no more than any other Christian can they take refuge in a facile complacency. They can take comfort from Vatican II, which reasserted the age-old values of contemplative life and of monasticism, but they must also answer the Council's challenge to renew and adapt themselves.

It is . . . significant that Paul VI took the opportunity, during a Council that has devoted itself to increasing our knowledge of the meaning of the Church and her work in the world today, of publicly reaffirming the historical and perennial importance of monasticism, by raising St. Benedict, father of the monks of the West, to the dignity of patron of Europe. The solemn speech made by the Pope, at the moving ceremony held in the reconstructed abbey of Monte Cassino, is an authoritative expression of what the Church thinks of the monastic life and what she expects from the monks of today and of the future.[2]

Conclusion. All that I have said can be summed up in one of the principles of monastic spirituality:

> In the Church, monastic life is not a ministry nor a particular function different from the sacerdotal or married state; it is based not on a particular sacrament; what is specific about it is that it is situated not in the order of the sacramental signs, but in that of the realities of grace signified by the sacraments. It is simply the place where everything is organized in order that the means of sanctification of which the Church has received the deposit may bear all the fruits of life in the Spirit. That is why monasticism is truly situated in the heart of the Church, whose whole mystery it in some way recapitulates. The monastic institution represents the manner of living that the Church, mistress of perfection, proposes to a man who does not want merely to live, but wants to develop in himself, by his own free consent, the germ of grace deposited in his heart by the proclamation of the Word of God and the celebration of the mystery of cult. Under this title, monasticism constitutes the most interior aspect of the ecclesial tradition and takes on the value of an example for every Christian.
>
> On the other hand, in the measure in which practice of the means of sanctification has borne fruit in the monk, he enjoys, thanks to his prayer and holy life, as every friend of God, a very efficacious power of intercession, which constitutes a spiritual priesthood. At the same time, the holy monks and the monastery where they live exercise, by the radiation of the spiritual beauty that emanates from it, a powerful attraction to souls and help to introduce these souls to the mystery of the kingdom of God, whose secret presence on earth they manifest.[3]

[2] Paul Molinari, in Supplement to *The Way*, May 1966, p. 36.
[3] *Principes de Spiritualité Monastique* (Abbaye de Bellefontaine, 1962), pp. 18–19.

Monasticism in Ecclesial Community
Archbishop D. S. Lourdusamy

CONDITIONS FOR BETTER INCORPORATION IN THE CHURCH

The Church is engaged today in an all-round and deep-level renewal. Since the fate of monasticism, through the centuries, has been associated with that of the Church, an imperative condition for its continued and better integration in the Church is a program of updating and renewal of monastic life.

Basic elements of monasticism to be preserved. There are certain elements that seem to be basic to monasticism in whatever age or civilization it finds itself. It would seem that such basic elements, however they be renewed and adapted, must be present if monasticism is to be itself and to deserve its name.

The monastic life, developing as it did from the eremitical life, is always in some way a *fuga mundi*, a flight from the world. We must understand very well what the "world" means. Too often it has been identified with the material elements of existence, as if these were inherently evil. In practice the world has too often meant ordinary life outside the cloister. We must interpret the word "world," as St. John so often does, in the sense of something organized against God. The *fuga mundi* means basically a fear of sin and of everything, however good it may be, that could be for an individual an occasion of sin. Karl Rahner has pointed out that unless a person appreciates the goodness of an ordinary existence, unless he is in love with life, he cannot make an authentic renunciation of that life. For him entrance into a monastery or religious life would be no more than an escape from the challenges of ordinary existence, an option for security and mediocrity.[4]

As a *fuga mundi*, monastic life has an essentially eschatological dimension. It is an anticipation of death and resurrection, of a *transitus* through which all are destined to pass, and through which we must pass with Christ if we are to enter into eternal life. In the atmosphere in which eremitical and monastic life developed, martyrdom was regarded as the supreme form of Christian death, the most perfect configuration to Christ, the most perfect imitation of him. Monasticism was a substitute for martyrdom. In the Celtic churches it was referred to as a white or green martyrdom. It thus aimed at the consummation of Christian life.

The fact is that monasticism is not a distinct life lived along with or parallel to the Christian vocation. A true monk is none other than a

---

[4] "Theology of the Religious Life," in *Religious in the Modern World*, p. 58.

true Christian. He is a man who takes his baptism into Christ crucified with the utmost seriousness. He spends his whole life drawing out to the full the implications of the grace of baptism. It has been pointed out in the Constitution on the Church (n. 39) that the evangelical counsels are not for the privileged few: their practice is open to all. The practice of the precepts is ordained to the practice of the counsels, the counsels being no more than the perfection of the precepts. A Christian who makes no attempt to practice the counsels will hardly succeed in observing the precepts.

What distinguishes monastic life from lay Christian life is not so much the practice of the counsels, but rather their perfect and constant practice to the extent of making two of them—those two that precisely point emphatically to the transcendent-eschatological nature of the Church—the object of a vow. If monks make this radical option, very often the reason is that this is the only way they can live their Christian life. They have to be totalitarians: total sinners or total saints. For many persons monastic (or religious) vocation is the form that Christian vocation itself must take. They are persons who by temperament are either all for God and their neighbor or all for self. There is no middle way.

Monks, therefore, through their *fuga mundi* and their eschatological preferences, are simply what Cassian calls *renuntiantes*. They are men engaged in spiritual combat with the devil, with the principle of evil, with everything opposed to God. In late Old Testament and in New Testament times, the desert was popularly thought to be the habitation of devils. Jesus is tempted in the desert. The expelled demon wanders about waterless places (Mt. 12:43). The early anchorites took this literally. They went into the desert to wrestle with Satan. They found him, however, not so much on the desert sands as in the depths of their own being. It was this theme of St. Anthony's combat with Satan that provided Renaissance artists with one of their favorite subjects. The anchorite, the original monk, the *monos*, ventured out to the desert in order to be *solus cum Deo, solus cum diabolo*. It is evident that cenobitism, the development of the anchorite life, must retain this emphasis on the overcoming of Satan in the monk's own personal life. His first job is to allow God to sanctify him.

Dangers in monasticism. England is full of ruins, monastic ruins. They stand as a gaunt warning to modern monks of the possible fate that could overtake them. To be a monk is to answer a call, but monasticism itself is not only a way of life but also an institution. Like all institutions, it experiences its periods of growth, its golden age, its decline and obsolescence.

English monasticism collapsed under the weight of the wealth that the centuries had accumulated. When you combine three elements: the physical stability of the monastery, the frugality of the monks and the generosity of the faithful, the result can be a very wealthy monastery. To this day there is nothing that causes so much resentment on the part of the local people in an agricultural society as a monastic passion for land. It was one of the insights of St. Francis of Assisi that it is not enough for the individual monk to be poor. The community as a community must be poor also. History teaches us the lesson that the accumulation of wealth is one of the occupational hazards of monasticism.

There is also a danger of estheticism. Monasteries can become museums, conservatories of medieval tradition. There can be an element of the theatricality in the recitation of the Office, a performance to impress visitors.

> Monasteries did not come into existence as a source of spiritual and esthetic pleasure for more educated and cultivated Catholics. Part of the problem current monasticism faces is that it has acquiesced to this common notion and has often made of its liturgy a theatrical performance with flowing cowls, hooded heads and ethereal chanting —much of which came from a romantic, Tennysonian concept of the medieval cloister worship, rather than a deep-felt liturgical sensitivity to what was meaningful for the spiritual life of the participating monk.[5]

There is the danger of having a whole community of priests. Must cenobites be ordained priests? If they are ordained priests, is it not a shameful waste to restrict their pastoral work? If they acually engage in pastoral work, is it possible to retain the vital meaning of monasticism as a *fuga mundi?* Is teaching a solution? It has been widely adopted by English Benedictines; but is not the role of the Church in education an issue under consideration by today's questioning Church?

Finally, there is the possibility of an invasion of influence from later forms of the religious life. One can hardly deny that the Jesuits have influenced the Benedictines at least as much as the Benedictines the Jesuits. If too many influences begin to play on the basic concepts of monastic life, it is difficult to see how this life can be reinvigorated and

---

[5] R. G. Weakland, O.S.B., in *New Blackfriars*, 1965, p. 513.

bear its own peculiar witness today. A sturdy original growth has a much better chance of making sense than an amalgam in which the lines are blurred.

Basic renewal. In general we must try today to make the monastery a sign that will be authentic, that is, meaningful, sincere and therefore effective—a sign of the kingdom of God. The monastery should be a finger pointing to the transcendence of God, reminding men of God's love, of its imperiousness, of the totalitarian demands that this love, devouring and purifying, makes in man. As a consequence the monastery has a role to play today that is peculiarly relevant. There is so much stress on the demands, the values and the validity of life on earth that we must not forget that there is a world to come. The function of the monastery is therefore to remind men that the fashion, the "scheme," of this world is passing away: the world as we experience it will not last forever, and in consequence we must use it as though we used it not (1 Cor. 7:31).

The indispensable service of monasticism, a service that pastoral work can supplement but never replace, is to remind us of the essentially nomadic character of human existence: that we are men on a pilgrimage, seeking a city with foundations, whose maker and builder is God (Heb. 11:16). How, then, are we to secure the monastery's authenticity as a sign?

The first of these means of renewal is poverty. It is evident that the monastery and all who are in it should be poor. It should be noted that Vatican II's Decree on the Appropriate Renewal of the Religious Life speaks of "communities" rather than of individual religious monks. The community is not a means by which the individual perfects himself. Rather it is the community itself, as a community, that must strive after this perfection. If the community is an eschatological community, a sign and sample of what the whole Christian community will be at the end of time, it is evident that it must be God-centered. The fine, fortress-like monasteries of Romanesque Europe bore testimony to the feudal importance of the abbot, but today such monasteries can hardly point to the kingdom of God.

The buildings, furniture, vessels, clothes and even church adornments should be simple and modest. To be poor does not mean to be dirty or ugly. It means to be unpretentious.

It may be asked whether monasteries with very many monks can be truly a community, and further whether they can be truly poor. It has been suggested that a norm of twelve to twenty monks should be

Monasticism in Ecclesial Community
Archbishop D. S. Lourdusamy

accepted, and that for training of young monks a central larger monastery might be acceptable.[6]

The poverty of the monastery will have to take into account the total life of the surroundings: the conditions of life of the nation in general and of the neighbors in particular. Friendly relations with the people of the neighborhood, an aspect of hospitality, a virtue traditionally associated with monasticism, is also part of the practice of poverty. The monks of the desert worked so as to have something to give to the poor.

Today these friendly relationships will have to be extended also to a study of the culture of the neighboring people, especially in the East. The Council's Decree on the Church's Missionary Activity several times insists on the divinely implanted elements of the various cultures and rites found among the peoples of the earth. It is part of the monk's task to investigate these, to discover any forms of local mysticism that have authentic elements, and to integrate these with their own spiritual life. To become signs to men one has to come as close to them as possible within the limits of one's vocation. This, after all, is what the incarnation is about.

A second factor is the meaning of authority and obedience—a crucial question in the Church's life today. In this matter, monastic and religious life are passing through their own aggiornamento.

The tradition of the Benedictines is to emphasize the familial nature of the community, with the leader designated as abbot, father. The Jesuits, on the other hand, have emphasized a more centralized, organized and bureaucratic type of religious life. Both concepts need clarification today.

It is well known that religious obedience originated in the master-disciple relationship between an experienced anchorite and a young aspirant for life in the desert. This concept was taken over by the cenobites. But very soon the concept was juridicized, as is evident from the additions made to the rule of Pachomius in later translations.[7] In the Middle Ages the abbot was often indistinguishable from a secular prince and was adorned with *pontificalia*. In the end he became rather a ruler than the father he originally was intended to be.

Today even the master-disciple relationship is a doubtful basis from

---

[6] Cf. G. M. Colombas, "Pour un Monastère Simple," in *Vie Spirituelle*, January 1966, p. 77.

[7] Cf. M. M. Van Molle, "Premières Règles de Vie Commune," in *Supplement to Vie Spirituelle*, February 1968, pp. 108–27.

which to begin reform. When this relationship was originally developed, the master was indeed a *magister* and had much to teach that the young man did not know. Today education is more widespread: specialization is a necessity. It often happens that in many spheres a monk knows more than his abbot.

Nevertheless, the central element in the master-disciple relationship may be retained and made the basis to build upon. In former times the master was at least an inspiration to the young man. What is needed today in monasteries is men of charismatic quality who will lead the young by inspiring them through the authenticity of their own life and experience. They must be men who can rouse enthusiasm rather than appeal to some extraneous communication of power that enables them to command. They have to be brothers among brothers, men who will not quench the Spirit but will spend their lives seeking the will of God and with their brothers bending all their energies to fulfill it.

A third factor of renewal lies in the Divine Office. In his book *Monastic Renewal*, Dom Cary-Elwes suggests that monks began to lose their influence for good in medieval society when the Office became too long, a process that began with the Cluniac reform. An English Benedictine wrote an article in the *Clergy Review* in 1966 entitled "Opus Dei or Onus Diei." In it he says:

> The Office should be so arranged that it will not be too long. There could be fewer psalms, for instance, and more pauses. In every area of liturgical life it is essential to introduce into the rites themselves more frequent and longer pauses if the liturgy is not to degenerate into mere ritualism. It has been well said that a liturgy without silence is a liturgy without a future.[8]

A generous interspersal of readings and chants with pauses will help effect a reform much needed in the Church today, namely, the reintegration of mental prayer into liturgical prayer. Dom Jean Leclercq has written a well-known article in *Maison Dieu*[9] in which he shows that the modern division between these two types of prayer was something unknown to medieval piety and that it has resulted in the impoverishment of both. In authentic Christian prayer there is a rhythm and pattern that we forget at our peril: *lectio-meditatio-oratio*. The Word of

---

[8] Cf. *Lumière et Vie*, 51, 10 (1966), 748; 72, p. 54.
[9] 69 (1962), 39–55.

Monasticism in Ecclesial Community
Archbishop D. S. Lourdusamy

God, assimilated in silence, expressing itself climactically in a final, lapidary community prayer—this is the classical structure that should be present in all forms of prayer. Where are we to find this prayer if not in the liturgy, and especially in the Divine Office?

If the Office were thus simplified and made easier to assimilate, it would become again what it originally was, the prayer of the Church. It is false to the origins of the Office to think of it merely as a prayer for the Church recited by those deputed for the purpose. In its origin it was indeed the prayer of all the local Church, at least of its fervent members. It can become so again if it is simplified and made accessible as a fount of true piety by the use of meditative pauses.

Auxiliary to the Divine Office is the *lectio divina*. The prime source of this exercise is the Bible itself. But other subjects for reading are commentaries on Scripture, liturgical texts and in general prayers and other writings with a biblical background. The monk's schedule should be so arranged that he can immerse himself in this kind of reading, which will be a continuation of—and a preparation for—the worship of God in church.

The last of these means of renewal is the eremitical way of life. The roots of monasticism reach deep into it. St. Basil reacted against eremitism, but in his rule (1, 3–5) St. Benedict made allowance for it for those who were first trained to community life. Some hermitages could be provided in every monastery, simpler than the monastery itself, to which those with the vocation could repair for a time or for life, always depending on the abbot and the community. Thus an element would be restored to monasticism that was one of its formative aspects.

In "The Night Spirit and the Dawn Air," Thomas Merton wrote:

> To be a solitary but not an individualist: concerned not merely with perfecting one's life (this, as Marx saw, is an indecent luxury and full of illusion). One's solitude belongs to the world and to God. Are these just words?
>
> Solitude has its own special work: a deepening of awareness that the world needs. A struggle against alienation. True solitude is deeply aware of the world's needs. It does not hold the world at arm's length.[10]

Part of the renewal of monasticism, as of so much else, depends on a return to the sources: *Revertimini ad fontes*. The monk, intent on

---

[10] *New Blackfriars*, 1965, p. 690.

renewal, will neglect history at his peril. He has to see the whole history of monasticism: its origins, its legitimate developments, its cancerous growths, the traps into which it has fallen in the past.

To quote Thomas Merton again, this time from "The Council and Religious Life":

> More than anyone else the monks have naturally identified themselves with the medieval culture and society built by their monastic forebears. More than anyone else, therefore, they have to recognize that if "monasticism" means purely and simply "medieval" and "western European" monasticism, it is likely to disappear. An aggiornamento of monasticism which would be nothing more than an effort to recapture the spirit and rebuild the structure of the great medieval reforms of Cluny, Citraux and the rest, can result in little more than an exercise in archaism.[11]

MONASTICISM, A PROVIDENTIAL STEPPINGSTONE FOR INCORPORATING THE CHURCH IN MISSION LANDS, ESPECIALLY INDIA

Thanks to the Council, we have become more aware that the Church is essentially missionary. And since monasticism is closely integrated into the life and mystery of the Church, and since contemplative life belongs to the fullness of the Church's presence, it is only normal that it should be established everywhere, especially in mission lands. Thus monasticism has a role to play in the missionary activities of the Church, in the proclamation of the Word and in the forming of new Christian communities in the young Churches.

Importance of monasteries in the young Churches. Pius XI wanted monasteries to go into the mission lands. In his apostolic letter *Umbrilatem* (1923), he wrote: "If the Superiors of these [monastic] orders establish houses in the mission fields, they will do something especially salutary for the multitude of the heathen, and more acceptable and pleasing to Us than can be believed." The same pontiff, in his encyclical *Rerum Ecclesiae*, urged superiors of contemplative orders "to take care that the practice of the more austere life of contemplation be introduced in the mission fields, especially among the people of the East, so naturally inclined to the life of solitude, prayer and contemplation."

[11] *New Blackfriars*, 1965, p. 6.

Monasticism in Ecclesial Community
Archbishop D. S. Lourdusamy

And now the Decree on the Church's Missionary Activity (n. 18) has solemnly invited them to go into the missions, but with the warning that since evangelization supposes acculturation, instead of simply importing their Western forms of monastic life, they should discover and integrate all the religious and contemplative traditions of the land.

> Working to plant the Church, and thoroughly enriched with the treasures of mysticism adorning the Church's religious tradition, religious communities should strive to give expression to these treasures and to hand them on in a manner harmonious with the nature and genius of each nation. Let them reflect attentively on how Christian religious life may be able to assimilate the ascetic and contemplative traditions whose seeds were sometimes already planted by God in ancient cultures prior to the preaching of the gospel. . . . Worthy of special mention are the various projects aimed at helping contemplative life take root.

Monastic foundations in India. Fortunately, the last few decades have witnessed the rapid founding of monasteries in the various countries of Africa and Asia. As a participant from India I am glad to state that attempts have been made in India, too, for the last twenty years to make monasteries places of genuine encounter between the Church and Hinduism. In spite of initial difficulties and failures, we can still boast of three foundations:

1. The Bendictine monastery of Siluvaigiri, founded in Salem District in 1952[12] by two Indian priests and transferred to Bangalore in 1957.[13] It is known as Asirvanam and counts at present thirty monks, with Dom Emmanuel de Meester, O.S.B., as prior, and is dependent on the Abbaye St.-André, Bruges, Belgium.

2. The Cistercian monastery of Kurisumala, in Kerala, founded by Dom Francis Acharya, O.C.S.O., and Dom Bede Griffiths, O.S.B.,[14] integrating itself into the monastic traditions of the Syro-Malankar Rite.

---

[12] Cf. Kaipanplakal, O.S.B., "Siluvaigiri Ashram," in *The Clergy Monthly Supplement*, 1952, pp. 156–158.

[13] Cf. E. de Meester, O.S.B., *The Benedictine Order*.

[14] Cf. A Cistercian Monk, *Kurisumala Ashram* (Tiruvalla, 1958); F. Mahieu, "Kurisumala Ashram," in *The Clergy Monthly Supplement*, 1959, pp. 202–04; "L'Ashram de Kurisumala," in *Bulletin du Cercle S. Jean-Baptiste*, March 1961; "Monasticism in India," in *The Clergy Monthly Supplement*, 1964, pp. 45–60; also several articles in *Église Vivante*.

3. The hermitage of Shantivanam, Tannirpalli, in the diocese of Tiruchirapalli, founded by Father Jules Monchanin (Parama Arubi Ananda) and Father Henri le Saux (Abhishiktananda).[15] Eleven years after the death of Father Monchanin it is being revived today by Dom Bede Griffiths as a Cistercian monastery.

Is monasticism the most efficient and best adapted missionary method? Now the crucial question is to situate monasticism in present-day India and to assess its role in the mission of the Church there. This question has been discussed in India in several books and articles during the last two decades. Though there is no general agreement on its relevance as the most efficient and best adapted missionary method, everybody is aware of its spiritual value and its lawful place in the Church in India.[16]

The chief exponent of this idea has been Father Jules Monchanin. His ideas can be summed up thus, as far as possible in his own words:

> India has received from the Almighty an uncommon gift, an unquenchable thirst for whatever is spiritual. From Vedic times a countless host of her sons have been great seekers of God. Century after century there arose seers and poets, singing the joys and sorrows

---

[15] *An Indian Benedictine Ashram* (Tiruchirapalli, 1950); J. Monchanin, S.A.M., and H. le Saux, O.S.B., *A Benedictine Ashram* (Douglas: Times Press, 1964); J. Monchanin and H. Le Saux, *Ermites du Saccidananda* (Paris: Casterman, 1956); *L'Abbé Jules Monchanin* (Paris, 1960); J. Bayart, S. J., "An Indian Benedictine Ashram," in *The Clergy Monthly Supplement*, 1952, pp. 76–81; E. Duperray, "Sur les Pas de l'Abbé Monchanin," in *Bulletin du Cercle S. Jean-Baptiste*, January 1962; J.–F. Six, "L'Abbé Jules Monchanin," in *Études*, October 1962, pp. 70–79; E. Duperray, "L'Abbé Monchanin," in *Parole et Mission*, No. 1; H. de Lufac, S. J., "Images de l'Abbé Monchanin" (Paris: Aubier, 1968).

[16] Cf. H. le Saux, "Le Monachisme Chrétien aux Indes," in *Vie Spirituelle*, supplement, September 15, 1956, pp. 283–316; "Christian Sannyasis," in *The Clergy Monthly Supplement*, 1958, p. 106ff.; J. Monchanin, "Le Monachisme et l'Inde," in *Église vivante*, 1952, p. 206ff.; "L'Heure de l'Inde," *ibid.*, 1955, pp. 30–38; "L'Inde et la Contemplation," in *Dieu Vivant*, 3 (1945), 13–46; "The Christian Approach to Hinduism," in *The Clergy Monthly Supplement*, 1952, p. 46ff.; D.S. Amalorpavadass, "L'Inde à la Rencontre du Seigneur" (Paris: Spes, 1964), pp. 66–70; "La Destinée de l'Église dans l'Inde d'Aujourd'hui," (Paris: Fayard-Mame, 1967), pp. 37–42, 46–50, 88–92; especially the last chapter, "Une Rencontre de l'Hindouisme au Niveau de l'Experience de Dieu," pp. 309–28; S. V. Swami, "Contemplative Life in India," in *The Examiner*, Bombay, January 13, 1968, p. 23; January 20, 1968, p. 37.

of a soul in the quest of the One, and philosophers reminding every man of the supremacy of contemplation. . . . Hundreds of thousands of men and women, both inside Hinduism and outside it, have consecrated themselves entirely to that end. Such a dedication, a very movement toward God, constitutes the essence of Indian monasticism.

We may rightly think that such a marvelous seed was not planted in vain by God in the Indian soul. Just as the Logos was mysteriously paving the way for his advent, and the Holy Spirit was stimulating from within the research of the most pure among the Greek sages, the Logos and the Spirit are still at work in a similar manner in the depth of the Indian soul. Unfortunately, Indian wisdom is tainted with erroneous tendencies and looks as if it has not yet found its own equilibrium . . . but we can hope that (like Greece) India, once baptized to the fullness of her body and soul, and to the depth of her age-long quest of Brahman, will reject pantheistic tendencies and discover in the splendors of the Holy Spirit the true mysticism . . . and will bring forth for the good of mankind and the Church, and ultimately for God's glory, an unparalleled galaxy of saints and doctors. Should India fail in that task, we cannot understand, humanly speaking, how the Mystical Body of Christ could reach its quantitative and qualitative fullness in his eschatological advent.[17]

Not only has India to receive something essential from Christianity to attain its age-old objectives, but India has also, in Father Monanchin's words, "a message of her own to deliver within the Church and to the world at large, but it will be only after finding her own achievement in Christ."

It was chiefly in her monks that India's message of spirituality found its best expression. It was her monks who fully experienced what was latent in her soul. Monasticism has been forever the most genuine fruit of her heart. . . . Is there not in all this a providential hint that also in India, once Christianized, monasticism is to get a prominent place; that the very message that India has to deliver—both as India and as Christian India—will be delivered mainly through monks, that is, those of her sons who are completely dedicated to divine contemplation; that in the Mystical Body, India's function will

---

[17] *A Benedictine Ashram* (Douglas: Times Press, 1964), pp. 15–17.

be principally a contemplative one, a function bearing a special testimony . . . to the essentially spiritual value of the Church, ultimately to the divine transcendency, to the Absolute? May we not also rightly say that it is such a testimony of pure spirituality that India herself is now expecting from the Church? Would not India fully open her mind and heart to the message of the risen Christ if she perceived that the Church is, above all, and essentially, a being humbly prostrate at the feet of the almighty and transcendent God, silently recollected in the embrace of the "Indwelling One"?[18]

India today calls for a wide diversity of approach. Though I subscribe in general to the opinion that contemplative life should be widely fostered, I should like to make a few further remarks.

1. India is not a monolith, and hence a priori any one solution, however good, cannot be proposed as best or unique. Moreover, as you know well, India is today passing through a crisis of values. Though the traditional values of India are spiritual, and spirituality held primacy of place, today India is passing through a severe crisis. This began with the definite establishment of the British control in India at the end of the eighteenth century and the spread of English education in the nineteenth. Though we appreciate the advantages of this education, we cannot fail to stress that it was by nature secularized, materialistic, positivistic and rationalistic. As a result it shook the spiritual equilibrium of the country and its fidelity to its ancestral customs. Today this crisis has reached a climax. The whole world—both the developed and the developing nations—are entering into an international planetary civilization that, while bringing gigantic progress, menaces every traditional culture with extinction.

On this subject, I would like to refer you to the doctoral thesis of Father D. S. Amalorpavadass,[19] where this crisis is thoroughly examined. The author asks the following questions and tries to answer them: Has India really abandoned its traditional spiritual values in order to adopt new ones? If there is a change in values, has it affected the whole population? What is the degree of change among those who have abandoned tradition? How does this change affect our approaches and methods of evangelization?

Some think that, in spite of appearances, India remains faithful to its

---

[18] *Ibid.*, pp. 24–25.
[19] *Destinée de l'Eglise dans l'Inde d'Aujourd'hui* (Paris, 1967), Chap. I, "La Crise des Valeurs en Inde," pp. 35–64, 89–92.

Monasticism in Ecclesial Community
Archbishop D. S. Lourdusamy

traditional values and that the change is only superficial. This is the way of thinking of what we may call idealists; others, who want to be realists, consider the spirituality of India as a thing of the past. In their eyes, the country is becoming more Westernized day by day and is adopting the material values of the West. Finally, there are those who avoid all generalizations and try to judge the reality in a balanced manner. In short, we can say that the crisis of values has thus far spared the rural population, who make up eighty percent of the country, and in urban milieus it provokes different reactions: an attitude of conservative defensiveness, a brutal rupture with the spiritual tradition to the advantage of the material values in Western civilization, or a quest for an equilibrium and a synthesis between the spiritual heritage and new values capable of purifying, updating and enriching Hinduism.[20]

2. If this is the situation, there is evidently no single solution valid for every place and all times. The diversity of mentalities, milieus and values, in the context of an evolving society, imposes on the Church a corresponding diversity of missionary approach and Christian presence. Let us not, therefore, exaggerate the case and say that India will be converted only by monasticism and that the real encounter between India and the Church will take place only in monasticism and contemplation. Let us not estimate other methods of evangelization.[21]

3. Perhaps it is more correct to say that hitherto the values of monasticism have not been sufficiently understood and esteemed by the Church in India. This form of Christian presence did not sufficiently draw our attention. The credit for having called attention to it goes to Father Robert de Nobili, S. J., four centuries ago, and two decades ago to Father Jules Monchanin, S.A.M., and his colleagues. Without, therefore, excluding or diminishing the value of other forms of Christian presence, action and service, we should lay stress on the primacy of contemplation in Christianity and monasticism as an institution favoring it.

4. It may be we shall need patience. Perhaps we shall have to pass through certain stages before monasteries can become centers of cultural integration and rendezvous for interreligious dialogue. The Church in India will have to learn to appreciate the contemplative life and come to recognize the value of monasticism. As Dom Bede Griffiths observes:

> One feels that the Indian Church is not yet mature for a meeting with Hinduism at its deepest level. Yet one can hope that if contem-

---

[20] *Ibid.*, pp. 45, 46, 57, 64.
[21] *Ibid.*, pp. 90–92.

plative life can be established within the Church, in a way attractive to the Catholics, it could eventually furnish a meeting point that would provoke contact with the Hindu tradition. It is only when contemplative life has taken root and begun to grow in this way that we can hope for this contact with the living sources of Hindu spirituality, through which the Church can, after all, enrich herself.[22]

CONCLUSION

In conclusion, I should like to quote once again Father Monchanin and Father le Saux. Their wish for India, expressed in *A Benedictine Ashram* (pp. 27–28) can easily be enlarged for all the young churches of Asia and Africa:

> Since monasticism has always held so important and conspicuous a place in Indian life from the very start, since it is likely to hold it even in the Indian Church, we may confidently hope that God will grant the age-long but always vigorous and sappy stem of Christian monasticism to shoot over our land a fresh and young branch with thick foliage, bearing abundant fruit. . . . A day will come—no matter how long hence—when God will give the Indian Church an Anthony or a Benedict who will make Indian monasticism come into its own and give it a form at once traditional and new, adorned with the purified spiritual splendor of its past legacies. But it is already time that the sons of India realize their obligation in this regard and prepare to gird themselves up humbly but steadily for the hour appointed by God.

SYNTHESIS OF GROUP DISCUSSIONS

December 14, 1968

ORGANIZATIONAL PROJECTS

Questions for discussion.[1]

1. *Should future meetings like the Bangkok conference be organized on a general or a regional basis?*

---

[22] "Hindouisme et Christianisme en Inde," in *Parole et Mission*, No. 10.
[1] The questions are based on the questionnaire, Part IV (Appendix B, p. 279). See also the summary of replies to Part IV (Appendix B, pp. 315–321).

2. Would an institute for the study of monastic questions in the Asian context be useful? Would a secretariat or center of information, as a first step to such an institute, be desirable?
3. Is it advisable to establish an organization to serve as a link between Asian monasteries and to promote their various interests?
4. How are superiors to be elected, and for how long should they serve?

1. *General and regional meetings.* All were unanimous in recognizing the benefits of general meetings like this one at Bangkok. But there are obvious difficulties in traveling from place to place. Hence it appeared that they should be held at relatively long intervals, every five or six years, for example. Regional meetings would also be very useful and could take place more often: every year or two. Their frequency was left to the initiative of each group, and the meetings were to be organized by a coordinator chosen for each region.

2. *Institute for the study of monastic questions, and a secretariat.* An institute of this sort seemed desirable but just now impossible to put into operation. While waiting for a more opportune time, it was suggested that monks could be sent to study such questions in other monasteries.

The creation of a secretariat or center of information was found, on the contrary, to be of urgent necessity—something to be decided on immediately. A general secretariat seemed to be too vast and too cumbersome for the moment. The delegates preferred regional secretariats united at the top. In this case, in order to supply centralization, those regions with more means might aid those with less. General information would be given out in care of the A.I.M. It would be good, also, to be in closer contact with the Roman secretariats and those of the Order about questions that concern them.

A "Newsletter" was planned by the group of monasteries in the Far East. News would be collected at Manila, where it would be edited and printed. The review would at first be published twice a year. Each issue would be dedicated to an aspect of the monastic life: for example, liturgy, formation and so on. The first number was anticipated for June, 1969.

In order to help groups that could not produce such a letter at present, it was agreed, after discussion, to dedicate a few pages to their news and to communicate information about them.

3. *Creation of an organization to serve as a link between monasteries.* Following the example of the monasteries of Africa and Latin America, the groups decided to create a connecting organization, called Union Monastique (Monastic Union), among the superiors of Asiatic monasteries grouped in regional conferences. The number of these regions is four: (1) India and Ceylon; (2) South Vietnam and the neighboring countries; (3) the monasteries of the Far East: South Korea, Japan, Hong Kong, Taiwan, the Philippines, Indonesia; (4) New Zealand and Australia.

The delegates named as president Dom Odo Haas, O.S.B., abbot of Waekwan, South Korea, and as regional coordinators: Mother Assunta Filser, O.S.B., prioress of Manila, for the group of the Far East; Dom Thomas Chau Van Dang, prior of Thien An, for the group of South Vietnam; Dom Mayeul de Dreuille, of Asirvanam, for the group of India; Dom Simon Tonini, O.S.B. Sylv., for the group of New Zealand and Australia.

The role of Union Monastique is, first of all, to establish regional secretariats and ensure relations among them. It is also to organize with them, in monasteries where interested monks could group themselves, seminars to study common questions with the aid of specialists. The secretariats could also promote the circulation of lecturers or of retreat masters and organize all services judged useful for the common good. Finally, an important part of this role is to represent the interests of monasteries before higher authorities.

It is quite clear, however, that the Union will fully respect the autonomy of each monastery and will not have anything to do with their organization into orders and into congregations. It is an organization of service and of unity.

4. *Election and tenure of superiors.* On the question of the designation of superiors by democratic procedures, there seemed to be unanimous agreement that elections should be carried out by democratic procedures as soon as a monastery had acquired a certain stability and independence. As for the length of tenure, it was felt by the contemplative monasteries that they should retain the traditional form of superiorship, while allowing for the possibility of changing a superior without formality if this was necessary. For this purpose an election was recommended for a fixed period (six or eight years), indefinitely renewable.

Certain more active congregations, where the superior is more a coordinator, seemed satisfied with their system of election for six years, renewable once only.

PRAYER
(In French)

Thou who sendest forth the light and dost make it wane; thou who makest the sun to shine upon the just and the unjust, upon the good and bad; thou who makest the dawn and dost enlighten the universe, do thou illumine our hearts, Master of all. Grant that we may please thee on this present day by preserving us from all sin, every wicked deed; by protecting us against darts flying by day and against all hostile powers, through the prayers of our Lady, the immaculate Mother of God, of the heavenly and immaterial powers who serve thee, and of all the saints who have pleased thee throughout the ages. For it becomes thee to take pity and to save us, O thou our God, and it is to thee that we render glory, Father, Son and Holy Spirit, now and for ever, world without end. Amen.

FIRST READING
(In French)

This is what must be done by him who is wise, who is seeking after good and has acquired peace.

Let him be diligent, loyal, perfectly loyal, docile, meek, humble, content, easily satisfied. Let him not be entangled in worldly business, let him not burden himself with riches, let him control his senses. Let him be wise, without pride, without family ties. Let him not do anything mean, anything of which the wise might possibly disapprove.

Let all beings be happy. Let them be in joy and security.

All that is living, weak or strong, tall, big or medium, short or small, visible or invisible, near or far, already born or yet to be born —let all these beings be happy.

Let no one deceive another or despise any being, however lowly it may be. Let no one, through anger or hate, wish evil for another.

Just as a mother in danger of death watches over and protects her only child, so with a boundless spirit should we cherish all living things, love the whole world, above, below and all about, without limit, with a benevolent and infinite kindness. Standing and walking, sitting or lying down, as long as we are awake, we must cultivate this thought. That is what is called the highest way of living. Abandoning false views, having profound inner sight, virtuous, freed from sensual appetites, he who is perfect will no longer know rebirth.

—*Suttanipata* (Buddhist)

SECOND READING
(*In English*)

And thus I understand that whatever man or woman with firm will chooses God in this life, for love, he may be sure that he is loved without end: which endless love works in him that grace. For he wills that we be as assured in hope of the bliss of heaven while we are here as we shall be in sureness while we are there. And ever the more pleasure and joy we take in this sureness, with reverence and meekness, the better pleased is he, as it was shown. This reverence that I mean is a holy, courteous dread of our Lord, to which meekness is united: and that is, that a creature sees the Lord marvelous great, and itself marvelous little. For these virtues are had endlessly by those loved of God, and this may now be seen and felt in measure through the gracious presence of our Lord when it is seen: which presence in all things is most desired, for it works marvelous assuredness in true faith, and sure hope, by greatness of charity, in dread that is sweet and delectable.

It is God's will that I see myself as much bound to him in love as if he had done for me alone all that he has done; and thus should every soul think inwardly of its Lover. That is to say, the charity of God makes in us such a unity that, when it is truly seen, no man can part himself from it for anything other. And thus ought our soul to think that God has done for it all that he has done.

And this he shows to make us to love him and naught dread but him. For it is his will that we perceive that all the might of our enemy is taken into our Friend's hand; and therefore the soul that knows assuredly this, he shall not dread but him that he loves. All other dread he sets among passions and bodily sicknesses and imaginations. And therefore though we be in so much pain, woe and distress that it seems to us we can think of naught but of that which we are in, or of that which we feel, yet as soon as we may, we pass lightly over and set it at naught. And why? Because God wills that we know him; and if we know him and love him and reverently dread him, we shall have peace and be in great rest, and all that he does shall be great pleasure to us. And this our Lord showed in these words: "Why should it then aggrieve you to suffer awhile, since it is my will and my worship?"

—Julian of Norwich (Chapter 65)

SEVENTH DAY

Sunday, December 15

The entire Christian world, and others as well, by the dramatic intervention of God in this week, in taking from us the most known of our participants, have had their attention drawn to the problem of monasticism in the Orient. It is up to us to see that that interest fructifies into action.

—Dom Rembert Weakland, O.S.B.

Conclusions of the Conference[1]

Like the Church itself, Christian monasticism must be missionary. In a word, it must strive to bear witness to the gospel for Christians and non-Christians alike. This it will accomplish if it is open to the values proper to the peoples among whom it has been introduced and if it contributes to their progress. We have come together here, from different monastic families in all parts of Asia, precisely to study the problems raised by the introduction of Christian monasticism into this continent.

I

In the areas we come from, monasticism is the Church institution closest to the non-Christian religions and is possibly the best means of approach to them. Thus one of the major objectives of Christian monks in Asia is to make contacts with monks of other religions.

We are well aware of the very great differences between the religions in the various parts of Asia and between the forms of monasticism here, as well as of the dynamism of these cultures now in process of evolution. Following the example of Thomas Merton, who so generously undertook this same sort of research, we must discover in them the total Christ and thus lift them up to his fullness. We think, as Thomas Merton did, that in these Asian countries, where a serious and highly esteemed form of non-Christian eremitical life already exists, one of the needs of the Church is to establish Christian hermits in order to show that mystical prayer exists also among Christians.

We must accept in our monasteries, it would seem, such customs from among these peoples' different cultural expressions as faithfully express the authentic principles of monastic life. One task of the Church in our various countries is to seek out all that is good in their traditions so as to conserve it and give it a more modern expression.

[1] Approved by the final session at Bangkok, on December 15, 1968.

Communities must be awakened to the fact of these problems and be kept informed about how they are being worked out. A knowledge of local cultures should become a normal part of the formation of the young monks and nuns. Furthermore, this formation would gain much if each of its different stages were made more flexible. The monastic "constitutions" should allow for adaptation to the specific character of each people.

Lastly, we should give special attention to the warmth of the welcome extended to non-Christian monks who may visit the monastery.

II

In our discussions, constant emphasis was given to two particular aspects of the part to be played by a monastery in these developing countries. The monastery is first of all a spiritual center, a witness to the eschatological character of the Church, with every one of its activities directed to God. The specific contribution of monasticism to progress is prayer, for it is this that will give a spiritual dimension to the work of our contemporaries.

On the other hand, since the monastery is an integral part of a human environment, it must also express Christ's charity toward men. Charity is not simply vertical; it is also horizontal. It seems that in our times men want their contemplation to be nurtured by a seeking for Christ in mankind.

This twin duty of reaching toward God and of social charity creates a tension that finds various solutions according to the location and traditions of the monasteries. Some insist on the principle that monasticism has no "secondary aim"; others emphasize the duty of Christian charity as incumbent on every man and institution.

Certainly, however, the value of our witness depends above all on the authenticity and sincerity of our search for God. Our progress must be in Christ. Our mission, like his, is to bring about an inner change in men and to give a Christian motivation to progress. Hence the importance of free and personal encounter with God, something that must be encouraged both in the monks themselves and in all who come to the monastery for retreats. Therein lies, too, one of our profoundest points of contact with the Asian religions, centered as they are on personal experience of the divine.

Special attention must be paid to the attitude of the young people who enter the monastery. They belong to a generation athirst for progress, one that is more or less consciously preparing a socio-economic revolution. They cannot be suddenly cut off from this sort of commitment without serious risk of disturbance. Rather, it should be recognized that they constitute a vital link for the monastery with the world, keeping it in touch with its evolution.

With regard to actual social work, it seems better to fit in with a governmental or regional plan rather than to embark on individual projects. It also seems proper for the different monastic organizations to open themselves not only to Catholics, but to everyone.

It is desirable for a monastery to be as independent as possible of any regular help from abroad or from purely capitalistic sources. This suggestion does not, however, exclude accepting temporary help for a definite project.

Speaking more generally, social work undertaken by the monastery calls for flexibility both in organization and in the daily schedule, but it should in no instance deflect the monastery from its specific vocation and work. On the level of the individual, it is for superiors to discern and respect the true spiritual aspirations of each member.

Another aspect of the monasteries' contribution to progress is the virtue of poverty, understood as being an evangelical value consisting in sincerity, detachment and willingness to share. It has an infinite number of aspects, and it is good that these should be represented by a variety of monasteries of different traditions and dimensions.

It appears, however, that in the various Asian countries we should provide especially for the creation of small monasteries, either in the form of communities of a limited number—not exceeding thirty—or of experimental groups dependent on a central monastery. Such small communities have the advantage of allowing a simpler form of life and making adaptation to local conditions easier.

About the site of a monastery, all were unanimous in wishing it to be sufficiently tranquil to safeguard monastic recollection and yet easy of access, that is to say, near an important urban center, which should also be a center of intellectual activity. This proximity would allow the religious to enrich their own culture as well as to serve the particular needs of those frequenting such a center. One of the objectives of A.I.M. should be to assist monasteries in choosing those places best adapted for establishing monasticism in areas where it does not already exist.

In promoting monasticism there must be absolutely no question of propaganda. We must be simply what we are, in a realistic and human way, and we must give honest information about ourselves to those young people who show interest. It would be useful for the monasteries to cooperate in producing and distributing whatever literature is needed.

Lastly, in order to facilitate exchange of information as well as representation of monastic interests to the higher authorities, it seemed opportune to create a monastic union of the superiors of Asia, subdivided into "regional conferences." A president was named, as well as regional coordinators.

III

In conclusion, it should be emphasized that the monk must be a man of peace, one who has acquired, by the grace of God, the smiling serenity typical of the monks of the other Eastern religions. The monastery, where often men from very different backgrounds live together, must exhibit true charity among its members and toward its neighbors—something that will be evident to each people and to the world at large. A peaceful relationship with others will be easier to maintain if monks avoid entering into local political quarrels; but that fact should not prevent monasteries from making every effort to promote social justice.

Neither Communism nor any movement of secularization will be overcome by violence. They will be overcome only by a spiritual force stronger than themselves. In the struggle for peace, everyone assuredly wishes for the silencing of armaments; but it is our duty, at the same time, to arouse in ourselves a tremendous passion, both of the mind and of the heart, so that, following after Christ, our lives may be entirely dedicated to God and to men.

CONCLUDING REMARKS OF DOM REMBERT G. WEAKLAND, O.S.B.

My dear Confreres:

My task is not to act as a judge as to the success or failure of this week. First of all, it is impossible to judge accurately the effects of a week of this sort on the participants. Only you can answer that question, and perhaps you will not be able to answer it accurately until months from now, when you have returned home and have assimilated the papers, dialogues and events of this week and shared them with your communities. Nor will it be possible to judge the effects of this week on the history of monasticism in the Orient. The contact with the Patriarch of the Buddhist monks is symbolic and significant, but only the future will tell its full impact.

One thing, though, I feel I can say with certitude: the monks of the world have had their attention drawn to the Orient. Whether they wish to or not, they have suddenly become aware of our conference and have had their attention drawn here. But not only the monks of the world: the entire Christian world, and others as well, by the dramatic intervention of God in this week, in taking from us the most known of our participants, have had their attention drawn to the problem of monasticism in the Orient. It is up to us to see that that interest fructifies into action and active concern for monasticism in the Orient.

In my opening remarks, I said I hoped this congress would help us realize who and what we are at this moment. The discussion of definitions and the different views presented have convinced me that the full complexity of monasticism in the Orient as well as in the West is represented among you. And of this I am glad. It is good that we are unable to define ourselves clearly at this moment, because we are living and growing and changing and transforming. And yet I feel that we were instinctively one unit; that there were bonds of agreement uniting us, even if they were tenuous and were more characterized by common searching than by common solutions. Perhaps Father Merton's lecture was the clearest in stating the prophetic role of monasticism, however that prophetic role may be dressed and clothed in the concrete.

The congress has made all of us aware of the futility of generalizations about the Orient. In almost every case when the cultural and religious patterns were being described for one country, each of you was, I am sure, making mental observations about the one where you are located, and later you would say how different the situation was in your locality. This was true especially when discussing the influence of Buddhism, Confucianism or whatever it may be. You became aware of the difference of each area. From this it should be clear to you now that these same cultures, including the one in which you have settled, are not static but rapidly changing. You have all made clear your awareness of these changes. Since you are all working in cultures that have a different mixture of common basic elements that are changing at different speeds under the influence of Western infiltration, it is no wonder that no one clear, unique solution for monasticism in the Orient can or should be presented to you.

The solution to your adaptation must and should be different for each area in which you are working. The beauty of the monastic witness, with its flexibility and need to sink its roots into the living local communities where it finds itself, becomes now more evident here in the Orient. There is deep beauty in this variety. I have seen it in my wanderings before this conference. I will not—I cannot—say that one solution is right, one is wrong; but all have their reason to exist and contribute to the whole. There is no blueprint for monasticism in the Orient. There is only a changing, shifting blueprint for each house. No one here can or should make that blueprint for you. You and your individual communities must make your own blueprints. There is no single answer for all.

I had hoped this conference would be informative. The facts seem to me to prove that it has been. Not all the information may be of practical use today or tomorrow for you, but the general value of any information in broadening your scope of vision and perspectives will always be present.

I also hoped you would gain courage from the contacts with others facing similar problems. On this level, I can say it was a clear enrichment of my life to have met all of you and to have been able to share with you this week some aspects of our very being that makes each of us grow as children of Christ and sons of St. Benedict. None of us will return home the same from these contacts. Such personal sharings cannot be put on a scale or placed on a graph, but they go to make up our ultimate being. You all must have the courage to be yourselves and to be free to share with others.

We have shared our concerns to maintain our search for Christ in

Final Remarks
Rembert Weakland, O.S.B.

these cultures where we are sinking roots. We have tried to get some insights into how people here think about God and about prayer. We have considered their concepts of simplicity and poverty. We have talked of our attempts to find Christ and the monastic way of life in these elements. In all of this we have shown our desire to continue the search for the living Christ here.

It has also been a dramatic week. One of the most known searchers among us was unable to share his insights to the fullest with us because God called him. It is our duty now to continue the search that brought him this far away from his home monastery. His death here in the Orient is certainly not in vain. It must serve as a further impetus to us all to finish the work he, too, began.

Most of all, this has been a week to be experienced. It can hardly be described. It had to be experienced. We began as a group of strangers. We end as friends. We came to know our differences this week; I hope we came also to reassess them. Our common concern is that the gospel message, with its monastic dimension as a way of living that message, be planted deep in the Oriental soil and that in doing so we do not destroy, but rather shelter and protect, the basic Christian elements we find here.

My thanks to all the organizers again. My thanks to all of those who spoke and prepared lectures. My thanks to all of you for being here.

APPENDICES

Appendix A

TELEGRAM OF HIS HOLINESS PAUL VI

BANGKOK

HIS HOLINESS, PATERNALLY ENCOURAGING THE MONASTIC SUPERIORS CONVENING AT BANGKOK TO STUDY THE MONASTIC PROBLEMS OF THE FAR EAST, LOOKS WITH FAVOR ON THIS OCCASION FOR ENGAGING OR DEEPENING CONTACTS WITH NON-CHRISTIAN MONASTICISM IN THE SPIRIT OF THE RECENT CONCILIAR DOCUMENTS. I SEND WITH ALL MY HEART TO THE MOST REVEREND BENEDICTINE ABBOTS, AND TO ALL PARTICIPANTS ENGAGED IN THIS FRUITFUL WORK, THE DESIRED APOSTOLIC BENEDICTION.

CARDINAL CICOGNANI

THE VATICAN
DECEMBER 9, 1968

Sacra Congregatio Pro Gentium Evangelizatione
Seu de Propaganda Fide

Rome, December 5, 1968

Most Reverend Father:

This Sacred Congregation of Propaganda Fide has been particularly happy to learn that a meeting of monastic superiors of the Far East is going to be held at Bangkok under your presidency from the eighth to the fifteenth of this December.

From the earliest times of the Church, the number of the saved has increased thanks to the practice of the apostolic life, as the evangelist St. Luke describes it for us in the Acts of the Apostles. In the course of centuries, the monastic order has contributed, in a remarkable fashion, to the planting of the Church in the Occidental world, and we are not unaware here of all that the missions owe to the monasteries, whose prayer and generosity as well as presence in the mission countries constitute one of the important elements of evangelization.

This Sacred Congregation Pro Gentium Evangelizatione was always solicitous to see respected the local usages of the countries to be evangelized. As early as 1459, in fact, in the Instructions given to vicars apostolic leaving for the realms of Tonkin and of Cochin China, the Sacred Congregation wrote: "Do not introduce among them our country, but the faith, this faith that neither rejects nor wounds either the rites or the customs of any people, providing that they are not detestable, but, much to the contrary, wishes that they be kept and protected. Never place on a parallel the usages of these peoples with those of Europe, but quite to the contrary, force yourselves to become habituated to them. Admire and praise that which merits praise."

Above all, the recent Council has insisted that the religious life be adapted to the particular situation of the missions (Decree on the Church's Missionary Activity, nn. 18 and 40). This is why we ardently wish that your meeting—of which we will be glad to know the conclusions—may be able to encourage an authentic adaptation of monasticism to local conditions and to facilitate its implantation into the socio-cultural milieu to be evangelized, in particular in the great Asiatic continent, where flourishing monasteries already exist and where the religious life has been always held in particular esteem.

Calling down the abundance of divine benediction on the work of your congress, I am happy to profit by this occasion to renew to you, Most Reverend Father, the expression of my esteem and to assure you of my kindest regards.

Sincerely and devotedly yours,

G. P. Cardinal Agagianian, Prefect
Edward Pecorais, Under-Secretary

Most Reverend Father Rembert Weakland
Abbot Primate of the Confederated Benedictines

TELEGRAMS OF THE ABBOT PRIMATE

HIS HOLINESS PAUL VI
VATICAN CITY

MONKS AND NUNS GATHERED TOGETHER IN BANGKOK STUDYING THE MONASTIC PROBLEM OF THE FAR EAST SINCERELY THANK YOUR HOLINESS FOR YOUR PATERNAL ENCOURAGEMENT. THEY HOPE TO HAVE RESPONDED TO THE DESIRE OF YOUR HOLINESS IN WELCOMING THE SUPREME PATRIARCH OF THE BUDDHISTS. WE ASK YOUR BLESSING ON OUR FUTURE WORK.

> WEAKLAND
> ABBOT PRIMATE

HIS EMINENCE CARDINAL AGAGIANIAN
PIAZZA DI SPAGNA, ROMA

MONKS AND NUNS GATHERED TOGETHER AT BANGKOK STUDYING THE MONASTIC PROBLEM OF THE FAR EAST THANK YOUR EMINENCE FOR THE ENCOURAGING LETTER OF THE FIFTH OF DECEMBER. THEY WILLINGLY PROMISE MISSIONARY EFFORTS IN THE DIRECTION INDICATED.

> WEAKLAND
> ABBOT PRIMATE

SCROLL PRESENTED TO THE SUPREME PATRIARCH OF THAI BUDDHISM
December 9, 1968

In the month of December, of the year nineteen hundred sixty-eight, the monks of the Christian religion living in Asia convened at Bangkok under the presidency of their head, the Father Abbot Primate of the Benedictines, Dom Rembert Weakland. They have been happy to receive the hospitality of Thailand. In this country, where Buddhist monks have been so numerous down so many centuries, they have profited by the presence of this ancient and very rich tradition of the spiritual life. It is a joy to express their gratitude to His Holiness, the Supreme Patriarch of the Buddhists, who has benevolently paid them the honor of visiting their meeting, and they wish that for him all the desires of his heart may be realized.

Appendix B

PREPARATORY QUESTIONNAIRE[1]

I. PROBLEMS OF FORMATION IN THE MONASTIC LIFE

A. Influence of the environment:
   1. From what social environment do the postulants come?
   2. What influence do these environments have on their behavior?
      a. What elements of behavior specific to environment are manifested in the behavior of the young monks?
      b. What customs and institutions are to be integrated in community life in order to make it intelligible, entirely adapted to the native monks and favorable to a monasticism rooted in the country and fulfilling its aspirations?

B. The monastic virtues:
   1. What are your views on obedience and liberty; co-responsibility?
   2. What do you think about fraternal relationships; the unity of the community (often made up of people from extremely varied origins)?
   3. How is the monk's vocation understood?
      a. Is the monastic priesthood desired? If so, why?
      b. How is the organization of studies envisaged?
   4. How do the individual monks envisage and practice their personal poverty?
   5. Problems concerning prayer.
      (Under this heading we wish to consider the part monks have to play in the development of the Word of God in His Church, spoken of in the Constitution on Divine Revelation, n. 8: "This tradition, which comes from the apostles, develops in the Church with the help of the Holy Spirit. For there is growth in the understanding of the realities and the words that have been handed down. This happens through contemplation and study on the part of believers, who treasure these things in their hearts, through intimate understanding of the spiritual things they experience.")
      a. Liturgy: In keeping with the spirit of the restoration of the liturgy, how can we take into account, in our celebration of the cult, "the traditions and genius of individual peoples" (Constitution on the Sacred Liturgy, n. 40, 1)?

[1] This set of questions was sent to prospective delegates early in 1968. Summaries of the replies are given in the remaining sections of Appendix B.

b. What forms of personal prayer do you consider most suited to the mentality of the native monks?
  6. How are separation from the world, and enclosure, effectively realized?
  7. Stages of the monastic life: What suggestions have you concerning the postulancy and the delay necessary before a definitive commitment?

II. THE MONASTERY IN THE LOCAL CHURCH COMMUNITY

A. How do you personally, the local Christians, the local hierarchy, look upon:
  1. the presence of Christian monasticism, affirming the contemplative and absolute character of the Christian mystery, in the heart of local Churches where religious life is almost exclusively represented by active congregations?
  2. the aid that the monastery can offer from the point of view of (a) spiritual development (retreats, etc.), (b) liturgy, (c) culture (publications, translations, sacred art)?

B. How can the monastic community serve the local Church in its effort to become open to the cultural and religious values of the country?

C. Experts point out the importance of the movement of "secularization," which is becoming daily more manifest in the heart of non-Christian religious structures in different Asiatic countries. How may we contribute, in this process of secularization, to maintaining the true spiritual values proper to Asian cultures?

D. How are the relationships with the hierarchy and the clergy understood?

E. What do you consider the ecumenical role of monasticism in the heart of the local Church where other Christian confessions exist?

III. THE MONASTERY IN THE COUNTRY

A. In the sociological context of each country, how can the monastery give an intelligible Christian witness of charity, prayer, poverty?

B. How can our monasticism undertake and develop truly religious exchanges with representatives of non-Christian monasticism?

C. How can monks and communities participate, in keeping with the teaching of the encyclical *Populorum Progressio*, in the real development of the human environment in which they find themselves (social justice, peace and all the different points of the 1967 Christmas message of Paul VI)?

D. What part can the monastic community play in the evangelization of the aborigines (mountain tribes and others)? Ought we not to foresee and

Appendix B

hasten among these peoples the foundation of contemplative communities according to the directives of Vatican II: "The contemplative life belongs to the fullness of the Church's presence and should therefore be everywhere established" (Decree on the Church's Missionary Activity, n. 18)?

E. What have you to say about the site of the monastery and its relationships with the country?

IV. INSTITUTIONAL QUESTIONS

A. In order to respond to the very complex situations we have to face, would it not be a good thing to consider:
   1. varying forms of monastic life
      a. within the same community: cenobitical life, eremitical life, small groups supported by a community of traditional style?
      b. within monasteries of different, but complementary, types, to better adapt themselves to the varied environments of certain countries?
   2. Some sort of union between the monasteries (as in the communities of Africa and of Latin America) in order to favor mutual help and a certain unity?

SUMMARY OF THE REPLIES TO PARTS I AND II OF THE PREPARATORY QUESTIONNAIRE[2]

Prepared by Jean Leclercq, O.S.B.

PRELIMINARY REMARKS

The first two questions concern the nature of Christian monasticism and its relations with Asian traditions. A divergence of opinions appears in connection with these two points, and we may attempt to clarify them by means of the following distinctions.

Two conceptions of Christian monasticism. For some, monasticism is a "celibate life lived in a community." Its occupations are those that may be carried out by any group of Christians living the celibate life in common. In mission countries they are missionary in nature (care of parishes, schools, hospitals, etc.), and the problems that arise as a result of this approach are missionary problems. Here and there, for example in Korea, missionary monks from the West notice a tendency toward a contemplative type of monastic life, something that has been arrived at by the Asian religious themselves and could possibly develop in a spiritual climate they themselves would have to create.

For the majority, monasticism is the life lived by Christians who withdraw from the world in order to devote themselves, together, to prayer, asceticism and work.

Aspects of Christian monasticism in different countries. Of all the Eastern countries, India is the most important by reason of its past and present influence. In India itself three kinds of Christian monks are to be found. The Keralians in Kerala continue to observe the Syriac Rite and exhibit real homogeneity. The Keralians outside Kerala, who have been uprooted, desire as much Westernization as possible and are drawn to the priesthood as much as to monastic life. Among the non-Keralians there is a great variety of forms, but there is also profound agreement in conceiving the monastic life to be contemplative.

Outside India the situation is complex and varied. In Thailand, Jesuits and the priests of the Paris Foreign Missions have grasped the importance and the meaning of Buddhist monasticism and thus the necessity of having

---

[2] When this report was drafted, in August 1968, twenty replies had been received. Some of them were more than twenty pages long. So rich were they in facts and ideas that it would have been impossible to summarize them. Hence it seemed preferable to give here an overall view of their responses to each of the points dealt with and to select suggestive passages.

a Christian monasticism. In Korea, on the other hand, the conflict between Buddhism and Confucianism makes this sort of understanding less easy.

In Japan, whose development is now in full progress, the few examples of Christian monasticism are deeply marked by the West. But a Jesuit, Father Monsterleet, writes:

> I very much wish to see a monastery of contemplative Benedictine monks and another of Benedictine nuns set up in Japan; they should take their inspiration from the Zen monasteries (cf. Father F. Enomiya-Lassalle, S. J., and Father H. Dumoulin, S. J., at Sophia University). But especially the monastery would have to be open to outside people, so that they could profit from the monastery's silence and liturgy. I would also like the monks to serve the Church by translating spiritual works.

In Vietnam, Christian monasticism is marked by the forms of life and piety of the founding monastery, whether twenty or fifty years ago; by the results of the country's relationship with the United States; by the fact that a large membership has been sought and obtained, and that monasticism has engaged itself in ownership and production, thus exposing itself to certain dangers, which many see quite clearly. In Cambodia, again, the situation of monasticism, as of the whole Church, is determined by the fact that part of the Christians are Vietnamese.

In Indonesia, the Philippines and other countries, the situations differ, too.

Each one who has replied to the questionnaire has done so according to the situation in his particular country. Thus the documentation obtained from their reports is complementary rather than repetitive.

Different types within each country. Two conceptions and tendencies in Christian monasticism are represented by two types of Asians. In each country of Asia there are, one is tempted to say, two different Asian worlds.

Many, and not only among the Asians, insist upon the indigenization of the monasticism brought from the West, or, better still, on the creation of a typical Asian monasticism.

Some, on the other hand, favor the Westernization of those Asians who have become monks and the conforming of Asian monasticism to the mode of existence and thought proper to the West. Each of these seeks to realize his own plan according to his origin, his formation, his personality, his location and the conditions of the founding of the monastery he is in charge of.

As is only natural, each representative of these two tendencies presents his program as the best. In fact, both methods exist, and both are, for the moment, legitimate, whatever may be the prognostications for the future.

The conception inherited from history in the West and that suggested by the Asian Church as it is at present. The Benedictines and Cistercians are limited—in their culture and their openness to the present—by the past, distant or recent, upon which they depend.

The Jesuits as well as the Paris Foreign Missionaries have a freer conception of what monasticism should be in Asia. For them there is no doubt that it must be entirely contemplative and adapted to the country. Consequently they are more inventive, more creative. Dom Francis Acharya, O.C.S.O., and Dom Bede Griffiths, O.S.B., as well as Sister Praxede, agree with them; and various evidence proves that their views are not considered eccentric or more or less extravagant by the Catholics in Asia.

Two mentalities. There is a preconciliar mentality, which coincides with the one prevalent during the period of colonization and the evangelization that accompanied it. In the replies, it is described as being "aggressive, proselytizing, domineering, self-sufficient" and linked to an "anti-Asian prejudice."

There is also a postconciliar (as well as postcolonial) mentality. It consists, with regard to Asians, their religions and their monasticisms, as Father A. Gomane, S.J., has said, in "coming as brothers, not as rivals."

Thus we may conclude that there is room today for a sort of "monastic ecumenism." Every advantage is to be gained from allowing the representatives of the different tendencies, mentalities and realizations we have noted to get to know one another, to understand one another, to esteem one another and to draw together, completing and helping one another. Such should be one of the aims of the monastic meeting at Bangkok.

I. PROBLEMS OF FORMATION IN THE MONASTIC LIFE

The various responses to Part I of the questionnaire are here arranged in a simpler manner under seven general headings.

Recruitment and influence of the environment. In general, Asians are recognized as having a capacity for deep peace, for prayer, simple living and austerity, which prepare conditions favorable to the monastic life. Since candidates for Christian monastic life are, on the whole, of a poorer origin, their entry into Western style religious life is considered both by themselves and by their society as being a promotion and a raising of their standard of living.

Several Westerners point out that the patriarchal structure of the family is not very favorable to the development of personality. But others, including some Asians, affirm that one of the benefits of Hindu or Buddhist monasticism is to liberate personalities. Christian monasticism, then, must also be able to do this.

The purpose of the monastic life. Monasticism answers a need of the Asian man, in conformity with his religious traditions, in which meditation and self-control hold a large place. It also fulfills the need of making up for a lack in the Church in Asia, which is solely "activist" and "philanthropic," giving rise to the "heresy of good works." It is wanting in those two signs of Christian vitality: the missionary sense and the contemplative sense (a want not made up for by the hidden presence of a few Carmels of Western style). Consequently, it is said almost unanimously, the Church is recognized not as a witness to the spiritual life, but as an organization of help and progress, certainly powerful, yet not disinterested because motivated by proselytism.

"An average Hindu would not think of going to a Catholic priest in order to learn how to pray. His deepest sympathies and admiration are reserved for his holy men," says Father Mathias, S.J.

Thus the goal of A.I.M. cannot be to contribute to the establishing of monasticism in India or in other countries where it existed long before Christianity—it would be just as pretentious, it has been pointed out, as to wish to "establish urban life in New York City"—but to the introduction of monasticism in the Church of Asia, where it is almost totally wanting.

In actual fact, to Asians the Western style monastic life often appears not as a means of salvation and of sanctification, but as an occasion for either economic promotion by means of raising of the standard of living or for intellectual promotion because of its making study possible. The quality of the monasticism introduced, then, depends on what is promised to the candidates or what the existing institutions lead them to hope for: access to studies and the priesthood or a vocation to prayer and a simple life. This vocation is given to some, and certain missionary monks notice that Asian Christians are beginning to discover it. The aim of the monastic life should be to offer them the possibility of realizing this vocation.

Religious traditions in Asia and Christian monasticism. More than in ways of acting, of eating, dressing, offering hospitality, which are by no means negligible but can remain accessory, Christian monasticism must enter into deep spiritual contact with Asia, and first of all with the fact of the existence of an ancient monasticism, widespread and varied.

Here, by way of example, are statements taken from replies received concerning first Hinduism and then Buddhism. Father S. Ryan, S.J., writes:

> Asians are still sensitive to Western dominance, still suspicious of the white men's superiority complex and secret devaluation of colored races. This fear can remain below the level of consciousness and cause trouble. Hence manifest equality from the start, avoidance of imposition of any item or custom from the West that is not essential to the gospel. Life must be centered on the gospel essentials; the rest must be left to evolve naturally in the indigenous culture. In the beginning, therefore, structures and worship will be simple, as seen in the Gospels; they will gradually build

themselves a body through vital assimilation. An imported body can only be a dead body, as Church history in India has amply proved. Care should be taken to appoint or elect Indians or Asians superiors as soon as possible, even from the beginning. And the others must be willing to remain under them and not quit. This point is particularly to be attended to among women.

In India, the monk is one who realizes and reveals by the witness of his life the fact that this phenomenal world is not the ultimate Reality, is not the one necessary Reality; and the fact that *karuna*, or compassion, is the ultimate solution to the problem of the pain of existence. The Christian adds a third dimension: the vocation of the monastic community is to realize and manifest the ideal society that God intends for mankind: a brotherhood deeply united, open to God and to man in work, peace and prayer.

Mother Adele Fiske, R.S.C.J., who is one of those who have seen the most Buddhist and Hindu monasteries in the most Asian countries, writes:

> The monastic concept in India seems to me so different from the Christian that I do not see how a monastery could witness to charity, prayer, poverty, except by adopting the Indian pattern. But again, this pattern is not uniform, as each geographical area and each sect (for example, Virashaivism in Mysore, or the Vaishavite sects in Mathura) vary in aims and structure. The one who has most assimilated the eremitical pattern seems to be Dom Le Saux, but he does not aim at a monastery. Another point is that most sadhus move freely, and although their allegiance is to their *guru*, they do not seem permanently bound to a community.

From a Buddhist country, Father Moling, S.J., writes:

> The fact is that the Catholics here in Thailand have had no training in contemplative life and have rather been taught to live and behave differently, never to do what the Buddhists do. It is therefore not sure that Catholics will like the idea of becoming a "monk," as the Buddhists do. Besides, to be a Buddhist monk does not imply an obligation for life; they remain free to leave the monastery at any time they please. I suggest that we consider the possibility of giving young men the possibility of becoming monks *ad tempus* only, without obligation to stay for life or even for a definite period of time. This could be the way to make young Catholic men acquainted with the real monastic life, and I hope that some of these "temporary monks" could get the idea of becoming a monk for life.

Appendix B

Father E. Verdière, of the Paris Foreign Missions in Thailand, writes along the same lines:

According to the doctrine of Buddha, what is of primary importance is to arrive at perfection; consequently, anyone can live the experience of a monk, and it is a custom anchored in the Thai mentality that every young man must pass through the pagoda at least once during his life. The monk may live the contemplative life all through his life, but it is not a principle, and in fact there are relatively few who give themselves up to the monastic life during the whole of their existence. This is something that might certainly be considered in Christian monasticism, and a sounding of opinions among European and Thai missionaries shows that such an idea meets with much approval.

Christian monasticism in Thailand is completely nonexistent. The Christians as well as pagans ignore that there is such a thing, or do not realize what it is. The Thai language even is ignorant of the word. The term that is translated by "monk" really means hermit. The presence of contemplative Christians, apart from the spiritual influence on the people, both Christian and pagan, would also have a witness value: it would certainly be a revelation to see Christian monks giving themselves up to contemplation, without necessarily systematically eliminating the pastoral side.

On the other hand, an effective collaboration in the work of penetration into Thai culture, in view of a deeper assimilation of Christian culture, is something that may not be neglected.

There is certainly a movement of secularization. But Buddhism in Thailand has such a hold that it is deeply rooted in morals and customs. Even if the religious spirit tends to go down, the outer religious framework is far from having been touched. For example, the number of monks is 151,560 plus 87,010 whom we would call seminarians, in 22,402 pagodas.

Christian monasticism would have a special effect if it gave the example of a monastic life really lived, really impregnated with a religious spirit. But it goes without saying that this influence must not be rated too high in a country where the proportion of Catholics is very small (0.6 percent).

It would seem that at the present time both hierarchy and clergy are among those who are most favorable to the establishment of monasticism in Thailand, but always with the idea that it must be adapted as much as possible to the Thai mentality.

Besides respect for the local language and the duty to study it that are incumbent on all, other typical sorts of behavior in Asian monasticism are characterized by Father Rayan, S.J., as follows:

Peace, deep peace and prayerfulness; poverty and detachment, with simplicity of life and simple austerity; hospitality; availability, approachability—these are traits of Indian, and I suppose Asian, spiritual life and must shine in monastic life. Only these will make this sort of life intelligible. There may be added the use of clothing according to native ascetic tradition, and vegetarianism, which is associated with refinement of spirit, purity, peace and universal compassion.

It is not sufficient, then, merely to adopt outward ways of behaving. A start must be made by entering into the spirit that gives them their meaning.

Certain Westerners consider that it would be impossible for them to adopt the Asian spirit and mentality: the most they can do is to favor a dialogue between themselves and the Asians that would be stimulating and enriching for both parties. Others think it is possible and necessary for Christian monks in Asia, including even Westerners, to assimilate certain elements of the traditional religions and of Asian monasticism. Nevertheless, Christians—Asians or Westerners—cannot claim these values to be found in Hinduism and Buddhism as something to which they have a right without meriting them. They will come to merit them in learning to know, respect and esteem them. They would have to make it known and accepted that they take a certain inspiration from these values. And if they are asked if they belong to one or other Hindu order or mission, they will be able to justify the fact that they take inspiration from them and yet are Christians, and they will thus be accepted—as experience has shown is possible.

Before adopting Asian ways, Westerners will have to begin by giving up, as far as possible, their own ways as far as food, clothing and habitat are concerned, and then initiate themselves into the spiritual experiences of Hinduism and Buddhism by spending some time in the ashrams. The characteristics observed in these ashrams are poverty, simplicity, the great importance given to prayer, reading, hospitality, the austere practice of Yoga or other methods that favor recollection and self-control; absence of juridicism in the life, of rubricism in prayer; finally, the variety of kinds of religious life, all the way from communities to hermits, between which come the wandering monks—all this, let it be said in passing, is close to primitive Christian monasticism. Among the vows taken by the monks are numbered nonviolence, truth, celibacy, poverty, labor, freedom from fear, self-control, solidarity with one's neighbors.

Monastic virtues. The vows of the Hindu or Buddhist monk do not coincide with those of the Christian monk—though, in fact they cover approximately the same areas. It is therefore pointed out that the virtues are given different names on both sides, and that it is not without profit to know what virtues are expected of a monk in Asia. These consist of distinguishing the

APPENDIX B   287

divine, or spiritual, from what is transitory; in not being attached to objects that cause pleasure, because they give rise to desire, possession, recompense; in maintaining mental and spiritual equilibrium; courage under difficulties and sufferings of every kind; the practice of meditation; the cultivation of self-denial, faith, desire for union with God.

Here are some of the virtues that have been considered traditional in Christian monasticism:

Obedience. Insistence is made on the necessity of favoring the sense of personal responsibility by not multiplying the obligations in detail, and by cultivating the community sense so profound in many Asians. One reply seems to reconcile all the aspects that need reconciling:

> Obedience corresponds to authority, which, according to the gospel, is leadership in service; it is a function of charity, springing from the greater love that brought the brothers together to serve, and in which alone the group continues to exist as a religious group. The superior is in the first place the sacrament of this love and this union, revealing and fostering them; consequently he is the sacrament of ordered life and service. Hence Christian authority can work only through dialogue and sharing of responsibility: the community is the subject of responsibility, which coalesces from the responsibilities that individuals freely disposed of by themselves, on entering the religious group. Obedience is the willed state and attitude by which personal responsibility maintains itself open to the influence and enrichment that comes from the responsibility of others; the will to co-responsibility is obedience. Hence obedience is a school of freedom of others and through them of Christ.

Several Westerners remark that it is difficult to get certain Asians to follow a fixed time schedule (for example, eating at times fixed in advance). One may ask whether that is a primary need; certain practices of Eastern Christian monasticism, even to our day, may lead one to think that there is nothing very important in that fact. Likewise, the wish expressed by Asians to have more "free time" at their disposal is probably more justified than certain persons would seem to think.

Humility. The temptation to always "save one's face" or to give way to ambition seems to exist in the East just as it does in the West, under slightly different psychological forms, and this is one more reason for cultivating profound humility.

Brotherly relations. As everywhere, the possibility of selfishness exists in the Far East; but the Asians offer great resources for the sense of community. For example, the Trappists of Indonesia reply:

The spirit of helpfulness *(gotong-royong)*, sublimated into a spirit of Christian charity, must be promoted in order to maintain and develop the unity of the monastic family. This spirit of help must not be limited to the sphere of material things, but must also be introduced into the spiritual realm. It cannot be fully realized if, within the monastery, one is not authorized to have normal and human contacts with one's brothers, without prejudice to the importance of silence and recollection. A healthy contact is a condition *sine qua non* for dialogue, which, whether officially organized or spontaneous, is very necessary for brotherly relationships.

This spirit of helpfulness can also be furthered by help in the sphere of studies, *lectio divina* and so on.

Withdrawal from the world. The essential observance consists in not going out of the monastery without a reason, because one remains drawn by the spiritual center. Material enclosure is not seen to be necessary. Here are extracts from two replies that touch on the basic problem and suggest solutions. Father S. Rayan, S.J., writes:

The world from which we are separated is the world for which Jesus would not pray: the power that deliberately stands against God—but not the world that God so loved as to give his Son for its salvation. Hence enclosure is in the heart. Here perhaps a radical rethinking is required to help monasticism continue along the lines of the Incarnation and of divine involvement with the world. The monk will live with and within the concerns and anxieties of modern man and become the relation of the world to God, the presence in the world of God's peace and charity, in a word, the divine transparency for the world.

There should be an arrangement in the monastery itself, not in an outside house, for all sorts of people to come and live and share the life of the monks as fully as they want. Postulants could live here for a time, and receive special instruction in the rule and in prayer, though wearing no special habit. They will enter when they are judged ready to. Christian faith is man's definitive engagement; it deepens and blossoms with the growth of charity. Entrance into religion is one such point of growth; the development will continue. Is not the rest mainly a legal affair, and need much thought be given to it? Faith orients life definitively, and then a man progresses endlessly. And in one sense every act each day is definitive. Keeping legal thinking to the minimum is essential for religious life in Asia.

The Trappists of Indonesia write:

The spirit of helpfulness *(gotong-royong)* must be introduced into our community, either in the relationships that our monastic community has with society—the monastery is not a walled-in castle, but a member of society—or in the mutual relations between the monks themselves. They ought to live in a fraternal atmosphere of mutual help. Consequently, absolute silence cannot be maintained. In the practice of silence, which nevertheless keeps its original importance, there ought to be a certain liberty.

According to the local custom, when receiving families in the guest house, meals may be taken with the guests. Visits to the family should be allowed in the case of the death of a close relative. As to other occasions, for example, weddings, religious profession or ordination of next of kin, and so on, there should be no fixed rule for allowing visits to the family. Each case should be prudently considered, bearing in mind the charity that is due to the family, but without prejudice to the respect due to withdrawal from the world.

Prayer. Two facts are to be remarked here. First, a preference given, in many places, to contemplation and meditation, based on Scripture and tradition as they are already practiced by Hindu and Buddhist monks. This preference is in conformity with the practice in ancient Christian monasticism. Furthermore, the Divine Office has been readily accepted, even if it has not been adapted to the psychology of the country: "We like to say the Office, because it makes us proud [of being monks]." Nevertheless, in certain localities there is already an attempt at making the liturgy simpler and freer.

Here is a program, suggested by Father S. Rayan, S.J.:

> Start with the essentials of the liturgy, as they did in the early Church, and then let it grow through contact with indigenous cult and culture, through constant dialogue within the community regarding new shapes and forms, and through a process of responsible experiment. Each community in Asia will have to find its own way, and by pooling of experience build an indigenous liturgy. Along with the Bible, use with insight hymns, texts, tunes, symbols and gestures of indigenous cult after making sure they have no unsavory connotation in the modern man's mind. We shall fill them with the Paschal mystery and the sentiments of this mystery.
>
> Let there be an inward and peaceful presence before God; affectionate perusal of Holy Scripture in the presence of him who speaks through them; simple contemplation of nature and of events in the manner of the Bible. All this should become increasingly interior and peaceful. It will have to be carefully taught to the Asian monk, since the Asian Church's tradition of prayer is repetition of formulas.
>
> There should be also a creative and ever evolving liturgy—through deepening insight into the providential meaning of the religions that have

appeared in history, and the relation of these religions to Christ and the Church; through an integrated spirituality in which Western Christian experience will combine with Asian experience; through newer and profounder understanding of Scripture, as mentioned above.

Lastly, Father Bulatao, from the Philippines, shows that the problem of the liturgy is connected with that of the community spirit. His witness is interesting because it shows us how an Asian sees Westerners:

> My only comment on your program is that I feel there should be some discussion of "community spirit" in your conference. Many contemplative (and noncontemplative) communities I have seen are not really communities, but merely conglomerations of individuals. There is complete lack of a deep communication between the members, and mutual distrust keeps the individuals from becoming a group.
>
> I think of the liturgy as the expression of community spirit. When this community spirit is lacking, the liturgy is expression without substance, a mere ritual, the conjoint worship of individuals. Accordingly, there is need to create a spirit of community among contemplatives.
>
> There are at present new, secular technologies for the improvement of interpersonal communication and the creation of true community. These technologies consist mainly of discussion groups set up to discuss existential relationships in the community. The goal is to create an open society where a man has freedom to be himself and to express himself, and not to put on an appearance for the sake of legalisms. Also one seeks to create an atmosphere of real respect for each other as persons of absolute value. In such an atmosphere both the individual and the group can grow.
>
> We Jesuits of the East Asian Province have just finished one week's conference in Hong Kong. We feel that we want to form a closer community with the region around us, but to do so we must first form a real community among ourselves.

Father Bulatao was kind enough to add to his reply a remarkable report on "indigenization." The Hong Kong meeting to which he refers will be dealt with later on.

Poverty. This subject has already been alluded to in the replies quoted above, as well as under labor and hospitality. Here is still another witness:

> Poverty is not considered as being a reality, for the economic standard of the monastery is higher than that of the environment from which the postulants come. Generally, on entering the monastery, one leaves little to receive more. It may be added, however, that our way of living is more sober than that of the religious of other orders or congregations.

And a program, suggested by Father Rayan:

> Be clad in simple garments; live in simple cottages; let the cell be simple but beautifully painted in colors and symbols, with only a few books, writing materials and a cot that serves also for table and chair. . . . The library will have have all conveniences for study. Travel simply, as the poor of the locality do, carrying their own baggage. Have something to share with the very needy; live by your own work, and work so as to have something to give. But common poverty is important; the house should look modest. All are to work, and that not only on the farm but also in factories; for this area of modern life should not be left alone without the presence of peace and prayer.

Formation. Many suggest that the time preceding the final commitment should be fairly long, and even last for a period that has not been determined beforehand. Certain persons, as has already been seen, suggest that one might be able to engage oneself in the Christian monastic life temporarily, as in Buddhist monasticism.

Whatever may be the case, there is a desire for a great deal more suppleness than the present Latin legislation allows. The discussions at Bangkok will show whether it is suitable to formulate a *votum* on this subject to be transmitted to the authorities. Moreover, this agrees with the desire expressed in many places in the West.

Many remark that up to now monks have depended upon means of formation (seminaries, scholasticates) that had not been conceived with the monastic life in mind. On several sides it is insisted that formation in Holy Scripture be intensified, as well as formation in the liturgy, the Fathers of the Church and recent theology. Also there may be some initiation into the Hindu and Buddhist traditions, even into Confucianism and other traditions, depending on the country.

A program has been suggested by Father Rayan:

> All should study from the start and continue through life the following: the local language, the cultural language of the country, the languages of the Bible (some perhaps could study Greek and others Hebrew). They should also study the Bible closely and scientifically, the Sacred Scriptures of the country, and the religions of the world, which bear the seeds of the Word and are waiting to develop into the Church in God's time, through peaceful contact with the gospel in us. A ten-year or twelve-year program should lay the foundations on which each can build, with the help of a library. Some at least can attend secular universities: this presence and contact will be beneficial both to the monks and to society at large. There

should be some course for all, though only a few will receive ministerial ordination.

Here is what has been achieved by the Trappists of Indonesia:

The period of postulancy lasts about a year, followed by at least two years' novitiate. The minimum period of temporary vows is three years.

The classes given in the novitiate are designed for postulants and novices in the first two years of monastic life. There is a daily lesson of forty-five minutes. The matter taught includes a general introduction to Holy Scripture, the Psalms, the spiritual life, the Rule of St. Benedict, the history of the Order, prayer, the constitutions and singing. In addition, once a week, instruction is given that may from time to time take the form of dialogue. Twice a month the novices, in turn, give a talk to the others between thirty and forty-five minutes long, based on their reading. On this occasion criticism is offered and questions are asked.

Once the novitiate lessons are ended, the young brothers, who normally remain up to two years in the novitiate after their temporary profession, follow courses given in the juniorate for a period that has not yet been determined, but continues at the most up to the taking of solemn vows. They are given the opportunity to take lessons three times a week in a foreign language. This year [1968] they may choose either German or Dutch. Twice a week there is a special lesson of forty-five minutes on subjects decided upon each year. The other members of the community who feel the need may attend these lessons. Each year an exegesis of St. John's Gospel is given during the first semester, and during the second, one on Christology. Last year the matter taught comprised Church history, history of Christian spirituality and special questions concerning the spiritual life. Other subjects on the program are Vatican II, the Cistercian Fathers, one or two treatises on dogmatic theology and on moral theology, patrology and so on.

The problem of the priesthood. Many observe that among the monks priesthood is looked upon in the same way it is looked upon outside monasticism, that is to say, it is often considered as an occasion of promotion—of honor for the priest and for his family, and of material advantages—though the monk is scarcely inclined to accept the pastoral charges and responsibilities that go with it. Entry into the monastery gives the means of studying in the Western style. "Under these conditions," states one of the replies, "it is very difficult to have people appreciate the value of monastic life in itself." It does not help to insist that this situation has been created by the Westerners themselves, who arrive already ordained, and that the solution to this problem must also be first found in the West.

It is also noted that the fact of being raised to the priesthood, with the social, economic and intellectual promotion it comprises, is what most differentiates Christian monasticism from the humble, simple and poor life that is normally (for there are exceptions) that of the monk according to Asian tradition. From this point of view, the priesthood of the monks seems to be the major obstacle to any understanding that Buddhists and Hindus might have of the monastic life and, in consequence, of the introduction of Christian monasticism in Asia.

On this point Father Rayan is very clear-sighted:

> By baptism all share in the priesthood of Christ and grow in it as charity grows, and this is the eternal priesthood. Of this vital priesthood, the ministerial priesthood is but a sacrament or sign. There should therefore be in a community only as many "ministers" as are required to serve the needs of the community. In Asia, priesthood has an aura of prestige and power that is too closely associated with the Christian religion. What is needed today in Asia is a clearer witness and example of gospel life. The measure of religious and Christian life here bears small proportion to the number of ministers and activities.

Indigenization. Certain conclusions are to be drawn from the replies to the first part of the questionnaire. One of the replies acknowledges that "creativity has been stifled" by the fact that Western forms have been imposed upon the Asians and that as a result sometimes the Asian Christian is "more conservative (and more European) than the missionary himself." It is added that this situation occurs in monasticism also.

Here is witness from Father Paramananda Divarkar, S.J., along the same lines:

> My feeling, from whatever little experience I have here in my own country, is that monastic life—and indeed all religious life—suffers from a serious defect that is rooted in the quality of the Christian life here. Our Christians are very devout and faithful, but in general they seem to lack a certain vitality; their life does not spring from a transforming Christian experience. I have often said—though it is a cruel statement—that we are a secondhand Church, lacking in creative energy. This difficulty manifests itself even more clearly in the religious life: young aspirants learn to conform, and they do it very well; but they do not seem to be transformed. Though India has a monastic tradition of its own and attempts have been made to Christianize it, one gets the impression, in general, that Christian monasticism here is a thing from outside, something whose ways one can learn but whose spirit one has not wholly captured. Despite attempts at adaptation, the monasteries we have still appear as imitations, not as

something rising from an inner necessity. Perhaps I am exaggerating this point, but to me this is the root difficulty that must be resolved before we can proceed farther.

Thus the Christians in Asia must be given back their freedom by disengaging their Christianity from the recent Western forms in which it has been clothed. This does not mean that they must be made to imitate Hindu or Buddhist forms, either ancient or renewed. A Benedictine nun declares: "We should give greater encouragement to authentic ideas, customs and ways of Christian living." Thus, over and above the traditions of Western Christianity and those of non-Christian Asia, we are brought back to the source: the gospel. Liberty with regard to the past and with regard to laws established in and for other continents, confidence in the fruitfulness of the Christian message, in what it possesses that is fundamental and universal, will allow us to center everything on the gospel and will prevent our imposing on Asian monasticism a European look that the gospel does not ask for.

It will then be possible to create in each country an original Asian monasticism, one that is not a copy of any other but that incorporates the values of others, those of the Christian West and Near East as well as those of non-Christian Asia. Here are two witnesses in this connection:

> We ourselves must try to be respectful of, open to and sympathetic toward the cultural and religious values of the country we work in, sympathetic toward its cultural and religious values, and strive to make this respect and sympathy flow into our contacts, our teaching and the like, with our students and with people in general. When the chance offers itself, we should try to integrate these values in our Christian community life and radiate them in the surrounding Christian and non-Christian community.

And again:

> The role of the monks from Europe and America in this part of the world is not to bring over Benedictine, Cistercian, Carmelite and other traditions and adapt them more or less to the conditions of climate, culture and so forth. . . . The Christian monastic life, here, must start off from the traditional monastic life (which began at least ten centuries before St. Benedict himself) and incorporate the wealth of Christian monasticism, and first of all that of the Desert Fathers, in such a way as to bring it to evangelical perfection; it is in view of this that the Spirit has made it known to the best of the wise men here. That supposes among the pioneers a sort of novitiate among the monks. Then, slowly, after maturation and intimate osmosis, a Christian monasticism will appear that will be the continuation and the sublimation of this long waiting.

When we read such witnesses and the elements of the program that have already been quoted, and when we take note of what has already been realized we are led to ask certain loyal questions. Is Western Christian monasticism actually capable of establishing Christian monasticism in Asia? Ought we give up the task and wait for the time when Christianity becomes Asian and engenders its own monasticism? Otherwise, one risks having in Asia a few colonies of monks as alien as the few schools of Yoga to be found near certain capitals in Europe and America.

Perhaps for the immediate future we ought to begin by just watching Asians—monks and others—live, studying their traditions, learning their languages, reading their books, trying to understand their mentality, broadening our culture, recognizing with modesty, according to the words of Father F. Enomiya-Lassalle, S. J., that the Eastern religions "have made better use of man's natural faculties than Christianity has."

One must also learn to judge the authenticity of a monastic establishment not from its outer prosperity (numbers, duration, foundations)—for a man who remains alone may see more clearly and find himself nearer the sources—but according to its conformity with the gospel demands and the evangelization of cultures. We must also get used to greater variety and adaptability in forms of life and institutions than has been known in the West during the last few centuries.

Thus we see that the solution to the problems is to be sought in the West as much as in Asia. And already there are certain indications to give us confidence. Thus, when the Western Benedictine abbots drew up their "Propositions," they only dared to use the term "contemplative life" once, and that by way of allusion and almost with an apology for doing so, whereas Jesuit missionaries and even some Benedictines in Asia are not afraid to speak of it. Western monasticism has something to learn, or to relearn, from that of the Far East, and we can say that this process has already started.

Finally, a recent manifestation of the Church's vitality in Asia—analogous in the missionary sphere to what the Bangkok meeting should be in the monastic sphere—recalls one of the elements for solving the problem that has already been mentioned in several replies.

When the Jesuit meeting of missionaries and missiologists took place in Hong Kong in April 1968, an Asian missionary began by warning the Church in Asia against "imitating the irrelevant churches of the West." Another spoke of "indigenization"—how to make Christianity present in Asia in an authentically indigenous way. A third called for more Asian leadership, and this marked the turning point. As one Asian put it: "We realized for the first time that we were really being listened to." The account of this congress —we are still waiting for the proceedings to be published—is already a model and a warning for us. Among other things, we can read there that the Asians urged non-Asians to "try to enter into our minds and hearts" and help bring an end to "paternalism, condescension and contempt"—all so many leftovers from colonial days. Though non-Asians outnumbered Asians, a committee was made up of four Asians and one non-Asian. Lastly, the memory was invoked of two confreres who had worked in China, not far from Hong Kong: Father Matteo Ricci, S. J., and Father Pierre Teilhard de Chardin, S. J.[3]

II. THE MONASTERY IN THE LOCAL CHURCH COMMUNITY

The replies to this part of the questionnaire were generally shorter, and the summary will be also, because their content depends largely upon what has already been said in connection with Part I.

The first contribution that monasticism has to make to the life of the Church in Asia is to manifest that aspect of the Church which the Vatican Council has several times called "contemplation"[4] and that form of life which it has called, following tradition, the "contemplative life."[5] It is, then, incumbent upon Christian monks in Asia to make themselves accepted as such, to arouse interest in that aspect of the Church which it is their vocation to represent among the hierarchy, the clergy and the faithful. That is what Father E. de Meester has done by the letter he addressed to the Seminary of India before a reunion during which all the aspects of the Church were to be studied. He also had printed and sent to all the bishops of India a pamphlet setting forth the teaching of Vatican II on the contemplative life.

Here are some extracts from his letter:

> It is commonplace to say that Indians are contemplative minded. History has produced in this country an extraordinary flourishing of monastic vocations with Buddhism, and even now in our own time Hinduism produces hundreds of ashrams and *maths*, thousands of *sannyasis* and *sadhus*. Yet it must be recognized that our Catholics have completely lost that contemplative dimension of their Christianity. It would be easy to give many instances of the lack of interest of priests and laymen in the monastic life.
>
> Although the holy men of Hinduism were constantly concerned with

---

[3] Cf. C. J. McNaspy, S.J., "A Meeting in Hong Kong," *America*, June 22, 1968, pp. 792–93. The proceedings have been published under the title *East Asian Jesuit Secretariat Conference—Hong Kong*, April 16–20, 1968 (New York: Jesuit Missions, 1968).

[4] See Constitution on the Sacred Liturgy, n. 2; Constitution on the Church, n. 1; Decree on the Ministry and Life of Priests, n. 13; Constitution on the Church in the Modern World, nn. 8, 56–57, 59; Constitution on Divine Revelation, n. 7–8.

[5] See Decree on the Church's Missionary Activity, nn. 18, 40; Decree on the Bishops' Pastoral Office in the Church, n. 35; Decree on the Appropriate Renewal of the Religious Life, n. 7.

the absoluteness of God, many of our young people seem to fear the "God alone" motive, which is the fundamental motive of monastic life; they prefer this motive to be watered down with external activities, which they consider ordinarily in a very naturalistic manner. For them a monastic life has thus no meaning at all, and they fail to understand the apostolic value of contemplative life, and that "every believer who sanctifies himself takes part in the mystery of universal redemption." And furthermore, that "it is his privilege that he cannot save himself alone; his personal sanctification is also an apostolate, a work of redemption in Christ."

I may also mention what Monsignor Eugène de Souza wrote in *Points de Vue sur la Vie Monastique* (Montserrat, 1964). He sees "in the contemplative presence, which monasticism makes possible, a compensation, a remedy for the heresy of good works, which, he declares, is already very widespread and has done serious damage to the spiritual structure of our country."

I think, thus, that greater account should be taken by the hierarchy of the texts of the Popes on the contemplative life and of the teaching of the Vatican Council that the contemplative life "belongs to the fullness of the Church's presence and ought to be established everywhere in the infant church."

The existence of flourishing monasteries is absolutely necessary for a deep spirituality among priests and laymen. Unless we have a good number of men and women dedicated to contemplative life, we shall never be able to create a liturgy that will be the fruit of the Indian soil, for the liturgy is only the result of the contemplation of the Christian mystery; nor can a real dialogue be initiated with the non-Christians, since a true dialogue can only start from a deep experience of the inner life in Christ.

Here are still other witnesses. The first comes from an American Benedictine of Taiwan:

> Once the monastery's objective has been determined, it can be an effective witness to the Christian community with a character that is distinct from that of active congregations. It can serve as a center for the application and implementation of the documents of Vatican II. It can be of service to the local Church as a refuge of spiritual development and a cultural center to welcome scholars who are willing to devote their energies and talents to the arts in and for the Church. It can also serve as an experimental center for a liturgy peculiar to the Chinese.
>
> It is hoped that they will gradually accept the presence of a Christian monasticism in their midst and take advantage of what it can contribute to their spiritual formation.

Since the community has been welcomed by the local hierarchy, it should be ready to render service to the diocese while at the same time maintaining its identity as primarily a contemplative order.

Father A. Goman, S. J., writes from Thailand:

In a country where the Buddhist religion (of Hinayana, or the Little Vehicle) presents itself essentially in a monastic and community form, the Catholic Church must absolutely present this aspect that is essential to it and that so far is completely unknown to the Buddhists. This aspect cannot fail to attract them, since it is one familiar to them; the Church would inspire them with greater respect, and in the comparison they would be led to make between the two monasticisms, they would see more clearly the differences: the Buddhist monk seeks to save himself, and his social role consists above all in showing the way of salvation *out of* the world; the Christian monk serves God and men *in* the world, which he wishes to save. This monastic presence would give them the key to the Christian apostolate by showing that God is the source of it; without this presence it is difficult sometimes to make it understood that our action is something more than philanthropy.

In order to play its role, the Church, in its monastic and community aspect, must be clothed in the fashion of the country: a great deal of adaptation will probably be necessary from many points of view. A monastic center would also render great services to the Church if retreats could be organized there.

And Father Rayan says:

The monks' own existence is to be a manifest brotherhood and a communion of love. Their life of work will set a pattern of living by honest toil, producing a surplus for the benefit of others, sharing wealth, manifesting thus that the meaning of wealth is fraternity, revealing the spiritual and personal dimensions of work. They will put their collective and traditional experience and skill at the service of the villages around them and even make them the gift of their time and work—what Vinoba calls *sram-dan*. They will treat all with equally high reverence so as to transform society with the values of the personal.

They could play a significant role in increasing literacy and giving adult education and thus develop God's unlettered children. Ideas of cooperation and unity and sharing of life and labor and the fruits of labor could be inculated and fostered. They will be instruments of social and personal reconciliation and peace. It will be a great social and Christian service to prepare the people for change, to create the will to change and inject into traditional social stagnation a dynamism of sound social revolution. It will promote hope and optimism and the will to work.

Hospitality is important as well as availability; part of the monk's labor will be for the poorest of the locality. Monks will visit the poor, deal with all in sweetness and peace, honor the lowly, treat all with equal charity and consideration. The monastery should be known as a house of peace and prayer; prayer programs ought to be organized so many times a week for people to attend, with readings, chants, silences and meditation, but without pomp or anything that is untrue. There must be poverty, living by one's own work; constant effort and self-examination will be required to keep close to the level of life of the country's poor. A surplus must be produced, earned and secured for the poor of the locality.

What is needed is a monasticism that will work with the people; that will help develop liturgy and culture; that will act as a spiritual leaven—giving retreats, teaching catechism, visiting the sick, reconciling people, teaching people to work, introducing new techniques, helping the emergence of new insights into the words and deeds of God recorded in the Bible, through new scrutiny in the light and in the context of Asia's religious perceptions, and giving these insights to the world through publications that both illuminate and invite to further probing.

The monks, rich in prayer and spiritual wisdom, will be at the disposal of the bishop and clergy to serve, without detriment to the spirit and ideal of monasticism, as retreat masters, catechists, publishers, organizers of the liturgy, music and art, and so on.

The monastery will be a home for all, a place of meeting, understanding and charity, of openness and hospitality; a center of study, a point of contact in depth and sweet meditation and confidence and peace.

Two main ideas emerge from all these statements:
1. In conformity with its tradition in Christian history and with what it often is in the Asian traditions, monasticism will have to carry out different forms of radiation, of spiritual and material help, which will not be the same as the apostolic and pastoral activities of the clergy and the missionaries but will be in harmony with the specific traits of a life that is willing to be of the "contemplative" type.

As Father Rayan says: "Let monasteries be present among the aboriginals; but not to 'convert' in the classical sense; they will be there to give the people an experience of the Church and of Christ, a contact with Christ's charity and prayer. In confrontation with these, the grace that is in them will mature in God's time and God's ways."

2. Since monasticism is that which is closest in the Church to the mon-

asticism so important in the Asian religions, it is especially fitted to contribute to approaching these religions and their monasticism, to integrate certain forms of meditation and expression in worship. Hence its liturgical role. This is, in fact, already carried out in several localities in collaboration with the diocesan, regional or national liturgical commissions.

Here, for example, is what the Trappists of Indonesia say:

> As for us, we know very well that the presence of Christian monasticism attests to the contemplative and absolute character of the Christian mystery. And as for the faithful, I think they are not in a position to grasp clearly, and with any depth of though, the role of the monastic vocation within the Church's life, though it must be said that they have a vague notion of the meaning of the monastic life.
>
> From the hierarchy we get sympathetic understanding. We all agree— the faithful and the hierarchy are of the same mind—that the monastery must contribute to the spiritual, liturgical and cultural development in such measure as is possible. In fact, our monastery has already opened its doors to retreatants, priests, religious and laymen, though only in small numbers on account of the limited number of rooms in our guest house.
>
> Generally speaking, we do not give retreats outside the monastery. Perhaps we could make exceptions in favor of other contemplative monasteries in the country.
>
> In matters of liturgy, especially in the domain of sacred music, our monastery has contributed much to the efforts of the local Church during these last years. But nothing has yet been done in the cultural sphere, for want of competent persons.

As to the work of rapprochement between the Christian Churches (i.e., ecumenism) or between the other religions, the replies say very little, except for Kerala, where there are Eastern Churches of different rites. Elsewhere relationships have been established with Anglicans or with the Protestants. The Trappists of Indonesia write: "In this sphere we have not yet done very much. We have helped the Muslims of our village to level the ground for the building of their mosque."

We may conclude these replies with a quotation from Martin Buber: "Every real life is a meeting."

SUMMARY OF REPLIES TO PART III
THE MONASTERY IN THE COUNTRY
Prepared by C. P. Tholens, O.S.B.

The first question of this section was about how, in the sociological context of each country, the monastery can give an intelligible Christian witness to charity, prayer and poverty.

A. *Poverty.* On the whole, the replies to the questionnaire show that the monasteries in Asia feel a certain difficulty concerning the witness of evangelical poverty. "The monk who thinks he is poor has ceased to be so; likewise, every monastery that thinks it is poor is a counter-witness to itself." Also, "the needs of even a small community call for land, buildings, material, which class the monks among the rich."
The difficulty arises partly from this fact:

> For most of the aspirants, entry into the monastery signifies a considerable raising of their standard of living. They are not psychologically ready, then, for renouncing material wealth, and they do not know the real value of money. Left to themselves they are inclined to spend money without any thought of economy and they are scarcely impressed by the example of a life of poverty.

Another reason for the difficulty of practicing poverty lies in the fact that it is considered in these countries as an evil to combat: "In our age of rapid economic progress, it is difficult to freely assume poverty in solidarity with those who do not yet benefit by this progress."
It seems that we must conclude, as Dom André Louf said in 1965 at the monastic meeting at Bouaké, in Africa, where the subject of poverty was studied and discussed at length:

> Poverty is essentially a grace, a grace for the Church, a grace for each one of us. It seems that we can never reproach anyone with not being poor, because it is something that we cannot choose. No, we cannot "choose" poverty . . . it would be still another act of a rich man. To be truly poor, we have to let ourselves be chosen by the Lord, because it is a very particular grace, and we can only await this grace from God. Every monk, however, should await and ask for this grace, both for himself and for his community.

Nevertheless, we must know how to impose an attitude upon ourselves. This fact is emphasized by the following reflections:

Our neighbors can at least notice that in the monastery there is real poverty: first from the fact that the monks work manually; then from the fact that the monks do not have the use even of the objects that even the poor have: good clothes for holidays, radio, gold watches, jewels. The best informed can know that the monks may possess nothing of their own, that they may not dispose of personal money, that they have to ask everything from the superior.

By the simplicity of our houses and our clothing, we must aim at not going beyond the standard of living of the middle class, according to local circumstances.

The poverty lived in this attitude would be of the open-handed sort, which gives readily, and does not hold to monastery possessions, which lives simply and spends little (at least ordinarily), so that what is left over may be given to the less favored.

One must live by means of his work; a constant effort and an examination of conscience should be demanded in order to keep oneself at the level of the life of the poor in the country. A surplus must be produced; it must be earned and assured for the country's poor.

We shall give a witness of poverty, in spite of appearances, if we can at least keep up our social attitudes, using our wealth (which, of course, must be considered as relative) in order to raise the level of local society, being always disposed to lighten the sufferings of the poor. In short, we shall give a witness of poverty in working to earn our living and in always developing within us the spirit of sociability.

We must little by little work to do away with all false conceptions and direct our attempts toward programs implied by this effort. That would show our will to share our possessions and to serve the real needs of our neighbors.[6]

Prayer. Here are some replies:

In these Buddhist countries, the value of prayer, of intercession, is recognized. The *bonzes* (monks) are considered as being the models of the Buddhist faith and as mediators. But education, more and more widespread, does not favor religious thought. Whatever the case, those independent persons who continue to practice have esteem for men of prayer and understand our message as Catholic monks, but they do not

---

[6] *Rythmes du Monde,* 1965, Nos. 1 and 2.

come into the churches and thus are not touched by liturgical prayer. Attempts at outward manifestations of piety, consisting of liturgies of the Word adapted to non-Christians, might give the sense of Catholic prayer. But it would perhaps be a good thing to select the participants; otherwise one would end up with a fairground atmosphere, such as to be noticed in the feasts held in the pagodas. For the rare Christians, a real effort must be made to offer them a prayer they can understand and make their own. The introduction of the local language is necessary. As to vocal and instrumental music, its use is to be commended as long as it really is a help to prayer.

We must work at giving our neighbors an intelligible liturgy. And, of course, we must give the witness of our personal lives as lives of prayer.

The Oriental conception consists in the awareness of the presence of a deity, which affects their daily life. . . . Our prayer must bear witness to the eternal presence of the only true God, and it must show that all our actions are directed in this sense.

[We need] programs of study and prayer in common; we must make an effort to understand the prayer of others, their faith, their mysticism and their eschatological hope; we must be signs of the kingdom, by transparency of the life of prayer, but also realize a presence in the local milieu . . . attempting to give the Divine Office a worthy and appropriate form, acting as a mediating community.

The monks of Kurisumala have recently been asked by the Commission for Liturgy of the Episcopal Conference to start thinking about the creation of a new Indian rite. An Indian witness gives further weight to the question:

We could envisage the suggestion, truly revolutionary, of replacing certain parts of the Divine Office by sacred Hindu texts that contain especially beautiful and profound prayers. On the whole, the Offices celebrated in the churches of our monasteries should create an atmosphere of devotion, especially by the meditative recitation of the Divine Office, in which lay people could take part, even Buddhists. Indian religious music should be used in the official liturgy, just as certain more popular religious songs, which the Indians like very much, should be exploited.

In India, the monk is the one who realizes and reveals by his life that this world of phenomena is not the last reality, is not the sole necessary reality. . . . Christian monasticism adds another dimension, which is to realize and manifest the ideal society God desires for mankind: a deeply united brotherhood, open to God and to men, in work, peace and prayer.

... Peace, deep peace and the faculty of prayer; poverty and detachment, with a simple life and a simple austerity; hospitality, serviceability, easiness of approach—such are the traits of Indian and Asian spiritual life that must shine forth in the monastic life. We might add that the choice of clothes according to the native ascetic tradition and vegetarianism are associated with the refining of the mind, purity, peace and universal compassion.

Charity. These replies were received:

Hospitality and availability are of equal importance. Part of the work of the monks would be to help the poor of the country. The monks could visit the poor, helping them in gentleness and peace; they ought to honor those who are in any way oppressed, and should treat all men with the same charity and consideration.

Charity within the community "must be a working virtue for the service of the surrounding community and for the local churches. That implies a serious knowledge of the problems of society and the will to contribute, according to possibilities, to the solution of social problems."

B. The second question was about how Christian monasticism can undertake and develop truly religious exchanges with the representatives of non-Christian monasticism.

In his report "Problems of Christian Monasticism in Asia,"[7] Dom Jean Leclercq, O.S.B., writes:

After the Council, there is no longer any need for Catholics to justify the necessity of an "approach" to Hinduism and to Buddhism. It is part of this "meeting of religions," of this "dialogue for," for which so many will be working from now on. It presupposes that we admit that there is in these traditions a considerable fund of truth that must be sought. For monasticism, which concerns us here, there is the same sort of duty. Between Christian and Hindu monasticism, there exist resemblances in different areas: in historical evolution, in practices and forms of existence, above all in spiritual attitudes.

Cardinal Marella, President of the Secretariat for non-Christian Religions, wrote to the Apostolic Delegate of Bangkok:

In these contacts we must not aim at immediate success, but sow seeds that one day, perhaps still far off, will yield fruit.... We must not, today, judge or condemn the attitudes taken by Catholics of other times with

[7] *Vie Religieuse et Vie Contemplative* (Paris: Lethielleux, 1969), p. 231.

regard to non-Christian religions; but we must now go beyond this stage and adopt a more positive attitude, avoiding anything that might lead either to syncretism or to religious indifference. We must also forget and forgive the persecutions suffered in the past, whenever they took place. We must bear in mind the favor that was almost everywhere shown to Christian missionaries. We must be open to all natural values—not merely material and temporal ones, but also religious ones—of humanity as a whole.... This is to be accomplished by means of dialogue, which is encounter, exchange, in an atmosphere of friendship: none of these occasions must be missed. The first condition is that, on both sides, we learn to know one another better. And we know that the human virtues to be found in Buddhism—kindliness, compassion for those who suffer, acceptance of pain, search for interior peace, condemnation of violence, respect for the dead, desire to acquire merits for a future life—have their origin in the Word enlightening every man, as the Council has explained. Really, what counts is that Christianity should not seem to be a ghetto, but should show its true universal nature, its force for good, capable of winning sympathies in the different religious milieus, with prudence and dignity, without either syncretism or concessions.

Christian monasticism as it presently exists in Asia has not yet attained this lofty point of view. Here is the opinion of an expert:

The Christian expression in Vietnam has been one-sidedly Westernized. ... There is a conviction that all that is native is "pagan," thus diabolic. ... Architecture, objects used for worship, everything is in a style of European art that is without style.... This "anti-pagan" prejudice is still reigning and is a great obstacle to the openness of Christianity to the values of the other religions strongly represented in the country. Our monks have been formed along these lines of thought. Practically none among them yet dares to get in contact with a *bonze*.

But it is not always like that:

It must be remarked that these contacts between Christian and non-Christian monasticism were almost unheard of in India until quite recently. It was our privilege to receive very early some *sadhus* in our guest house. Since then, several have been coming regularly for a time of silence. We also have periodical meetings with swamis. All this remains very limited, however, and without any great impact on a real religious exchange between us and them. We ought to have deeper contacts so that they could bear fruit in mutual enrichment and in friendship. We must try to arrive at mutual esteem and appreciation. This stage is only attained when we discover, or rather, when we "realize" a divine presence in the life of our brothers, a real action of God; it is only that which can bring about mutual understanding and truly fruitful exchanges. Perhaps we may remark here that Catholics often have the tendency to obscure their Christian witness, their divine sonship, by accidental, even sometimes trivial, devotions and practices, whereas our Hindu brothers live more often in an almost constant recognition of the divine presence in nature as well as in the depths of the heart. In order to develop understanding and friendship, there can be nothing better than to prolong our stay among them.

Other difficulties must be pointed out:

> The local language is very poorly known by the European religious, and Pali is unknown even to the native monks themselves. And then there is the "alien," which applies not only to European monks but even to the monks of the territory, since they have rejected the national religion.

The difficulties, however, do not come only from the Christian monks. The non-Christian monks often create difficulties:

> Among the *bonzes* there is fear of an encroachment, fear of indoctrination, of proselytism. They are very sensitive about this point. They cannot believe we are disinterested. Then there is the doctrinal ignorance on the part of a large majority of the *bonzes*, even perhaps of all those in the countryside. In the pagoda, apart from the daily recitation of Pali texts, understood by almost none, and the exhortation to practice morals and the ritual, there is scarcely any other intellectual formation. All this helps to reduce the possibility of fruitful dialogue. What do exist, and must be cultivated, are friendly relationships, conversations on the human level. Work in common with them is hardly possible, for up to now the *bonzes* have scarcely been concerned with social work.

(We shall see later that this is not universally true.)

In many replies from our Christian monasteries we notice a desire for rapprochement. The religious are searching, and one can already see in which direction the solutions lie. An expert writes:

> We must suppress the barriers of misunderstanding and distrust and set up a dialogue that may lead to a mutual interest and to the service of the people. . . . We must set up dialogue with Christian and non-Christian communities in order to create a really fraternal atmosphere. We must approach problems of doctrine and unity gradually.

Personal contacts must be developed, combined activities and so on must be started by men who have prepared for this by suitable formation.

I suggest visits, temporary stays, or even permanent ones in a Hindu ashram, sharing the life of the Hindu monks in everything, inviting them in exchange into our monasteries and welcoming them into our communities as brothers. But the precondition for this sort of development and its inevitable consequences would be that our monasteries would have to change a great many of their customs and their ways of living. Otherwise there would be the danger that the Hindus would feel as if they were strangers and be embarrassed. But there is no doubt that living contact with Hindu monasticism would enrich and reward our Christian monastic community.

Study of different religious traditions is also a question of prudence, as another expert, Prof. J. Wils, of the University of Nijmegen, points out:

> We have not yet sufficiently gone into the cultures from which these religions have sprung. Furthermore, many of these non-Christian religions themselves are faced with a chrisis; they do not know very well how to solve modern problems.

This is confirmed by a witness from Korea:

> The whole Korean culture has its origin in Buddhism and Confucianism. But the modern Korean has turned away from them. Why is this so? For a long time, too long, the Koreans believed that Buddhism and Confucianism were the only valid standards of life, and they long held to their ancient customs. For this reason they have not always followed the progress of science in modern civilization. That is why in the underdeveloped villages only the most ignorant still hold to their old faith, being incapable of following the process of modern culture. Educated youth in the towns, and especially in student circles, is avid to open its heart and mind to modern Western ideas. It is certain that here and there a few learned Buddhists are trying to bring about an aggiornamento of their Buddhist and Confucian doctrine in order to integrate it with the modern world. Nevertheless most young Koreans maintain that we ought rather to spread the true ideas, habits and styles of Christian living than try to integrate the ideas of Buddhism or Confucianism into a modern Korea.

None of this, however, seems to be of such nature as to hinder a useful dialogue with non-Christian monks. Quite the contrary, since the modern Asian world finds itself about to lose every notion of religious transcendence, it will be up to Christian and non-Christian monks to take up together a serious study of this problem wherever it seems possible.

This is exactly what Dom Bede Griffiths foresees in his book *Christian Ashram:*

> It is necessary for us, therefore, to approach the people of these different religious traditions not as our enemies but as our friends, who share in part the truth we are called to preach. At the present time, in particular, when the majority of young men all over the world are turning from their traditional religion toward atheism and skepticism, we should surely recognize the value of these traditions. What is needed is some kind of ecumenical movement among the world religions comparable to that which already exists among Christians. If we are now beginning to approach our separated fellow Christians as our brothers and not as our enemies, it is surely time that we begin to approach our fellow men in other religious traditions in the same way.

In conclusion, the reader's attention is again called to Dom Leclercq's report: "Problems of Christian Monasticism in Asia."[8]

C. The third question was about how monks and communities can participate, in keeping with the encyclical *Populorum Progressio,* in the real development of their environment.

We must approach this subject with a quotation of Gunnar Myrdal, in his book *Asian Drama,* cited by one of the experts in response to the questionnaire:

> The immediate necessity of this country is its human development and a process of education that would allow Asians to take their own destinies in hand and to agree to bear the responsibility for a progress that is specific to Asia. Only Asians can save Asia. The missionary can help them help themselves. And this is perhaps the specific and immediate mission that is asked of the Church today, and it is perhaps that also which we must realize.

And indeed, there are new duties for Christians in the Third World, and monks cannot refuse to take an interest in them. It is the duty of the Church in Asia to begin to realize, or at least to serve, the human and lawful aspirations of the Asian peoples. The Church must make an effort to develop a sense of social responsibilities.

And the monastic communities must not forget that they are sociological entities in these different countries. In a special way, they have to collaborate

---

[8] *Ibid.*

with those who bear social responsibilities. They must, so to speak, think of these responsibilities on an inter-Asian level. And just because they are for the most part institutions that have come from the West, they must contribute to awaken the rest of the world, where most of their recruits still come from, to the terribly urgent problems of international justice.

When a monastic community wishes to live the Christian life in an exemplary way, it cannot avoid the problems that are imposed upon it by the human context itself. It will always have to take at least two things into consideration: (1) These countries of Asia are extraordinarily socially retarded, which calls for justice and charity, without delay, on the part of all. (2) The young people who enter these monasteries in Asia cannot be totally isolated, without causing serious troubles, from the social and political context of their country. The elite of the young people of these countries is above all a political elite that is preparing, at least unconsciously, a socio-economic revolution. Unfortunately the young Catholics seem to belong, for the greater part, to a certain conservative type. But that situation cannot last. And so Catholic youth will soon have to join in with the political and cultural milieu of their countries.

In all of this, the young monks have an enormous task to carry out. This socioeconomic revolution is the price to be paid for technical and political development; there is thus a danger that the new civilization will despiritualize Asian culture. Young native Christian monks will have to do a great deal to help their Hindu, Buddhist, and Muslim brothers maintain the spiritual dimension of their life. That would not mean that the monastery would have to become the "world"; but it means just what Brother Roger Schutz, the prior of Taizé, has so well expressed in his *Unanimity in Pluralism*:[9]

> In the pluralist and secular societies, more than ever before there is a need for places where transcendence is more felt, places where the City of God meets the city of men. The Christian today must be found where the vertical God links up with the community of mankind. A non-integrated contemplative life is no longer understood by contemporary man. But the Christian who has let himself be entirely absorbed by the human milieu is not recognized any more.

In spite of the heavy uncertainty that weighs on monasticism in the face of the modern world, and even though non-Christian Asian monasticism has not always managed to find the happy medium between a justified preoccupation with the future of this world and what we might call eschatology, we nevertheless find among Asian monks eloquent examples of the very real influence they have over the peoples among whom they live. In the first place there can be noticed, especially in the countries of Southeast Asia, the

[9] Taizé Press, 1966.

phenomenon of the alliance of Buddhism with nationalism. In this connection should be read *The Lotus in the Sea of Fire*, by the Vietnamese scholar, Thich Nhat Hanh.[10]

In this marvelous little book, the author, a contemplative monk, says:

> Within the strength of the various nationalist movements, Buddhism is an important element, and its potentialities for guiding the development of new societies need to be explored more fully than they have been. The West has never recognized this, but when it looks at Buddhism tends to make a comparison between its subtle and ingrained relationship to the people and the highly organized, highly structured organization of such religions as Catholicism. The Christian missionaries are far more capable in terms of organization than the local Buddhist institutions. The extensive Western resources behind them make it possible for them to establish impressive schools, hospitals and other forms of social organization. . . . But when one goes more deeply, one discovers that the strength of Buddhism lies not in organization, but in deep roots of psychological and moral values held by the people. . . . The living spiritual force of Buddhism cannot be so easily grasped—statistically, least of all. It represents more a spiritual fluid, an inner attitude, a disposition, than a specific program, let alone ideology.

In the preface to this book, Thomas Merton makes the following remark:

> This new Buddhism is not immersed in an eternal trance. Nor is it engaged in a fanatical self-glorifying quest for political power. It is not remote or withdrawn from the sufferings of ordinary men and their problems in a world of revolution. It seeks to help them solve these problems.

A similar "political clarification" is happening in Hinduism in India. Gandhi has written in the magazine *Harijan*:

> Man's ultimate aim is the realization of God, and all his activities—social, political, religious—have to be guided by the ultimate aim of the vision of God. The immediate service of all human beings (sarvodaya) becomes a necessary part of endeavor, simply because the only way to find God is to see him in his creation and to be one with it. This can only be done through the service of all. I am a part and parcel of the whole, and I cannot find him apart from the rest of humanity. My countrymen are my nearest neighbors. They have become so helpless, so resourceless, so inert, that I must concentrate myself on serving them. If I could persuade

---

[10] SCM Press Ltd., 1967.

APPENDIX B 311

myself that I could find him in a Himalayan cave, I would proceed there immediately. But I know that I cannot find him apart from humanity.

This passage is truly revealing of the change that has taken place in modern India. A disciple of Gandhi, Vinoba Bhave, realized this ideal by identifying himself with the poor of the country. He goes about the whole of India preaching *sarvodaya* and the renunciation of rights to property in favor of the poorest among the people. We must admit that this is a society based on the principles of the gospel, a society of free men who organize their life in cooperation, assuring order and peace. Christian monasticism has only to enter this movement. (Further information about this point may be obtained from Dom Bede Griffith's book *Christian Ashram*.)

Two replies to the questionnaire make suggestions along these lines:

> Monks will take part in the true development of the human milieu in which they live by cooperation and active participation in organized groups for social service; by favoring the installation of credit unions, etc., avoiding cases of personal dispute so as not to be implied in lawsuits.

It is pointed out, however, that with all the good will in the world, the duty of participating in the country's progress is not always easy:

> In speaking of active charity, we have underlined the difficulties that are met with when one tries to raise the standard of living of the poor around one, whose plight has resulted from lack of a sense of economy and lack of foresight on the part of the inhabitants. Their carefree attitude and the modesty of their wants are some of the lovable characteristics of their temperament, but it is just these that make them easy victims of others, often strangers, who exploit them.
>
> And then certain measures taken by the government create considerable obstacles. The government forbids any association, any trade union. It has nationalized large sectors of national life and organized cooperatives, but on the level of social security, health insurance, work insurance, old age pensions, there is nothing. A Catholic daily had come into being, but once it went beyond the sphere of spiritual formation and started speaking of social things, it was attacked and had to be done away with. Any initiatives in favor of peace and any other major undertaking would come up against opposition by the government, which does not wish to be given foreign advice. The schools are perhaps the only possibility left, but there again they are closely supervised and menaced by nationalization.

There are other aspects:

> The specific existence of the monk must be a manifestation of fraternity and a communion of love. The life of work within the monastery must be

an example of an honest life of labor, producing a surplus to be used in the service of neighbors, sharing any wealth and thus proving that wealth is for the service of the brotherhood, and revealing the personal and spiritual dimensions of work. The monks should put their collective experience and knowledge to the service of neighboring villages and should even make a gift of their time and of their work, which is what Vinoba Bhave calls *sram-dan*.

They must treat all men with respect so as, by honoring personal values, to transform society. They could play an important part in helping the people to achieve literacy, giving real education to adults, and thus work toward the development of the sons of God. The ideas of cooperation, unity, sharing of life, work and even the fruits of work must be instilled, encouraged and spread by the monks. They should be instruments of reconciliation and social peace . . . preparing the people for changes; they should create the will to change, inject into the local traditional social stagnation a dynamic of healthy social revolution, promote hope, optimism and the will to work. . . . All that would be Christian and it would be social service of great importance.

Ought we to speak of Communism? We should be hiding our heads in the sand were we to refuse to do so. Dom Leclercq writes:

Finally, we cannot ignore the role played by modern ideologies, especially by Communism. Whatever may be the immediate policy of each country, its influence is at work everywhere in Asia. It will not fail to have consequences, which we do not have to attempt to foresee here. But it is certain that it must be taken into account. Certain traditional values, certain mental, family, social and political structures will be transformed or eliminated. The separation from the West might become deeper. The chief victim, or at least the first, in the cultural sphere, already seems to be what is called "the old Confucianist universe." This makes us think of what Paul VI, in his message of January 1967 to continental China, named "the passing of ancient and static traditional forms of its culture to those inevitable and new ones that result from the industrial and social structures of modern life."

And it is through all this that we have to find our way. No one would do any good by dealing with this life-or-death question in a purely and simply negative fashion. M. M. Thomas of Bangalore makes the following remark in *Herder Korrespondenz* (68, 172): "Through the revolutions in Asia is manifested the demand to become man in the fullest and richest sense of the word."

Appendix B

We are touching here upon a very delicate question; but we would show culpable irresponsibility in refusing to face the problems set by the phenomenon of Communism, or rather, Marxism, as much on the level of ideas as on that of real and forced encounter. It seems that in the Bangkok meeting this subject should not be passed over in silence. We must insist upon having a deep knowledge of the great social and political documents of the Church: the encyclicals *Mater et Magistra, Pacem in Terris* and *Populorum Progressio,* and the Constitution on the Church in the Modern World.

It might be found interesting to note the remark made by Archbishop Yu Pin in an interview granted to Father Mario von Galli (*Ruhr-Wort*, Vol. 6, No. 24) concerning the attitude of the West with regard to China. He complained of the policy of the West and of all Western Catholicism, which he could not understand:

> One cannot make the wheel of history turn back. It is not the Church's mission to protect itself against China by means of a policy of power, as is hoped sometimes even in Vatican circles; but, on the contrary, it is quite in keeping with the part it has to play to study very carefully the points of contact that China has with Christianity and to seek courageously to develop them, even by adopting entirely new ways.

There is one such new way practiced by the non-Christian monks of Asia along which Christian monasticism must resolutely set out: nonviolence. Indeed, Communism will never be overcome by violence. It will be overcome only by a spiritual force stronger than itself. Vinoba Bhave, who has already been mentioned, believes in two basic principles for succeeding in his efforts: *satya* (truth) and *ahimsa* (nonviolence). He thus goes in a direction entirely opposed to Communism. By "truth" Vinoba means, as did Gandhi, obedience to the inner light and to the voice of conscience, which is that of God; by *ahimsa* he means that no kind of violence may be used in the pursuit of an ideal. He asks for the giving up of all passion and self-interest, a total renunciation that he himself learned from Mahatma Gandhi. It is clear that this virtue of nonviolence cannot be practiced as an isolated virtue. It has very close bonds with other Christian virtues such as poverty, chastity, obedience.

It is among the monks that this ideal could take root and develop. It is a serious matter: it calls for immediate deep reflection and study to assure a decisive future for Christianity and monasticism in Asia.

Conclusion. The replies to the third part of the questionnaire for the Bangkok program have revealed problems, opportunities, solutions, hopes and fears. Let us conclude with a few words from Dom Leclercq, who writes:[11]

---

[11] *Op. cit.,* pp. 232–233.

At the present time, the solution of the problems that have already been posed appears to consist neither in a return to the pure and simple Asian past nor in an imitation of the West. It consists rather in the creation of Asian cultures that conform to both the psychology and the traditions of the different peoples, while profiting from modern technology and its consequences in the domains of thought and action. Asia is being given a wonderful chance. Monasticism, in its own modest place, must be open to this great work.

A great deal of thought, study and dialogue will be needed. It is to be sincerely hoped that our efforts will proceed along these lines and that there will be a follow-up of the results by all Christian monks in Asia.

SUMMARY OF THE REPLIES TO PART IV

Prepared by Marie De Floris, O.S.B.

INSTITUTIONAL QUESTIONS

The questions asked in the fourth part dealt with two themes.

The first concerned the diversity of forms of the monastic life. It was asked whether the possibility should be considered of the coexistence in the same community of both the cenobitic and the eremitic form of life; whether the creation of small monastic groups, dependent upon a community of the traditional type should be favored; whether monasteries of varying but complementary style should be founded, in order to assure a better adaptation to the widely varied circumstances of certain countries.

The second theme suggested that thought should be given to the opportunity of establishing a certain link between the monasteries in order to further mutual help and sufficient unit, as has been done for the communities of Africa and Latin America.

In this summary, the replies are given in the order of the questionnaire.

A. Respondents discussing the diverse forms of monastic life have expressed the following opinions.

Eremitism. Only one reply makes explicit mention of this matter. A prior writes from Taiwan:

> I would be in favor of a great deal of flexibility in the monastic life, both within single communities (especially within large communities) and among different communities. I would like, for instance, to see large, active cenobitic communities make available a few small hermitages or cottages where individual members could retire for short periods of more quiet prayer and reflection.

The remarks of another correspondent, Dom Francis Acharya, of Kurisumala, India, may perhaps be interpreted as a wish to be open to the charism of eremitism:

> In India the Church should allow monasticism to develop along charismatic lines, as happened in the beginnings of the monastic life in so many countries. We cannot see how we can bring to Christ the great variety of riches accumulated in the past, and still present in contemporary Hindu monasticism, within the frame of the existing canonical structures of the Church.

Small monastic groups. If a certain reserve is shown with regard to eremitism, there is nevertheless unanimity as to the wish to favor multiplication of small monastic groups, united in a loose and flexible organization around a big community of the traditional type.

This unanimity of desire is supported by varying arguments:

1. The reply quoted above appeals to the variety of monastic charisms, reflecting the unfathomable richness of the grace of Christ.

2. Another reason frequently given is the necessity of imposing with greater evidence and authority the witness to poverty and simplicity. A Christian swami writes:

> It is my bishop's and my own opinion that preference is to be given to small groups. No big establishments like our abbeys in Europe are needed. Small groups will have the agility and adaptability necessary in our rapidly changing times. Small groups do not need much organization; they can lead a simple life, can more easily keep in contact with the people of the locality. It seems to be the call of our time that monks should live among their Christian brethren, not in strict separation from them.

Another community records that it was led to form a smaller monastic group in order to satisfy the aspirations of a certain number of monks wishing to lead a more strictly contemplative life, with more austerity and poverty than were considered compatible with the life in the mother community.

Father P. Moyersoen, S. J., rector of St. Stanislaus College in Sitagarhor, Bihar, India, writes:

> A big problem in India (and the whole East) is that of poverty—both personal and community poverty. Many of our religious in India, who come from very poor families or from well-to-do families accustomed to a simple style of life, cannot take the vow of poverty without first becoming rich. What can then be their spirit of poverty, unless they are highly spiritual? More serious is the problem of large monasteries (and large religious houses) that give at least the impression of affluence. Where then can be the "common witness to the poverty of Christ" so important in the East? This is why I firmly believe we must think of small monasteries, of at most ten monks or nuns. Larger monasteries for the training of young monks should be the exception.

3. A community in Cambodia points out that this multiplication of small monastic groups would answer the desires of the local clergy:

> The bishop and priests (nearly all foreigners) would like to see small groups of monks dotted over the mission territory, giving an example of poverty and labor and living in more direct contact with the people. These groups, composed of a few members, should be established preferably in

rural areas and in the heart of non-Christian populations. They would probably call for a simpler Office, one accessible to uneducated recruits; a more flexible enclosure; and fewer observances.

Organization. The respondents seem to wish that these monasteries, or rather these monastic groups, should be connected with each other by very much more supple bonds than is generally the case in the West. We find this point of view strongly emphasized in a reply coming from Dom Acharya, in India:

> The Latin Code is far too rigid to allow the creation of an authentic Indian monasticism, one that would be truly indigenous. The Oriental Code is more articulate, as it has a properly monastic legislation (which is not found in the Latin Code), providing for a greater variety of expressions. Monasteries are always open to the eremitical life. Besides monasteries of common life, there are the Lauras, the Sketes, the Metochia. Moreover, Oriental monasticism has no division of the monks into organization as orders, congregations and so on, but only one monastic order to which belong all monks and nuns. The monastic state is also more independent from the priesthood than in the West. The grouping of monasteries is more flexible, generally in federations.

Another correspondent remarks:

> Monastic foundations in India cannot be simply an "implantation" of ready-made, Western trading founding groups. Rather they must come out of the soil of the country itself; otherwise they will remain a foreign body.
>
> Regarding varying forms of monastic life, we have to leave behind all our typical Western inclination to systematize, to institutionalize, to discriminate, to make our religious life uniform. Two years in a Hindu ashram have taught me that strict discipline and uniformity are not necessarily an indication of spiritual striving, as is thought in our Western monasteries. I came to the conclusion that much freedom should be given to the individual to develop his own personality; the frame should be wide enough to embrace all the different aspirations of monastic life in one community, without discriminating too much between cenobites and hermits. Especially we have to take in consideration that Asians have a very different mentality; they are more emotional, less rational, more given up to intuition and to the moment.

Though all communities would like to see the founding of small monastic groups, nevertheless most of them insist on pointing out the difficulties they foresee in the realization of such a project.

1. The first difficulty, a fundamental one, is mentioned by an Indian religious, rector of an important Jesuit College:

> I have now only one remark to make, but I think it touches a fundamental point: my feeling, from whatever little experience I have had here in my own country, is that our monastic life—and indeed all religious life—suffers from a serious defect that is rooted in the quality of the Christian life here. Our Christians are very devout and faithful, but in general they seem to lack a certain vitality; their life does not spring from a transforming Christian experience. I have often said—though it is a cruel statement—that we are a secondhand Church, lacking in creative energy. This difficulty manifests itself even more clearly in the religious life: young aspirants learn to conform and they do it very well; but they do not seem to be transformed. Though India has a monastic tradition of its own and attempts have been made to Christianize it, one gets the impression, in general, that Christian monasticism here is a thing from outside, something whose ways one can learn but whose spirit one has not wholly captured. Despite attempts at adaptation, the monasteries we have still appear as imitations, not as something arising from an inner necessity. Perhaps I am exaggerating this point, but to me this is the root difficulty that must be resolved before we can proceed farther.

2. A second difficulty, already mentioned, is stressed by several respondents in mentioning the rigidity of the Western Code, which does not leave sufficient room for adapting the juridical situation to the necessities of actual existence.

3. Another difficulty arises from the fact that almost inevitably the small groups, though founded in a burst of fervor, once they are institutionalized become "established," in their turn, after the manner of the founding community and thus cease to fulfill their vocation as witnesses.

The community of Waegwan, in South Korea, gives the example of its own experience:

> The high standard of living results first from the fact that the monastery was planned and equipped by Europeans according to their needs. It is difficult to lower it for practical reasons and also because many weak-spirited persons among Europeans, and Koreans as well, would not accept such a reduction now.
>
> The second reason for a high living standard is the community life itself. In a large community modern facilities are often more economical (e.g., high buildings, central heating). Food has to be provided according to the standard not of the healthier and more ascetical, but of the weaker members.
>
> As a consequence, the new foundation in Pusan, which some of us had

Appendix B

hoped would be closer to the common life of Koreans, seems to be going in the same direction as the abbey here.

4. A Vietnamese monk, though suggesting the foundation of small groups, insists that they should be formed with great prudence in order to avoid any break between the communities:

> Is it possible to make efficacious and realistic suggestions to communities concerning the trying out of new forms, in particular of very small communities? We are still so allergic to everything that concerns "novelty" that such suggestions seem to bring about ruptures within the communities. If an attempt were to be allowed spontaneously and in all sincerity, it would be acceptable, but that presupposes that the community is already well ahead with its renewal. Otherwise, an attempt allowed grudgingly, perhaps brought about thanks to the strong insistence of the Order, risks accentuating the dissension.
>
> This is said with the assumption that the mother community continues to have rights over the trial one. That would be the ideal situation, but it appears really much more theoretical than practical. There must be either "renewal" from within or a "new creation"—and this would finally have more chance of being realized in complete liberty.

5. A final difficulty arises from the mentality of the native monks. A superior writes:

> Among the foreign monks are certain ones who would accept this new form, at once simpler and poorer. But the native monks, more eager to obtain human promotion, are not favorable to this more humble life.

In conclusion, we may say that the monastic communities of Asia unanimously wish to see the creation of smaller monastic groups; they nevertheless are conscious of the difficulties of such an undertaking. They wish the smaller monastic groups to be attached to larger communities, thus assuring the formation of young recruits. This change would have to be carried out in stages, as the community of Rawaseneng, in Indonesia, very clearly states:

> The traditional community, sufficiently adapted of course, represents to our eyes a first stage. The next stage would be to seek another form of monastic life, more adapted to the locality. For the moment, we are still in the first stage. We must faithfully transmit the monastic ideal traditional in the Church (i.e., the Western Church). Indonesian monks must endeavor to understand this monastic tradition and make it their own. It is only then that they will be able to "Indonesianize" it, that is, to express it

after their own manner in forms more adapted to the genius of their own people. But there is a long way to go.

B. Concerning the link to be set up between monasteries, the replies are most clearly summed up in that given by the community of Taiwan:

> The sort of loose union that has a healthy respect for monastic pluralism and is merely intended to facilitate the exchange of ideas, encourage mutual help and the like, would be desirable. The type of juridical union that would attempt to impose uniformity of practice and the rest, would of course be undesirable.

That is the gist of the other replies, except that some mention "regional" unions and seem to wish that these unions should include only the communities of a single, well-specified geographical or cultural unit.

The community of Kep, in Cambodia, says:

> Liaison between monasteries is obviously desirable, but it is certain that the very great differences of culture, mentality and conception of the monastic life will make this sort of union less rigid than it is elsewhere.

To conclude this section dealing with the liaison to be set up between monasteries in Asia, we record a suggestion with obvious interest for all. From three different sources mention is made of a "center of monastic studies" for the communities of Asia.

In September 1967, in a letter addressed to Dom Jean Leclercq, two monks from Vietnam had already suggested this project:

> We hope ... you will not forget the profound desire that we expressed in our letter of May 13, 1967. Everything must be done to establish an institute of monastic studies in Vietnam. To start with one could select a monastery as temporary residence, send competent professors there, set up a good monastic library, help gifted young monks to study abroad, form a team of good translators, set up a printing press. ... This is very important if we want to establish Christian monasticism on the solid foundations of the pure ancient monastic tradition and the local ascetic and contemplative traditions.

Father P. Moyersoen, S. J., writes:

> To develop a Christian monasticism that incorporates all that is best in Hindu or Buddhist tradition will require much study. You will need to have experts from among you, men who will begin by studying Sanskrit and can themselves go deep into the study of Hindu and Buddhist Scriptures. You might have to think of a center of your own for that purpose, perhaps one center for the whole East.

Appendix B

But it is an Indian, Father Raymond Pannikar, who in a memorandum has explained his ideas with the greatest precision. He sets out from the fundamental conviction that monasticism, devoted to the seeking after pure truth, represents a common basis at the heart of all cultures and all traditions. As he puts it:

> This is why we envisage a monastic study center in which a dozen or so monks from a variety of backgrounds, Buddhist, Christian, Hindu, Muslim, and so on, will live together for a year or two. The external framework of shared work and meals, study and recollection, is adaptable to a great variety of needs. Yet it is designed to cultivate self-discipline, silence, detachment, simplicity, harmony with the rhythm of nature and all the essentials of monastic training. The monks selected for this venture must be well grounded in their own tradition and sufficiently formed by it to bear witness to it simply by what they are. The nature of a study center demands, however, that they also be articulate and alert to the questions and tasks confronting monasticism and religion today. Personal friendships can be of incalculable value for this endeavor. But we must squarely face the problems that present barriers to our deepest understanding, come to grips with them and deal with them constructively in a joint effort.

Father Pannikar sets out his ideas precisely, under three headings:

1. *What?* Monks (three for each religion) would for a certain period gather together with members of the lay society and with "students of monastic life" with a view to establishing contacts among themselves.

2. *Why?* Monks speak the same language throughout the world; the center would be able to help them become aware of this fact, so that they might really communicate among themselves, strengthen the bond between them and eventually make their contribution to concord among men.

3. *How?* The activities of the study center could be divided among three types of participants:

   a. *Monks.* Three monks of the same monastic tradition would spend one or two years together and give themselves up to the study of different forms of monastic life and the effects they have on life in society as a whole.

   b. *Long-term Students.* Such students would be attached to one or other of the monastic trends and live the common life with "their" nucleus. Academic encounters would assure links between all and the necessary mixing of ideas.

   c. *Short-term Guests.* These would be specialists in research, industry, education, social service. They would come for short stays in order to share their knowledge with both monks and students, in conferences and discussions.

Appendix C

EXCERPTS FROM
"CHRISTIANITY CONFRONTS HINDUISM"[1]
John Moffitt

In any valid dialogue between religions, it has been said many times, both sides must be willing to listen to each other—be they Catholics or Protestants or Jews or Hindus or Buddhists or Muslims—not only in respect but also with love. Each must be confident, too, that from the confrontation a result will issue that is beneficial to both. . . .

It is central to the thinking of Christians that ours is the "fulfillment" of the non-Christian religions. But merely *telling* sophisticated "heathens" that our own faith embodies all that their faith is reaching toward is not usually the way to help them discover, through grace, who and what Jesus Christ is. Before we are in a position to tell Hindus, for instance, that our faith embodies all the best of theirs and more besides, we must intimately know what their faith embodies. We must be able to describe their faith in a way that satisfies them. We have long since abandoned the attitude that would condemn the religious beliefs of non-Christians as outright falsehoods. But too often we still seek to "preach the gospel" to these men without first acquainting ourselves—as St. Paul certainly did when he preached to the Greeks of the "unknown God"—with what they actually believe. This sort of indifference to the content of the faiths of others (to which I would couple the willingness to believe uncritically what other Western Christians have written about them) is the greatest single obstacle to true dialogue with non-Christians in the Orient. . . .

We are not seeking through the dialogue for a new, "universal" religion, an eclectic invention that will somehow satisfy everybody. The goal we seek is to be attained neither through indifference nor through any muting of disparities nor by any misguided zeal, but rather by humbly facing the total structure of the other religion and of the mystery of its persistence through millenniums. What that goal is, indeed, we can only dimly surmise. That it can be attained we must believe. In the dialogue with Protestant Christianity, Anglicanism and the Orthodox Church, advances have been made that no one would have thought possible even a few years ago. So too, I believe,

---

[1] This paper was prepared as background material for the delegates to the Bangkok conference. It was published in *Theological Studies*, 30, No. 2 (June 1969), pp. 207–224, and is used here in abbreviated form by permission.

there will be unforeseen advances in the dialogue with non-Christians—especially with Hindus. All that is needed is a willingness on both sides to wait for some sort of change of thinking, a mutation in spiritual sensitivity, as it were, that neither party to the dialogue can foresee—and that affronts neither. . . .

What we shall need, as certain writers have already pointed out, is a thoroughgoing objectivity. This is not easy to achieve. But to the extent that we are faithful to our own beliefs for their own sake (not for the sake of proving them superior to any others), and to the extent that we live up to them, to that extent we can dare to be and manage to be objective. It is out of this sort of fearless and prayerful approach that we can hope for the change of thinking, on the part of both sides of the dialogue, that I have spoken of. In order to grasp better what I mean by honest dialogue, we shall have to consider a few pertinent facts about Hinduism and Christianity as they come into confrontation. Yet before we begin to speak about similarities and disparities, let us first determine just what we mean by the terms "Hinduism" and "Christianity."

Since we must all begin, as Jacques-Albert Cuttat has pointed out,[2] with our own particular religious experience, I shall here define Christianity as the religion of the Roman Catholic Church. The problem of how to define Hinduism is more complicated. If, as Cuttat has suggested, the question in any such confrontation is which of the two religions is capable of including the other without mutilating its essential positive values, or better, which of the two is comprehensive enough to assume the other and perfect it, then how we define Hinduism means a great deal. . . .

Despite a natural Christian desire to identify as Hinduism something that approaches Christianity, we are forced, I believe, to settle on the Advaita or nondualistic Vedanta as being what truly represents Hinduism—for the single reason that Shankaracharya's school is the only one that claims to have no quarrel with anyone, but rather to respect all phases of Hindu belief as different levels of understanding of the one indivisible Reality.

I should even go a step farther and state that, in my belief, the Advaita Vedanta of Shankaracharya, as illuminated and revivified by the experiences and teaching of the modern *avatara*, Ramakrishna, in the nineteenth century, is what we should seek to dialogue with. Each of the devotional sects, and perhaps even the sect of Shankaracharya itself, has tended to affirm itself as the fulfillment of all the others. In Ramakrishna's interpretation of Vedanta alone do we find a thoroughgoing acceptance of all sects as valid ways to one and the same goal of God-consciousness. . . .

[2] See his essay, "Expérience Chrétienne et Spiritualité Orientale," in *La Mystique et les Mystiques* (Paris, 1965). Cuttat's ideas on Hinduism have been examined critically by Father Mariasusai Dhavamony, S. J., in an excellent article, "Christian Experience and Hindu Spirituality," in *Gregorianium*, 48 (1967), 776–791.

Cuttat declares that if there is between man and God, who is the absolute Person, a distance across which man is confronted with God, who reveals himself to him, then the Oriental spiritual experience can be "assumed" into Christian experience without mutilating its essential values. This might possibly be true were we to accept dualistic Hinduism as the true measure of Hinduism. But it is precisely this "distance" between man and God, in His essence, that nondualistic Vedanta denies—on the basis of the mystical experience of the Hindu seers as well as the evidence of Scripture. How the nondualistic teaching can be assumed into Christianity without mutilating this "positive value" is difficult to understand. Moreover, were Hinduism to be thus "included" in Christianity, another most characteristic doctrine, that of the cosmic and the individual *maya*, would also have to be rejected. It is this doctrine that explains that the phenomenal world and the individual soul, while utterly factual from the world's point of view, are perceived as a result of misapprehension and are not ultimately real.

The only way in which Hinduism could be assumed into Christianity, it would appear, would be to show that the "attributeless" suprapersonal Reality, or Nirguna Brahman, of Advaita Vedanta, was in actuality one with the personal, creative God, the Trinity, of Christianity. But to prove this would involve long and painstaking inquiry into the true meaning of the term "personal" in both religions. Another way might be, as I myself once thought, to show that the experience of the nonduality of Atman and Brahman, even though a mystical experience, was heretical not only from the Christian point of view but also from that of all the other Hindu schools. Yet to exclude nondualism, when more crucial texts in the Hindu Scriptures support than oppose it, now seems to me highly questionable. And to decide that Christians have a right to determine what is essential and what nonessential in a religion other than their own is to beg the question.

Thus we are faced with a serious difficulty if we insist, as Cuttat does, that in any confrontation between religions one of the religions must be able to include the other; for only by an arbitrary omission of certain facts can we assert that no mutilation of values would occur—and especially when the religions happen to be Christianity and an Oriental religion. . . .

If we look objectively at the totality of Hindu doctrines, both nondualistic and dualistic or devotional, what do we observe? Aside from the unique nondualistic doctrine of the essential identity of Atman and Brahman, the immortal soul and the transcendental Reality, we notice certain striking similarities between the beliefs of Hindus (based either on revealed Scripture or on the experience of mystical philosophers) and those of Christians (based likewise on revealed Scripture and the definitions of the magisterium of the Church). We notice, too, of course, important differences.

In the first place, there is a striking similarity in the idea of a personal

God. The personal God of Hinduism—whether he is thought of as formless yet endowed with attributes (Saguna Brahman) or as having form as well as attributes (the various deities, such as Shiva and Kali)—is the ruler of the universe, and it is through his grace that the soul is eventually joined with him in loving, eternal relationship. Yet there is, at the same time, an important difference in the fact that God as conceived in Vedanta does not create the universe out of nothing, as Christians believe God creates the world. He creates out of the eternally existing basic matter of the physical world, through an impulse of will. What seems the most striking difference of all, the suprapersonal Reality posited by nondualism, which transcends all normal definitions of personality, may turn out on examination to be not very different from the Divine Ground of Christian mystics—such as the pseudo-Dionysius or Meister Eckhart—who was to be known through "unknowing." The highest affirmation of Vedanta is not something utterly incomprehensible to Christian mystics.

To consider the concept of the Godhead a bit further, we find some interesting parallels in the concept of the Trinity. It has been urged that there is an approach to the Christian concept of the Trinity in the classical trinity of Hindu mythology: Brahma, the Creator; Vishnu, the Preserver; Siva, the Dissolver. True, these are in some sense persons. But a far more meaningful parallel, it seems to me, is to be found in the nondualistic concept of the Nirguna or pure Brahman as Satchidananda—*Sat* or absolute existence, *Chit* or absolute awareness, *Ananda* or absolute bliss—in which these three "aspects" of the Godhead are not separate from each other, but each and all are inseparable from Reality. Moreover, as I have said, in the Qualified Nondualist and the Dualist schools of Vedanta, that Brahman or God is conceived as recreating the world or, more exactly, reprojecting it, by an act of will out of the eternally preexisting subtle matter. At the same time, in the Nondualist school, though this "creating" is accepted as fact from the empirical point of view, from the point of view of Brahman the universe is conceived to appear as a result of *maya*, an inexplicable power said to inhere in Brahman.

Here, then, we have the concept of a personal God willing the "creation" of a fresh cycle of cosmic existence, together with the subtler concept of matter itself being created, as it were, "out of nothing." It should be noted that both the concept of eternal cycles of existence initiated by the personal God and the concept of a deluding *maya*, which first veils Reality and then projects the world of forms, are based on the spiritual experiences of seers, not simply on speculation. Interestingly enough, from the Hindu point of view it could easily seem that the Christian concept of a single creation by a personal God out of nothing represented only a single stage of the series they had conceived, and that in this one respect Hinduism might be said to be able to "include" Christianity—were the Hindus interested in attempting this sort of rebuttal.

From the devotional Scriptures, further, has come the doctrine of the *avatara* or incarnation of Vishnu, the Preserver. The incarnation is not conceived as the Second Person of a Trinity, the perfect image of the Father, but rather as an appearance of God, who manifests himself whenever virtue declines and vice prevails, for the upholding of righteousness and the destruction of wickedness. One exception to the *avatara* explanation is the Lord Krishna. Usually called an incarnation by Westerners, he is actually worshipped by his followers, whose number is very large, as the totality of Vishnu or the Godhead.

Though there is no exact parallel to the doctrine of the Incarnation as it is found in Christianity, there is a fascinating hint of the Logos doctrine. It is the doctrine of the *Sphota*, the eternal Word, from which all sounds and thus all names derive. (Sound, not light, is considered by Hindus as coming first in the order of evolution of the material universe.) The primal word that includes all utterable sounds is, according to Vedanta, the word Aum (Om); there is an elaborate analysis of its meaning in Vedantic scholastic philosophy. "In the beginning was the *Sphota*," the Hindus would say.

Radically different, apparently, are the Christian and Hindu concepts of the fate of the soul. In contrast to the Christian affirmation that the soul is created out of nothing at or about the time of conception, Hinduism asserts that the soul in its essence is eternal existence-awareness-bliss; that it has simply forgotten its true nature and hence must pass from life to life until it remembers who it is and learns that no desire brings satisfaction but the desire for God. (Some advanced Vedantic thinkers have gone so far as to say that the whole doctrine of rebirth is not necessarily a logical, but is rather a psychological, truth to impress men with the urgency of striving in this life for perfection and love of God.) Hinduism maintains that there is no example of something that, not having existed before, continues to have existence eternally, after its creation. Perhaps the difference is not as great as it at first appears to be, for in talking about the soul Hindus and Christians are not always talking about the same thing. It is the individual soul after it has been deluded by *maya* that corresponds to the Christian soul, and that soul in a sense may be said to have been created out of nothing through *maya*.

The Hindus maintain, however, that the true nature of the individual soul, the absolute Atman, keeps breaking through—a fact that is responsible for the belief innate in every man that he possesses free will. Here again we see a parallel to Christian doctrine, where God is said to have created man with free will either to love and obey him or to reject him. This freedom, the Hindus say, is of the soul's very essence. Indeed, it might well appear to a Hindu that the biblical statement that man is created "in the image of God" is simply another way of saying that the human soul is, in essence, divine. . . .

Appendix C

I have already mentioned Hindu arguments about the soul's preexistence. Just how and when the individual soul enters its new abode is a favorite topic of discussion with scholastic philosophers in India, though today the explanations seem archaic. Their elaborate theories, however, are matched by those of our own contemporary thinkers, who are faced with the difficulty of showing just when God creates and inbreathes the soul into the fetus—a task made embarrassing by the fact that there is a stage in its development before one knows whether there will be a single child or a multiple birth. That there is a soul, however, and that that soul's highest destiny is to know God and enjoy him, both religions affirm. There can be no doubt that in general they are talking about the same entity.

In addition to all these similarities, there are a number of other important details in which the two religions come close to each other—without ever, of course, totally meeting. The means in Hinduism through which the soul's life on earth is guided and brought into touch with God's grace include these: birth ceremonies, confirmation (the sacred thread ceremony), penance, the partaking of sanctified food, marriage, holy orders, death ceremonies. Though none of these corresponds exactly to any one of the Christian sacraments, they are similar enough in purpose to permit of fruitful investigation. The concept of grace is stressed as strongly in Hindu religious thought as in Christian. Even nondualists agree that, in the relative world, everything in the way of spiritual advancement depends on God's grace. Though human effort is important, nothing succeeds without divine cooperation. As an old saying in India puts it: "If you take one step toward God, God comes toward you by ten steps."

Though Scripture is given a different emphasis in the two religions, there are in both of them many books accepted as divinely inspired, as the revelation of God's truth to men. In Judaism and Christianity the books that belong to the canon were determined by priests and Church Fathers. In India, since there was no teaching authority, the books that constituted Scripture were probably determined by ancient seers and prophets. (The Vedas are held to be identical in each cosmic cycle.) The Hindu Scriptures themselves, however, make the statement that in the state of God-consciousness "the Vedas are no Vedas." Scripture itself bears witness to the fact that there is a state of consciousness beyond itself.

It is difficult to determine how a Christian could convince a believing Hindu that the Bible (much of which was composed at a period later than the Vedic age) is the only true Scripture. That Christ accepted the Old Testament as the word of God, and the Church Fathers the New Testament, is a compelling argument for a Christian, but hardly for a Hindu, who cannot grasp the fact that Krishna is not God every bit as much as Christ. Yet the Hindu would accept the Bible, along with the Vedas, as the word of God....

The several aspects of Hindu religious life I have outlined represent only a fraction of the total complex of Hinduism. In discussing them I am painfully aware of my own inadequacy. It is possible that in numerous instances my own interpretations have been swayed by Western prejudice or lack of penetration. Hinduism is a particularly rich religion, one that has dealt with all the major issues of the spiritual life, and a bewildering array of the minor issues. It is impossible to do complete justice to it by means of simple generalities such as those I have been compelled to employ. Nevertheless, having considered all these striking similarities and almost as striking disparities between the two religions, we are now, I believe, in a position to examine some of the consequences of an honest confrontation between Christianity and Hinduism.

As I have said earlier, to the extent that we are faithful to our own beliefs, to that extent we can dare to be objective. And to be objective means to be willing to see similarities as well as disparities. Anyone with the slightest amount of candor must grant that so vast an array of profound spiritual insights as has been manifested in Hinduism cannot possibly be the work of man unaided by divine grace. We need not—indeed, we cannot—state precisely, at this point, to what degree the Hindu vision is the product of divine inspiration and to what degree the result of man's imagination. What is required of us now is a painstaking study, in all charity, of the implications of the great body of Hindu beliefs.

As we proceed to that prudent and loving study of Hinduism called for by the Declaration on Non-Christian Religions, there are certain pitfalls to be strenuously avoided. We must not seek at the start to equate any one item of Hindu belief with its counterpart in Christianity in the mistaken notion that we shall thereby enable members of the other faith to accept the main body of our dogma. Such an attempt has already been made in several instances. It has even been suggested that Christ and the Atman, the absolute, indefinable Reality underlying the individual soul, are identical. The theory, however, ignores the vast amount of contradictory meanings connoted by the two terms; obviously, the word "Christ" here would have to be understood in a very special way.

Again, even while admitting the similarities between the two faiths, Christians must not forget the radical differences between them: the reality of sin (which to Hinduism is only error), the reality of the world as God's creation, the fact of a soul moving toward a realization of its higher potentialities (rather than trying to rid itself of encrustations and uncover what it already is, as suggested by Vedanta), the primacy of personality. None of these seem to be stressed in Hinduism. . . .

Hindus think we Christians are naive in saying that ours is the only truth, that Christ alone is "the way, the truth, and the life." "Everybody says his own watch alone is right," said Ramakrishna humorously, referring not only to the Hindu sects. Nevertheless, as Christians we know we have been given the truth, for Christ himself has told us so. And we have been told by him to go and share that truth with the nations. How best to share it with the Orient we have obviously not yet learned. In all the hundreds of years of Christian missionary activity in India (over 1,900 years, if St. Thomas the Apostle was indeed the first Christian to visit the country), we have converted less than 2 percent of the population. What has been wanting, I submit, is sufficient respect and love for Hinduism and the Hindu culture in general.

Surely our best way of preaching the gospel is to live it. And surely our missionaries have been trying, often heroically, to live it according to their own lights. But too many have forgotten that part of living the gospel is not to limit one's practice of Christianity. The great Jesuit Robert de Nobili did not forget that fact, nor did Matteo Ricci in China—both certainly very good Christians. They were never condescending. They lived the gospel mentally and spiritually as well as physically and morally. If we modern Christians can learn to do so, we shall not only be fostering the dialogue; we shall also find ourselves subtly broadened and enriched without sacrificing anything of our own fundamental truth. "A dog," goes a Hindu proverb, "can recognize his own master no matter what disguise he puts on." Have we been failing to recognize our own Master where he appears in other faiths?

On the other hand, Hindus, too, know they have the truth. The Rig-Veda, one of their revealed scriptures, declared perhaps 1,500 years before Christ: "Truth is one: the sages give it differing names." And so they "accept" all faiths as true paths to God and want to enjoy them all—though, it often seems to me, as *they* interpret them. Nevertheless, traditionally they have not sought to persuade others to accept their own vision of religious truth. . . .

If Hindus must learn to understand Christianity as Christians see it, we Christians must learn as well to understand Hinduism as Hindus see it. At the same time, as the dialogue progresses, we may begin to see a little better what both Hinduism and Christianity are saying beyond their differing dogmatic affirmations.

Perhaps what Hinduism, as corrected and integrated by the nondualistic Vedanta of Shankaracharya and Ramakrishna, is really saying—beyond its affirmation of the nonduality of the Godhead and the "divinity" of the soul —is that the *experience* of God's loving, guiding, saving presence, however imperfectly described in certain of the religions, is found to be identical or at least highly similar by mystics in all the advanced religions, and that in that sense all religions are efficacious as ways to him. Perhaps it is also saying that since we are differing human beings, in differing traditions, the ways of serving God are as numerous as there are different individuals.

Perhaps what Christianity, as guided by the Holy Spirit through the Church, is saying—beyond its specific message of salvation through Christ and his one Church—is that though man's chief end is indeed to know and love and serve his Father, the only true God, the formulation of the experience of that God is not equally accurate in all religions, and in so far as men's religion is based on faith in what a particular Scripture has taught, one religion is indeed superior to another—and one is supreme. Perhaps it is also saying that since we must think in terms of our own tradition, our loyalty belongs to our own traditional dogma alone. Despite these differing emphases, however, both Hinduism and Christianity place God at the very center of human existence.

In *The Love of Learning and the Desire for God*, Dom Jean Leclercq has pointed out that the basis of Western monasticism is that same yearning for the highest spiritual experience that is the basis of the whole of traditional Hindu society, monastic and sacerdotal and secular. Thus it is perhaps Christian monks who, while holding fast to their faith in the uniqueness of Christ, can be most faithful to the dialogue—without rejection or misinterpretation, respectfully and lovingly seeking for that objectivity that alone makes dialogue come alive. For their part, Hindu monks and priests and laymen have shown themselves to be more than well-disposed toward loving and respectful dialogue with other faiths. As we have seen, what they most need is to see Christianity as it is, rather than as something completely reconcilable with Hinduism.

But Christians, too, may need a radical change of understanding with regard to Hinduism. As a result of unprejudiced study, it may well become plain that a preponderance of basic Hindu belief is indeed divinely inspired. In that event, Christians will have to grant that Hinduism may actually be more valid for most of its faithful than a literal, Western-oriented Christianity. The Spirit may be working in ways that we only dimly perceive. Should this prove to be so, to become more effective apostles they will need to place far greater stress on that aspect of Christ which Hindus can readily grasp: the nonhistorical Christ, the Second Person of the Trinity. I venture to say that it might well be the dream of a Hindu deeply versed in Christian doctrine that Christians should one day grant it is that Christ, through the Holy Spirit, who is manifesting himself in all the higher religions.

I believe Christians owe it to themselves to give the implications of this thought serious consideration. For if Christ by his sacrifice and death redeemed all men, there is no reason why that same Christ cannot speak to all men through all revelations to the human spirit. I do not accept this idea as a truth that has been demonstrated beyond doubt; what I suggest is that, in view of the richness of the Oriental religions, we should in all humility be willing to treat it as a possibility. Perhaps there is much that Christ has thus spoken to others that we have forgotten or not yet recognized in our own revelation. What we must guard against, at all events, is a premature assumption that God intends that everyone in the Orient should be a professing Christian.

It is impossible for Hindus to grasp the statement that their religion,

Appendix C

whatever its particular sectarian form, is not inspired by God but is, as Christians have said, a "yearning" toward the knowledge of the fullness of Christ. The old, comfortable phrase *Anima naturaliter christiana* says the truth only halfway. It represents a way of thinking that is not acceptable to non-Christians—unless they are indeed chosen by God to become professed followers of Christ. St. Augustine, however, put it slightly differently: "What is now called the Christian religion existed even among the ancients and was not lacking from the beginning of the human race until 'Christ came in the flesh.' From that time, true religion, which already existed, began to be called Christian" (*Retractations*, 1, 12, 3). This is the sort of statement a Hindu can grasp. . . .

I submit that only a radical change in our thinking about Hinduism will suffice to convince Hindus that we do not condescend toward them or secretly wish to convert them into something they are not. About that change in our thinking, I have suggested that greater stress on the non-historical Christ may be the key to progress in the dialogue. If such an approach can bring Hindus to understand the meaning of Christ, what have we to fear? We who know something of the riches of Christ do not need to defend ourselves with any sort of iron curtain. In allowing for the working of the Holy Spirit in ways we do not suspect, surely we are not in any manner betraying our own faith in Christ. And if we insist on the old, literal, unyielding approach, what hope is there of success—indeed, what meaning is there in the dialogue?

Appendix D

LIST OF PARTICIPANTS AT THE BANGKOK CONFERENCE

The conference was presided over by the Most Reverend Dom Rembert Weakland, O.S.B., Abbot Primate of the Benedictine Order.

MONASTIC DELEGATES

AUSTRALIA
- Arcadia — Dom Simon Tonini, O.S.B., Sylv., Prior
- Tarrawarra — Dom Anselm Parker, O.C.S.O., Prior

CAMBODIA
- Kep — Dom Ernest Drouet, O.S.B., Prior
- Dom J. Badré, O.S.B.

CEYLON
- Ampitiya — Dom I. Robinson, O.S.B., Prior

CHINA (TAIWAN)
- Chyayi — Dom Timothy Marceau, O.S.B., Prior
- Hsin Chiang — Dom Paul Maher, O.S.B., Prior
- Tanshui — Sister Glenore Riedner, O.S.B., Prioress

HONG KONG
- Lantao — Dom Simeon Chang, O.C.S.O., Prior

INDIA
- Asirvanam — Dom Emmanuel de Meester, O.S.B., Prior
  - Dom Mayeul de Dreuille, O.S.B.
  - Dom Placide Arakkel, O.S.B., Sub-Prior
- Bangalore — Sister Teresita D'Silva, O.S.B.
- Shantivanam — Dom Bede Griffiths, O.S.B., Prior
- Tondarnad — Dom D. P. Vadakepattani, O.S.B., Sylv., Prior

JAPAN
- Hokkaido-Muroran — Sister Shaun O'Meara, O.S.B., Superior
- Seiboen — Mother Christiana, O.C.S.O., Abbess
  - Sister Marie de la Croix, O.C.S.O.

NEW ZEALAND
- Kopua — Dom Joachim Murphy, O.C.S.O., Abbot

APPENDIX D

PHILIPPINES
    Manila   Dom Celestine Say, O.S.B., Prior
                                 Dom Bernardo Perez, O.S.B.
                                 Mother Assumpta Filser, O.S.B., Prioress
                                 Sister M. Simeona Ricalde, O.S.B., Sub-Prioress
    Vigan   Mother Rosemarie, O.S.B., Prioress
                                 Mother Scholastique, O.S.B.

SOUTH KOREA
    Taegu   Mother Edeltrude Weist, O.S.B., Prioress
                                 Sister Beda Kim, O.S.B.
    Waegwan   Dom Odo Haas, O.S.B., Abbot

VIETNAM
    Chau Son   Dom Léon Chinh, S. O. Cist., Novice Master
    My Ca   Dom Maur Nguyen Cong Dang, S. O. Cist., Prior
    Phuoc Son   Dom Maxime Thong, S.O.Cist., Prior
                                 Dom Jean Lam, S. O. Cist., Juniorate Director
    Thien An   Dom Thomas Chau Van Dang, O.S.B., Prior
    Thu Duc   Mother Marie-Bénédicte Gautier, O.S.B., Prioress
                                 Sister Marie-Bénédicte Cuc, O.S.B.

DELEGATES FROM SOME OF THE FOUNDING ABBEYS

ENGLAND
    Ryde (Bangalore)   Mother B. Smeyers, O.S.B., Abbess

UNITED STATES
    St. Procope–Lisle
      (Chayi, Taiwan)   Dom D. Kucera, O.S.B., Abbot
    St. Vincent–Latrobe
      (Hsin Chiang, Taiwan) Dom Egbert H. Donovan, O.S.B., Archabbot

EXPERTS

INDIA
    Bangalore   Monsignor D. S. Lourdusamy, Archbishop
    Brahma Vidya Mandir Sister Shraddhananda Bahin
    Kottayam, Kerala   Sadhu Ittyavirah
    Kurisumala   Dom M. F. Acharya, O.S.C.O., Prior

INDONESIA
    Rawaseneng   *Dom M. Frans Hardjawijata, O.C.S.O.*

JAPAN
    Tokyo (Sophia
        University)   *Father F. Enomiya-Lassalle, S.J.*

LUXEMBOURG
    Clervaux (Abbey of
        St. Maurice)   *Dom Jean Leclercq, O.S.B.*

THAILAND
    Bangkok (Chulalongkorn
        University)   *Father Jacques Amyot, S.J.*

UNITED STATES
    Kentucky (Abbey of
        Gethsemani)   *Father M. Louis, O.C.S.O.*
    New York (America
        magazine)   *Mr. John Moffitt*

VIETNAM
    Thien An   *Dom Marie-Joseph Ngoc Hoang, O.S.B.*

MEMBERS OF THE A.I.M. SECRETARIAT

FRANCE
    Paris (Vanves)   *Dom Marie de Floris, O.S.B., Abbot*
                                         Mother Pia Valeri, O.S.B.
                                         Mother M. Bernard Said, O.S.B.
                                         Mme. L. Marchal
                                         Mlle. J. Brouet

HOLLAND
    Slangenburg   *Dom P. C. Tholens, O.S.B., Abbot*

ITALY
    Rome   *Dom Paul Gordon, O.S.B.*

AUDITORS

BELGIUM
    Bruges (Abbey of
        St.-André: *Rythmes*
        du Monde)   *Dom François de Grunne, O.S.B.*

APPENDIX D 335

FRANCE
    Paris (Informations
        Catholiques Inter-
        nationales)   M. Jean Vogel

ITALY
    Bologna   Don G. Dossetti
                        Don U. Neri
    Rome (R.A.I.)   M. La Valle
                        Mme. La Valle

JAPAN
    Takamori   Father Shigeto Oshido, O. P.

THAILAND
    Bangkok (Paris
        Foreign Missions)   Father E. Verdière, M.E.P.
    Interpreters   Mr. Adri Schrama
                        Sister Patrice
                        Sister Marthe

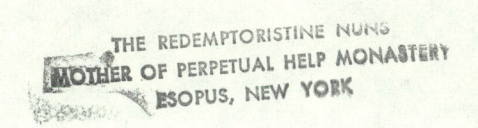

Redemptoristine Nuns
Mother of Perpetual Help Monastery
Esopus, New York 12429

255 NEW
/ Moffitt, John
A New charter for monasticism